Blackhood Against
the Police Power

Blackhood Against
the Police Power

PUNISHMENT AND DISAVOWAL IN THE "POST-RACIAL" ERA

Tryon P. Woods

Michigan State University Press | East Lansing

♾ The paper used in this publication meets the minimum requirements
of ANSI/NISO Z39.48-1992 (R 1997) (Permanence of Paper).

Michigan State University Press
East Lansing, Michigan 48823-5245

Printed and bound in the United States of America.

28 27 26 25 24 23 22 21 20 19   1 2 3 4 5 6 7 8 9 10

LIBRARY OF CONGRESS CATALOGING-IN-PUBLICATION DATA
Library of Congress Cataloging-in-Publication Data
Names: Woods, Tryon P., author.
Title: Blackhood against the police power : punishment and disavowal in the "post-racial" era / Tryon P. Woods.
Description: East Lansing : Michigan State University Press, [2019] | Includes bibliographical references and index.
Identifiers: LCCN 2018035321| ISBN 9781611863185 (cloth : alk. paper) | ISBN 9781609175979 (pdf)
| ISBN 9781628953633 (epub) | ISBN 9781628963649 (kindle)
Subjects: LCSH: Police brutality—United States. | United States—Race relations—Political aspects.
| African Americans—Social conditions.
Classification: LCC HV8141 .W66 2019 | DDC 363.2/32—dc23
LC record available at https://lccn.loc.gov/2018035321

Book design by Charlie Sharp, Sharp Designs, East Lansing, MI
Cover design by Shaun Allshouse, www.shaunallshouse.com

Michigan State University Press is a member of the Green Press Initiative and is committed to developing
and encouraging ecologically responsible publishing practices. For more information about the Green
Press Initiative and the use of recycled paper in book publishing, please visit www.greenpressinitiative.org.

Visit Michigan State University Press at *www.msupress.org*

Robert Thomas Bowen Jr., 1968–1991
forever a brother, always a reminder

Thelma Renee Foote, 1956–2007
forever a singular spirit, always an example

In the last quarter, sweetheart,
anything can happen.
And will.

Toni Cade Bambara, *The Salt Eaters*

Contents

Preface

In a global semantic field structured by anti-black solidarity, it stands to reason that the potential energy of a black, or blackened, position holds out a singularly transformative possibility, an energy generated by virtue of its relation to others in a field of force.

—Jared Sexton, "Afro-Pessimism: The Unclear Word," 2016

This book addresses the punishment of "race" and the disavowal of sexual violence central to the contemporary "post-racial" culture of politics. It asserts that the "post-racial" bears an antiblack animus that we should read as desiring the end of blackness. The book makes the following four interventions into how we conceptualize our present moment:

1. Redefine policing as a sociohistorical process of implementing and reproducing the modern world's onto-epistemic structure of antiblackness.

2. Redefine racism, policing's other name, as an act of sexual violence that produces the punishment of race.
3. Critique leading antiracist discourse for its complicity with antiblack policing.
4. Account for the way in which the original 1960s conception of black studies offers a corrective to the deficiencies in today's critical discourse on race and sex.

Following these four lines of intervention, I show that the post-racial is more than simply the latest iteration of antiblackness in which our society has long been mired. Only a historically grounded study can adequately ascertain the full meaning of the present; properly contextualized, we see that history does not repeat itself so much as its relations of force proceed, profoundly contested, but as yet unvanquished and continuous. Likewise, despite the national mythology of American exceptionalism and progress, proclaiming that the present period has shorn itself of the worst violence of the previous era, the contemporary culture of politics is what it is precisely because the black freedom struggle continues to lean into the ongoing destruction, mayhem, and atrocity of the modern world. This book pinpoints the unique manner in which antiblack sexual violence, constitutive of the modern world since the dawn of racial slavery, wraps itself in the guise of a new discourse of disavowal.

I wrote this book during the first decade and a half of the twenty-first century: begun around 2006, it was finally completed in 2016. For much of this time, I used the working title, "'Post-racial' is the New Antiblack," to declare the specific deception of the "post-racial." Eventually, the present title, *Blackhood Against the Police Power*, emerged as the book's framework clarified. The presidency of Barack Obama came and went. I have retained "post-racial" in the book's subtitle, nonetheless, because although this marker is most closely associated with the rise of Obama in 2008, I aim to demonstrate how it pronounces a historical moment in an ongoing culture of politics, and that it does not primarily spring from nor revolve around the state, changes to the political economy, or the details of electoral politics. Although the emergence of the Donald Trump presidency has evoked horror and end-of-times apoplexy from liberals and the Left, its racism, misogyny (including against Mother Earth), homophobia, and general unabashed elitism and cronyism are not retrograde, anathema, or the harbinger of fascism—all of those things, and more, have long been the order of the day. Due especially to its sexual politics, the 2016 presidential contest between Trump and Hillary Clinton was depicted as evidence that electoral politics have really gotten out of hand. From the perspective of the black freedom struggle, however, recall that things have been out of hand, as it were, since at least the time of the first U.S. presidential election, when the slaveholding class anointed one of its own to oversee the consolidation of what Gerald Horne argues is properly understood as the American counterrevolution against the enslaved. Obama and Trump are two sides of the same coin, two strains of the same mold, two spurs of the same razor wire.

One of the reasons why new personnel in the White House does not mean a change in the post-racial culture of politics is that antiblackness is well entrenched not only in plain sight, as Wahneema Lubiano has taught us, but moreover, in the very places that present themselves as antiracist and multicultural.[1] Recently, my wife and I met with the director of our youngest daughter's school to discuss where she would attend sixth grade the following year. My wife is black and I am white; our daughters are black. The school director, a white man, extolled the virtues of the school, emphasizing in particular its commitment to diversity. The coffee table around which we sat prominently displayed a copy of *Hamilton: A Revolution*, by Lin-Manuel Miranda and Jeremy McCarter, the libretto and back story to the Broadway hit show. At one point in the meeting, out of the blue, the director placed his hands on top of the book and pushed it toward us, telling us how much he loves *Hamilton*. As it happens, this gesture of identification and desire by the school director, non sequitur aside, has become commonplace: *Hamilton* has sent white people with emotional investments in not being racist over the moon. They trip over themselves telling each other and their nonwhite friends how they have memorized the soundtrack; they seem to feel that giving *Hamilton* as housewarming and holiday gifts, or showing it off to the parents of a black child in the school for which they serve as director, authenticates their commitment to diversity. These are the "good" whites. Given that *Hamilton* adds black and brown faces to a national mythology without altering that narrative in any substantive manner, this possessive and performative frenzy is telling. Miranda,

Hamilton's creator and star, and his crew portray the most prominent slavehold-ers and slave traders of the white nation's founding generation beatboxing and rapping—the counterrevolutionaries against black freedom in a strange type of blackface. The mystification aims to have it both ways: condemn slavery as evil and then resurrect the people who perpetrated it as "self-made" men and the social structures based on it as multicultural and inclusive, minus the chattel condition.[2] Slave traders with soul!

The connection between *Hamilton*'s blackface performance and state practices of antiblackness is a symbiotic one. Obama's "state minstrelsy" (to borrow a term that Lubiano employed to describe Supreme Court Justice Clarence Thomas's confirmation hearings in 1991) was most evident not when he twice hosted Miranda and the cast of *Hamilton* at the White House, but in moments such as his stump speech for presidential candidate Hillary Clinton at North Carolina A&T University in October 2016. It was students from A&T who launched the sit-in movement in 1960 at the local Greensboro Woolworth's lunch counter. By 2016, however, the first black president was pandering to his audience—journalist Utrice Leid described it as a "carnival barker" performance, invoking the grotesque and the absurd—at the historically black university against which he had levied funding cuts larger than any previous administration, all while he had elsewhere featured education prominently in his economic stimulus package.[3] We have sunk a long way since the days when students at HBCUs and other campuses around the country rose up against precisely this kind of historical treachery. As Leid noted, because of what he has done to black people, the students at A&T should never have permitted Obama onto campus in the first place. Post-racial aims to distract and deceive; the deception is ongoing.

In short, things are not as they appear. All writing bears an autobiographical imprint, no matter how muted or densely layered into the written work. As a white scholar working in black studies, I confront the ongoing historical violence of white appropriation of black struggle. I respect the perspective that holds white people such as me, and our work, at a critical distance: such suspicion is historically warranted, ethically sound, and ultimately, necessary for self-defense. I welcome the close scrutiny, not in hopes that a rigorous vetting will vindicate my credentials, but rather because antiracism cannot rest on identity or proprietary claims: who can say and do what about it.⁴ An autobiographical dimension of this book is my effort to blacken my praxis. This commitment does not entail denying or hiding my whiteness, nor does it presuppose that I become less white along the way, that there will be a litmus at which point I have reached a state of sufficient blackening. As I elaborate across the pages of this book, an ethical relationship to the black freedom struggle requires that racial analysis move away from its preoccupation with the empirical and the performative and begin to more scrupulously encompass the structural dimension of the world. My experiences, therefore, are not at issue.

Although white people do not exist in the world uniformly due to differences in gender, sexuality, and class, in the least, one of my goals in this book is to recalibrate the ethics of gender and sex studies to the protocols of antiblackness. If my experiences alone were the issue, I could certainly tell numerous stories about how my white maleness has played out advantageously for me, regardless of my actions, as well as how it has been used against me in different moments. All of this is beside the point that I seek to sharpen, however, which is that my gender and sexuality function as modalities of my whiteness. Indeed, although I am well aware that "gender" and "sexuality" are not reducible to each other, I will often formulate them together as "gender-sex" throughout this study in order to stress a more fundamental structure of power for which gender and sexuality are expressions.

Although always personal (the terror and the rage!), this state of affairs is not an individual one. I do not embrace my whiteness; rather, I strive to tell the truth about it, including accepting how profoundly pathological and diabolical it is. Again, regardless of how much I may as an individual white person reactively insist on the gross difference between myself and the image of me created in culture as antiblack, it is still part of my visage in the world all the same. In other words, there is no such thing, in terms of the structure of this world, as "good" and "bad" whites. Across the diversity of our behaviors and beliefs (the empirical), it is our very existence as the authors and beneficiaries of a world-rupturing violence that is the problem (the structural). By my estimation, then, the only ethical way of being white in the world is to tell the truth about antiblackness and to embark wholeheartedly on the affirmation of blackness, as if life itself hangs in the balance—which it does. This is an existential problem for me as a white person in a way that is connected to but different from the struggle for survival that black people face. The problem of black social death issues from and implicitly indicts nonblacks for being socially alive, prior to our actions in the world.[5] Consequently, as I prosecute humanity for its pathological consumption of blackness, I am ultimately seeking my own destruction.

■   ■   ■

The Introduction identifies critical features of the current moment in black historical struggle that inform the intervention I explore through *Blackhood Against the Police Power*. I identify the terms of what I call the "post-racial" quarantine, its "post–black people" impulse, and the consequences of this structure of desire for black thought. The time of the post-racial is dangerous not only to black people, but to thought itself, a tendency I name and explore as "post–black studies." I further consider this study's relationship to black studies, to the leadership of black women and to black feminism in particular, and to the seam in black critical thought recently identified as "afro-pessimism." Chapter 1, "The Time of Blackened Ethics," begins investigation of how the police power operates as the culture of politics in the post-racial period. I explore how contesting the world that the police power has made, and remakes on a daily basis, requires critiquing it in a language it does not already colonize. While genealogy is the favored modality for situating the terms of a historically grounded study, I argue for its subversion with respect to the self-activity of blackhood against the police power across the generations. I explore how the production of knowledge about the social, and our understanding of ethical action therein, is indelibly transformed when we place blackness and the gratuitous violence through which it emerges in the modern world at the center of our analysis. How does a blackened inquiry take us beyond the usual pronouncements of "racial bias," "excessive force," or "homophobia," and toward a more fundamental grasp of the antiblack sexual violence underwriting this society? Chapter 1 delineates the methods of analysis faithful to black struggle that I corral toward the intervention blackhood offers.

Chapter 2, "The Inadmissible Career of Social Death," argues that the conditions of black existence in the modern world, the status of social death, constitute inadmissible evidence in the courts of public and academic discourse. Toward this end, I examine black "missing persons" and the manner in which the leading critical study of race and sex reinforces the social death of blackness by producing persons who are missing as black. Consistent with the protocols of fungible blackness wherein society appropriates for itself the very products or terms of black culture that it had used to pathologize black people, the discourse on "social death" has been adopted by some ethnic studies and queer studies scholars, while the labors of some black studies scholars to evaluate "the social life of social death" are degraded and trivialized.[6] Along these lines, I read Lisa Marie Cacho's *Social Death: Racialized Rightlessness and the Criminalization of the Unprotected* and Alexander Weheliye's *Habeas Viscus: Racializing Assemblages, Biopolitics, and Black Feminist Theories of the Human* for the ways in which blackness goes "missing and murdered." This chapter presents the most extended focus on academic discourse in *Blackhood Against the Police Power*. My aim with this chapter is to situate what may appear to be largely academic preoccupations within the real-world context in which the ideas live. The various ways in which black people are rendered missing and murdered across space and time, therefore, bookend this engagement with the academic discourse of "social death." Social death, however, is revealed as all too consequential in the disappearances of murdered black women in Rocky Mount, North Carolina, in the early 2000s. Belated discoveries of decomposing black bodies must spur us to hasten the decomposition of the leading discursive policing of questions of race, sex, and power.

The phrase "missing and murdered" comes from the Atlanta black child murders of 1979–1981. The Atlanta case, and Toni Cade Bambara's compendium to that period of black historical struggle, *Those Bones Are Not My Child*, serves as the terrain on which I rebut the disappearance of blackness from the critical discourse on race and sex, and from the world, in chapter 3, "From Blackland, with Love." Bambara's conception of "blackhood" lends this argument rigor and positions this chapter as the centerpiece of the book. I argue that Bambara charts the way to a more ethical and viable mode of liberation movement. Through blackhood, then, this chapter shows how displacing gender-sex in black praxis can elucidate the centrality of self-defense and political clarity for self-determination. Humanism's discourses of the body ("gender-sex") stand as an intransigent impediment to an ethical embrace of the only discourse of embodiment we need for self-determination: blackhood. The Atlanta "missing and murdered," as local residents referred to the case, stand in this chapter for how the seizure and fungibility of black bodies respond to Pan-African self-determination against a slaveholding society. I suggest that blackhood ferrets a way through this landscape. How does blackhood stand against today's leading critical discourse on race and sex that renders black people missing and murdered?

In chapter 4, "All The Things Your Movement Could Be by Now If It Were to Center Black Self-Determination," I turn to one of the more salient arenas for the post-racial retrenchment of antiblackness: the movement to reform the criminal justice system. The most prominent issues in the present reform period are stop-and-frisk policing and mass incarceration. I address how the anti-stop-and-frisk movement is itself a component of the police power, situating the recent court decision against the New York Police Department in *Floyd, et al. v. City of New York, et al.* in its proper historical context: the emergence of the Fourth Amendment to the U.S. Constitution as central to the preservation of the slavocracy. With the protection against search and seizure understood as counterrevolutionary, rather than revolutionary, I critique contemporary Fourth Amendment jurisprudence, calling for the end of "reasonable suspicion" and arguing that *Floyd* actually preserves the police power, rather than constraining it. At issue here is the displacement of black studies from the study of law and policing that contributes to misconstruing both racism and its remedies. This inquiry into what is happening on the street with the police (the backups) leads into an inquiry into the nature of the debate about policing and punishment animating civil society (the front lines) in cases such as the killings of Trayvon Martin and Jordan Davis. A critical reading of Michelle Alexander's *The New Jim Crow: Mass Incarceration in the Age of Colorblindness* and Ruth Gilmore's *Golden Gulag: Prisons, Surplus, Crisis, and Opposition in Globalizing California* assesses how the critics of police and prisons can also be the police power themselves.

Chapter 5, "On Performance and Position, Erotically," extends the analysis of sexual violence as the essence of racialization introduced in earlier chapters. Under examination in this chapter are the ethical coordinates of performance studies of blackness and resistance to antiblack violence in order to excavate the limits of performing black liberation. The customary discourse on "intersectionality" is put under pressure, revealing a distinct queer antiblackness to leading critical work on performativity and the punishment and policing of black people. I use hip hop and Lil Wayne's song "Beat It Like a Cop" to illustrate the possibilities and constraints of performance, and also the centrality of blackness to interrogations of gender-sex. I call into question the displacement of blackness in certain queer political formation, recalling in response Cathy Cohen's clarion to notice how blackness *is* queer.

Chapter 6, "Torture Outside of Pain in the Black Studies Tradition," investigates the meaning of torture under conditions of antiblackness, returning to the role of antiblack sexual violence within the black liberation imaginary. I begin with the slave-devouring dogs deployed by the various slaving Europeans in the Caribbean and Southern United States, and then read contemporary cases of policing such as the death of Sandra Bland in this historical light. This reevaluation of torture sets the stage for a critical confrontation with the recent film *What Happened, Miss Simone?*, documentarian Liz Garbus's take on Nina Simone. Garbus's treatment of the context for black movement extends my meditations on torture, the representation of post-racialism, and the attempt to quarantine black self-determination. The historical context presented in *What Happened, Miss Simone?* is also the time of Bambara's formulation of blackhood during the Black Arts Movement, and together they open an understanding of how black people struggle outside of pain.

Following the coda, which offers a concise refrain and extension of the argument established during the preceding chapters, the reader of *Blackhood Against the Police Power* will reach the final pages without encountering conclusions or prescriptions. No solutions here. The answers to our common immiseration as human beings, or to the fundamental dehumanization of black people at the heart of it all, will not come from scholarship, critical thought, scientific inquiry, or philosophical meditations. My contribution to knowledge aims to reformulate how we view the world, but it is remedial and counteractive, necessitated by decade after decade, generation upon generation, of disavowal, displacement, and distancing of a truth borne of black struggle and self-determination. Blackhood is not the answer; it is merely a call to repurpose our energies, to reestablish an ethical accountability to blackness, and to cut through the dissemblance of law, gender-sex, and performativity. I believe that this recalibration to the foundation of human liberation is of vital importance so we are primed to support movement toward total reconstruction, by way of utter destruction, when the time is right, and so that we can better recognize the present flights and fights of marronage in our midst. As Nina Simone asked her audience before she performed at one of the large rallies during the civil rights era: "Is your mind ready? Is your body ready?" No solutions in these pages or any pages; solutions are only out there—intellectual tasks following street tasks.

Acknowledgments

First thanks go to Julie L. Loehr, Editor-in-Chief at Michigan State University Press, and all of the outstanding staff at the press, who collectively marshaled this project across the finish line. Thank you as well to Steven Moore for the index. This book went through the academic-peer-review wringer: eight different reviews at three different university presses, with four different editors, across three years. I am honored by every reader (most of whom remain anonymous to me) and editor who took the time to engage the project and provide feedback. I am most humbled by Joy James's support: Joy was the first reviewer and the one who steadfastly endorsed the project from beginning to end. Frank Wilderson and Jared Sexton's comradely intervention way back in 2004–2005 was instrumental in the path I have pursued since then and I am grateful for it. The book itself, however, would not be what it has become, because I would not be who I have become, without the friendship and collaborations of Deborah Bowen, Donald Tibbs, and Khalil Saucier.

Each and every sentence of *Blackhood Against the Police Power* was written while supporting my family by teaching full-time, sometimes at as many as three different universities concurrently. The book's publication timeline reflects this path, but I also hope that this context of family and labor has found its way into the integrity and urgency of insight to which the book aspires.

While a long while in the making in the brief context of my own life, this book is not even a blip in the scrolls of black liberation praxis, an inexorable movement across the time and space of modern human existence for almost a millennium and the only social movement with the potential to free all human beings from oppression, a struggle so utterly banal and protracted that it will forever exceed adequate representation. Toni Cade Bambara, whose ethereal leadership gently guides my aims as an educator, once responded with her customary wit and blunt beauty to an interviewer's question regarding justice, community, and other matters of getting whole, to which she had dedicated her life's work:

> INTERVIEWER: Do you think fiction is the most effective way to do this?
>
> BAMBARA: I don't think fiction is the most effective way to do it. The most effective way to do it, *is to do it!*

I have encountered a number of people in my life who are simply getting on with this work, and each has contributed not only to my own personal development but, more importantly, to the indomitable flow of energy that will not suffer anything less than the truth of the inner eye. In the most inimitable opening sentence to a novel ever written (in my humble opinion), Bambara the healer had her character Minnie Ransom, the healer in *The Salt Eaters*, inquire of Velma Henry, and of us all, "Are you sure, sweetheart, that you want to be well?" Minnie later elaborates, in a sort of way: "I like to caution folks, that's all. No sense us wasting each other's time, sweetheart. A lot of weight when you're well. Now, you just hold that thought."

If having experienced this book, the reader has found his or her time not spent in vain, it is largely due to the weight of this tradition impressing itself upon my work. Beyond the ancestors—those who pillaged and those who survived the pillaging—there is also the breath, the soul, and the mystery. Along that flowing river, I learned integrity of thought, intention, and action from people of all walks of life, people I worked with, observed, listened to, read about, shared a subway car with, or broke bread with over the years, faces and feelings too numerous to recall and too supernal to name, but I must tag a small group of people who have instructed me, held me accountable over the years, or provided important or timely support, without whose care I would not have anything to say worth hearing. Jared Sexton and Frank Wilderson; Greg Thomas; Joy James; Denise Ferreira da Silva and George Lipsitz; Franco Barchiesi; Keisha-Khan Perry; my brothers Donald Tibbs and Khalil Saucier; my aunt Barbara Woods; my parents Doug and Susan Woods, my sister Betsy McNeil, and my wife's parents Bob Bowen and Loyce Foucher; the children, including all of my nieces and nephews on both coasts, and many more beyond blood and marriage, without whom it all falls apart; and above all, to the three people who are my heart, lungs, and legs: my beautiful and extraordinary daughters Naomi Marie and Assana Simone, and my wife, the peerless, sun-shy-fine and universe-wise Deborah Bowen—you propel me in search of greater vulnerability, honesty, and strength so that you may find shade when the heat is heavy, light when the darkness crowds in, passion and courage when the mediocrity drags around you, safety when the draft is too strong, and grace through the turbulence and along the concourse of your own lives in this stormy land.

Introduction

What are we pretending not to know today, dear?

—Toni Cade Bambara, *Those Bones Are Not My Child*, 1999

I n the early morning hours of New Year's Day 2009, the Bay Area Rapid
Transit (BART) police murdered Oscar Grant in Oakland, CA. Grant had
been on his way home with his friends after celebrating New Year's Eve in
San Francisco. The BART train in which they were riding was jam-packed
with hundreds of other New Year's Eve revelers. There had been a scuffle at one
point in one of the train's cars; a train conductor reported a fight with a possible
weapon to BART police, who greeted the train at the next station, Fruitvale.
BART officers immediately singled out Grant and several of his friends from the
crowded train cars, lined them up against the wall of the station's platform, and
proceeded to arrest them. Grant and his friends attempted to ascertain from
the officers why they had been taken off the train and why they were being
arrested. At one point, one of the lead officers assaulted one of the friends,
punching him in the face. Eventually the officers put Grant facedown on the

ground; one officer had his knee on Grant's neck, another officer had Grant's arms held behind his back, and at this point Officer Johannes Mehserle stood up, told the other officers to step back, drew his gun, and shot one bullet into Grant's back. The bullet went through Grant, ricocheted off of the pavement on which he was already prostrated, and returned to his body, puncturing his lung. Grant died from his wounds some seven hours later in the hospital.

Scores of passengers witnessed the entire sequence of events as the packed BART train stood idling in the station during the fifteen minutes in which Grant and his friends were being detained prior to his killing. Many video recordings were made of the event on passenger cell phones, with many passengers' loud objections audible on all recordings, soon turning to horrified gasps at the shooting, and then expressions of anger as the police quickly ordered the train out of the station, whisking away the witnesses to the crime. This high degree of visibility and video documentation alone, from multiple angles no less, separates the Grant case from the litany of other cases of police violence that otherwise present the commonality of police officers and the victims they shoot dead. The average annual number of killings decreed by the police themselves to be "justifiable homicides" exceeds four hundred.[1] Due to the widely circulated video footage of his death and the persistent public pressure that the Oakland community brought to bear on the district attorney, Officer Mehserle was actually prosecuted for his crime, a course of events atypical for police violence. Mehserle was eventually convicted of involuntary manslaughter and served less than two years in an isolated wing of the Los Angeles County Jail. He was released on parole on May 3, 2011.

Two years later, in January 2013, Ryan Coogler's film adaptation of the final forty-eight hours of Oscar Grant's life debuted at the Sundance Film Festival as *Fruitvale*, where it won the U.S. Grand Jury Prize and the Audience Award, before going into limited release later that summer retitled as *Fruitvale Station*. It earned one of the highest openings of any film in limited release, one of the best openings for a Sundance festival top prizewinner, and through early 2014, has grossed over $21 million worldwide in combined box office and DVD/Blu-ray sales.[2] When the film opened in the San Francisco Bay Area, an advert poster appeared in the very same Fruitvale station that was the scene of the crime. BART provided full location access to Coogler's film crew, making

Fruitvale station itself available for three four-hour nights, including one night of filming from inside a BART train car. During its run in area movie theaters, there were sixty-five posters for *Fruitvale Station* in thirty-two BART stations. Contacted by the *San Francisco Chronicle* at the time, BART spokeswoman Luna Salaver stated, "There was no debate whether to allow 'Fruitvale Station' [advertisements] on BART. None whatsoever." Salaver went on to say, "We really support Ryan. He's just an amazing person. I think Ryan had said it was his intention to show his love for Oakland and the people of Oakland, and he really succeeded." Speaking on behalf of the department whose agents did more than anyone else to confirm Grant's devalued humanity, Salaver went on to add: "The film is really about humanizing Oscar Grant, and Ryan did a superb job."[3]

Oscar Grant's death is hypervisible as a spectacle of state violence. The problem with hypervisibility is that it absorbs all attention, relegating other aspects of the social to the shadows. The spectacular event obscures the range of racist violence, its daily operation in the lives of all black people, and the absence of any recourse through which to remedy these disruptions. In the shadows of Grant's murder, for instance, urban school districts across California and around the nation have been steadily closing down schools, laying off teachers, and investing public money into privately run charter schools, a process that has a grossly disproportionate negative impact on already destabilized black communities. Not only do we typically fail to view this cycle of divestment and reinvestment in school systems—a process best described as "education gentrification"—as racial violence, additionally, school-reform discourse trumpets the process as good for the very communities that it harms, as the award-winning 2010 documentary *Waiting for Superman* depicts. At first blush, *Fruitvale Station* would appear to put racist violence on blast, the film's popularity an indication of a shift in public sentiment against the legitimacy of the manner of policing it displays. BART's public rhetoric endorsing the film's message, not to mention its cooperation with the filmmaker and its willingness to profit from selling advertising space for the film, however, suggest something else is afoot. Perhaps *Fruitvale Station* does something more than merely condemn police practices. Since the film is not much more than a stylized elaboration of the events recorded by handheld cell phones and broadcast around the world, we need to also inquire as to the political effects of the bystander recordings of police violence: What does the spectacle mean, what are the effects of its hypervisibility, and what are the relations of power in which both the spectacular instances of racist violence and their mundane, everyday corollaries emerge?

In response to the 1992 acquittal of the Los Angeles Police Department officers who attacked Rodney King, perhaps the first entry in the now voluminous archive of video recordings of antiblack violence, the critic Sylvia Wynter penned "No Humans Involved: An Open Letter to My Colleagues." "NHI" is an acronym used by the police to designate crimes committed against black people, prostitutes, drug addicts, or the homeless. Wynter pointedly asked her colleagues in academia, and educators everywhere, "what is wrong with our education?" She asserts that the social crisis is being perpetrated and managed by our students, the people who are products of the very educational system in which antiblack violence is normalized across the curriculum. "If, as Ralph Ellison alerted us to in *The Invisible Man*," writes Wynter, "we see each other only through the 'inner eyes' with which we look through our physical eyes upon reality, the question we must confront in the wake of the Rodney King Event becomes: What is our responsibility for the making of those 'inner eyes'?" She continues:

> What have we had to do, and still have to do, with the putting in place of the classifying logic of that shared mode of "subjective understanding" in whose "inner eyes" young Black males can be perceived as being *justly* shut out from what Helen Fein calls the "universe of moral obligation" that bonds the interests of the Simi Valley jurors as Whites and non-Blacks (one Asian, one Hispanic) to the interests of the White policemen and the Los Angeles judicial office-holders who are our graduates?[4]

Recalling sociologist St. Clair Drake's notion of "street tasks" and "intellectual tasks," Wynter affirmed the essential activity of the streets, the organizing, protesting, petitioning, and rhetoric, both of the 1960s and of the spring of 1992 when Los Angeles rose up against the King verdict. Wynter reminds us, however, that for Drake "street tasks" are necessarily complemented by "intellectual tasks": action must provoke an "epistemological break" with the prevailing categories of thought that govern the social order, how it conceives of itself, and the paradigms it upholds and through which it institutes the world.[5] Whereas the street tasks of the 1960s ignited the movement to create black studies, Wynter's call to arms in 1992 is that the post–civil rights era of antiblack policing warrants a renewed intellectual task.

Ryan Coogler, the writer-director of *Fruitvale Station*, has explained that his intention with the film was to disrupt the flat, one-dimensional portrayals of Grant that predominated during the trial following his death: "Oscar was either cast as a saint who had never done anything wrong in his life, or he was painted as a monster who got what he deserved that night."[6] Humanizing Grant, as the BART spokeswoman noted, was indeed Coogler's primary aim: "What I felt was lost was the fact that this guy was a normal person. He had relationships."[7] Coogler's vision, then, of a humanized Grant rests in a universal appeal: "I hope that people will watch the film regardless of where they are from, regardless of what their political views are, and regardless of what their ethnicity is, see the film and see a little bit of themselves in the human being in the film."[8] Can *Fruitvale Station* actually humanize what has already been decreed beyond the pale—short of, as James Baldwin once wrote, a metamorphosis "so violent as to blow . . . all of us away"?[9] Under what terms can blackness, the position of NHI, be made universally accessible?

To extend Wynter's analysis in "No Human Involved," black people have no room with which to maneuver themselves into humanity within the existing social order. The counterargument to the presumption of black inhumanity (*Fruitvale Station*, for instance) does little to unsettle a world instituted through the categorical violence of NHI, as long as it issues from, or is read within, the same epistemic framework in whose logic the plight of blackness, in Wynter's terms, "is neither posable nor resolvable."[10] Wynter goes on to note that today's intellectuals refrain from "marrying" their thought to this state of affairs, from grounding their perspectives and analyses of the world within the singular position of black existence. Ostensibly, the reason for this difficulty is that the NHI are unfit for any of the redeemable social categories (labor, multicultural coalition, feminism, displaced migrant or refugee) legible within the order, and they are unidentifiable within any of the contemporary social movements of interest (Occupy Wall Street, antitrafficking, human rights, environment). In response, Wynter pointedly asks, referring to the 1992 Los Angeles uprising: "How then did they change the course of human history in two days?"[11] She concludes by challenging her colleagues in the university in a similar manner, laying down the intellectual task of our time, to marry our thought to the NHI, to calibrate our ensemble of questions to the suffering of not only "the unarmed young black man," the ubiquitous victim of state violence, but also to the questions posed by the street tasks as they erupt in Oakland, or Staten Island, or Ferguson, Missouri, or Sanford, Florida. Perhaps we might better see Grant's humanity if *Fruitvale Station* had begun where it left off, with the street tasks set off by murder's routine performance. Or as a student pointedly asked in response to my presentation of the questions arising in this case, the film "might have humanized Oscar Grant, but what about the rest of us black people?"

What Is Policing?

Policing is not what we think it is. I mean this in two ways: first, policing by law enforcement is not what we think it is; and second, policing by law enforcement is not even really policing—in the sense that it is subordinate, ancillary, and inferior to the historical processes that position, profile, patrol, punish, and purge the principal "criminal" threat within the social body. Let us begin with what policing is and what it is not. I led off with the Oscar Grant case to establish what policing is not. Policing by law enforcement cannot hold the center: no one case of police conduct, or pattern of behaviors, can define the unjust world we inhabit, the problem to be overcome through protracted social struggle. I would like to be able to discuss Grant's murder as if it were *the* current illustration of the problem to be examined. Given the political stakes, the human lives that hang in the balance, the pressures to do so are intense. But I can't. As Greg Thomas has noted, you cannot begin with a single illustrative case, no matter how powerful, poignant, and current, because as soon as you do, the next one has already superseded that case.[12] This state of affairs presents two important warnings for us. First, Officer Mehserle's shooting of Grant was a death foretold. It was foretold by the litany of antiblack violence that preceded his murder and that has followed it as a matter of course. Second, to focus on any one of these cases of policing, in fact, is to buy into the logic of white supremacy that zealously grips the fallacy that these moments of violence are just that—moments, incidents of excess, cases of excessive force or violence—when in fact everyday life in an antiblack society such as ours is excessively violent for black people in ways too numerous to delineate here.

I raise Grant's case, and those of some of the many black men, women, and children taken from us prematurely, to name names against the dark void of amnesia. I do so to mark the passing of another bright human being at the hands of antiblack violence, to honor the protracted efforts of the black community across the ages to hold its young and raise up life, nonetheless. In so doing, I enjoin the tradition of black studies and black social movement in offering an ethical accounting of the world as it is, not as we would pretend it to be. One of the many paradoxes at the heart of a society based in slavery is that all of us, to greater or lesser degrees, have learned to speak and to be struck dumb at the same time. For example, conceptualizing "justice" in the face of such obvious injustice may in fact be premature given that much of society cowers in the face of reality's true name.

This book grapples with the dead end of "justice" discourse, calling us to arm ourselves with "ethics," instead. Frank Wilderson notes the difference:

> I might have *feelings* about justice, for example I *feel* that the killing of Oscar Grant by a BART police officer was unjust; and that the verdict in the case (involuntary manslaughter) is also unjust. But justice is not a register that I trade in as a theorist. And perhaps not even as a politico. I am interested in *ethics*, which is to say that I am interested in explaining relations of power. You might say that both of my books are arguing that the existence of the world, meaning the existence of the modern era, is unjust. It would be hard to find a corner of justice within an unjust paradigm, unless you made a provisional move away from explaining the paradigm.[13]

Following Wilderson, I am concerned with how antiracism can direct justice into a cul-de-sac within an unjust paradigm. Antiblackness necessarily paves the way for such provisional departures from an ethical accounting of the world we live in today. Beginning with the power relations in which we find policing raises six basic starting points for recalibrating how we position the police in the paradigm—six points for the six bullets that Officer Darren Wilson shot into seventeen-year-old Michael Brown of Ferguson, Missouri, on August 9, 2014.

1. Most of the harm caused to our society—in terms of financial loss, bodily injury, and premature death—comes from the realm of white-collar crime and state crime, not from street crime, and yet we focus the overwhelming brunt of our attention, resources, and fear on the latter realm of criminal behaviors. I call this the "justice contradiction": society focuses mostly on those behaviors that cause the least amount of harm, socially speaking, while devoting the least amount of attention to those behaviors that wreak the most destruction on society.

2. The justice contradiction turns our attention away from crime and onto the police themselves: we have a *policing* problem, not a crime problem per se. Members of all races and classes participate in law breaking, yet whites and the wealthy go relatively unpoliced and decriminalized. This means that what gets counted as "crime," and who shows up as "criminal," is not a reflection of what is actually happening in terms of law-breaking behavior but is merely a catalog of police behavior, not to mention an index of the law's disposition itself.

3. Given this policing problem, we face the reality that we are not policed for what we do, but for who we are or what we represent in the historical structure. Policing is thus a cultural and structural phenomenon; it is not principally about enforcing law, making us safe, or keeping a lid on chaos.

4. The content of this cultural problem is antiblackness, and the historical structure that it maintains is racial slavery. I will discuss slavery at length throughout this study, but for my purposes here in sketching what policing is and what it is not, I call attention to the fact that the historical context of slavery as the formative crucible for modern policing presents three crucial insights to incorporate into

the analysis. First, modern policing formed through the policing of blackness; second, modern policing has always been militaristic with respect to black people; third, modern policing is a key mechanism for racialization. Policing is a function of racism, not the other way around, reminding us that racism is first and foremost an act of violence and that which we call "race" is the aftereffect of this violence. To wit: racism is Officer Darren Wilson approaching Michael Brown and shooting him for walking in the street in the middle of the day on August 9, 2014, in Ferguson, Missouri; "race" is Michael Brown lying dead in the street. Or racism is the Ferguson police leaving Michael Brown's body lying in the middle of the street uncovered for four hours; "race" is the community left to stand by, for four hours, witness to Michael Brown's dehumanization, which was their own.

5. Many of the recent calls for reforming police behavior all miss the fundamental point of what the police are about. Suggestions have been made that the police shouldn't have so much military weaponry; or that they should wear body cameras at all times to record their behaviors; or that they should be better trained. Since the videotaped beating of Rodney King by the Los Angeles Police Department in 1991, there is a vast archive of visual documentation of police violence, but none of it has curbed police impunity. The reason, as I will explore later in this study, is that "crime" is a racial and political construct that cannot apply to the police themselves, or the racialized structures on which this society is based would collapse. Cities pay out millions of dollars annually managing this contradiction, in the form of civil suit settlements with the victims of policing. But police officers are never held criminally liable for their actions (with the rare individual exceptions proving the rule). What this means is that taxpayers— presumably inclusive of the victims' families—end up paying restitution to themselves for the violence that their public servants (the cops) perpetrate on them. The calculus of it all is that black bodies are worth more dead than alive.[14] It is time to read this reality for what it is: two bodies of law, criminal and civil, one for human beings, one for dehumanized beings.

6. The prerogative to ignore police violence is part of what it means to be white or nonblack, to be human. One of the most common ways in which white society ignores police violence is to accept what the police tell us: that the streets are a war zone, that they patrol the front lines, that they are in the trenches fighting hard on our behalf, making tough split-second decisions of life and death. This is not true. First of all, policing is only slightly above average in terms of occupational dangers, far below truck driver, construction worker, agricultural worker, landscaper, miner, and fisherman.[15] The inflated perception of danger is solely attributable to the fear of blackness. Second, the police are not even the front line. Civil society is the front line, and the police are merely the backups, reinforcing the terms of antiblackness that society establishes. For four hundred years of slavery, followed by one hundred years of lynching, it was everyday white people who policed all black people. While this duty largely transferred to the state in the form of the cops by the 1970s (which means it has only been in their hands for a mere four decades), the recent killings of Trayvon Martin, Renisha McBride, Jordan Davis, and others at the hands of non–police officers remind us that this police power rests first with civil society, not with law enforcement.

With these six bullets serving as our point of departure, we can note that the police are many things, but law enforcement is not one of them. Moreover, the police are secondary to the police power of civil society from which the criminal justice apparatus derives its power. The cops do not have power of their own (except situationally, of course); theirs is merely an expression of power located elsewhere in society: they are an appendage of power, not power itself. While the criminal justice system at times may operate autonomously from these power relations, like an appendage that has turned on its host, holding the social body hostage to terms that it now wields against society rather than receives from it, criminal justice remains merely symptomatic of the structure's disposition. Since I am interested in lodging as devastating a critique as I can formulate against the power relations that snatch away black life with impunity, I will not tarry around with symptoms. I seek a deeper cut.

The Post-Racial Quarantine

The contemporary discourse on post-racialism animating the post–civil rights period reveals how today's culture of politics serves as the principal mode of policing in the antiblack world. Proponents of the post-racial claim that ours is a time in which race truly no longer matters in shaping social processes and lived experiences. Against this proposition, critics of the post-racial assiduously refute such claims, asserting to the contrary that racism persists in both inter-personal and institutionalized forms. In this study, I find that neither position accurately addresses how post-racialism represents the latest discursive reit-eration of antiblackness, specifically, and as such, how it reproduces essential features of antiblack racism that have structured the world across the better part of a millennium.

Consequently, my concern in this book is to address, first, the ways in which the historical materiality of antiblack sexual violence continues to constitute the base of the social; and second, to forward an engagement with how this historicity is misrepresented in the epistemological violence of the North Atlantic academy and its institutionalization of the study of racial, sex, and gender difference. I am interested in why it is that the increased visibility of critical fields of inquiry devoted to the study of race and people of color has not illuminated the quality of black suffering but, rather, has contributed to an eclipse of the black struggle's protracted agitation for the liberation of human-ity in full: is this state of affairs a constituent element of the post-racial? Ours is a time of unprecedented black dispossession and criminalization, a moment in which contemporary multicultural and post-racial discourse that avers a perverse inversion of racial hierarchy is corrupting the social, identifying black "reverse racism" and intransigent pathology as the paramount impediments to democratic cohesion, further muting and transmogrifying the historical strug-gles for black liberation into the cellblocks and prison yards of an uninhabitable social incarceration. I view this situation as proceeding from a signal desire to quarantine the ethical demands of the black freedom struggle in its inexorable path across the generations. As a modest contribution to the diverse response from black studies quarters to this state of affairs, then, the present study is an ethico-political engagement with the antiblack world—with, namely, the specific context of black bodily subjection that underwrites the production of knowledge about humanity and the social.

The post-racial moment arrests us by way of a paradox of epic hypervisibility. On the one hand, we are instructed to heed the dawn of a new era: most prominent among these markers, of course, being the 2008 election of Barack Obama as the first black president of a nation founded on the transatlantic enslavement of his African ancestors. While electoral politics may be a feature of the political economy, it is also productive of the symbolic economy of the nation-state—and this was no more the case than with the election of President Obama.[16] Representations of black people in popular culture (such as in films like *Training Day*, *Monster's Ball*, *Antwone Fisher*, *Precious*, and *The Help*) under the sign of the post-racial continue to be construed in sexually pathological terms that warrant state control or extermination, as desirous of sexual subjection to white patriarchy, and in need of white benevolence to find voice and liberation; the causes of black suffering are located intramurally or interpersonally, within the black community; and black death or sexual violence against black people is proffered as the precondition for black entrance into civil society, or the human family, under severe terms of erasure. Despite the racist content of these narratives, they function as evidence of a new post-racial reality, often simply because they are promoted by certain black elites—the president, black celebrities, black intellectuals and pundits. On the contrary, the hypervisible symbols of black success complement, rather than contradict, ongoing black immiseration.[17] This study treats this situation as indicative of a persistent desire for and loathing of that which continues to hold society together: black death and bodily subjection.

The post-racial moment is also marked by the ongoing social concern with issues that shape black lived experience, such as public education and the criminal justice system. The plight of the most disadvantaged children in society, with black and brown kids portrayed most prominently under this sign, is consistently deployed to warrant the massive structural reforms that the United States has pursued in how it educates its young in the post-racial era. This too misconstrues what is actually happening in education reform, where we see the discipline, punishment, and containment of black and brown children extended, not ameliorated—now as much through curricula, privatization, "choice," and "objective" performance barometers as through the increased application of detention, suspension, ongoing segregation, and even criminal prosecution for in-school behavior. All told, these features of education reform amount to racialized corporal punishment. Criminal justice, meanwhile, has increasingly come under popular scrutiny, with the system's deeply entrenched racism thoroughly exposed in mainstream media venues. Voters across the nation have steadily decriminalized marijuana, a response to the futility and social degradation wrought by the war on drugs perhaps, while the electorate has sought to both end the death penalty and make it more difficult for death row inmates to appeal their sentences.[18] In the academy, a nascent "critical prison studies" or "carceral state studies" has mushroomed across the disciplines, with historical accounts of the early twentieth-century and the post-1970s periods receiving heaviest attention.

Ironically, partly due to the nature of the aforementioned discourses on social problems, black suffering remains hidden in plain sight, pleasurable entertainment for civil society, normalized in its ubiquity, or its ordinariness displaced and obscured as other oppressed groups blame black people for their own oppression. Black death continues to shape the historical milieu of the post-racial. An endless litany of violent murder and mayhem targeting black people during the Obama years underscores the fact that the post-racial connects the present to each and every preceding historical period in a continuous structure of antiblack violence. As with slavery, lynching, Jim Crow, COINTELPRO (the FBI's Counter-Intelligence Program), and the wars on crime, gangs, and drugs, our present era is profoundly mired in both the theatrics of black death—the performance of spectacular state violence or antiblackness or both, as in the multitude of police murders or in incidents of nonblacks attacking black people—and the banality of antiblack violence, cordoning off black people from life through overlapping systems and environments of toxicity and danger.

Most critical treatments of the post-racial remain mired in this either/or dichotomy, compelled to either disavow violence as such, to assert that what is, is not, or to document and re-present the persistence of heinous racial violence, egregious discriminatory treatment, and unacceptable inequalities, as if these pairings were not already inherently redundant, in order to refute claims of the post-racial. In so doing, such critical treatments of contemporary racism further insulate from view the fact that the social itself, its very terms of engagement, structures of thought, psychic life, and ethical coordinates, are composed through routine violence against black bodies. Indeed, this is a key meaning of the post-racial policing of the social as I define it in this study: to compel a retestimony of racial injury that only further obscures the actual nature of suffering under racial regime. Studies that treat post-racial discourse dismissively not only miss what is particular to the present moment, but, ironically, they also further mystify the historical reality of race. Historicizing the post-racial ultimately means working through the ways in which the relations of slavery constitute (*present* tense) contemporary society; such an explication of slavery will, accordingly, occupy much of this book. The present study resituates our understanding of policing as an expression of culture that forecloses an ethical confrontation with the essential antiblack sexual violence that structures the very questions we formulate about injustice.

Post–Black People

The cultural authority of the police power expresses itself as an implicit desire to not simply be done with racial discourse, but more pointedly, to be done with black people. In this way, the police power accommodates both racist and avowedly antiracist discourse, insofar as they both share an epistemology of the social that subordinates black suffering and self-possession to other, nonblack political interests. The desire with respect to racial discourse, then, is more pointedly an aspiration for the end of racial blackness as an ethically particular structural position. Consider this claim more fully: the current discourse of post-racialism bespeaks nonblack society's desire to not have to be bothered, once and for all, with the insatiate demands of the black freedom struggle—in short, for black people to stop being *black*. Since the human race is normatively white, racialized human beings exist as a nonwhite subspecies of humanity, with the negation of white being its supposed opposite, black. For this reason, Lewis Gordon suggests that in the antiblack world there is but one race—black—and to be racialized is to be pushed down toward blackness, while to be deracialized is to move up toward whiteness.[19] This means that race is itself a product of racism, not the other way around; it is a function of the dominance that white society claims for itself and expresses through the prerogative to explain the hierarchy created by such dominance in terms of racialization and to name the society it creates as "natural." And therein lies the rub: the attempt to deal with the consequences of racism by "transcending *race*," or by renaming the social space "post-racial," aspires to a raceless future while ultimately advocating the elimination not of racist domination per se, but rather of what it creates—*race*—or, more to the point, black people.[20]

We can support this claim further with respect to four points that are illuminated by the Great White House Beer Summit of 2009. As the reader will likely recall, in July 2009 Harvard University professor Henry Louis Gates Jr. was arrested by the Cambridge police for entering his own home. In the initial aftermath, President Obama termed the Cambridge police action "stupid" and a case of racial profiling, the reality of which he personally testified to having endured during his time in Chicago. He then was compelled to retract both of these statements, instead characterizing the incident as one where both men—Dr. Gates and the arresting officer, Sergeant James Crowley—"probably overreacted." The president subsequently invited both men to join him for beers at the White House, a spectacle designed to emphasize that racial conflict is ultimately an interpersonal matter of miscommunication. Instead of renewing the discussion of racial profiling that had gained national prominence prior to September 11, 2001, we were left with the American beer industry complaining that the president served foreign lagers instead of domestic ales.[21]

The White House Beer Summit illustrates my assertion that our present post-racial discourse desires the elimination of black people in four respects. First, the specter of black criminality reveals itself as the other side of the colorblind coin. Pathological blackness proves itself a defining racial discourse capable of disciplining even the president's bully pulpit: the president had to distance his office from his own personal experience with racial profiling. The specter of black criminality—the basis of racial profiling's legitimacy—is revealed as integral to colorblind ideology. Fred Moten explains this context: "The cultural and political discourse on black pathology has been so pervasive that it could be said to constitute the background against which all representations of blacks, blackness, or (the color) black take place."[22]

Secondly, black subjection is central to the coherence of U.S. society. The emergence of post-racialism raises the vision of racial uplift and progress in the midst of the highest rates of black captivity and poverty in history by way of the redeployment of racist tropes of black criminality. In fact, as Joy James incisively showed in her analysis of the elections of President Obama and Massachusetts governor Deval Patrick, rather than destabilize the basic structure of antiblackness, the convergence of notions of racial progress and multicultural democracy that mark this historical moment actually reinvigorates "the disciplinary narratives of anti-black racism."[23] Obama, and the post-racial moment itself, emerges *because of* pathological blackness, not in spite of it. Having a black person in the presidency simply means that the beer summit was a meeting between the president and himself: the Racially Profiled and the Racial Profiler-in-Chief, with the body currently occupying the office of the president falling squarely in the camp of the former (the Racially Profiled), while that body's office itself oversees the latter (the Racial Profiler-in-Chief). With Gates over to the House, the schizophrenic mania doubles: both Obama and Gates, hailing from that highly selective and suspect cadre known as the "black elite," have played no small part in transmitting the fallacy of black pathology in order to distinguish themselves from the black masses. For instance, in a 1998 PBS *Frontline* documentary, Gates interviews his Harvard colleague William Julius Wilson about the "two nations of black America," to which Wilson responds, "To think that our situation is comparable to that of the inner-city black is ridiculous." Gates concurs: "I find it hard to concede that these hoodlums are part of the same community I belong to. . . . This guy from the street seemed like a Martian to me."[24] When it was his turn, however, to be treated like a common hoodlum in his own home, presumably it did not occur to Gates that it was his proverbial chickens coming home to roost on his well-appointed Cambridge stoop.

With respect to the formation of the post-racial, the black revolution—and all meaningful assertions of black self-possession, no matter how mundane and pedestrian, such as entering one's own home—must be killed off in order that the colorblind nation, with its enormous market and cultural interests in blackness, may live. This recognition resounds in the black studies archive. For instance, Cornel West, following Richard Wright, observes "black subordination constitutes the necessary condition for the flourishing of American democracy, the tragic prerequisite for America itself."[25] Similarly, Frank Wilderson asserts that "America generates the coherence of White life" by killing off the black subject.[26] While the president of the United States is frequently referred to in white nationalist terms as the "most powerful man on Earth," the annals of black studies and recent events such as the Great White House Beer Summit remind us that President Obama was only vested with power, let alone gender, putatively.

The third supporting point, then, is that by examining post-racialism in terms of its roots in black self-possession and state violence we can better discern the intrinsic antiblackness of both conservative and liberal variants of colorblindness and the various Left-progressive iterations of multiculturalism and multiracialism that mark the post-racial present, some of which expressed triumph in the Obama election. As Jared Sexton has so incisively demonstrated in his study of the subject, multiracialism is aligned with the post-1960s neo-conservative discourse of "reverse racism." In this vein, the increasing diversity or multiculturalism of U.S. society confronts an undue influence wielded by black people over federal policy and the remodeling of national culture as a result of the civil rights era. According to this view, the improper material and political empowerment of the black community refracts the social imprimatur censuring overt racism into an "oppressive black power" against whites and nonblack people of color.[27] That is to say, multicultural discourse presumes that blacks have inverted racial hierarchy, that black politics must be detrimental to a multicultural and multiracial society, and thus, the superficial and uncritical celebration of the multicultural functions as a quarantine of racial blackness—and what better than for a black face (Obama) to signify this capture.[28] In an observation of enormous import for the present study, Sexton explains that this convergence reveals "the inverse historical relation between white supremacy's tolerance for multiracial formations and the relative strength of the black liberation struggle. When black resistance is thought by state and civil society to be effectively contained or neutralized, both practically and symbolically, the color line becomes considerably more fluid."[29]

Lastly, Sexton's trenchant analysis about the connection between the efficacy of black liberation and the acceptance of multiculturalism weighs heavily on how we evaluate contemporary race and sex scholarship. The degree to which the conceptual and political protocols of multiculturalism have become hegemonic in the critical study of race and sex in the post-racial era also seems to register the extent to which black radicalism is sequestered within the academy and in civil society at large from authorizing an analysis of what it means to suffer in the twenty-first century. On this score, my concern is to explore the degree to which the post-racial is as much a feature of the political multicultural Left as it is of the liberal mainstream or the conservative Right. This study, then, is as concerned with reading the making of the modern world through the history of antiblack sexual violence as it is with assessing how this foundational violence is obscured or falls out altogether from critical treatments of racism and sexual oppression. Sexton's leading insight here is anticipated by Gordon who approaches from a different valence my argument that post-racialism represents the latest effort to do away with black people. Gordon emphatically stakes out the ground of accountability for assessing how the post-racial shapes contemporary critical thought on racial regime: "there is no way to reject the thesis that there is something wrong with being black beyond the willingness to 'be' black—not in terms of convenient fads of playing blackness, but by paying the social costs of antiblackness on a global scale."[30] To properly ascertain how Gordon's standard applies to the critical study of race and sex, we need to elaborate on the original black studies paradigm from which this book emerges.

Post–Black Studies

This book's framework is situated in the leading conception of black studies coming out of the Black Power era. The founding black studies formation never reflected a consensus on what black studies should look like, and internal debate has always marked the movement. This certainly has been true of its institutionalized period after it entered the academy under its own name as a result of the student and community-based organizing on and around college campuses in the late 1960s.[31] Without sorting out all of these different tendencies here, the black studies project that I am calling upon in this study coalesced and distilled a long-standing tradition of radical black thought into a guiding interpretive paradigm alternative to the mainstream order of knowledge. The present study tacks toward this course. In 1995, Elizabeth Alexander published her now well-known essay "'Can You Be BLACK and Look at This': Reading the Rodney King Videos," in both the Thelma Golden edited volume *Black Male: Representations of Masculinity in Contemporary American Art*, occasioned by the Whitney Museum exhibition and public forum of the same name, and in the Black Public Sphere project that originated as a special issue of the journal *Public Culture*. In her milestone intervention in the annals of black cultural studies, Alexander arranges a series of texts representing black horror—the video of the Rodney King beating, slave narratives, the photograph of Emmett Till's mutilated corpse, and Pat Ward Williams's artistic confrontation with lynching photography presented at the Whitney exhibit—to stress that these cases "reminded us that there is such a thing as 'bottom line blackness' with regard to violence."[32] As Alexander observes, even in the brief archive she compiles in her essay, black people carry the history of horror on their very flesh, the collective memory of which is a resurrection and the visual re-presentation of which, it is claimed, repeatedly spurs insurrection. Alexander's reading of the violence of black existence compels us to discover what happens to the ethics of our political analysis when we behold the complexities and pluralities of contemporary subordination within the context of the essential structural antagonism of antiblackness—the violence of "bottom line blackness."

The leading paradigms guiding the study of race and sex across the disciplines and even within the interdisciplinary field of black studies have failed to situate the study of black existence within its essential structuring antagonism, Alexander's violence of "bottom line blackness." This failure—which I will argue is in fact an essential feature of the larger structural violence organizing the social—is devastating: despite the fact that "intersectionality" is now de rigueur in the academy, and that gender and sexuality are now popular topics in black studies, any analysis into what Wilderson terms the "culture of politics" configuring blackness as humanity's absence that does not delve into the implications of the violence of "bottom line blackness" is incapable, by definition, of approaching an ethical reading of conjunctural politics, the complexities subtending the concept, if not the rhetoric, of the "intersection," because there is no adequate understanding of the multiple articulations of gender, sex, nation, empire, class, or any other coupling of power and difference without first positing the terms of antiblackness. "Intersectionality" now functions as a disciplining mechanism across academic fields, eclipsing the insights of black studies and subordinating blackness to the politically suspect coalition discourse of "people of color" (as opposed to actual on-the-ground coalition work between differently positioned groups). This is *post–black studies*, which is to say, the culture of politics that would cordon off from serious intellectual study in the academic disciplines the very axial dilemmas that black social movement poses to the antiblack world—in Wynter's terms, again, questions regarding the station of blackness that are "neither posable nor resolvable" within today's prevailing multiculturalist framework. I am interested in how the police power expresses itself as post–black studies through the very topics of study identified with black life (policing, punishment, popular culture) and through those issues (sexuality, gender politics, antiessentialist identity) on which new academic fields (queer studies, performance studies, gender studies, queer of color critique) establish their turf partly by distancing themselves from a perceived retrograde seam with respect to said issues within black studies ("oppressive blackness").

Post–black studies, as the academic discourse of the post-racial moment, reiterates antiblackness by unmooring its conjunctural politics of the intersection from the exorbitant force blackness represents for modern knowledge.[33] As formulated throughout post–black studies, the intersection becomes a meeting place of identities, rather than a reading of the relations of power wherein the discourse on blackness "as a problem for thought" inheres within relation itself.[34] The main problem with post–black studies, why it ultimately predicates itself on a deracinated conception of power, is that it fails to respect the singular grammar of suffering that blackness reserves for New World Africans.

Blackened Paradigm Shifts

One of the many trenchant themes running through Wynter's work is the notion of mistaking the map for the territory. Her account of this inversion addresses itself to the rise and fall of black studies "in its original thrust, before its later cooptation into the mainstream of the very order of knowledge whose 'truth' in 'some abstract universal sense' it had arisen to contest."[35] Black studies emerged out of the collective "street tasks" of Black Power, its anti-integrationist politics, the eruption of black inner cities in 1968, and the foundations hewn by a network of black educational institutions that were working toward the establishment of an independent black university.[36] The original transgressive orientation of black studies programs, along with that of the Black Arts and Black Aesthetic Movements, explains Wynter, was "rechanneled as they came to be defined (and in many cases, actively to define themselves so) in new 'multicultural terms' as African-American Studies; as such, this field appeared as but one of the many diverse 'Ethnic Studies' that now served to re-verify the very thesis of Liberal universalism against which the challenges of all three movements had been directed in the first place."[37] We can view two of the central reasons for this cooptation of black studies in terms of a dual-counterinsurgency strategy to meet the threat posed by the black movement's "street tasks" and "intellectual tasks." First, the curtailment, by means of the various methods of state repression in the community, of black uprising and social movement from which black studies drew its strength was coupled with an attempted ideological cleansing of Black Power in the university. While the police murdered, prosecuted, and harassed black activists, entities such as the Ford Foundation were policing the ideological content of the black studies programs, providing funding for those geared toward integration, and not supporting those bearing nationalist, separatist, or Black Power ideas.[38]

The second component of the dual counterinsurgency that brought down the original 1960s conception of black studies came from within the black academy itself. As Wynter describes it, "the hegemonic rise of a black (soon to be 'African-American') poststructuralist and 'multicultural' literary theory and criticism spearheaded by Henry Louis Gates, Jr." policed the alternative aesthetic and imaginative possibility so powerfully mobilized under the sign of blackness during the street tasks of the 1960s, theorized by the artists and intellectuals of the Black Aesthetic and Black Arts Movements, and brought into the academy as the liberation struggle's "epistemological break" with the

Western knowledge regime. Gates's poststructuralist critique charged the original black studies formation with an inversion of the "racial essentialism" intrinsic to the Western construction of pathological blackness, of installing blackness, notes Wynter, as "another transcendent signified."[39] Gates and the poststructuralist multiculturalism replaced the galvanizing energy of blackness with what Wynter describes as "the reformist call for an alternative 'African-American' literary canon ostensibly able to complement the Euro-American literary one and, therefore, to do for the now newly incorporated black middle classes what the Euro-American literary canon did and continues to do for the generic, because white, and hegemonically Euroamerican middle classes."[40]

The diminution of the original black studies formation, as with that of the black radical tradition itself in the annals of Western civilization, as Cedric Robinson has demonstrated in his classic study *Black Marxism: The Making of the Black Radical Tradition*, serves the purpose of retrenching the present order of knowledge and its claim as the universal Truth to which there is no outside, to which there can be no alternative. This mystification is what Wynter describes as mistaking the map for the territory: the representation of what in fact is a decidedly relativistic worldview and a framework of violence mistaken for reality. The institutionalization of black studies, along with the various ethnic studies entities, did not produce intellectual emancipation commensurate with the prodigious cataclysm of the long civil rights and anticolonial period. Paradoxically, the complete social tumult of the multiple social movements assailing the Westernized structures of the global world system, and the upheaval of all received categories of subjectivity therein, ultimately did not find its influence on our ways of knowing. Citing the literary critic Wlad Godzich's observation that this paradox reveals a deep-seated reluctance to recognize the relationship "between the epistemology of knowledge and the liberation of people," Wynter suggests that this averseness expressed itself as profound hostility from the academic mainstream against the particularist claims of the black movement over and against both liberalism's and Marxism's universalism. In the midst of a global crisis in labor's struggle against capital during the 1970s and 1980s, the conditions facing the white working classes came to stand in for *the* generic human issue.[41] The liberal-Marxist universalism remapped the territory of social change by incorporating the various social movements as features of the universal Euro-American-centered mainstream scholarship, sanitizing the black studies challenge to *relativize* the Western paradigm.[42]

In many respects, social analysis in the Western tradition remains colonized by the itinerary of Marxism's and liberalism's universalist assumptive logics. Even studies of culture and race apply concepts and analytics derived from political economy in which oppression is contrasted with, and at the same time integrated into, the supposedly universal suffering of Westernized labor. Throughout this study I will examine in detail the numerous ruptures that slavery instigates throughout the canon of Marxist political economy and historiography, largely derived from the fact that Marxism's emphasis on the relation between labor and capital is displaced by the gratuitous violence of antiblackness, the antirelation of power essential to the modern world. Similarly, black studies in its original thrust, as Wynter puts it, reveals the academy's critical discourse on "race, gender, class, and sexuality" as largely impotent for countering the imperialism of white supremacy. In addition to an overly general analysis of the color line and a misplaced priority on the wage relation and the grammar of exploitation, the contemporary rhetoric is inadequate because it is largely mute with respect to the fact that sexualities are formulated, ritually propounded, and theorized *as* race. As Thomas notes, sexuality is promulgated in the service of a global historical traffic in white supremacy and antiblackness.[43] Feminism, gender studies, and queer studies have proceeded as if the very notion and material reality of Western civilization has not been founded on a primary and sexually graphic opposition between black and nonblack persons. By contrast, black studies has always registered this fact—and not as a discrete category of analysis distinct from what it means to be racialized in an antiblack world. The maps of the academic mainstream—including the various ethnic studies fields of inquiry—have revealed themselves incapable of charting the multidimensional terrain of black subjection and, as a result, the horizon of human liberation.

Wynter is clear that "the eventual defeat of the Black Aesthetic and Black Arts Movement as well as of Black Studies in its original conception resulted from the very process that had occasioned their initial triumph."[44] By this

Wynter means the black movements' revalorization of blackness, of the sign of nonbeing, as systematically devalorized by the present epistemological order. The revalorization of blackness in the work of black writers in the 1960s and 1970s, therefore, offers an entry point for extending the incomplete task of getting to the heart of the matter—the territory itself, not its maps and itineraries of misdirection. For example, in her groundbreaking anthology *The Black Woman*, published in 1970, Toni Cade Bambara laid out the terms for addressing the sexual violence of white supremacy under the sign of blackness. Bambara pointedly states: "Perhaps we need to let go of all notions of manhood and femininity and concentrate on Blackhood."[45] By "blackhood," Bambara means a unified Self over and against the bodily disaggregation of Western white supremacy.

Bambara's revalorization of blackness, through the notion "blackhood," allows us to revisit the original conception of black studies and, in so doing, shift the focus of racial analytic away from white supremacy and its various supplementary discourses of the body (sexuality, gender) and onto the more fundamental problem of antiblackness. While I will discuss both in the course of this study, centering antiblackness in the investigation of the post-racial is crucial. The time of post-racialism, or what Wilderson terms the "context of enunciation," includes shifts in racial demographics, a waning of racist vitriolic against all nonwhites uniformly, the hegemony of a multicultural or multiracial analytic that patently refuses the black/white binary as having any purchase on new realities, new depths to the crisis of capitalist production that, in turn, has compelled a renewed disciplining of Left politics to view capital as the primary engine of human subjugation under which all other forces are subsumed, and a deepening of the structural dispossession of both black and nonblack peoples of color.[46] The fact that these seemingly contradictory forces are not at all disabling to the reproduction of a post-racial imaginary is precisely the problem that requires excavation, and the structure of antiblackness is central to unpacking this problem. Across all of the changes that post-racialism represents, its enduring power is the further mystification of how racism and white supremacy come to be contested, destabilized, and retrenched through antiblackness—racism for an antiracist age.

Black Feminism's Betrayal

By centering my study around Bambara's "blackhood" and the principles of black power that have informed the black studies movement prior to, and, in rare instances, following, its institutional formations in the white academy, I am not evoking nostalgia for the 1960s or proposing a return to an unfinished liberation moment. Walter Rodney makes an observation about the worldwide black struggle that is prescient for the problem I am addressing in *Blackhood Against the Police Power*. Referring to Amilcar Cabral's status in the pantheon of black revolutionaries, Rodney notes,

> More than that, there is also the problem that so long as one does not make a revolution, one tends to be continually at a disadvantage when facing up to other people who have made a revolution. It is very easy for Cabral's view to be generalized because those views represent the views of a revolution, and a revolution that has succeeded, not just of a revolutionary.[47]

Of course, Guinea-Bissau may have won its war for independence from Portugal, but its decolonization has not yet been successful because black liberation the world over remains unrealized. Nonetheless, the burden to which Rodney refers is augmented when black people have repeatedly made a revolution, only to have freedom repetitively deferred, as is the case in North America. Defeat and failure, in this situation, are not a simple function of faulty tactics and ideology, given the massive intractability of the obstacle to be overcome. Nonetheless, the inheritance is complex: Which lessons from the past do we draw guidance from and how?

The dual counterinsurgency that eviscerated black studies from within as its base was undermined from without bears particular consequences for how to understand black feminism in relation to blackhood and the multicultural academy's post-racial quarantine of black power. *Blackhood Against the Police Power* would not be possible without black women's leadership in the struggle for black liberation. Although I am indebted to, and draw extensively from, black women thinkers such as Toni Cade Bambara, Elaine Brown, Safiya Bukhari, Saidiya Hartman, Joy James, Audre Lorde, Toni Morrison, Assata

Shakur, Hortense Spillers, and Sylvia Wynter, among many others, I distinguish this study from black feminism per se, past or present. In fact, whether black feminism has encountered a theoretical dead-end or its own institutionalized decadence, this study emerges out of black feminism's conceptual and political limitations and is posed as a respectful riposte to the crisis of contemporary black studies, which is the ongoing crisis of black liberation, of which black feminism today is an expression. The war against blackness in the present period has been waged in the same manner that it has been since the dawn of the African slave trade in the ninth-century Indian Ocean: a panoply of gratuitous violence, from kidnappings to sadomasochistic torture and sexual assault to the criminalization of any and all expressions of black self-possession. And the language in which this war against blackness is represented has also been consistent across the millennium-plus: in terms of a graphic and normative language of sex and gender, the basic codes imputing black savagery and conferring white civilization. The difficulty today is that this gender and sex politics includes a progressive and antiracist dimension: black feminism. How black feminism becomes part of the problem that it arises to confront is a story that has yet to be told, the full telling of which is beyond the scope of this study. As a minor step toward such an accounting, I outline key points regarding black feminism's co-optation against black power that situate the present investigation.

Daniel Patrick Moynihan's 1965 report "The Negro Family: The Case for National Action" was more than an indication of the "liberal retreat from race" and a shift in federal policy away from addressing white racism and its institutional life across American society and toward prosecuting the supposed deficiencies of black people themselves.[48] The Moynihan Report represented the attenuation of the resistance to desegregation and the preemptive groundwork for undermining the nascent Black Power movement. It also stands as a defining lightning rod for post–civil rights black feminism. While the duty to police black self-determination was shifting during the civil rights period from everyday white people in communities across the country, where it had served as the basic glue of modern society throughout the slavocracy and the century of lynching, to a law enforcement apparatus that was becoming newly professionalized and coordinated across local, regional, and national jurisdictions expressly to contain black mass mobilization, the Moynihan Report signifies a repurposing underway in the sexual terms of this antiblack violence.[49] Although lynching has not altogether ceased, the discourse of lynching in which the mythological black rapist threatens the purity of white femininity, and by extension, the stability of white society, was superseded by a discourse in which the black family posed the primary danger, namely its matriarchal structure that was said to engender sexual degeneracy and chaos. In Thomas's words, these are "the carnal dynamics of white domination" and "the erotic brutality of what is termed race."[50] Put differently, the terms of this latest attack on the black movement in the 1960s affirm the basic disqualification of black people from the gendered constructs of modern civilization.

Although it is but one illustration of modern society's antiblackness, the Moynihan Report represents the terms in which the vicious and sadistic attacks on black self determination in the COINTELPRO period were legitimated and redirected at the same time. Racist warfare became intelligible principally as gender and sex politics, such that by the 1980s black feminist texts began to appear in greater numbers, recording the void in which black women's issues had been disappeared, swallowed up by sexist assumptions about race and racist assumptions about sex. Chauvinism, sexism, homophobia, and misogyny are indeed ample not simply in the wider society, but also throughout the black movement, including black studies. It is important, however, to call this intramural violence by its proper name: antiblackness. I am reframing it as antiblackness because it denigrates and subjugates black women and queers in the names Western civilization creates to position blacks as subhuman. Conversely, black women's challenge to this gender and sex violence present within the movement, and rampant throughout the larger society, seeks to subvert the gendered power dynamics by redeploying the same terms that white racist culture uses in its discourses of the body to naturalize antiblack desire. Although black feminism gives renewed voice to black female subjectivity, black female sexual desire, black queer identities, and black gender and sex equality, it does so by relying on the normative codes of race—gender and sex. In advancing a reconstruction of the meaning of gender and sexuality, it has worked within the normative codes of antiblackness, or what Wynter refers to as the "genres" of Man. When black feminism engages the terms of antiblackness thusly, it is not antiblack because it does not seek to extend black oppression. Nonetheless, Hortense Spillers's characterization of society's compact with black women, "that is to say, the agreement to go hungry (on all the registers)," is not entirely accurate.[51] Black men are bribed to enter patriarchy, at the expense of black women, queers, and children, but black feminists are similarly induced to embody gender as equally central to their liberation, when in fact both operations of gender "sell the poison by way of the decoy," as Spillers puts it.[52]

Black feminism's reply, of course, has long been that since gender is an inseparable and irrefutable dimension of black women's existence, it is essential to black liberation in toto.[53] Black women continue to be targets of harassment and racist sexual violence from all quarters, including in the academy, making black feminism often seem necessary and strategic, in the least. This reality cannot be minimized or overstated. And yet, there are costs here that need accounting for. What is the "poison" for which gender and sex politics are "decoys"? Without minimizing black feminism's historic role in checking the unbridled erotic rampage of racist culture, it is time to take stock of its own internal limits. All discourse has its material effects, and the concrete realities out of which black feminism emerged included the repression by terror of a militant blackness that had congealed during the Black Power era but that emanates from long-standing traditions of black self-defense and self-determination, and the blaming of the victims of the state's counterinsurgency to the tune of black hypersexuality (chauvinist brothers, on the one hand, and sisters-out-of-place, on the other hand).[54] While every institution in the black community was blitzed between the 1950s and the 1990s by assassination and criminalization, deindustrialization, restructuring of the welfare state, and the epidemics of HIV/AIDS and crack cocaine, racial debate largely devolved around the terms crystalized in the Moynihan Report. Whereas the Black Arts Movement positioned blackness as "primal and essential," while simultaneously transforming it "into a *critical* posture" capable of strident critiques of an essential blackness, the Moynihan Report's decoy function dispatched black revolutionary thought from black discourse like moths swallowed in the flame.[55] *Fire!!* of the Harlem Renaissance became *Black Fire* in the Black Power era, followed later by *Words of Fire* and *Sisterfire* from black feminists in the 1990s.[56] *Fire!!* was a literary magazine produced by Langston Hughes, Zora

Neale Hurston, Wallace Thurman, Gwendolyn Bennett, Bruce Nugent, and other black artists in 1920s New York City that explored black sexual realities. *Fire!!* suffered from the lack of an independent political and economic base of support in the black community and folded after just one issue. By the time of the Black Arts Movement, during the Black Power era, a robust black public sphere sustained numerous black literary publications, such as *Black Fire*, which remains in print thanks to one of the few remaining such institutions, Baltimore's Black Classic Press. *Words of Fire* and *Sisterfire* are both published by mainstream white publishing houses. While the latter fire-texts rightfully align themselves with the august tradition of black letters going back to the landmark *Black Fire*, and to *Fire!!* before it, the commercial viability of black feminism after the suppression of black power bespeaks both the tokenistic treatment of black arts in the post–civil rights era and the co-opted frame in which black feminism is legible to the mainstream, including corporate academia.[57]

As noted earlier in this chapter, the black academy (including black feminism) also conspired in transmuting this critical feature of black power—an essentially critical / critically essential blackness—from asset to fatal flaw. Claiming the progressive mantel of "antiessentialism," this attack on black critique was patently opportunistic, as well. As Spillers explains, by the Black Power era the black movement had yoked blackness "to a symbolic program of philosophical 'disobedience' (a systematic skepticism and refusal)" available to anyone or any position that was willing to pursue creative destruction and invention through thinking.[58] Blackness, as a mode of iconoclastic thought, opened up a strategy for imagination and critique that made it a fertile site for multiculturalism, women of color political formations, and the various identity movements. These late arrivals, however, did not always extend the interests of black people; more to the point, their critical programs rested upon displacing blackness from its essential place in explaining the onto-epistemic structure of the modern world. This state of affairs produces dire consequences for black thought and for black lives.

One example from 2015–2017 illustrates how black feminism is vulnerable to co-optation in the absence of black power. In this period, we witnessed the almost daily outpouring of (mostly white) women accusing politicians and powerful men in the entertainment industries of sexual harassment and assault. Given that this violence has been going on routinely for a very long time, we might wonder why the accusations are finally being heard now. Powerful white men are being fired from their jobs merely on the face of accusations, without evidence, due process, or legal conviction—and I do not mean to imply that these men are being railroaded, assuming they were in fact at fault, but instead I emphasize the summary judgments against them to underscore that this process is atypical for white men who are ordinarily allowed to retain their innocence even after a thorough exposure of the damning evidence against them, including the occasional criminal conviction. Although certainly the climate of the Donald Trump presidency is a factor here, I suggest that we cannot overlook the Movement for Black Lives (M4BL) as part of the explanation for why this modicum of accountability for long-standing patterns of misogyny is occurring now. M4BL refocused the nation's attention onto the violence of policing, and yet police officers continue their daily assaults unabated. In late September 2017, when a teenager accused two New York Police Department officers of arresting her in Coney Island and raping her while she was in handcuffs, it was only the latest incident of cops raping young girls during the period of M4BL.

Even irony is overwhelmed by history: it would be historically consistent if the most immediate outcome of M4BL, initiated in its current historical iteration by three black feminists, were that elite white men are held accountable for their assaults on (mostly) white women. It is common knowledge, for instance, that white women have been the primary beneficiaries of affirmative action policies that were the outgrowth of civil rights organizing by black people; black activists and scholars have also noted that the primary result of the movement against violence against women—criminalizing domestic violence—has largely translated into more punitive state control in black lives, despite prominent leadership by black feminists in the anti-violence campaign.[59] While black people must do the heavy lifting of communal organizing and put their lives on the line to highlight the violence, white women can raise their voices *as individuals with jobs* to interrupt workplace harassment. Presumably there are white men accused during this period of #MeToo who are also assaulting women and girls of color, but considering Bill Clinton, Dominique Strauss-Kahn, and numerous other powerful white men who are accused of assaulting black women but are never held accountable, it is clear that being white and female is the prerequisite for victimhood. This truth is well known, but if the M4BL can indirectly lead to an expanded sphere of safety for white women of a certain class status, with no commensurate protection for black people, then this is how blackness is used to meet nonblack needs and an example of how the ethical dilemmas of civil society are parasitic on antiblack sexual violence. My suggestion that the protocols of black feminism as they have developed in the post–civil rights period are also part of this dynamic where M4BL can foment vindication for white, not black, victims of violence is a difficult proposition requiring measured scrutiny.

The elevation of black feminism, its affinities with identity politics (fraught tensions with, and dissensions from, identitarianism notwithstanding), and the suppression of black power indict the period of historical struggle, not simply black feminists as individuals. Individual thinkers are products of their time, as much as they create the times. For instance, Haki Madhubuti connects Gwendolyn Brooks's evolution from a "negro poet" to a "black poet" to Brooks's aesthetic and political response to the direction of black struggle in the 1960s.[60] Coming out of the Black Power era, then, black women thinkers did, in fact, outline alternatives to the feminist embrace of gender and sex categories. Bambara took stock of the terms of racist abuse extolled in the Moynihan Report and responded by explicitly calling for the abandonment of these categories of gender and sex altogether, and as a result, a rethinking of the meaning of blackness. In 1971, writing from her jail cell at the Women's House of Detention in lower Manhattan, Angela Y. Davis, as well, contributed a formidable intervention into gendered thought. Davis's "Reflections on the Black Woman's Role in the Community of Slaves" directly replied to the Moynihan Report, but did so in a manner that also sought to undermine the very terms employed in Moynihan's sexual racism. Davis's methods in "Reflections" also stand directly opposed to the terms that served as the basis for black feminism as it would develop from the late 1970s onward—including in Davis's own work ever since she rewrote "Reflections" a decade later for inclusion in her book of essays, *Women, Race, and Class*.[61] In "Reflections," Davis strips biologism from sex and deconstructs conventional Western notions of sex and gender, writing that for slavery to work, "the black woman had to be annulled as woman," and through sexual assault the slave master had "to establish her as a female *animal*." [62] Had Davis and Bambara's methods gained traction—in other words, had the historical context of a robust black power ethic in which they made their interventions not been thoroughly repressed—we might not have been left with the winnowed capacity for interrogating, and the resulting accommodation of, the basic sexual concepts through which antiblackness operates. With black power neutralized, the 1980s find Davis reframing her reading of black women's ungendering in "Reflections" into "standards for a new womanhood," signaling the black feminist attempt to work within the narrow confines imposed by what Thomas refers to as "the gender conceits of empire." [63]

Without the context of black power to back them up, black women thinkers working in the post–civil rights period found themselves further isolated, maligned, and under assault. Spillers reflects that when she published "Mama's Baby, Papa's Maybe" in 1987, her intention was to bolster herself, to live to fight another day: "I became very good at being a marksman and ducking." [64] Wynter, as well, comments that once she realized that the consciousness Western society has imposed upon her "does not function for my best interest," she understood that the black studies movement was nothing less than a "war against 'consciousness.'" [65] I cite these black women's martial language because the hegemony enjoyed by black feminism in the post-racial period has included denouncing such militancy as masculinist, chauvinist, inflammatory, or aggressive when it is expressed by black men, when in fact it is merely being descriptive and empirical. When it condones this hegemonic censure of militancy, black feminism contributes to post–black studies. Against this gender-sex common-sense, the history of black struggle teaches us two important lessons: first, when critique is on point, it is interpreted as "militant"; and second, militancy does not have a gender. Militancy is *un*gendering for black liberation: it is an erotic praxis that counters the sexual violence of the Middle Passage and enslavement that created the racist construal of black sexual beings as bestial and deployed gender constructs to naturalize this order of knowledge.

In one of the landmark black feminist texts, *All the Women Are White, All the Blacks Are Men, But Some of Us Are Brave*, Gloria T. Hull and Barbara Smith write:

Unfortunately, as women's studies has become both more institutionalized and at the same time more precarious within traditional academic structures, the radical life-changing vision of what women's studies can accomplish has constantly been diminished in exchange for acceptance, respectability, and the career advancement of individuals. This trend in women's studies is a trap that Black women's studies cannot afford to fall into.[66]

Despite the abundant and invaluable contributions, black feminism has fallen into the trap. Again, my interest is not to indict individual black feminists, nor to stake out a position against black feminism, let alone black women, but rather to highlight the absence of a vibrant and critical black public sphere capable of providing the basis for black self-determination that would imagine blackness apart from the categories of antiblackness set forth by Western slaveholding society. The withering of independent black institutions with the capacity for creative autonomy has left an overwhelmingly homogeneous culture of politics in which we must struggle to rethink the battle lines. Black thought is left to duck for cover and lob largely impotent mortars with imprecision. *Blackhood Against the Police Power*'s "context of enunciation" is related to black feminism's in that as its author I am located in the university, a product of the historical forces that have delegitimized black power, and thus party to the various discourses and disciplines that I strive to interrogate. I make no claims to being situated otherwise. Through the intellectual scaffolding of this study, however, I work to hold myself accountable to a paradigm of thought that emanates from autonomous black struggle. I do not presume to be immune from the mistakes that I criticize in others, nor do I assume that my consciousness is not polluted by the historical period and processes of which I am a product. It has been said that being a product of a racist society is like being a fish in water: the fish doesn't even know it's wet. This study recognizes that not only do we need to be aware of the water in which we swim (consciousness), but that working toward reestablishing independent black studies is a crucial step in the wholesale restructuring of our environments. Without this deeper cut, we are left exposed to the creeping political conservatism that is as present within black studies today as it was at the time of Booker T. Washington in 1895. The limitations of black feminism are closely tied to its institutional capture and the absence of sustainable black independent intellectual spaces. Stepping out from black feminism is now a necessary move in the "intellectual tasks" of black liberation.

Criticism by Any Other Name

An important seam in the contemporary black studies project from which I draw, toward autonomous black thought, comes under the label of "afro-pessimism." Although the term has a longer and more troubling history behind it, in its most recent iteration, Saidiya Hartman is usually credited with using the term "afro-pessimism" in response to a reviewer who labeled her book *Scenes of Subjection: Terror, Slavery, and Self-Making in Nineteenth-Century America* "pessimistic."[67] The main elaborators of the recent approach to black studies in the North American academy that has come to be called "afro-pessimist" are Frank B. Wilderson III and Jared Sexton. To my knowledge, at the time of this writing, they remain the only two scholars with a substantial body of published scholarship who readily identify their work as "afro-pessimist." Other scholars bear affinities with afro-pessimism, or are associated by others with it, but many of these same scholars would bristle at being labeled as such, and more importantly, many of them also bear as many contradictory strains as they do likenesses with the work of Wilderson and Sexton (Hartman included). The two books that I have edited with Khalil Saucier, *On Marronage: Ethical Confrontations with Antiblackness* and *Conceptual Aphasia in Black: Displacing Racial Formation*, are the only volumes to curate significant treatments of the afro-pessimist approach (at least at the time of this writing), and both collections present a roster of authors whose relationship to the label "afro-pessimist" varies.[68] The current version of afro-pessimism (there is a prior afro-pessimism, to which I will turn momentarily) congealed as an identifiable approach to black studies during the early 2000s when Wilderson and Sexton were graduate students at the University of California, Berkeley, where Hartman was a professor at the time. Since it is a technique of co-optation in Western society to filter a resistant body of knowledge through the personalities of its most recognizable authors, thereby dislocating thought from the traditions that call it forth, isolating individual thinkers from the communities out of which they emerge, figuring the epistemic challenge posed as the musings of extremists, or elevating it as the work of exceptional brilliance that presumably cannot be extended dialogically, only shot down or copied, out of respect for the individuals in question and for the black studies tradition that is fortified through their work, I will desist from saying anything further about the personal biographies of afro-pessimism's most identifiable proponents. The context for its emergence, however, does indeed matter, as I will explore further below.

When I began writing this book around 2006, this latest iteration of afro-pessimism was largely unheard of but swiftly became a bad word, both within black studies and outside of it. The small handful of scholars associated with it were treated with a leprous antipathy. Although this censorship remains largely in force around the North American academy, by the time I completed the book, nearly a decade later, afro-pessimism was enjoying a certain cachet. Having reviewed a number of scholarly articles for journals during this time that attempted to deal with afro-pessimism, and having sat through numerous academic conference presentations in which it was, variously, the elephant, the bogeyman, or the celebrity in the room, it appears that the approach remains both very much misunderstood and still in development. Although I do not presume that the defensiveness and hostility with which it continues to be received is because of a simple lack of understanding—often it is due to an astute recognition that foundational concepts are quaking—it is my intention that *Blackhood Against the Police Power* demonstrate the necessity of dealing seriously with the implications of the afro-pessimist approach.

It is testament to both the formidable trailblazing of Wilderson and Sexton, on the one hand, and to the deep-seated but largely disavowed truths about our world that this latest iteration of afro-pessimism is revealing, on the other hand, that in such a short time people are already referring to a "canon" of afro-pessimism. I do not believe that there is such a canon, and for reasons that I explore in the first chapter of *Blackhood Against the Police Power* regarding genealogy, I do not believe that there ever will be or should be such a canon. Presumably, some would point to the various sources that I draw from in this study as the canon, and yet I suggest that "canon" mystifies what is at work here. Afro-pessimism is not about compulsory texts or requisite references. It is an assault on the paradigm of knowledge that a slaveholding society demands to reproduce itself and, in particular, on the ways of knowing that same said social formation requires to fortify its post-racial and multicultural visage. In this introduction and in the first chapter, I elaborate on the key features of the paradigmatic intervention it pursues, but it is clear that afro-pessimism is squarely within the tradition of black studies' interrogation of Western society's core assumptions.

What does it mean, exactly, to be afro-pessimist in the present period? Sexton has expounded on this question amid the rancor, ad hominem attacks, and political intransigence that has greeted afro-pessimism in the academy.[69] Deborah Bowen states it rather more straightforwardly: "An afro-pessimist is just a black pessimist. It's a black person who is frustrated with the reality that we have not come as far as we like to think we have."[70] Hartman's reviewer labeled *Scenes of Subjection* "pessimistic" because the book endeavored to show that emancipation and its freedom discourse did not ameliorate the condition of enslavement, but instead was the site of its reelaboration and extension. Hartman explains her "pessimism" thusly:

> But I think there's a certain integrationist rights agenda that subjects who are variously positioned on the color line can take up. And that project is something I consider obscene: the attempt to make the narrative of defeat into an opportunity for celebration, the desire to look at the ravages and the brutality of the last few centuries, but to still find a way to feel good about ourselves. That's not my project at all, though I think it's actually the project of a number of people.[71]

Whereas much of black historiography keeps pointing back to the strides of civil rights, or to this or that act of resistance or agentic moment, the black pessimist acknowledges that the war on black survival continues, unabated and unbroken by Jubilee, formal legal equality, Oprah, you name it. In this sense, then, we might say that afro-pessimists abound in black history. David Walker published *An Appeal to the Coloured Citizens of the World* in 1829, calling for black unity, action, and self-determination informed by deep suspicion regarding the inclinations of the slaveholding class, inclusive of white abolitionists. Walker's contemporary Martin R. Delany facilitated John Brown's preparations for the Harper's Ferry raid, and whether in his novel *Blake* or in his 1854 pamphlet *The Political Destiny of the Colored Race on the American Continent*, Delany left record of a nascent black nationalism, of the intransigence of antiblackness, or of the need for black emigration out of the United States—either way, a decidedly sober early analysis of the forces arrayed against black life in the modern era. We might even read Marcus Garvey's leadership of the United Negro Improvement Association in the early twentieth century as an expression of a certain form of pessimism regarding the potentiality and desirability for black inclusion in the white nation. W. E. B. Du Bois's early critique of Garveyism, in this sense, expressed his faith at that time in his life of the possibility for black inclusion, a position he would later revise.

In his 1963 "Message to the Grassroots" speech, Malcolm X told his audience that "integration" meant infiltration of the black revolution, citing how the March on Washington earlier that year was designed to preempt the black grassroots from taking to the streets to shut down government.[72] The legal scholars who started the critical race theory movement in the 1980s were scorned for asserting the rather pedestrian claim that racism is endemic to U.S. society and for pillorying First Amendment piety for its racist and sexist violence, among other sensible but discomfiting ideas.[73] Derrick Bell, in particular, was castigated for his allegory about aliens from outer space that arrive to offer America an end to all of its ills—debt, disease, environmental destruction, crime, poverty, and so on—in exchange for giving up its black citizens to some unknown fate at the hands of the space traders.[74] As a veteran of the civil rights struggle living through the throes of the post–civil rights backlash of the 1980s, Bell recognized that black people remained expendable—or in terms that afro-pessimism has recently popularized, *fungible*. As a result of this sober diagnosis, Bell advocated "racial realism" in which the black struggle would be free to "think and plan within a space of reality, rather than idealism."[75] To borrow Wilderson's words, the "pessimist" moments in black historical struggle, then, are *enabling* of black life, not disabling, because they refuse to adjust an analysis of the terror encompassing black existence to "some kind of coherent, hopeful solution to things."[76]

We might say, despite the theoretical language in which some scholars work, that the afro-pessimist (at least in its current incarnation in North American black studies discourse) is just someone who calls a spade a spade. Although afro-pessimism has been disparaged at times for flaunting or caricaturing black experience, it may in fact be the case that afro-pessimist analysis more closely corroborates what ordinary black folk encounter than what has been the standard fare in black scholarship recently. Its popularity among some black high school students, driven largely by black debate club networks, testifies to afro-pessimist plain wisdom. The problem, then, that afro-pessimism represents for black studies is greater than the reluctance to give up the presumption of a previous generation's hard fought gains. It emerges in this moment of the post-racial era's post–black studies, a time in which antiracism and antiblackness commingle with each other, precisely because it responds to the long-standing crisis in black intellectual struggle. In his first editorial in November 1910 for *The Crisis*, the magazine he would edit for many years on behalf of the National Association for the Advancement of Colored People, Du Bois announced that the magazine "takes its name from the fact that the editors believe that this is a critical time in the history of the advancement of men."[77] By 1932, Carter G. Woodson had reformulated his various comments and objections to the state of black education into the intervention posed in his seminal *The Mis-Education of the Negro*. In the late spring of 1962, just before his death at age sixty-seven, E. Franklin Frazier returned to Atlanta where he had previously taught at Morehouse College and Fisk University until his article "The Pathology of Race Prejudice," in which he argued that whites are driven mad by their "Negro-complex," an "insanity" compelling otherwise "normal" white people to conduct revolting acts of cruelty against black people, led to death threats against him and his family.[78] In his return to Atlanta, Frazier gave a lecture on "the failure of the Negro intellectual." Of course, it would not be until Harold Cruse's *The Crisis of the Negro Intellectual* in 1967 that this practice of dissent and self-critique within the black movement would reach its most cogent apogee. As Nathan Hare would observe in Joyce Ladner's *The Death of White Sociology*, "the paradox is that only Cruse, who was not college-trained, has been able, in this era, to write such a book"—an incisive observation that Woodson had anticipated and that weighs significantly on our present moment.[79]

Each generation, in other words, has inveighed against the colonizing effect of an education that might benefit individual black people but does not serve the interests of blacks *as a people*; against that class of elites trained *away from* accountability to the black community; and against the profound black *dis*unity that is the outcome of these dynamics. Lerone Bennett noted in "The Betrayal of the Betrayal: The Crisis of the Black Middle Class" that "the historic role of the middle sector of an oppressed group is betrayal," while Fanon's *The Wretched of the Earth* dealt at length and in scathing terms with this state of affairs, with the role of the colonized elite in transmitting the line between the so-called civilized sectors of society and the so-called savage natives: "Objectively, the intellectual behaves in this phase like a common opportunist. In fact he has not stopped maneuvering."[80] Adolph Reed Jr. historicizes this opportunism by individual black elites in the contemporary period in his biting essay "'What Are the Drums Saying, Booker?': The Curious Role of the Black Public Intellectual." Reed argues that the race spokesperson badge worn by Booker T. Washington at the turn of the twentieth century, as designated by white elites rather than by any black constituency or movement, derived from the white nation's abandonment of the Reconstruction Era's racial democracy.[81] While Washington's promotion of the kind of education for blacks that his white benefactors approved of has been well documented, the commentary has usually held culpable Washington the individual, when in fact his rise to influence was only possible because white terrorism and betrayal decimated the broad, democratic political participation of black citizens. "The idea of the free-floating race spokesman was a pathological effect of the disfranchisement specific to the segregation era, the condition to which Washington contributed," explains Reed, and black leadership ever since has been hounded by "Washington's unacknowledged legacy . . . that any black individual's participation in public life always strives to express the will of the racial collectivity."[82]

Whereas the focus of Reed's essay is a handful of so-called "black public intellectuals" that he finds all too willing to update Washington's role in representing the race to the nonblack world, my interest is with how the recent afro-pessimism is a response to the larger undermining of black political mobilization that has made possible the outsized influence of individual scholars who acquiesce to a culture of politics that studiously seeks to quarantine black power in thought and practice. To the names that Reed calls out, we could add many more, the majority of whom would not be known beyond the academy, or perhaps even outside their specific institutions, but who collectively contribute to the crisis of black studies. It is often the well-heeled black intellectual who seems to be most vociferous in denouncing the afro-pessimist intervention, sometimes without actually studying its claims. Following Reed's insight that the presence of a robust black public sphere determines the nature of intellectual struggle, afro-pessimism seems to be a response to the manner in which the crisis of the surround institutionalizes the co-optation of the critical posture of black thought in the present period.

Blackhood Against the Police Power, as a text that draws insight from an afro-pessimist framework, offers three innovations that aim to extend the co-operative intervention and, in so doing, address its weaknesses and upgrade the power of collective analysis it makes possible. First, I address afro-pessimism's underdeveloped sense of its own historical position; second, I intentionally work with scholarly contributions that are positioned as oppositional to each other, separated by the emphasis on individual agency and collective efficacy; and third, I renovate afro-pessimism's take on gender-sex, not by coupling it with black feminism, but by deconstructing the latter by way of its own key insights. One of the major limitations of afro-pessimism as articulated by Wilderson and Sexton is that the tradition it calls forth clashes with the tradition in which it is rightfully situated. Long before Hartman, the term "afro-pessimism" was originally coined to refer to a body of scholarship, journalism, commentary, and policy prognostications about the continent of Africa postindependence. The main feature of this original afro-pessimism is the notion that Africa's destiny lies in war, violence, disease, corruption, and hopelessness due to the incapacity of Africans to make improvements in the state of health, poverty, development, peace, and governance since the end of the colonial period. As Thomas points out, this original afro-pessimism "functioned like a sociological 'culture of poverty' or 'culture of pathology' discourse not for Black ghettos in the diaspora but for the entire African continent (and, by extension, the diaspora) with a tacit historical and environmental determinism."[83] As V. Y. Mudimbe explained in his classic *The Invention of Africa: Gnosis, Philosophy, and the Order of Knowledge*, such claims about Africa do not, in fact, refer to a geographically bounded population entity, but rather that "Africa" means black people residing on the continent.[84] The tropes guiding this afro-pessimism connect its postcolonial emergence with the nineteenth-century racist tracts on civilization and history created to justify Western colonization.[85]

The problem is that this old afro-pessimism is not that old and it certainly is not past; it is very much still with us, as Toussaint Nothias's useful analysis of recent media coverage of Africa shows.[86] Wilderson and Sexton do not address the connections between the new afro-pessimism, on the one hand, and the long-standing recognition throughout the African diaspora that the term is a sign of neocolonial violence, on the other hand.[87] Yet, as Thomas's critical reading of the new afro-pessimism, what he calls "Afro-pessimism (2.0)," shows, there are indeed connections that warrant careful consideration. First, as Thomas puts it, "there is little if any Africa to this discourse at all, its nominal Afro-hyphenation notwithstanding."[88] It is not that Wilderson and Sexton do not include Africa and its diaspora beyond North America in the ambit of their theoretical interventions (although considerably more work needs to be done by the new afro-pessimism in this regard). Rather, the absence of Africa in Wilderson and Sexton's afro-pessimism lies with how African and African diasporic thought is muted in their formulation of afro-pessimism (selective uses of Fanon, an isolated discussion of Steve Biko, and a brief critique of Achille Mbembe standing in for a larger Pan-African body of thought).[89] Indeed, their engagement with black thought does not reveal its roots much beyond the time and space of the post–civil rights North American academy.

For Thomas, this void of African and African diasporic thought underwrites the continuities of pessimist ideology between afro-pessimism "1.0" and "2.0." He recalls that Cheikh Anta Diop's classic contributions to Pan-Africanism gave extensive exposure to the instrumental role of pessimism in European imperialism: in *The Cultural Unity of Black Africa*, Diop connected Western society's culture of "war, violence, crime, and conquests" to its signature "metaphysical systems" of pessimism; he further asserts that "from the time of Ancient Egypt to the present, the African has never thought of founding a durable moral or metaphysical system that is based on pessimism"; and in *Civilization or Barbarism: An Authentic Anthropology*, Diop challenged Ernest Renan's Eurocentric assumption that "only pessimism is fecund," asking in turn, if Africa could "save

Western man from his pessimism and individualistic solitude?"[90] Thomas notes that while Diop may be the "most monumental historian of the Black world," alongside Du Bois, he is but one in a tradition of Pan-African thinkers who explicitly reject a pessimist orientation to black futures as a design of Western imperialism and a racist conceit, from Ifi Amadiume to Cedric Robinson.[91]

It is a decided weakness of the recent afro-pessimism at this juncture in its development that it has as yet left this inheritance underexamined, and as a consequence, left its theoretical scaffolding more shallow and its discursive maneuvers more narrow than the sophistication of its insights demands. The task at hand requires the construction of a theoretical architecture as deep as the millennium of black freedom moves and a discursive apparatus as sweeping as the global reach of blackness and the planetary travels of black people. At this point, one of the consequences of this unfinished construction is a mystification of the differing levels at which optimism and pessimism are pitched in the varied debates that afro-pessimism old and new yoke together. The old afro-pessimism rehearsed a worn racist conception about blackness as the locus of all that is backward, savage, and undesirable into a prediction about black capacity. The notion that African societies would never "develop" bypasses the historic and present global relations of dominance in which Africa is enmeshed, of which the imperialism of "development" discourse itself is a constituent element, but it also rests on an assumptive logic that says black people cannot act and create their own history. Pan-African thought, from Du Bois to Diop to Robinson, responds to this "colonial cultural pathology" and has endeavored for just shy of a century to dismantle it, marshalling a comprehensive optimism of spirit, analysis, and action in reply.[92]

The new afro-pessimism emerges in the post-racial multicultural milieu and its ossification in the U.S. academy—in other words, two decades plus onward from the suppression of Black Power and its zenith of self-determination in black thought and struggle. This "context of enunciation" for the new afro-pessimism, as I have outlined in this introduction and that I seek to elaborate in detail across the chapters to follow, means that the theoretical armament must adapt to the shifting lines of force in the present period, while honing more closely on the scales of coercion that persist, continuously, across historical periods. The new afro-pessimism, then, scrutinizes the nonblack world, its material, epistemic, and ontic structures, its filiations, and its desires that prevent it from abandoning the perquisites of antiblackness. In other words, the old afro-pessimism was pessimistic about *black* capacities, while the new afro-pessimism is pessimistic about *nonblack* capacities for change. This is why two positions on either side of a supposedly impassable divide—new afro-pessimism and its objectors—can recognize their respective approaches as twin inflections of the same reality; and likewise, analysis that explicitly takes aim at the afro-pessimism of today, as Thomas does in his recent work, can stand as a vital coupling with, and necessary developmental corrective to, any afro-pessimist account.

The divide between the new afro-pessimism today and those who object to it is ostentatiously drawn along the question of agency. I aim to dispense with the superficiality of this divide by working with the deeper intentions of both sides. One of the ways in which afro-pessimist interventions today are dismissed is by blaming its authors for the turbulence that their insights arouse. Implicitly, these objections to afro-pessimism are saying that the mere presence of controversy, dissent, and critique are problems in and of themselves. On the contrary: the absence of controversy belies the presence of uniformity and a lack of serious critical content and ethical purpose. The arrival of the new afro-pessimism occasioned the first real controversy in the critical study of race and sex in a long while. For a time after its appearance, the supposed divide was characterized as between afro-pessimism and black optimism. Although Fred Moten coined the phrase to name his own scholarly and artistic program in his essay "Black Op," the term "black optimism" essentially describes the weft of Left racial analysis that has sought to contest the pathologizing of blackness and black movement, including in black studies, in the post–civil rights period.[93] In the broadest sense, it expresses the desire to resolve the ontological violence wherein black people are positioned as nonhuman, or to move beyond ontology altogether by imagining a universal humanity in which race no longer defines human existence. For black optimists, there is faith in the capacity of black people (along with others) to act on the world and eventually end racism. More often than not, however, the means come to stand in for the ends—in other words, for some black optimists, evidence of black agency doubles as evidence of actual social progress, and in this way, such work arcs back to the ever-present question of pathological blackness. Afro-pessimism, on the other hand, is not an argument for or against black agency, but rather views the modern world as founded on an a priori violence against black people that creates ontology as its effect. The world's onto-epistemic structure, therefore, is impervious to change through human action and discourse, except, perhaps, by means of an equally fundamental counterviolence.

Whereas afro-pessimism continues as a cogent and identifiable discourse, black optimism has faded out as such. The reason for this, I believe, is that the latter only arose as necessary in the moment that afro-pessimism burst on the scene as a challenge to the prevailing culture of politics gripping racial discourse. Black optimism allowed people to say, "we're not down with *that*." Since black optimism stood in for the normative mode of thought and the hegemonic methodology about race and sex critique, the need to name and sustain itself as a coherent program was no longer necessary as institutional forces (university presses, senior faculty, dissertation committees, tenure committees, hiring networks, peer review processes) took over the disciplining of the upstart afro-pessimism. This state of affairs is disastrous to the life of black studies, and thus to black liberation, because instead of supporting a robust arena for critique and debate, students and unprotected faculty are pressured, policed, and sanctioned for their engagement with afro-pessimism. The few tenured faculty working in an afro-pessimist vein are isolated and iced by their peers. Mind you, this scenario is not novel when it comes to new ideas in the academy, let alone to criticisms of received truth. The sad bit of the story is that black feminists, queers, progressives, and other scholars of color are among those implementing the institutional backlash against afro-pessimism.

It makes sense, therefore, that the other side of Moten's original formulation of "black op" wilted almost immediately. In a public talk given a year prior to the publication of "Black Op," Moten coupled "black optimism" with "black operations." Whereas black optimism, as I am arguing here, fades back into the surround, black operations too is lost, but for different reasons. Unlike the former, the implied guerilla and insurgent qualities of the latter may have been too hot to handle—or at least too ethical a burden to carry without a radical black public sphere to support the load. Indeed, even Moten has always emphasized optimism, with its future possibilities, over operations and its concomitant unsavory pragmatism ("by any means necessary") and counterviolence that today's protracted struggle would seem to require. As James has remarked, at this point it is all about "psy-ops"—psychological warfare.

Sexton and Moten, in fact, have published an extended dialogue about their respective approaches.[94] What is memorable about these exchanges is their clarification of the fine-grained distinction between the two positions, or "tendencies," as Sexton put it, and the deep respect and collegiality with which they conducted the debate. Although it might delineate a minor annex in the black studies archive, the genuine appreciation for the other's critical approach conveyed in their exchange stands out in the long history of black intellectual debate. Unfortunately, most of the people who align themselves with Moten's black optimism fail to grasp his nuanced distinction between black social death and the social life of blackness, and deign to assume his careful engagement with the work that afro-pessimism has produced. Indeed, it may in fact be more accurate to say that Moten is not even saying what the people who follow him think he is saying and that his popularity among these observers has more to do with his performance of what they impute onto him. Calvin Warren, for one, argues that Moten is seeking out a space between the two poles, what Warren names as a "black mysticism" that seeks to abandon ontology and politics altogether.[95] Although what Moten is doing is a topic for another time, it bears remembering that since thought is social, not individual, it is more properly understood as a collective intellect temporally entangled and expressing itself through individuals and their communal discourse at a moment in time.

Against this pressure to draw lines, and in harmony with the sociality of thought, I work with both sides of the supposed divide that has arisen around the new afro-pessimism and its objectors. Likewise, and despite the critical stance I articulated above, I pay close attention to black feminists and their perspective on the cases I investigate because it has been black women who have built the scaffolding for the deconstruction of gender and sex politics that I venture in this study. Indeed, I am reminded of the heated exchange between Zora Neale Hurston and Richard Wright in the late 1930s.[96] Each had taken issue with the other's gendered depictions of black sexuality, each calling into question the other's construal of black militancy. Hurston, in particular, was critical of the institutional formation of blackness during the Harlem Renaissance. The debate itself formulated a critical blackness essential to black power, while taken together, Hurston and Wright's respective positions leave a rich theoretical terrain on which today's students of black studies can evaluate contemporary cases. The point being, to recall a theme expressed by Steve Langley in Marlon Riggs's film *Tongues Untied* but that resonates across the generations, when life brings you up short, reach up and "snatch what's yours from the universe."[97] In the process, I hope to demonstrate to readers on both sides of this supposed afro-pessimism / black optimism divide, and to all those committed to the black freedom struggle, that we must be engaged with what engages the other: the tension can regenerate, not diminish.

While the old afro-pessimism is a discourse of Western imperialism found across the social sciences, as well as in journalist, international relations, and policy circles, the new afro-pessimism emerges from within black studies. The old afro-pessimism is implicitly a prognosis for black studies itself, that it will never generate the analytical refinement that stable civilizations require for knowledge production. Indeed, the old afro-pessimism is in fact part of the conditions of possibility for the new afro-pessimism in that the former helped legitimate the marginalization of black thought across the diaspora.[98] The suppression of black independent thought, as noted earlier in this chapter, paved the way for the rise of colorblindness, multiculturalism, and antiessentialism in racial theory, post-racialism, and the various ethnic studies formations—each different expressions of the displacement of black thought and Pan-Africanism in particular. The new afro-pessimism, then, is in some senses a product of the afterlife of the intensified counterinsurgency of the period 1950–present that has led to the isolation of Pan-African and black power epistemological and ontological traditions from the center of theoretical innovation in black studies. In light of this context, the new afro-pessimism responds to the collective political and critical stagnation in black studies, and aspires to hold black optimism accountable to the Pan-African traditions that precede the violence that constructed the New World in antiblack terms and to the habits of black power that have sustained this resistance ever since.

The new afro-pessimism is not presently up to the task that this historical moment has opened for it, however, because it remains underdeveloped with respect to Pan-Africanism and even to its own black studies lineage in North America. One illustration of this current shortcoming is that Wilderson and Sexton are often read outside of the black studies tradition. *Blackhood Against the Police Power* aims to demonstrate how this reading is done in error, but more importantly, it seeks to clarify the connections between the recent splash of afro-pessimism and the long-standing tradition of critique within the movement for black liberation. I suggest that the afro-pessimist approach is as incisive as it is because it draws upon insights that resonate across the black studies archive, but that its efficacy ultimately hinges on making these links explicit, and in so doing, realizing a deeper well from which to draw sustenance. The imperative, as I see it, is not unrelated to the recurring internal critique of black intellectuals across the generations, a la Du Bois, Hurston, Wright, Woodson, Frazier, Ladner, Hare, Cruse, Bambara, Davis, Reed, James, and Wynter noted already. For the afro-pessimist approach to make any inroads, it must be moored within a black studies tradition that clarifies the continuities across time and space as much as it nuances present configurations. At stake is the resuscitation of a critical black public sphere in which the issues of black struggle are debated and discussed in such a manner that holds all truth-telling accountable to black liberation. Black feminists, among others in the black studies tradition, of course, have voiced this same call before.[99] Today's resuscitation of this communal critique, however, owes to the labors of the afro-pessimists, and clarifying the connections between the present post-racial enclosure—including the attacks on the new afro-pessimism—and earlier moments in black liberation struggle is one modest contribution toward broadening and deepening the political participation necessary for exposing and overturning the slaveholding paradigm.

The third contribution that this study makes with respect to afro-pessimism is to directly confront the inadequacies of the leading approach to the study of gender and sex within black studies—that is, black feminism. *Blackhood Against the Police Power* does not work at cross-purposes with black feminism, any more than a new perspective on an old problem is necessarily at odds with older ways of looking at it. Although the potential revision is substantial in that it levies a paradigmatic intervention, the measure of my arguments in this book will not be a change in the tide. As an exercise in critical thought, it stands as a question, despite its many statements and claims; it offers a pro-visional opening, despite its numerous conclusions; it formulates a suggested intervention, despite its clear recommendations. The actual answers will come from the "street tasks" of communal struggle. I distill insights on gender and sex generated by Wynter and Thomas, especially, into the afro-pessimist perspective to which I believe their work is intimately connected. The issue is what happens to "gender-sex" when the paradigm of which it is a feature is pulled out from under it. I argue that gender-sex conceptually ruptures when we extend the insights of afro-pessimism, but this exposure is even more clearly elaborated in Wynter's rigorous and nuanced reading of the Western paradigm. My use of Thomas's work epitomizes the creative approach that I find necessary for adequately dealing with the topics of this study. Thomas has a profound grasp of the paradigm imposed by Euro-American slaveholding and colonizing society and brings forward a radical Pan-African sensibility largely muted in the new afro-pessimism. His mastery of Wynter's oeuvre and his masterful application of Pan-African thought to the sexual politics of empire are analytically analogous to afro-pessimism and corrective to its current weaknesses at the same time.

Decolonization Is Always Successful

Both Wilderson and Sexton have stated the afro-pessimist debt to black feminism; full explication of this debt beyond statements remains to be done. Black feminists working in an afro-pessimist vein have only begun to think these two things together. At the time of this writing, this elaboration remains in development and has mostly asserted that black feminism is prior to and makes possible the later development now known as afro-pessimism, and furthermore, that the historical basis for this precedence lies with the conten-tion that the modern world was constituted through gratuitous violence first against black *women*, as opposed to black people as a group.[100] I suggest that this is plateau work, at best: it remains on the same plane as black feminism generally, with the weaknesses that I have noted above. It assumes the form of a historical argument, but where there is in fact no historical basis, to my knowledge, for the heterosexist and genitalist claim that Western slaving societies were primarily driven by desire for African *female* bodies, any more than they were for Africans generally, what remains is simply the authority of black feminism's rhetorical strength—a power it borrows in this case from feminism, not from black struggle.

Also underway, but still in need of rigorous development, is the interface between black liberation and the movement against settler colonialism. The new afro-pessimism, in fact, features direct encounters with indigenous studies and settler colonial studies, provoking both countercritique and a flowering meditation by academics and activists across fields and knowledge formations on how to think the ongoing genocidal practices of slaveholding and settler colonial society together. Although there are important parallels between settler colonial studies and black studies—as in the former's assertion that native genocide operates as a structure, not as an event or an effect of the will, much like the afro-pessimist argument with respect to slavery—there remain severe gaps between the two.[101] The differences make integrated theory impossible at this point, indicating serious political problems in which American Indian and black relations are presently riven.[102] Among the signs of these political problems are settler colonial theory's failure to understand slavery as more than a coerced labor regime; a conception of racial slavery coming out of indigenous studies and settler colonial studies as something that develops through colonialism, rather than as its precondition; and a reliance by many settler colonial theorists on white historiography and social science when it comes to slavery and black struggle, leading to grim historical errors such as the fallacious assertion that there has been no significant black marronage in North America relative to the rest of the hemisphere and that the trade in African slaves was not fully established until the mid- to late seventeenth century.[103]

These conceptual and historical inaccuracies (which could be easily avoided through recourse to black studies) become the basis for indigenous and settler colonial studies' aphasia with respect to black positionality, rendering the foundational concepts of indigenous and settler colonial studies suspect. Indigenous scholars refer to African slaves as "arrivants," to the "coeval conditions of slavery and indentureship in the Americas," and to indigeneity as resistant to racialization due to American Indian "national assertions of sovereignty, self-determination, and land rights."[104] The very concept of "genocide" rent across indigenous and settler colonial studies thus winnows out the genocidal basis of the African slave trade and its afterlife. Either "genocide" as deployed in indigenous and settler colonial studies is too narrow or one dimensional or we need a different way into this historical process. Similarly, the worldwide scene of black genocide, inclusive of twelve centuries of the global African slave trade, African colonization, the renewed accumulation of black lands and black people in transit across the African continent and its Mediterranean borderlands with Europe, and so on and so forth, confounds the "site-specific" basis of indigeneity.[105] For this reason, I have argued elsewhere that slavery is the continual coaccumulation of black people and black lands, an argument I extend in chapter 3, "From Blackland, with Love." When we speak about "land" in the Pan-Africanist tradition, therefore, we are also referencing "body."[106] The indigenous discourse on "sovereignty" is likewise put under severe pressure through the structure of racial slavery, in which "the loss of sovereignty is a *fait accompli*, a byproduct rather than a precondition of enslavement," as Sexton puts it.[107] Wilderson's *Red, White & Black* explicates the manner in which native claims to self-determination are legible within the structure of settler colonialism precisely because such assertions by black people are not. For this reason, both Wilderson and Sexton argue, in differing ways, that "sovereignty" is a barrier not simply to American Indian and black political unity, but to indigenous efforts to redress settler colonialism itself: given that both settler colonialism and the political category of self-determination are products of black enslavement, indigenous claims to sovereignty inevitably seek purchase within the structure of antiblackness.

In short, *Blackhood Against the Police Power* does not extend the invisibility of indigenous peoples and epistemologies in its account of the post-racial era in their own land, despite not centering native perspectives. Rather, it invests in an analytics of black positionality and struggle necessary for entering questions of settler colonialism. It is the remedial work that must take place in order to contemplate what redress might mean. As Fanon makes clear, and Thomas reiterates, decolonization is always successful—if it fails, or has yet to succeed, then it is not yet properly decolonization. In order to be successful, I submit, it must consider the full ramifications of blackhood for these questions of gender-sex, land, and self-determination. As Madhubuti notes, Brooks was reclaimed for and by black power, and if there was a time for reclaiming manhood and womanhood, the masculine and the feminine, or for any deconstructed notion of gender and sexuality or space-specific sovereignty, that day is setting. Blackhood represents not a displacement of black feminism or queer blackness, but rather its necessary political denouement qua ethical extension. Moreover, it calls forth a lineage of black power that destabilizes leading racial theories and their dissenting opinions. Wynter's exhortation for thinkers to marry their concepts with the position of the NHI weighs on the internal conceptual schema of black feminism itself, confronts settler colonialism at its most basic fortifications, and addresses itself to the ongoing crisis in black studies, no less. Or as Brooks put it in her poem "Blackstone Rangers—As Seen by Disciplines": "There they are / Thirty at the corner / Black, raw, ready / Sores in the city / that do not want to heal."[108] Deal.

CHAPTER ONE

The Time of Blackened Ethics

From the incoherence of Black death, America generates the coherence of White life.

    —Frank B. Wilderson III, "The Prison Slave as Hegemony's (Silent) Scandal," 2007

Rather than a redaction of black struggle and standing in the modern world, I put on the table a reframing of what we know but disavow about our racist society. This reframing desists from the tendency, with which critical race and sex studies is rife, to assail the faulty premise of black pathology and thereby extend the interlocutory life of the very discourse being criticized within the assumptions of the critique.[1] Accordingly, this study of the "post-racial" does not present any new facts with which to counter the dominant framework of black pathology; this book is not a scholarly equivalent to a new evidentiary hearing of the case for black humanity. Instead, it is an evaluation of the most appropriate frame for explaining the disavowal of these facts and interpreting the violence represented in this abjuration.

    My argument that critical race and sex studies are all too frequently complicit in the very violence that ostensibly is their object of critique limns a deep disavowal animating the conjunction between racism and antiracism. In her essay "Poetry Is Not a Luxury," Audre Lorde presciently observes: "Sometimes we drug ourselves with dreams of new ideas. The head will save us. The brain alone will set us free. But there are no new ideas still waiting in the wings to save us as women, as human."[2] Lorde's insight resonates here because I do not purport to have access to greater powers of reason or rational deduction than other scholars of the topic. Rather, by abandoning the pretense of "new ideas" I am suggesting that what is needed is to listen anew to long-standing findings and perceptions in the black studies archive.

Lorde continues, "There are only old and forgotten ones, new combinations, extrapolations, and recognitions from within ourselves—along with the renewed courage to try them out. And we must constantly encourage ourselves and each other to attempt the heretical actions that our dreams imply, and so many of our old ideas disparage."[3] While this project revisits history, it does so cognizant of how the "crisis of knowledge" about humanity often compels a retreat into historicism, as Lewis Gordon explains, "in which there is believed to be the possibility of emerging rigorous because of an ultimate appeal to 'facts.'"[4] Black studies necessarily holds the archive and the empirical record at a critical distance because they are as rife with violent misrepresentations as they are fonts of discernment.

The specious appeal to "facts" and the "historical record" is a manifestation of another mistaken notion, namely that there is a method of study that will guide us out of the darkness. Frantz Fanon warns against refuge in methodology, proclaiming that "there is a point [in the human sciences] at which methods devour themselves."[5] Gordon elaborates on Fanon's reference to the cannibalism of methodology with his notion of "disciplinary decadence." Gordon uses *decadence* to emphasize that "the ontologizing or reification" of disciplinary thought and its institutionalization in terms of certain protocols ("methodology") occurs within, and is itself a sign of, the process of decay. Despite their pretense to naturalization or ahistoricism—in other words, the assertion that they are absolutes, that they do not have a time and place of emergence, conditions of possibility, an intrinsically political makeup—disciplines are human creations and, as such, reflect social conditions. Gordon observes that decadence has a debilitating paradox for epistemology: "As social conditions for the life of disciplines decline, so, too, do disciplines, but they do so . . . primarily through treating the proof of their decay as evidence of their health."[6] In order to effectively confront the prevailing order of knowledge, no matter the historical period, the best of black studies has always had to be more than the original interdiscipline. It has had to chip away at disciplinarity itself, to de-discipline knowledge production.

For instance, although "gender" and "sex" are not disciplines, per se, as objects of study they have realized an exteriorization of processes that are properly understood as interior to racial regime. We might say, then, that even as queer and gender studies has attacked the reification of gender and sex categories, they have reified the construction of "gender" and "sex" by giving it a life beyond racial violence. The contributions of queer and gender studies over recent decades have been numerous, and I intentionally gloss the innovations of this scholarship simply to make the point that antiblackness has provided the enabling fuel for queer and gender studies because it empowers nonblack genders and sexualities with a degree of fluidity and flexibility compared to a relatively static such social field for black people. The irony is that by exploring how gender and sex are embodied and performed, queer and gender studies have obscured the onto-epistemic structure of racism that delimits the meanings of black performativity relative to nonblack genders and sexualities.

The general failure of critical scholarship on race and sexuality to escape the entanglements of antiblack desire indexes precisely what Lorde refers to as a dream state: a set of libidinal investments that return progressive political projects to the site at which the ethical registers of black social movement are abandoned. Or, minimally, that remain blindly wedded to a set of remedies ("justice") that flaunt the propositions set forth by black struggle and ensconce ethicality within an antiblack politic. Along these lines, this chapter explores the lesson of black historical struggle that *perspective* is more vital than *method* for confronting the order of knowledge on which slaveholding rests. "Perspective" is understood to be inherently, and irreparably, subjective. As such, it amounts to a framework of analysis at the individual level. When we work at the level of the society, however, "perspective" becomes more than the aggregate of shared vantage points. It becomes *paradigm*.

The "time of blackened ethics" is a paradigm shift accountable to black freedom struggle across the generations. This chapter explains the features of this paradigm, and in so doing, sutures the recent contributions of the "afro-pessimists" to the black studies movement, argues against the place of "genealogy" in black studies, and begins the process of elucidating "blackhood" against the police power of the post-racial culture of politics. I anticipate that the most vexing parts of this book for readers will not be the militant blackness at the center of my analysis, but rather the treatment of gender and sex that such militancy produces. Let me be clear that they are one and the same: black militancy demands rethinking gender-sex. I am calling for the study of gender and sex *as* studies of antiblackness—no matter how the bodies in question are phenotypically constructed. To note the decadence of queer and gender studies is not to say gender and sex are not productive categories of inquiry; it simply means that such work may be counterproductive if it does not hold itself accountable to the structures of antiblackness in which gender and sex arise through their coupling with violence. The paradigm I lay out in this first chapter is key to understanding how queer and gender studies are patently parasitic on antiblackness and, by extension, on the black studies tradition that has singularly grappled with the holistic dimensions of this violence. I center the entire book around Bambara's concept of "blackhood" not to dispense with the study of gender and sex, but rather to bring an ethical rigor to it that, in my estimation, has been missing and has led to an avatar quality in which reality fades to black.

The Political Ontology of "Race"

The paradigm in need of specification is nothing less than the past millennium-plus in which one particular cultural conception of humanity has forcibly, steadily, and increasingly occupied global space as if it were the only way of understanding human beings and social life. In other words, one particularistic world of antiblackness has attempted to make itself into *the* world order. While this culture of antiblackness is most closely associated with the imperialism and settler colonialism of the rise of Europe, it is not reducible to this historical and geographic trajectory, as the Arab slave traders' desire for using Africans as exploited labor, sexual objects, and fungible status symbols in the Middle East and the Indian Ocean region as far back as the eighth century demonstrates.[7] This book's argument does not rest on an archaeological excavation of the original genesis of blackness, antiblackness, and racialism generally; it is concerned, rather, with understanding the operation of the worlds that antiblack violence creates. This agenda cannot take for granted, however, how things came to be. As such, this study approaches the question of black freedom as the key to human liberation itself, the emancipated person as trussed to independent territories, bodies, and minds. To contest the world the police power has made, and remakes on a daily basis, we must look for a critical language it does not already colonize. This chapter explores conceptual territory that in and of itself does not escape this capture, but does enjoin this collective practice of marronage. I illustrate the paradigmatic intervention recently formulated by the afro-pessimists to elucidate the onto-epistemic structure in which we must agitate for freedom through a brief examination of the Ramarley Graham case. Graham was an eighteen-year-old young black man shot to death by New York Police Department detectives in the bathroom of his apartment in the Bronx, on February 2, 2012, a few weeks prior to the better-known case of George Zimmerman's murder of Trayvon Martin in Sanford, Florida, on February 26, 2012. The police had followed Graham back to his apartment building and gained entry to the building by pointing a gun at another resident and his young child to force the resident to open the door. Within seconds after breaking into Graham's apartment, the police shot Graham in his own bathroom, claiming afterward that they believed he had a weapon, which he did not.

Critical coverage of the case by the media, as well as the calls for justice from the black community, focused largely on the police misjudgment of the danger Graham posed when they burst into his apartment to confront him. The Graham incident, it was said at the time, exposed police tactics as heavy-handed. Largely overlooked were the two main features of the case that foretold Graham's death. As with the Oscar Grant case, the police would not have been in a position to kill Graham had they not construed him as a criminal suspect in the first place, exclusive of any discernible behaviors that would have legally provided them with probable cause to make an arrest. Above all else, then, every single act of police violence that ends in death begins with an act of noticing, of apprehending blackness visually as suspect qua danger. Secondly, there would have been no shooting that day had the police not flagrantly flaunted constitutional requirements and illegally gained access to Graham's home. Seeing Graham is the first racist act; his bodily vulnerability, and the absolute dereliction of his home as a constitutionally protected zone of safety and privacy against unwarranted police intrusion, is the aftereffect of this violence, the meaning of "race."

Here we encounter the first constituent element of the black studies paradigm guiding this study: blackness is the product of a structure of gratuitous violence, as opposed to contingent violence. Black people experience violence and punishment not in response to some action or transgression on their part, such as law breaking (this would be contingent violence). Instead, blacks are subject to violence for being black, punishment for punishment's sake—a function of structural positionality in the antiblack world. Gratuitous violence produces a singular grammar of suffering, the hallmark of black existence relative to other positions in the structure of humanity. All ethical questions therein are authorized by this structure of gratuitous violence. As the afro-pessimists have shown, this defining fact of black existence is the scandal that is catastrophic for each and every humanistic discourse that society relies upon for its conceptual integrity and ethical coherence. When policing is formulated as a question of tactics, a matter of how society conducts itself—for example, did the officers obtain a warrant or probable cause before entering the home?—then the violence is contingent and the transgression lies with either the criminal suspect or with the officers. Somebody broke the law and unleashed the violence. To the contrary, when we recognize policing as the structure in which violence against black people is the precondition for society and all of its rules, including constitutional protections against "unreasonable search and seizure," then we have a very different situation. Police violence then becomes purely gratuitous and detached from the actions of a black "suspect."

The deafening silence on how the police obtained entry to Graham's apartment underscores the second constituent element of the black studies paradigm. The structure of gratuitous violence signifies blackness as the defining marker of the nonhuman. While the first element of the black studies paradigm is grounded in an empirical, sociohistorical reading of black life, the second feature of the paradigm attends to the ontological, axiological, and epistemological violence—or, a political ontology—constructing, enshrouding, entrenching, and extending the empirical. The political ontology of race is not a metaphysical notion, because it is the explicit outcome of a politics and thereby available to historical challenge through collective struggle. But it is not simply a description of political status either, because it functions as if it were a metaphysical property across the premodern, modern, and now postmodern eras.[8] We can see this captive state in the absolute vulnerability of black domesticity across time and space. Under slavery, the black family and "blood" were functionally outlawed, an impossibility, rendering inapplicable identities and categories of scholarly inquiry customary in the Eurocentric convention—gender, sexuality, labor, family, marriage, generations, ancestors—or, at best, leaving these classifications "indissociable from violence."[9] Under the contemporary war on drugs, the police practice of raiding black homes and neighborhoods becomes the context for the rise of militarized policing in the form of the now-ubiquitous SWAT, as well as asset forfeiture laws that permit law enforcement to confiscate the features of the black domestic sphere without criminal conviction or even due process. Structurally analogous to the slave quarters, black domesticity is neither private nor home: that there is no sanctuary for black bodies underscores how captivity is a constituent element of black life.[10]

The third element of the black studies paradigm expounds on blackness as absent presence, redirecting our analytic away from a preoccupation with political economy and instead toward a more robust apprehension of slavery as a structure of libidinal desire. Orlando Patterson's 1982 comparative study of slavery elucidates the culture of slavery via the concepts of natal alienation and generalized dishonor. In *Slavery and Social Death*, natal alienation refers to how the slave ceases to belong to a social order of either ascending or descending relations. In Patterson's succinct phrasing, the slave is "truly a genealogical isolate," existing within a social world that is not only unrecognized as such but, moreover, is explicitly proscribed by law.[11] Numerous documents in the black studies archive instruct us on the arc of this structure of violence as it came to be inscribed in legal, cultural, economic, and political narrative: the forcible removal of children and other family relations, the utter vulnerability of slave sexuality, and so on, into the contemporary era as noted above with the war on drugs and the prison-industrial complex. Dorothy Roberts's work on the junctures of the criminal justice and child welfare systems vividly documents this process of natal alienation today.[12] Perpetuity and inheritability both derive from natal alienation, which also generates what Patterson terms "generalized dishonor." Patterson uses "honor" to underscore the relationship between power, on the one hand, and recognition, value, and standing, on the other, leading him to assert that slavery really meant "the direct and insidious violence, the namelessness and invisibility, the endless personal violation, and the chronic inalienable dishonor."[13]

The essential vulnerability and generalized dishonor of blackness is only matched in the Graham case by the equally vital and banal role it plays in sustaining civil society's ethical dilemmas, as revealed in the trial of Graham's twin half-brothers on gun-related conspiracy charges. The presiding judge in the twins' case, Justice Edward McLaughlin, chastised the young men at sentencing: "No one, of course, is accusing either of you of holding the gun which killed your brother," Justice McLaughlin said. "But the acts of your conspiracy, spanning four years, including many shootings and ending just months before his death, is an unavoidable and integral part of the context in which that tragic event occurred and likely will be judged."[14] Justice McLaughlin is implying that it was reasonable for Graham's killer to violate without hesitation all constitutional protocols (not to mention his sworn duty as a "peace officer" to "protect life") because of the obvious danger in need of containment that Graham embodied, and at the same time, that it was equally reasonable for the officer to fear for his life when faced with an unarmed black man, given the confirmed criminality (according to the state) of two entirely different human beings, connected to Graham's case only by virtue of belonging to the same family of blackness. This is the generalized dishonor of the slave: all black people are equally suspect by association, as with one object so too with the next, for the association is not one of human relations, wherein the precepts of individuality, autonomous agency, and presumed innocence would otherwise need apply.

At the time that Justice McLaughlin made his remarks, in August 2012, Graham's killer, Officer Richard Haste, was facing a grand jury indictment for manslaughter. It is no less remarkable that a judge in one case can take the patently unethical move of making a prediction from the bench about the outcome of an altogether unrelated case that has yet to even reach trial. The Haste indictment was subsequently vacated by that case's presiding judge, and a second grand jury refused to indict the officer. Rather than face censure for what amounts to a preemptive acquittal of Officer Haste, Justice McLaughlin was perceived as a champion of public safety and a compassionate voice for justice. In chastising the Graham twins for indirectly causing the death of their half brother, the judge recalls the paternalizing force of the slave owner who terrorized the slaves for their own good. The humanity of the judge and the police officer is confirmed in the face of black nonhumanity, and in due course, the ethical dilemmas of civil society—war against crime or police brutality?—are satisfactorily elaborated.

The three components of the black studies paradigm identified above and deployed in this study aim to extend the epistemic break called for by the street tasks of the 1960s-era black liberation movement. First, blackness as a product of a structure of gratuitous violence departs profoundly from humanism's presumption that subjects experience violence only contingently or instrumentally, not to mention individually. Second, being structurally positioned by gratuitous violence signifies blackness as the defining marker of the nonhuman. As objectified sentient beings with "no ontological status," black people's existence both sutures the ethics of civil society—as in, binds together society's various debates, dilemmas, and moral controversies within acceptable limits that appear to be shared by all because all appear to enter the circumscribed terms willingly—and distresses the stability of ontology itself.[15] Third, the general dishonor and natal alienation of the slave suture a culture of politics that rests on black fungibility—the way in which black people enable society's most pressing debates and simultaneously are precluded from authorizing such deliberations about social life. Together, these elements comprise what the afro-pessimists have termed the political ontology of race.

The political ontology of race recognizes slavery not as a discrete historical event, nor as primarily a political economy organizing the reproduction of surplus value, but rather as a structure of libidinal desire that transcends any particular historically bounded political economy and arranges the symbolic universe according to its dictates. The libidinal economy of slavery hails the ongoing generalized dishonor of blackness, a singular status popularized in contemporary academic discourse as "social death." The afro-pessimists contribute refined theoretical terms to a long-standing recognition in black thought that calls into question the very assumptive logic undergirding both ends of the analytic concept so crucial to the critical study of race and sex: relations of power. The afro-pessimists distinguish between preconscious interests, unconscious identifications, and structural positionality, helping us today to lay further weight on the insights of earlier generations who noted how none of the various efforts of the black movement to combat the psychic alienation of antiblackness and to develop collective awareness of the methods of social control arrayed against black people have been able to approach the restoration of what has been defined a priori as an absence.

W. E. B. Du Bois, for instance, implicitly noted the failure to make such analytical distinctions at the level of representation, pitching his intervention into white supremacist historiography on the grounds of structural positionality. In his classic study *Black Reconstruction in America: An Essay Toward a History of the Part Which Black Folk Played in the Attempt to Reconstruct Democracy in America, 1860–1880,* Du Bois exposes the historical paradox of a nation founded on and deeply invested in slavery waging a death match with itself over how to conduct this system, not over whether or not it should continue. *Black Reconstruction* shows how the national dependence on captive black bodies, the labor movement's roots in racial violence, and most importantly, the collective mass action by the oppressed leads to Du Bois's recognition that the slaves forced the issue of their emancipation and that such freedom is an expression of revolutionary action.[16] *Black Reconstruction* provides the essential parameters for ascertaining the cultural, economic, and political lines of force inscribed inside of "freedom," and in so doing, exposes the necessity of advancing an understanding of black movement within the essential structural antagonism constituting the social. Change in the legal standing of black people did not alter the structural position of blackness: Du Bois aids us in this recognition by demonstrating how the outcomes of conflicts such as the Civil War are immaterial when compared to their utility in reconstituting the disposition of the social against black people. To recognize as much is to see the humanity in history's empty figure of the slave, of blackness; this visibility is an apocalyptic vision for the modern regime of power.

Du Bois's analysis that white people slaughtered over half a million of their brothers for the right to control the manner of black social death—a reality to which there was only minor dissenting opinions—leads directly to Fanon's explanation that blackness is an antirelation. That is, the impossible subjectivity of a sentient being who can have "no recognition in the eyes of" the Other—which, in turn, brings us to the afro-pessimist meditation on "relations of power" as a violent gloss on "the way in which power obtains *in* and *as* relation."[17] There is no such thing as reciprocal relations in an antiblack world where blacks are positioned as "the things against which all other subjects take their bearing."[18] Since gratuitous violence turns the black body into a fungible object and destroys the possibility of relation, the only way that black people can appear to participate in the world alongside human beings is by way of what Wilderson refers to as a "structural adjustment" wherein blacks are permitted to act as if they possess ontological capacity in exchange for remaining within the agreed upon limits of knowledge and ethics. For example, the objections to police stop-and-frisk of black pedestrians assert that black people's constitutional protections are violated in such practices, as if the Fourth Amendment protection against unwarranted search and seizure were not in fact created to oversee the seizure of black bodies. This "structural adjustment" is typical of what I refer to as the new post–black studies convention marking the contemporary post-racial period. Despite the immense diversity and complexity of factors and processes that make blackness imaginable and influential, and their articulation with the very epochal changes of modernity, we can say with certainty that blackness indicates an "existence without standing in the modern world system."[19]

Genealogy: A Subversion

As demonstrated through the Graham case, the black studies tradition that I am following in this study, in terms sharpened recently by the afro-pessimists, adheres closely to the historical structure of enslavement. This itinerary confounds the anticipation of an intellectual tradition deconstructed, a tracing backward of the emergence of a particular ideology or set of conceptual protocols guiding the study—a genealogy: Where did this concept originate, what are the progenitors of this analysis, where do you locate this idea in the story of origins, simply put, however plural and contradictory the path may be, perfunctory qualifications against the search for origins aside? What do you say about origins, however, when the study arises from the experience of originary displacement, the black hole of history that defies the expectation and privilege of traditional ontology?[20]

Genealogy itself has attained something of a fetish status in critical race and sex studies, trading on the affective impression that genealogies write history against itself by following the relations of power that inscribe themselves into historical narratives. Michel Foucault described genealogy as a particular kind of historical investigation into "those elements which we tend to feel [are] without history," such as sexuality, truth, or madness.[21] Foucauldian genealogy of the subject accounts "for the constitution of knowledges, discourses, domains of objects, and so on, without having to make reference to a subject which is either transcendental in relation to the field of events or runs in its empty sameness throughout the course of history."[22] Foucauldian genealogy has become popular in critical race and sex studies and in the field of ethnic studies in general for advancing an interventionist methodology into white supremacist socioeconomic formation. We have, for example, "a genealogy of black female sexuality," "feminist genealogies," "the racial genealogy of excellence," "the genealogy of women of color feminism," "a genealogy of the interdisciplines," and so on.[23] This promotion of Foucauldian methodology for the study of race is the multicultural academy's post-racial quarantine of independent black thought.

The popularity of Foucauldian genealogical treatments of racial regime and the material economies of sexuality point up how the subjects of every order (the scholars of such genealogies) tend to be enmeshed in producing the mode of being human hegemonic to that order, a practice of self-inscription that stands *within*, not outside, that discursive order—the affective register of genealogy's counterpolitics notwithstanding. Whereas Foucault's genealogy regards history as the organization and reorganization of power/knowledge regimes, with each new episteme signaling a break into a new order, from the millennium-plus paradigm of black struggle, these changes amount to quantitative disruptions that do not rise to the level of a qualitative transformation in how the world sees itself. As Sylvia Wynter puts it, a new episteme should signal an epistemological break*through* into a new way of being human—a movement in *beingness*, rather than simply a shift in the politics of "truth."[24] A genealogy of blackness is thwarted in its solicitation of the history of enslavement; the ontic relations therein exceed Foucault's grasp.

What is to be done with a genealogy of an absence? Fred Moten suggests that the significance of that absence lies in its dissembling quality for modern discourse: "What if the value of that absence or excess is given to us only in and by way of a kind of failure or inadequacy . . . so that the non-attainment of meaning or ontology, of source or origin, is the only way to approach the thing?"[25] Moten names this analytic "black operations," later shortened usefully and enigmatically to "black op."[26] Why does he not call it a "genealogy of blackness?" The black studies paradigm I am applying in this study raises the challenge that "genealogy" presupposes the work of various historical codes that resist historicizing even when the objective is to expose the conditions of possibility for history's narration. Where the onto-epistemic field of blackness is a void, genealogy finds itself muted. Genealogy presupposes bodily and cultural integrity; genealogy's subversion in the black studies tradition begins with the black subject's subversion through violence. Cornel West's genealogy in "The New Cultural Politics of Difference," an essay well cited during the ascent of the post–civil rights multicultural formation in the 1990s, supports this argument. West offers a genealogy of the present moment through recourse to three coordinates, none of which contemplates the structural impediments to bringing blackness into the living: the displacement of European high culture; the augmentation of the United States as a world power and the central engine of global cultural production; and the decolonization of the third world, including the advent of an African diasporic decolonial consciousness.[27] Slavery does not factor into his historical accounting of the present. West demonstrates the "structural adjustment" of blackness necessary for it to appear in "genealogy."

Alternatively, we might try to name black studies genealogies: Cheikh Anta Diop and Walter Rodney desediment European empire by recasting the history of Africa and the globe, releasing a metaphysics of relationality and sexuality from the narrow, racially exclusive binary of Eurocentric bourgeois heterosexual and homosexual civilization; Greg Thomas accomplishes the same feat for a post–Black Power generation; Saidiya Hartman's work highlights the inevitable failure of black counterhistorical recovery, precisely because these narratives can never be installed as history for the onto-epistemic field of blackness—the "time of slavery" remains in effect; and many more.[28] Yet in each of these instances and beyond, the critical project must confront the very terms of its own oblivion in order to register the historical codes themselves as structural coordinates of slavery's system. Indeed, one of the very few (anti) genealogical works in black studies to name itself as such, M. NourbeSe Philip's "Genealogy of Resistance," demonstrates that a reconstructive undertaking that is faithful to, rather than promiscuous with, history's compulsory obliteration of blackness must intentionally slay grammatical form and mine the truth that lies "in Silence/s. And words. In gaps. And synapses. In discovery. Surprising always in the correspondence and connections."[29]

The black revolutionary praxis, in critical-theoretical exposition and in lived social movement, subverts the very ground on which genealogy would take hold. There is no ground of blackness on which it can lay seed; black history continually implodes the very premise of genealogy. The insertion of black existence into the prevailing domain of history and the various academic disciplines through which ontology is elaborated not only destabilizes these fields and subverts the possibility of genealogy, it instigates a structural crisis in the field of knowledge itself.[30] The question arises, then, how does this black studies paradigm face its own historical standing when the very terms of history itself compel black subjection? Wynter suggests that this conundrum is largely unavoidable because the subjects of an order know it as it needs to be known, but never as it really is.[31] Emancipatory knowledge is no less compromised:

> If you are intellectuals and artists who belong to a subordinated group, you are necessarily going to be educated in the scholarly paradigms of the group who dominate you. But these paradigms, whatever their other emancipatory attributes, must have *always already* legitimated the subordination of your

group. Must have even induced us to accept our subordination through the mediation of *their* imaginary.[32]

The task of critique is to bring the effects of this imaginary and its capacity to define what is and is not possible into the orbit of our consciousness, and in so doing to intervene in its efficacy over us. Wynter nonetheless takes us a step further yet in pronouncing this critical liberating endeavor "paradoxical":

> So the ground of our mode of being human will itself be the a priori or ground of the history to which it gives rise. But the paradox here, of course, is that it cannot itself be historicized within the terms of the ethnohistory to which it will give rise: that code/mode must remain, as you say, unhistoricizable. As ours now remains for us.[33]

In turn, David Marriott extends Wynter's insights:

> Now, insofar as what cannot be historicized are the codes or genres that make History itself "historical," history is in some senses the least historical of discourses. It also seems reasonable to suppose that these codes, which are "historical" while being themselves never simply historical, are in some sense more originary than the narratives of history which they ground, and are thus the origin and possibility of History itself.[34]

Wynter and Marriott are explaining why the historical revisionism of black studies is necessary but insufficient, is demanded and treacherous, is imperative yet also easily compromised. Although the need to revisit history, to resituate analysis of the present in the historical context that continues to hold sway over the future, remains central to the radical black imaginary, the terms of this reimagining themselves require yet another level of interrogation and existential interruption.

The historical codes most insulated against, and thus most resistant to, radical deconstruction are those that serve as transcendental or transhistorical coordinates, the basis for an ontology and the structure of reason that arises to legitimate both existing practices of antiblack violence and the various strategies of resistance that the prevailing historical paradigm accommodates—race, sex, gender, and nation, for instance. It follows that these terms are the ones most in need of their own deconstruction given their central status as the currency in which power insulates itself against revolution. While this may be the case, it is more to the point that race, gender, sex, and nation are simply bound up in the articulation of any and every historical code: time, space, loss, mobility, agency, imagination, the body, violence, psyche, blood, kinship, biology, science, economy, and so forth. Moreover, as I explore throughout this study, race is the central logic expressed everywhere gender, sex, and nation are invoked. As Nahum Chandler writes, "There is no contemporary discourse that is free or independent of the itinerary of the concept of race."[35] It is perhaps a measure of the height of the obstacle that even after the voluminous critical and (re)historical work in the black studies tradition over the past century and a half we remain largely stalled at the threshold, poised at the precipice, of the "epistemic break" Wynter has called for, the production of a qualitatively distinct knowledge commensurate with the openings created by political struggle. Not a stillbirth, for history is not over and the struggle is protracted, and yet for Marriott, it is "alarmingly easy" under present conditions to confuse the lines of demarcation: "Still, if to witness the effects of European history was always to incur the charge that one was not yet sufficiently historical, then to sense the need to escape from history was already to know that one's debt to such narratives had to be acquitted."[36]

The awareness of this condition often hides out just beyond thought. A political unease distends into a yearning colored by frustrations with leading prescriptions. What do you call for when they keep killing your people? Why is it compulsory for the families of the deceased to perform the pathologies of nonviolence? How do calls for the community to be calm betray the notion that the violence of the state is always preferable to the violence of the masses? Why is the ethical dimension of counterviolence against the police automatically suppressed as impermissible knowledge? On this last question, a wide range of counterviolence animates the historical record, from Ismaaiyl Brinsley, Christopher Dorner, Micah Xavier Johnson, Lovelle Mixon in the contemporary period, to the Black Liberation Army (BLA) and the Deacons for Defense across the decades of the mid-twentieth century, to John Brown, Nat Turner, Denmark

Vesey, Nanny of the Maroons, the Quilombos dos Palmares, and numerous unnamed others during the slavocracy.

I am not suggesting that the recent attacks on police (Brinsley, Dorner, Johnson, Mixon, etc.) are synonymous with those of the BLA or a John Brown or slave rebels. Political consciousness and strategy, although not everything, do matter. There is more to be said along these lines. At the same time, however, I am indeed equating these different moments of counterviolence against the police power for their shared ethical quality in a world constituted in routine gratuitous antiblack sexual violence. Brinsley and company are pathologized in the same terms as were applied to the BLA, the Black Panthers, Robert F. Williams, Brown, and every enslaved African revolutionary in order to criminalize political resistance. Moreover, in the contemporary period, it is a feature of the post-racial that objections to the gratuitous violence of antiblackness can be superseded by the condemnation of gratuitous counterviolence as a reply to antiblackness. This fact reveals that the battle lines are not as they would appear: the terms of antiracism today are not fundamentally opposed to those of racism itself. In short, "excessive" policing is bad, but nowhere near as big of a concern to civil society as violence against police. Again, state violence is always and everywhere preferable to black violence. Here we can see antiracism's supplementary role in fortifying the ethical terms of the antiblack world. Malcolm X's assessment of "chickens coming home to roost" comes to mind, as does his speech "Message to the Grass Roots," laying down the clarity of counterviolence: "And if it is right for America to draft us, and teach us how to be violent in defense of her, then it is right for you and me to do whatever is necessary to defend our own people right here in this country."[37] Why does this communal self-defense frequently boil down to a focus on how black children dress and present themselves, as those of us who love all black children everywhere, not the least our own black offspring, so often end up doing—as if the sexual violence shadowing them were not purely a gratuitous and structural feature of being black, rather than tied to how they perform their blackness?

Lying inside these questions, like a snake in the grass or rot in the cradle, is the paradox to which Wynter draws our attention. The questions—themselves wretchedly inadequate responses to wrenching conditions—extend the interlocutory life of antiblackness within antiracist formations by means of the trope of black pathology. As Moten observes, they are different instantiations of the basic question, *what is wrong with black people?* Marriott states that this trope "relies on being voluntarily assumed by its subjects, who, terrorized by it, seduced by it, addicted to it, internalize the requirements for maintaining its hold. No one wants to be or be seen as the *negré.*"[38] The subversion of genealogy is itself a "black operation" that militates against this violent seduction by insisting on a paradigmatic analysis that does not presuppose the system in which violence produces subjects and is confronted by them, or confronts them as objects, and then, in a subsequent move, inserts the subjects of that violence into this preset system to engage in questions of how the system functions.[39] Instead, analysis would need to begin with an accounting of the constitution of the structure itself, and not simply how it operates or how the inaugural actions of the subject call the system into being.[40]

The originary structure in which the subject is assembled, and the edifice that is customarily presupposed or unthought, is no less than the system of racial slavery. This is the space of which Fanon famously wrote,

> Ontology—once it is finally admitted as leaving existence by the wayside— does not permit us to understand the being of the black man. For not only must the black man be black; he must be black in relation to the white man. Some critics will take it upon themselves to remind us that the proposition has a converse. I say that this is false. The black man has no ontological resistance in the eyes of the white man.[41]

Despite changes to the political economy over time ("leaving existence by the wayside"), in which formerly enslaved Africans become nominally equal subjects before the law, blackness continues to mark a void in the drama of value. According to this schema, whites can experience their humanity in contradistinction to blackness, while blacks can only ever encounter humanity's absence in each other. As such, racial slavery constitutes blackness as its constitutive supplement that exceeds and dissembles the disciplining narratives of the social. This is the analytical task, then, of the black studies paradigm I apply in this study: to ground inquiry in the formation, and continual reformation, of this world-defining system of accumulating black bodies. In Moten's terms:

"What is it to be an irreducibly disordering, deformational force while at the same time being absolutely indispensable to normative order, normative form?"[42] This research question, in all of its infinite permutations, nonetheless, is all too frequently bypassed in favor of explaining the operational dynamics of the system and its agents.

Structural Dis-adjustments

How do we analyze the constitution of the structure itself without minimizing or neglecting its operational dynamics and the suffering it produces? On August 2014, Christopher Lollie released on YouTube the video that he managed to take during a police attack on January 31, 2014, in St. Paul, Minnesota. Lollie had been waiting to pick up his children at a nearby downtown daycare center when a private security guard summoned a St. Paul police officer who proceeded to accost him for his identification. Knowing that the law does not require him to provide identification to police, Lollie politely declined, whereupon two more officers arrived, shot Lollie with a Taser, took him to the ground, and arrested him. After refusing a prosecutor's offer for a plea bargain, Lollie's case was dismissed in court, and he sued the city for violating his civil rights.[43]

A black father shot and arrested by the police on his way to picking up his children from daycare emphatically details the entirely banal violence of the antiblack world. Lollie's arrest occurred only yards away from his children's daycare center; he later described looking into the faces of his children's classmates as he laid pinned to the ground by the three officers. This is the terror of everyday blackness. In a similar fashion, Haile Gerima's classic of Pan-Africanist cinema, *Bush Mama*, depicts T.C. leaving the house one day for a job interview and ending up in jail, with nary an acknowledgement in the film's narrative that job interview-to-jail constitutes a detour in the path, or a deviation in the script, of everyday blackness. Gerima states: "Now one of the experiences of being black in America is not going where you want to go, being stopped. . . . It is a truthful representation to cut from him leaving for the job interview to a prison scene without justifying how he got in jail."[44] For Gerima, immobility is a constituent element of blackness in the modern world—"not going where you want to go"—and therefore it is a more perceptive and coherent representation of antiblack terror *not* to entertain the notion that the truth of black experience lies with cause-and-effect, within the fallacious realm of individual agency, as if T.C. or Chris Lollie had to do anything to occasion the respective detours in their days.

On August 18, 2006, seven black lesbian-identified and gender-noncon-forming young women, some of whom are mothers, were walking in the ostensibly gay-safe New York City neighborhood of the West Village when they were assaulted by a black man. The women defended themselves, but in the end, they were arrested and charged with assault, gang assault, and attempted murder—all while their assailant went uncharged. Three of the women pled guilty while the other four asserted their innocence but were convicted and received sentences ranging from three to eleven years.[45] An analysis by Laura Logan of the relationship between the media coverage of these black women and how their black refusal of victimization was transformed into black predation elucidated the following:

> Overall, almost two-thirds of the articles characterized the women as angry lesbians in one way or another, and nearly half also used animal imagery or language. They were "wild," a "wolf pack," and a "she-wolf pack." The women "pounced," "growled," and "roared," they "preyed upon" the victim—and several of the articles used such terms more than once. The message is that these women were dangerously wild, masculinized monsters.[46]

The New Jersey 4 (as the four women who served prison terms have come to be known because they were from Newark, New Jersey) meets up with Lollie's case and the story Gerima tells in *Bush Mama*. As with *Bush Mama*, so too nec-essarily with our present study of the post-racial as the latest epochal iteration of antiblackness: what happens when we bypass the normative explanatory frameworks and epistemic devices used to, alternately, interrogate, justify, and condemn the operation of "justice" in cases such as Lollie's and the NJ4? This is what I mean by "the time of blackened ethics": the production of knowledge about the social, and our understanding of ethical action therein, is indelibly transformed when we place blackness and the gratuitous violence through which it emerges in the modern world at the center of our analysis. How does a blackened inquiry take us beyond the usual pronouncements of "racial bias," "excessive force," or "homophobia" to produce a different explanation for the operation of antiblack violence in the Lollie and NJ4 cases, and any other case? Indeed, rather than the presumption that black gender-nonconforming women are being policed in terms of gender norms ("wild, masculinized monsters"), as Logan does above, what would it mean to see this bestial language as essential to the grammar of antiblackness and evidence of the gender inadmissibility for all black people under its terms?

What is happening when the police assault a black father on his way to pick up his children from daycare, or when black women are criminalized for defending themselves from attack, is not about a black *man*, or a black *woman*, or black *children*, or black *gender-sex*, but rather simply that each of these real-life referents embody the by nature irrational "name of what is evil," a "life unworthy of life."[47] We can acknowledge the multiple levels on which antiblack sexual violence works, the operational dynamics of the slave system and its afterlife, but only with reference to how "the master symbolic code of life and death," as Wynter puts it, constitutes the system's foundation. At the level of legal analysis—in other words, at the most superficial, or superstructural, operational level—the police violated Chris Lollie's constitutional right to be protected against unlawful search and seizure guaranteed under the Fourth Amendment. The police may only request identification if they have "reasonable suspicion" that a crime has been committed, is being committed, or is about to be committed. The violence against Lollie and the NJ4 is violence against *blackhood*. It is not a question of gender and sexuality supplementing or subtending or intersecting with racism. Both the Lollie and the NJ4 attacks were sexual assaults, in one sense because of the erotic lens through which blackness is coded as the "name of what is evil," and in yet another sense because they were both assaults on black social reproduction. In Gerima's *Bush Mama*, the state's ongoing effort to control Dorothy's womb climaxes with the attempted rape of her daughter Luann by a police officer who enters Dorothy's home while she is away at work, and the subsequent abortion-through-beating of Dorothy's fetus at the police station. While Dorothy's beating appears as her punishment for coming to Luann's rescue and killing the child rapist, for what was Luann being punished with sexual assault? Gerima prefigures Dorothy's punishment as the gratuitous act that it is by placing it prior to Luann's own encounter with gratuitous violence in the sequence of the film's narrative, rather than afterward. We see Dorothy huddled on the floor of the jail cell, blood from her forcibly aborted fetus on her clothes and on the floor; and then in the next set of frames, we see her arrive home to find the police officer on top of her daughter. Sexual punishment is the opening salvo for the state's actions against the black community, not a contingent response to black transgressions.

The police accosted Lollie, jumping on his prostrated body, in front of not only his children, but the entire preschool class of children as well. At least one of the NJ4 is a mother. As she prepared to leave her son behind to serve her prison sentence, he asked his mother to promise him that she will just walk away from the next incident she encounters (something she and her friends had in fact tried to do the first time) so that she would not be taken away from him again. Echoing the FBI's expressed intention with its Counter-Intelligence Program (COINTELPRO) to target the children of black activists, the Lollie and the NJ4 cases reduce black children as a class to the taxonomy of objects. This is the violence that splays human bodies into flesh, and fleshy parts, literally and imaginatively, thereby destroying "the possibility of ontology because it positions the Black in an infinite and indeterminately horrifying and open vulnerability, an object made available (which is to say fungible) for any subject" qua human.[48] As flesh, "black parent" is both structurally prohibited and an oxymoron at the level of representation. As Frank Wilderson explains, "Black children do not belong to Black mothers (or fathers), just as Black men and women don't belong to, and thus cannot claim, each other: flesh is always already claimed by direct relations of force."[49] Can our analytics correspond to this utter and wanton openness, the structural vulnerability that gratuitous violence produces? Or do we seek in our various calls for "justice" the structural adjustment of post–black studies, to recompose the fleshy disintegrated black bodies that were done wrong—as if any black body can authorize the representation of meaning (including the meaning of justice) when in fact it has no referent through which productive subjectivity gains voice?[50]

When the transcript of the grand jury testimony of Officer Darren Wilson in Ferguson, Missouri, was released to the public in late November 2014, the whole world was able to read in Wilson's words how he imagined Michael Brown in order to shoot him dead. According to Wilson, after he first shot Brown in self-defense, Brown "looked up at me and had the most intense aggressive face. The only way I can describe it, it looks like a demon, that's how angry he looked. He comes back towards me again."[51] Wilson testifies that after being shot once, Brown attacks him again before fleeing, wounded. Wilson explains that he then pursues Brown who eventually stops fleeing, turns, and comes at Wilson again, causing Wilson to shoot him five more times, until he is dead. Wilson's naming of Brown as a demon follows his description of the lethal threat he faced from Brown: "I felt that another one of those punches in my face could knock me out or worse. I mean it was, he's obviously bigger than I was and stronger and the, I've already taken two to the face and I didn't think I would, the third one could be fatal if he hit me right [*sic*]."[52] Wilson's view that his own death was imminent followed his testimony of being dwarfed by Brown's monstrous presence: "And when I grabbed him, the only way I can describe it is I felt like a five-year-old holding onto Hulk Hogan . . . that's just how big he felt and how small I felt just from grasping his arm."[53] Wilson also testified to the grand jury that he is six feet four inches tall, the same height as Brown, and weighed 210 pounds on the day he killed Brown. As I noted earlier, following Wynter, antiblackness apprehends the threat to be quarantined not as a race or a gender, large or small, or even as a criminal, but simply as the "name of what is evil." What happens as a result of the apprehension of this demonic evil, in due course, is what we come to call the name of "race."

Officer Wilson may have specifically articulated this trope of the devil in the Brown case, but it is no less implied in every other case of the policing of blackness. On May 20, 2014, university police assaulted Dr. Ersula Ore, a professor of English at Arizona State University, as she attempted to cross a street on campus on her way home from teaching class. The incident was recorded on the dashboard camera of the police car.[54] Officer Stewart Ferrin accosts Professor Ore with aggression and force, beginning with the (non)question, "Do you know what the sidewalk is for?!" He responds to her subsequent reasoned and respectful questioning of why he is arresting her by slamming her against the patrol car and then throwing her to the ground. The difference between Officer Wilson and Officer Ferrin is simply the degree of a priori intimidation experienced by the police and then brought to an encounter with black people unnecessarily initiated by the police themselves. After Wilson had shot Brown a second and third time, he says

> I remember seeing the smoke from the gun and I kind of looked at him and he's still coming at me, he hadn't slowed down. At this point I start backpedaling and again, I tell him get on the ground, get on the ground, he doesn't. I shoot another round of shots. Again, I don't recall how many it was or if I hit him every time. I know at least once because he flinched again. At this point it looked like he was almost bulking up to run through the shots, like it was making him mad that I'm shooting at him. And the face that he had was looking straight through me, like I wasn't even there, I wasn't even anything in his way. Well, he keeps coming at me after that again, during the pause I tell him to get on the ground, get on the ground, he still keeps coming at me, gets about 8 to 10 feet away. At this point I'm backing up pretty rapidly, I'm backpedaling pretty good because I know if he reaches me, he'll kill me. And he had started to lean forward as he got that close, like he was going to just tackle me, just go right through me.[55]

Wilson acts out his own personal horror fantasy sequence in characterizing Brown as a superhuman menace undeterred by bullets and hell-bent on attacking him. Officer Ferrin, for his part, acted in a manner suggesting that Professor Ore's threat to society as she crossed the street was equally evident and in need of violent repulsion. Ferrin attacked Ore with the authority of a man abusing a woman, but with the impunity of a white person using a black person. This is fungible blackness, an object of knowledge whose name is what is evil. Beyond this basic operation of the foundational symbolic code of life/death, the gendered differences between these police officers' shared Negrophobia (the disgust and lust for shameful, immoral blackness) is negligible and superficial. We might say that gender in these cases amounts to fear/awe (Wilson), on the one hand, and disgust/arousal (Ferrin), on the other hand; but we could just as easily read them in reverse. Both cases are simply variations on the theme of antiblack desire that imagines black sexuality as demonic and nonhuman and masculinity as the province of white male warrior-protectors. Moreover, cases such as these remind us to strip away the pretense of the construction of gender and sexuality as anything but the form of the symbolic code, and not the code itself.[56]

Michael Brown is dead, and the St. Louis County prosecutor declined to put his killer on trial, accepting Wilson's claim that his own life was in danger. Professor Ore, not her assailant, was charged with aggravated assault. In both instances, and every other besides, the victim of policing becomes the medium for realizing police impunity.[57] In legal terms, this is called "vicarious liability." Generally referring to the responsibility of a third party for the actions of the violator, vicarious liability has been applied in cases such as an archdiocese's responsibility for the actions of a priest, a parent culpable for the actions of a child, or a business liable for an accident on its premises. When applied to police behavior, the third party is also the victim who is responsible for his or her own violation at the hands of the police. It is as if the police are an automaton simply responding to threats as they appear before them, and the personhood of those they stop, notice, or profile is enlisted into the role of perpetrator. For the victim-perpetrator, what appears superficially as a contradiction is in fact evidence of the triple-objectification that the police power imposes: police objectify a black person in the first instance simply by seeing him or her as "suspect," "danger," or "evil"; this first act of objectification leads to and legitimates the second, the act of violence against blackness as the means through which whiteness, masculinity, and all of the various ethical dilemmas of human society are reproduced; the structure of impunity that oversees antiblack violence entails the third dimension of objectification, wherein the victim is antagonized from his or her own objectified body and transformed into the agent causing the body harm. In other words, Brown caused his own death, or committed suicide by means of police shooting. Ore is not only the victim of her own self-abuse, but she is criminally liable for it to boot. Her very existence is the justification for her own abuse. When we especially consider that in both cases, as is usually true in most instances of killing by police, Brown and Ore were engaged in forms of self-defense—Brown with his hands up in the universal mode of defenseless-defense and Ore verbally asserting her rights and attempting to deflect Officer Ferrin's hands from invading her body and touching her private parts—vicarious liability puts on display society's structural prohibition against recognizing "the abject status of the will-less object."[58]

Prosecutors apply a version of vicarious liability whenever they pursue felony murder charges against individuals who commit a felony that ends in a death, even if the person killed is their accomplice in the crime. In a recent Alabama case, Lakeith Smith was sentenced to thirty years for A'Donte Washington's death, even though Washington was killed by police officers and Smith never possessed a weapon. Smith and Washington were among a group of five teenagers allegedly involved in a burglary when police responded and killed Washington, and prosecutors charged Smith with his friend's murder. Normally, the charge of felony murder, however, requires at least three basic elements: a murder, a principal to the murder, and an accessory to the principal. Since a grand jury had already ruled Washington's death a justifiable homicide by police shooting, there was no murder—legally speaking—for which Smith could be charged as an accessory. By means of vicarious liability, Washington was the principal in his own nonmurder, with his friend Smith his accessory. In this case, once again, the law recognizes black life only to conscript it into criminal culpability for the harm enacted on it by others.[59]

Ultimately, Wilson's testimony is a litmus test for competing explanatory frameworks. Does the story that Wilson tells—and is retold by the state and media, and by half of the witnesses that the grand jury chose to believe, including one witness who has subsequently been proven a liar—of an unarmed black teenager attacking a police officer unprovoked and repeatedly charging the officer after having been repelled and shot numerous times sound believable to you?[60] Or, do you find it hard to believe that a young black teenager would act in this fashion, knowing as you do many young black men personally over the years, or perhaps having been one yourself at one point, and moreover knowing that black people in particular, and people in general, throughout history have studiously avoided encounters with police rather than instigate them as Wilson claims Brown did with him? These questions are simply the inverse of more pertinent questions: Is it believable that a police officer, armed and in control of a motor vehicle, finds his life threatened by an unarmed pedestrian? Or, do you find it more believable that police officers seek out such encounters with black people? Or, more to the point still: do the police regularly lie under oath?

These questions are in fact unanswerable, but not because we do not know the correct answers (we do). They impugn the police power of civil society, not simply the impunity of the state's agents. Their conclusions are foregone because while they appear to reference knowable "facts" or "lived experience," they actually jeopardize the very ground of reason, the idea of cartographic dominion over the terrain of black life. This is the time of blackened ethics that demands unadorned analysis and epistemic transformation, and generates the black studies paradigm that connects contemporary afro-pessimists to earlier black thinkers who dealt with slavery's comprehensive reality.

CHAPTER TWO

The Inadmissible Career of Social Death

You cannot solve the issue of "consciousness" in terms of their body
of knowledge.

—Sylvia Wynter, "PROUD FLESH Inter/Views: Sylvia Wynter," 2006

A s Assata Shakur lay in a New Jersey hospital in 1973 with a bullet lodged near her heart and her right arm paralyzed, accused of murder in the deaths of two New Jersey state troopers, her aunt Evelyn A. Williams took up her legal defense. Williams records her experiences defending Shakur and other black activists during the height of the Black Power era in her memoir *Inadmissible Evidence: The Story of the African-American Trial Lawyer Who Defended the Black Liberation Army*. Although she had been a long-time public advocate for equality and civil rights in her varied career as a social worker and an attorney, Williams recounts how she nonetheless found herself in a crash tutorial on an altogether different level of political ethics during Shakur's legal defense. Williams describes the striking schism between the consciousness of black activists and the normative order of knowledge by which their acts of liberation were adjudicated:

> Being a lawyer for a political prisoner is in no way comparable to representing the usual criminal defendant. The orientation of political prisoners is international, global rather than personal, philosophical, and critically analytical. They consider the legal situation in which they find themselves entrapped after they are arrested as simply a microcosm of the larger society's imprisonment of all of its Black citizens, and extrication from it must be defined by stratagems of political correctness. While occasionally they are forced to do so, they usually will not conform to the rules of the court, to the rules of criminal or civil procedure, or to the rules of evidence, not to mention the rules of prescribed courtroom decorum. Political prisoners scrutinize each motion their attorney files with an eye not for its legal competence or consequences but for its political ramifications in the overall, unceasing need to expose the society in its true light, not to extricate themselves from its grip. And they refuse to be deterred by fear of the system's retaliatory might or by the hope that submission to its rules would benefit them.[1]

Williams states that because of the conditions that produce their criminalization and incarceration, she believes that all black people caught up in the criminal justice system are political prisoners. Although this claim has been levied frequently across the black studies archive, in the context of Williams's unique observations regarding the particular tactics of black revolutionary criminal defendants, she also seems to imply that tactics similar to those practiced by Shakur during her defense are warranted in each and every instance of criminal defense proceeding. As Williams explains, "we made a pact: I would do my legal thing and she would do her necessary thing," meaning that Shakur would not compromise political strategy for legal strategy.[2]

In Williams's terms, black liberation politics constitute "inadmissible evidence" in a court of law, for to permit into the court record the dossier of transgressions against which the black movement agitates, not to mention the evidence of state illegality in its criminalization of the black community, not only would mean the destabilization of law's institutionality but, moreover, would likely impel a profound rupture in the very coherence of society itself. As Elaine Brown, former chairwoman of the Black Panther Party, scrupulously accounts in her exposé of "new age racism," *The Condemnation of Little B*, the magnitude and reach of the interrelated forces arrayed against black life that culminate in criminal proceedings against a black defendant literally encompasses every feature of the antiblack world, indicting urban redevelopment, segregation, deindustrialization, suburbanization, black land and wealth dispossession, the short-circuiting of the civil rights era, media conglomeration, the legacy of Enlightenment-era aesthetics, Richard Nixon's "war on crime," miseducation of black schoolchildren, welfare reform, constructed drug paranoias, HIV/AIDS nonprevention, black elites' abandonment of the black community, recycling the discourse of black pathology, and so on and so forth.[3] As Brown lays out, these forces (collectively comprising the police power of state and civil society) are contradictory and frequently at odds with each other in the short term; the criminalization of black children, women, and men lends the glue that coheres divergent quarters of society that would otherwise be immersed in self-destructive internecine conflicts. These are the historical lines of force against which Shakur and her comrades were militantly opposed; the essential investments in antiblackness in which these factors are constituted produce their inadmissibility in a court of law.

Is the court of public or academic discourse any less restrictive? Or are the tactics of containment simply more diverse? Are the terms of black life, what Shakur, Williams, and Brown are referencing as beyond the legibility of admissible evidence, themselves inadmissible to the critical study of race and sex? How do the leading scholarly treatments of race and sex politics serve the police power against blackness by delimiting the permissible questions, debates, perspectives, and paradigms as the price of the ticket for participating in the conversation itself? After being convicted at trial and serving six years in the maximum security wing of the Clinton Correctional Facility for Women in New Jersey, Shakur escaped prison and went into exile in Cuba, as is well known. In May 2013, on the fortieth anniversary of her arrest, the FBI inexplicably named Shakur to its Most Wanted Terrorists list, with an award of up to $2 million for her capture, causing her to occasionally go underground to avoid reward-seeking bounty hunters even while in exile. While the U.S. government continues to regard her as a notorious fugitive, she remains a revered figure in the annals of the black freedom movement, a maroon from the modern-day plantations on which slavery's afterlife continues to be prosecuted.

Prior to her trial in 1973, Shakur composed and recorded a statement addressed to the black community and broadcast over the radio. In it she reiterated her commitment to black liberation and underscored the paradigmatic fallacy of the state's case against her and the media's construction of black revolutionaries as murderers. She also apologized for being on the New Jersey Turnpike, a place known to be a checkpoint (then and now) where black mobility is curtailed through traffic stops, unlawful searches, and harassment. She stated, "Revolutionaries must never be in too much of a hurry or make careless decisions. He who runs when the sun is sleeping will stumble many times."4 This chapter makes daylight moves—careful, deliberate, and studied assessments before the sun's unflinching witness of evidence often hidden under cover of night. I will chart what from the perspective of marronage and militant black liberation is nothing less than the inadmissible career of social death, the crisis-in-waiting threatening the regime of truth prevailing over the better part of the previous millennium and in which the social and its various buttressing discourses are constituted. There are legal moves to be made, but as Williams explained, they must be subordinated to political strategy, which in turn, needs to be faithful to political analysis. Such is the intention of this book, and the present chapter lays out the terrain on which black studies confronts the social death of blackness, which is to say, how the field grapples with that which threatens its own existence and standing.

The constituent elements of the political ontology of race, the leading arc of black studies in its original inception—a structure of gratuitous violence, blackness as nonhumanity, and slavery as a structure of libidinal desire (as expressed through natal alienation and general dishonor)—comprise the condition of social death. Taken together, this framework offers a paradigm shift, a move to a new assumptive logic in which social death rather than proprietary claims defines power relations in the afterlife of slavery. In other words, slavery is not a relation of power characterized solely or even primarily by the control over labor power specifically, or by the property interests of the owner in the enslaved generally. The ensemble of questions, as Frank

Wilderson puts it, that social death presents for an examination of the present disables the various explanatory frameworks comprising the Western humanist paradigm hegemonic in the academy today. Discursively, "social death" calls upon a constellation of political contestations, existential struggles, and ethical coordinates.

This chapter considers the issues that congeal in social death in pursuit of a twofold agenda. First, it explicates the "time of blackened ethics" introduced in the previous chapter through genealogy's subversion. Of particular concern will be to explore the kind of analysis attentive to the originary displacement of the African from the human family. This includes reading the multicultural academy's leading critical discourse on race, sex, gender, class, and nation without presupposing the system of racial slavery that installs these forms of being human. As I showed in the preceding chapter, this exercise does not entail recourse to genealogy, but rather a stripping away of the scaffolding that imbues these historically specific terms with transcendental qualities, on the one hand, or positions them in an affective register of deconstruction delimited by slavery's un-deconstructed premise, on the other hand.

Second, it examines the failure on the part of post–black studies to adequately attend to racial slavery's constitutive role in the reproduction of consciousness. I review two examples of post–black studies treatments of the "intersections" of racism, gender dominance, and sexual politics to illuminate this problem. The secondary point here is that the vibrancy of post–black studies sustains the post-racial as the latest iteration of antiblack politics. The primary point is that this discursive violence against blackness is part and parcel of the ongoing sexual predation of the antiblack world against the black freedom struggle. Black "missing persons" lend my inquiry the requisite point of reference. Shakur's disappearance into the prison and then into exile is the price and the promise of the revolutionary and the maroon. Her political journey, including onto the FBI's Most Wanted list, perhaps anticipating the changing geopolitics between the United States and Cuba and the consequent possibility of heightened vulnerability for former political prisoners such as Shakur living in exile on the island, only underscores the essential absence against which she and her comrades were fighting in the first place. Beyond the questions of how a black person becomes vulnerable to disappearance, how such disappearance fails to register as an absence, and how such cases serve as an interdiction of the black subject who remains not-here in the everyday, there is the matter before us of how the leading critical discourse on race and sex is analytically equipped to confront this condition as the crux of what it means to conceptualize justice or its impossibility. How do the leading discourses of the critical study of race and sex, of the post-racial, produce black people as missing?

Grammars of Suffering and Struggle

When Carlesha Freeland-Gaither, a twenty-two-year-old black woman, was found alive in Jessup, Maryland, on November 5, 2014, after having been abducted three days earlier off of a Philadelphia street where she was walking home from visiting her godson, her rescue briefly made national headlines. While her family was overjoyed at her safe return, Freeland-Gaither's survival of her ordeal was but a momentary respite from one of the slave system's ongoing patterns. Despite being only 13 percent of the national population, black people account for nearly 40 percent of missing person cases.[5] Of the total number of missing persons of color reported to the FBI in 2010, 85 percent are black and 64,000 are black women.[6]

Most poor white children who are abducted do not galvanize intense media attention and a dedicated law enforcement response, but a black child never becomes the representative symbol of child endangerment in the manner of a Polly Klaas or an Elizabeth Smart—not to mention the inspirations for new legislation and criminal justice policy, as has been the case with missing white children.[7] The vast majority of disappeared black people generate no notice from mainstream society and its media and state officialdom. Or in the terms Frantz Fanon famously employed, the black person generates "no ontological resistance"—having no existence that registers as such, the disappearance of an absence is no disappearance at all. The disappeared black person—a paradox, a redundancy, or an oxymoron?—implicitly draws the reflexes of pathos to his or her persona like a moth to flames.[8] As Kali Gross observes, in the Freeland-Gaither case the initial presumptions by authorities placed the victim under scrutiny, and it was not until it emerged that she was a nursing assistant with the love and support of both of her parents and her community that she went from being another faceless statistic succumbing to violence to a "good" victim worthy of concern and protection.[9]

By contrast, Jackie Askins was an eighteen-year-old working in commercial sex in Philadelphia in 1987 when she was held captive, raped, and tortured for over two months before she was rescued. Reflecting on her (ongoing) ordeal thirty years later, Askins states that the most painful aspect of her experience, above all else, has been that she was never even "missing" while she was a prisoner in her torturer's basement.[10] The abductions and disappearances, and the symbolic murder of silence with which they are met, are twin symptoms of the cultural situation of black people as a wounding. Organizations such as the Black and Missing Foundation and Black and Missing But Not Forgotten testify to the fact that blacks remain strictly segregated from life, the ground of such supposition a reference to a continuous line of accumulated bodies that despite being branded with their owner's proprietary claims so that they may be returned upon escape, and because of the ontological isolation from kith and kin signified by such marking, disappear into the nexus of slave traders, bounty hunters, far-flung plantations, flesh-devouring bloodhounds, salacious white desires, and even sometimes the deep reaches of maroon outposts. In Wilderson's words, "the Dead have the Blacks among them."[11]

This situation can only be explained through the black studies paradigm grounded in the time of blackened ethics, which supplants the humanist paradigm to which the critical study of race and sex is largely faithful, including comparative ethnic and racial studies, critical ethnic studies, performance studies, and queer of color critique, as well as the integrationist and multi-culturalist proprieties informing aspects of the black studies field. The main point to introduce at this juncture is the distinction between "empirical" and "structural." For my purposes, "empirical" refers to lived experience, understood sociologically or phenomenologically; "structural" denotes how humanity is organized, ontologically. An analytic of blackened ethics works away from an overreliance on the empirical, the events of daily life, and toward situating these experiences within the gross power differentials that become visible as our awareness of the structure of existence clarifies. In other words, even though it happens disproportionately to the black community, not just black people go missing, maimed, and murdered—so what is the difference?

The difference lies in the structural realm: while nonblack people may share with blacks the experience of abduction or violence, at the structural level what nonblacks all have in common is that they are not black. In a world structured by a negative categorical imperative—"above all, don't be black"—this fact acts as a psychic buffer for nonblack peoples, a confirmation of existence, and, time and again, a source of political sustenance and mobilization.[12] Within this polarized structure of humanity, blackness stands in antagonistic relation to all other positions in order that these other positions may struggle to overcome their respective conflicts with and among each other. All one needs to do to improve one's social standing, no matter how despised, disposed, or dystopic it may be, or to gather legitimacy to one's political project, no matter how controversial or suspect, is to champion antiblackness or to simply distance oneself from blackness. This move is ubiquitous in modern democratic politics: whenever an electoral candidate positions herself for law and order or against crime variously construed, she is obliquely conjuring the unifying force of antiblackness. Empirical findings regarding the suffering of nonblacks implicitly confirm their belonging within the human family, however fallen, degraded, or immiserated such conditions may be, inferring that such oppression signifies a loss that justice might recover. Documenting the violence that black people endure, however, does not invoke questions of justice, but instead serves as affirmation of black pathology. This difference is a result of the structural informing how we understand the empirical. Lewis Gordon writes: "Blacks here suffer the phobogenic reality posed by the spirit of seriousness. In effect, they more than symbolize or signify various social pathologies—they become them. In our antiblack world, blacks *are* pathology."[13] The move away from the empirical as the sole litmus for suffering or political belonging permits posing the dangerous question of what it means for blackness to signify *the* singular "human surrogate," and thereby direct the black studies critique to the myriad recuperations of the social at the extraordinary expense of blackness.[14]

With only rare exceptions across the fields of critical race and sex scholarship, empirical findings are routinely conflated with structural analysis, raising four key points to bear in mind as I turn to examine the inadmissible career of social death. First, it reminds us that the way black people suffer and struggle in the world is qualitatively distinct from how nonblack people suffer because only black people the world over are positioned historically outside of ontology, as the position of nonexistence. Second, analyses of power that gloss this fundamental distinction tend to act as if the ontological terms of the social world are not what they are. In other words, most social analysis is levied on the grounds of social conflict, which at once overlooks and naturalizes the structural antagonism that blackness denotes in the modern world.

Third, because ontic relations operate as a grammar they remain largely taken for granted, and as a consequence, analysts who are not conscious of ontology present the world in terms that promiscuously conflate structural positions that are in fact irreconcilable. Wilderson explains that in semiotics and linguistics, grammar is the unspoken, assumed set of rules by which speech communication is possible. Let us call this the structure of speech acts. Similarly, with respect to political ethics, there is an ontological grammar, or a structure of suffering based upon a specific conception of power relations that delimits and crowds out other understandings of struggle. For instance, the specious suggestion that black people and nonblack people of color share the same struggle against the system of white supremacy and are thus equally disadvantaged by it.

Fourth, even when critics are aware of the ontologic differences between black and nonblack, sometimes a conscious or unconscious desire to see black people join the human family leads to an analytic emphasis on black agency, performance, or success as if this phenomenological dimension can affect the ontic relations of the antiblack world. It cannot be overestimated how seductive it is to bypass the implications of ontology, to act as if the world and the grammar of its political ethics is not structured in a categorical imperative to avoid being black at all costs. This is partly how the post-racial recruits both its adherents and dissenters to a common antiblack structure of feeling. I will explore in subsequent chapters how this desire plays out in the movement to curb police violence, as if these terms "police" and "violence" were not a redundant reference to a structural relationship, wherein policing is violence, rather than an unfortunate but necessary, occasional, and correctable part of the job. The notion that justice can be brought to bear against the police power is thus an expression of bad faith in that it turns away from a displeasing reality, the world as it is, constituted in the irreconcilable violence of antiblackness, in favor of embracing a more comforting falsehood, an imagined world of social conflict remediable through struggle and reform.

In the following sections of this chapter I explore the production of black people as "missing persons" in relation to the sequestration of the black studies movement's singular challenge to the onto-epistemic violence of a world order in which black abductees do not even register as missing. Since the intervention on offer from black studies is not simply an empirical one, my objective here is to examine black disappearances structurally, at the level of knowledge production about society, in order to demonstrate how committed antiracist scholars end up legitimating black disappearances from the world by excising black power from their analyses of race and sex politics.

The Black Studies Eclipse

Speaking at a 1971 symposium sponsored by Atlanta's Institute of the Black World, C. L. R. James made the observation that "all political power presents itself to the world within a certain framework of ideas. It is fatal to ignore this in any estimate of social forces in political action."[15] This insight has been a benchmark for not only the black studies tradition, but also virtually every intellectual project emanating from the conditions of the oppressed, from Marxism to feminism to anticolonialism. Critical intellectual production on race and sex politics in the United States associated with ethnic studies, for its part, is concerned with confronting the varied epistemic scaffolding of white supremacist nationalisms within which the prevailing social order is presented. Even as ethnic studies challenges a certain set of ideas associated with power, however, it does so by wielding a more fundamental knowledge system that it in fact shares with its object of critique. The reproduction of the problem of blackness is the outcome. In short, the leading critical discourse on race and sex has cornered what it means to be antiracist precisely for the reason that it advances within, not against, the basic structure of antiblackness that creates "race," and by extension, "sex," in the first place. Blackness remains central to any truth claims regarding race and sex, and yet the very saliency of these claims, their purchase on reality within the domain of mainstream common sense, rests with a disavowal of this centrality.

Ethnic studies texts such as Lisa Marie Cacho's *Social Death: Racialized Rightlessness and the Criminalization of the Unprotected* employ a comparative model that relies upon, implicitly or explicitly, what Wilderson terms "the ruse of analogy." Wilderson explains that the attempt to analogize between blackness and other structural positions is a ruse since black existence is "without analog."[16] The ruse of analogy thus erases black struggle, but moreover, it does so in order to sustain the ethicality of, in this case, nonblack people of color politics. In *Social Death*, Cacho employs a comparison between the tragic deaths by car accident (in separate incidents) suffered by her Chicano cousin (along with two of his friends), on the one hand, and a white professional baseball player, on the other, to accomplish her larger goal of making relationality intelligible outside of the conceptual universe that lends value its relational basis in the first place. Cacho explores the many racialized, gendered, and sexualized ways in which her cousin's life and death are devalued in relation to the valorization of the professional athlete, concluding that it "is difficult to value Brandon by the quality of his life experiences when time and space are organized through heteronormativity and dictated by capital accumulation," leading her to situate his "unintelligible ethics of deviance" in "queer time and space."[17]

I cite Cacho's critical reflections on value, through her memorializing of her cousin's tragic death, not to call into question her findings or her attempt to put her loss into perspective, but rather to point out how her interpretation of value draws upon key insights from black studies, all the while eclipsing the persistent black presence in any discussion of human valuation. Getting clear on this method for appropriating blackness is key for ascertaining how the post-racial relies upon the ethnic studies framework to crowd out the black grammar of struggle and the black studies project that aims to bring it to bear on knowledge. Cacho cites one of the two indispensable sources from the black studies archive on the matter, Lindon Barrett's *Blackness and Value: Seeing Double*, in order to establish her comparative analytic. Here is Cacho referencing Barrett at the outset of *Social Death*: "Value is made intelligible relationally. According to literary critic Lindon Barrett, value *needs* negativity.

As he theorizes, the 'object' of value needs an 'other' of value because 'for value negativity is a *resource*, an essential resource. The negative, the expended, the excessive invariably form the ground of possibilities for value.'"[18] The problem here is that this conception of value, pulled from the larger context of *Blackness and Value*, actually eviscerates Barrett's signal contribution to the study of value by denuding his insights of their point of reference—the singular position of blackness in the construction of human form in the modern world. Cacho arrogates blackness into simply "difference" or "other," indicating how the ethnic studies formation transmutes blackness into one of a multiplicity of structurally (if not historically) equivalent positions. What Cacho finds useful in *Blackness and Value* is nothing more than the insights of previous scholars on the matter of value up to Barrett, from Marx to Mary Douglas, Peter Stallybrass and Allon White, Jean Baudrillard, and Gayatri Spivak. Barrett's contribution is to mine this fruitful file on value from a black studies perspective to elucidate how blackness is the missing term in everyone's critical armory. If you leave off this part of the equation, as Cacho does, then you are simply using Barrett as little more than a literature review service.

Cacho is astute to look to Barrett for clarification of the symbology of value. Building from Douglas and Stallybrass and White, Barrett explores how value masks social relations and inevitably depends on a relationship rifled through with boundaries that would police and delimit exchange and transit within the relation. He shows how this boundary intrinsic to valuation means that an original violence always inheres in value: "Value is violence and, more to the point, value is violence disguised or dis-figured."[19] However, rather than take Barrett's deconstruction of value as her point of departure, Cacho reproduces the essential mystification that Marx originally explained as the purpose of value and to which Barrett labored to expose with respect to blackness. Cacho does not miss the importance of each of these points—value's masking of social relations, the boundaries it relies upon and reproduces, and the violence of the social conveyed in value's particular forms—but she deploys them to extrapolate from the world as it is to support her version of the world. In other words, she uses "social relations," "boundary," and "violence" unmoored from their historical and ontological premise in the production of blackness. Barrett writes of the process that Cacho in fact reproduces:

The specter of this examination is the specter of bla(n)ckness and, to restate an important point, bla(n)ckness is not adequately conceptualized in terms of the mere inversion suggested by the dynamics of concepts like invisibility, marginalization, or exile. For bla(n)ckness not only remarks the inversibility of two fields distinguished by a clearly (rationally) established boundary, but interrogates as well the inadmissibility of that boundary as a measure of the two fields.[20]

There is no law or formula governing how value works that can be applied in social analysis of nonblack subjects or topics without accounting for the centrality of blackness in the constitution of value itself. Blackness's position as the negation of value, as the definitive absence to humanity's presence, cannot simply be inverted or transgressed or substituted for another ontological position. This is Barrett's singular innovation on the robust roster of critical commentary on the topic up to the publication of *Blackness and Value*. Whereas Marx, and the legion of scholars of Marx, led by Spivak, have exhaustively deconstructed the commodity in capitalist ideology and political economy, there is a general aphasia in Marxism regarding what to do analytically with the fact that the black is the commodity.[21]

Cacho's estimation of how society construes Brandon's social worth is tied to her analysis of how he is positioned by capital's exploiting and alienating methods. What she misses is precisely what Barrett's study is all about: the very fact that her cousin (or herself, for that matter) is positioned in terms of a tragic choice—between being valued for the exploitation of his labor power, on the one hand, or being devalued for his response to the alienation that he experiences having his labor power commodified, on the other hand—is itself the indication that he is a human being immune from the suffering of accumulation and fungibility reserved for nonhuman objects.[22] While Brandon's labor power is commodified, the commodity itself is black, a thingness essential to the very ethical questions sustaining Cacho's meditations and broached under capitalism as ethics proper. Cacho conflates commodification of labor power and alienation under racial capital's regime with the singular commodification of personhood itself due to the relations of racial slavery and its afterlife. In so doing, she demonstrates what Barrett refers to as the "formidable resistance to examining the unthinkable logic rendering African Americans unthinkable."[23] It is the aim of this book to unravel these relations of social death masked in the discourse of ethnic studies, of which *Social Death* is emblematic.

The second vital black studies resource on value is bypassed entirely by Cacho. W. E. B. Du Bois's notion of "double-consciousness," proffered immediately on the heels of Marx's original deconstruction of value, should have forever altered the course of critical thought on the matter by bringing Marxist thought back down to Earth, recalibrating it for the world as it is, a world constituted in slave relations, rather than wage relations, the fantasy world imagined by Marx and continuously dreamed about by the multitudes of thinkers working from the assumptive logic of exploitation and alienation as the primary language of human suffering. Du Bois would go on to contribute mightily to revising Marxist thought, from his *Black Reconstruction* onward. But his earliest cut sliced to the bone: in an 1897 *Atlantic Monthly* article entitled "The Strivings of the Negro People," which was later republished in 1903 as "Of Our Spiritual Strivings," the first chapter of *The Souls of Black Folk*, Du Bois introduced the concepts of "the veil" and "double-consciousness" to address the fact that black people alone are alienated from their personhood, not simply from their labor power, and not as a result of capital's dominance but because of antiblackness.

> It is a peculiar sensation, this double-consciousness, this sense of always looking at one's self through the eyes of others, of measuring one's soul by the tape of a world that looks on in amused contempt and pity. One ever feels his two-ness—an American, a Negro; two souls, two thoughts, two unreconciled strivings; two warring ideals in one dark body, whose dogged strength alone keeps it from being torn asunder.[24]

Although "double-consciousness" is multilayered, the only interpretation that lends traction against the antiblack world is in precisely the one register regularly overlooked in the continual recitation of this concept across ethnic studies and critical race and sex studies generally. Du Bois is saying that to be human ("an American") he must be antiblack ("a Negro"). In other words, black people embody dis-value, and while there are certainly insights to be gleaned from this "peculiar" station, the antagonism is irreconcilable ("two unreconciled strivings"), and in the final analysis, then, the struggle is to not be antiblack: with "two warring ideals in one dark body, whose dogged strength alone keeps it from being torn asunder." As Sylvia Wynter reflects: "I suddenly began to see what DuBois was trying to get at and what Fanon was going to get at with Black 'self-alienation,' which is that '*I have a consciousness that does not function for my best interest!*' THERE HAS TO BE A *WAR* AGAINST 'CONSCIOUSNESS.' BLACK STUDIES WAS A WAR!"[25] Above all else, blackness is a cultural value of total negation that all racialized groups are institutionally shaped to know, in their bodies, as if it were natural and as if the culturally constructed categories of blackness and nonblackness were actually biological ones. Rather than lay the groundwork for a phenomenology of human valuation, or a sociogeny of value, to use Fanon's term, however, Du Bois's "double-consciousness" has been evoked endlessly as mere social conflict, well beyond its reference point, such that anybody can experience doubleness: "two warring ideals in one body" becomes another way of expressing alienation or dissonance between the self and some other entity variously constituted. The traffic in double-consciousness across the multicultural academy, then, is parasitic on blackness. This is the structural adjustment, or the political quarantining, of black studies in the first degree.

From Social Death to "Social Death"

As is often the case, nonblack society acquires for itself those products of black culture that it has long construed as evidence of black pathos. Once in nonblack hands, the supposed signs of black pathos become fashionable and cool. In a similar manner, ethnic studies and the critical study of race and sex within the multiculturalist paradigm displace the social death of blackness as structural condition, only to popularize the discourse of "social death" to describe lived experience for nonblack people of color and queers—as in Cacho's *Social Death*. With the advent of the modern world, slavery went from an event that anyone can be subject to, to an ontological condition in which Africans alone not only encountered the event, but were engulfed by it, permanently reconfigured from human bodies into black flesh. In Wilderson's terms, "slavery is *cathedralized*," and as a condition of ontology, rather than as an event of experience, produces a "people who, *a priori*, that is prior to the contingency of the 'transgressive act' (such as losing a war or being convicted of a crime), stand as socially dead in relation to the rest of the world."[26]

The perversity is that having quarantined the structural critique that black studies levies against Western humanism's field of knowledge by foregrounding the gratuitous antiblack violence constituting the social, the multiculturalist paradigm has appropriated "social death" discourse to explain an event of experience, rather than a condition of ontology. This appropriation is evidence of the fungibility of blackness, of the persistence of slave relations into the present day. Hartman explains: "The figurative capacities of blackness enable white [and nonblack] flights of fancy while increasing the likelihood of the captive's disappearance."[27] This is why I argue that the post-racial is best understood in terms of a compulsion to retestify to racial injury that only further obscures the actual nature of suffering under racial regime.

The increasingly popular use of "social death" discourse to analyze non-black suffering within ethnic studies, queer studies, and beyond operates through a few distinct genealogies, one of which features the direct appropriation of black studies: for example, extrapolating from Lindon Barrett's study of blackness and value to explain the criminalization of Latino and Asian immigrant communities, as with Cacho's *Social Death* book cited above, to which I now return.[28] Necessarily, blackness is omnipresent in her discussions of various cases of criminalized Latino and Asian immigrants, but since she treats it as merely another position along a continuum of racialization, a la African Americans, Mexican Americans, Vietnamese Americans, and so forth, her racial analysis remains at the level of experience. The lived tensions between black communities and Latino and Asian immigrant and refugee communities that emerge throughout Cacho's study are indeed complex. Her account exacerbates these tensions at the level of representation, however, because blackness remains purely a symbolic host for her primary concerns, which are with nonblack racialized subjects.

Cacho analyses how poor Southeast Asian immigrants are able to marshal civil rights law through the Fair Housing Act. Their success in mobilizing state resources to access better living conditions was not through the right to decent housing or antidiscrimination law applied to the real estate market; it could only be achieved through the right to be protected from black crime within the poor neighborhoods that they shared with their black neighbors. In other words, Asian immigrant access to safe housing effectively means moving away from poor black residents. The same spatial mobility and legal recourse available to Asians were not only denied to blacks in the same neighborhoods, but more to the point, explains Cacho, they were available to Southeast Asians because refugee neighborhoods were poor and black.[29] This state of affairs would be stunning in its naked antiblackness were it not so routine, systemic, and uncontroversial. What is alarming about Cacho's analysis, however, is how the actual social death of blackness that it lays bare fails to generate extended meditation on her part. Worse yet, it leads to a truncated circular reasoning that all too efficiently relegates blackness to the sidelines of social analysis. The sum total of Cacho's explanation for how poor black people endure social captivity and at the same time serve as the springboard for the social mobility of other racialized groups:

> African Americans in the inner city are not eligible for civil rights not only because racism is defined in law as personal prejudice but also because inner-city spaces are criminalized. Criminalization, as I have been arguing, not only forecloses empathy but does so through producing people and places always already subject to a form of discrimination believed to be both legitimate and deserved.[30]

This is circular reasoning at its best: black people are ineligible for civil rights relief because they live in criminalized spaces, which are so construed precisely because they live there. Analytically this circularity functions in Cacho's work to jettison the specific forces of antiblackness from her analysis. Black spaces are criminalized—so what more can we say? Cacho fails to even remark on the fact that the racialized structures of state and civil society that are her topic of study require divisions between black and nonblack nonwhite groups precisely to preserve the status of black nonhumanity that sustains the ethicality of the law and everyone else's humanity. *Social Death* (the book) reinscribes the actual social death (structural positionality) of blackness by deploying fungible blackness (social death) in order to disseminate "social death" (the discourse of aggrieved suffering) to its Latino and Asian immigrant communities of identification. Studies such as *Social Death*, in short, deploy "social death" not as descriptive of a structural positionality irredeemable under the present terms of order but, rather, to accentuate attention on the performative aspects of dominance with the objective of making claims for redress more persuasive—as in, the terms of exploitation have gotten so bad that they are best characterized in terms of "death."

A second genealogy that popularizes "social death" discourse to analyze nonblack grammars of suffering and struggle develops from Michel Foucault's concept of "biopolitics" into Achille Mbembe's notion of "necropolitics." Studies on the "governance of life and death" that operate within this fold include far-ranging topics from the national security state and the war on terror to immigration around the globe to new media technologies to neoliberalism.[31] The notion of racism here is based, in large part, on one subset of Foucault's lectures at the Collège de France, published as *Society Must Be Defended*, where he propounds race as a technology of biopower in which exclusions, divisions, and discipline are employed by the state to manage its population in the name of reproducing a way of life.[32] Mbembe revises Foucault to apply to the context of colonial and postcolonial Africa, where he argues that the state dispenses with the pretense of leveraging life toward the ends of replicating a certain civilization; rather, the "postcolony" in Africa is governed by death-dealing in which population management is pursued through mass killing.[33] Much of this Foucauldian genealogy implicitly or explicitly draws upon, in addition to Foucault, Jean-Paul Sartre, Hannah Arendt, and more recently, Giorgio Agamben's concepts of "bare life" and "state of exception."[34]

In the Foucauldian approach to "social death," Nazism, colonialism, capitalism, and totalitarianism in general provide the historical points of reference for theorizing the subordination of life to a regime of death. The argument, advanced in a variety of ways across varied topics, that the "state of exception" in fact describes the juridical order to which the entire population is subject, albeit unevenly, overrides the one ethical claim to exceptionality (blackness) in favor of a general, or generally accessible, condition of immiseration and injury (under heteronormativity, capital, American geopolitical dominance, and so forth). Alexander Weheliye's *Habeas Viscus: Racializing Assemblages, Biopolitics, and Black Feminist Theories of the Human* demonstrates the problem with applying this framework to investigate black grammars of suffering and struggle. Weheliye's work is particularly insidious for the black studies movement because he is institutionally affiliated with a prominent black studies degree program in the United States and he positions *Habeas Viscus* as a work of black studies, and yet substantively it conforms to the ethnic studies paradigm. In other words, *Habeas Viscus* illustrates how black studies is undermined from within.

Weheliye opens *Habeas Viscus* with the stated objective to employ "the vantage point of black studies" to rectify "the shortcomings of 'bare life and biopolitics discourse,'" and in so doing, to propose "alternate ways of conceptualizing the place of race" within modern politics.[35] He identifies Hortense Spillers and Sylvia Wynter as the black feminist theorists from which his analysis will most heavily draw, in particular Spillers's notion of the "flesh" (hence the book's title, "you shall have the flesh"). Unfortunately, this agenda proves to be a cover story for recanonizing Western thought and further marginalizing the political project of black studies, including those insights on offer from Spillers and Wynter themselves. In the process, Weheliye repeatedly repositions blackness as but one voice in the family of "racialized minority discourse" and replicates the liberal myth that "race" produces racism. In the end, *Habeas Viscus* lodges its objections to reading black suffering and struggle through the lens of social death without even confronting the various ways in which black studies is currently grappling with the realities that social death names.

Black studies scholars have decisively revealed Foucault and Agamben deficient on race, with both lacking the requisite understanding of slavery's centrality to social theorizing.[36] *Habeas Viscus* bypasses these critiques, however, and where the European theorists perform a classic Eurocentric disavowal of modernity's racializing dynamic by locating racism's origins with colonialism and situating Nazism as the pinnacle of biopower, Weheliye writes an even more devious disavowal of black studies. He replicates the notion that Nazism, or even colonialism, inaugurates bare life and the state of exception wherein the sovereign power operates in suspension of positive law, a preposterous assertion in light of racial slavery's prior instantiation of modern power in the ship's hold, on the auction blocks, across the plantations of the New World. There is no doubt that Weheliye is aware of the extant black studies critiques of Foucault and Agamben; their omission from *Habeas Viscus* is no mere oversight, nor misrecognition of the theoretical plane on which they operate, but rather points to Weheliye's disagreement on the political level at which the critiques are posed.

Weheliye's failure (or unwillingness) to definitively rebut the cathedralization of the Jewish Holocaust recanonizes Western thought and directly sabotages the black radical tradition. While Western culture generally beholds Nazism and fascism as anomalous and singular in its horror, as the most egregious violation of civilized society, the black studies library is replete with the recognition that Europe was simply being engulfed during the Jewish Holocaust with precisely the form of genocidal power it had unleashed on non-European peoples for hundreds of years through slavery and colonialism. Aimé Césaire, Oliver Cox, Shirley Graham Du Bois, W. E. B. Du Bois, Frantz Fanon, Amy Jacques Garvey, Marcus Garvey, C. L. R. James, Claudia Jones, George Padmore, William Patterson, Paul Robeson, and Richard Wright, among many others, all understood fascism not as a rupture in Western civilization's march of progress, but rather as its logical denouement, an extension of a global system rooted in decadent self-destructive racist ideologies and violence established through the slave trade. The fascist problem, then, is the impermissible knowledge that Western civilization has always and already been constituted as fascist with respect to non-Western peoples and to black people in particular.[37] Agamben, Foucault, and black studies saboteurs such as Weheliye should be seen within this penumbra of fascistic knowledge production. As black studies scholars across the generations have made clear, the purpose of reifying Nazism as *the* ethical conundrum in modern history is to secure the elision of the *Maafa*, the African Holocaust, from the realm of ethics proper, and thereby to solidify the essential ethicality of nonblack society. Frantz Fanon's famous observation in *Black Skin, White Masks* that the Jewish Holocaust was simply a "family feud" was aimed at recalibrating our understanding of ethics in this way. Centering racial slavery in our conception of ethics is literally unimaginable for Western civilization, as it would render white ethics impossible.

His basic allegiance to Western humanism established, it is unsurprising that Weheliye speaks almost entirely of "race" in unspecific, ungrounded terms, an odd tendency for an avowedly black studies text. When he does speak of blackness, he immediately situates it within a family of "racialized minority discourse"—black and critical ethnic studies, postcolonial theory, queer theory, and so forth. Jared Sexton has termed this practice "people-of-color-blindness," the refusal to admit that the different histories between blacks and other nonwhites correspond to discrepant structural positions and, accordingly, the insistence "upon the monolithic character of victimization under white supremacy." Sexton explains that not only is the full scope and weight of black suffering and struggle occluded in such a decentered paradigm, but also what disappears is a proper analysis of the true nature of nonblack nonwhite "material and symbolic power *relative* to the category of blackness."[38] In Weheliye's hands, it becomes a "brutal" mash-up of popular themes within ethnic studies: he rejects "resistance," and yet "assemblage" and "flesh" are his effort to "elude the violence."[39] Similarly, "comparison" is out, in favor of "relation" or "side by side," as in: "the concentration camp, the colonial outpost, and slave plantation suggest three of many relay points in the weave of modern politics, which are neither exceptional nor comparable, but simply relational."[40] As I noted earlier, without a rigorous contextualization of the structure in which blackness signifies nonhuman and nonblackness parasitically relies upon black subjection to reach human status, "relations" misdiagnoses how black is positioned vis-à-vis nonblack. Here is Weheliye again riffing off a world that does not exist: "The point to be made here does not concern replacing the camp with the plantation as the nomos and hidden matrix of current politics but that it is necessary to think through the commonalities and disparities between these two spaces without awakening the demon of comparison."[41] Unfortunately, it is far too late to have it all—slavery took that away forever.

All of this is a means to an end, to leverage control over the latest critical developments within black studies while keeping in play a decadent European critical theory tradition. Curiously, Weheliye does not actually grapple with how the lens of social death is utilized within black studies; instead, he employs Agamben's bare life as a proxy, objecting that it "leaves no room for alternate forms of life that elude the law's violent embrace."[42] He goes on to note that

Europe's Jewry found a mode of resistance that enabled their survival until liberation from the concentration camps—a violence, mind you, that was wholly contingent upon a very particular political economy (Nazism) in a given historical moment. Anti-Semitism may have a long history, but if I am permitted the critical posture of comparison for a moment, even in contexts marked by intensely violent persecution, Jews always knew that at least they were not black: they had standing and generated value as human beings. In other words, Weheliye makes his case for "the flesh provid[ing] a stepping stone toward new genres of human" only within a matrix of human qua human violence.[43] Were the concentration camp survivor a black person on a plantation in the Carolinas or in a slave market on Chartres Street in New Orleans, what new genre of human did the flesh promise? What was the promise of the flesh on a chain gang in an Alabama convict lease camp? What stepping stones toward freedom revealed themselves in the flesh to Freddie Gray, killed in Baltimore on April 12, 2015, for "making eye contact" with police officers? How does Sandra Bland's flesh "elude the violence," as Weheliye puts it, as she was hunted down by a Texas state trooper who made a U-turn immediately upon spotting her drive by, then proceeded to instigate a confrontation that led to her eventual lynching in a jail cell?[44]

Since Weheliye and his European theorists prefer not to stray too far afield, what about the black GIs who were among the earliest American soldiers to arrive at Buchenwald, Dachau, and other Nazi concentration camps: did their flesh step them into a new genre of human as they returned to the United States from their life-giving service in the "family feud" of World War II to a reenergized antiblack terror campaign that claimed fifty-six black lynch victims in the first fifteen months after Hitler's defeat, most of whom were returning veterans?[45] These black veterans and lynch victims, as with their enslaved ancestors before them and their post-racial era descendants after them, face a gratuitous violence productive of each and every political economy past and present. In the context of gratuitous violence, a distinctly antiblack phenomenon, the "flesh" marks not the space of freedom moves, but rather the remainder left over once each and every category of the subject (gender, sex, bodily integrity, agency) that Western consciousness presumes composes the human is stripped away—*this* is the condition of social death.

When measured against the ethical standards and analytical rigor of contemporary black studies' struggle with social death, *Habeas Viscus* is too politically treacherous and analytically unsound to be taken seriously as anything other than counterinsurgency. Weheliye waits until his concluding chapter, "Freedom," to chastise the black struggle directly:

> Black studies, if it is to remain critical and oppositional, cannot fall prey to juridical humanity and its concomitant pitfalls, since this only affects change in the domain of the map but not the territory. In order to do so, the hieroglyphics of the flesh should not be conceptualized as just exceptional or radically particular, since this habitually leads to the comparative tabulation of different systems of oppression that then serve as the basis for defining personhood as possession. . . . If we are to affect significant systemic changes, then we must locate at least some of the struggles for justice in the region of humanity as a relational ontological totality (an object of knowledge) that cannot be reduced to either the universal or particular.[46]

The singularity of blackness is a trap, in Weheliye's way of thinking. The only hope for the black movement, he is saying, is to abandon black consciousness and self-determination in favor of a multicultural politics unmoored from blackness—in short, to stop being black. In this sense, "relational ontological totality" means human beings beyond "race"—with neither the hindrances of Man's universalizing conception of "race," nor of black studies' baggage of an obdurate and inveterate blackness, a particularity that cannot be translated to humanity writ large. It may be dense and obtuse academese, but Weheliye is nonetheless rehearsing Rodney King's refrain: Why can't we all just get along? Where King's plea once took the edge off of black rebellion and state violence, Weheliye promotes post–black studies for the post-racial present.

The Flesh of Post–Black Studies

Cacho and Weheliye illuminate my argument in this chapter that engagements with "social death" belie more vital subtending disputes: objections to the discourse divulge an objection to the structural analysis that social death demands, while embracement of it from ethnic and queer studies affiliates discloses the continued parasitic relationship between these fields and black studies. Resistance to the evidence of social death and preference for "social death" as a descriptive of nonblack experience are the necessary props for the performative, rather than structural, conception of violence and struggle hegemonic in the critical study of race and sex. Suturing a gender and sex analysis onto black experience advances the performative notion of racism. These two elements of the multicultural paradigm—violence as contingent or performative, and gender and sex as discrete identities, albeit overlapping or intersecting with race—shroud the horror of black kidnappings and the unimaginable loss of all that is imaginable (nothing from nothingness). How do we know that black disappearances signify a terror distinct from that of non-black missing person cases? Beyond the statistical overrepresentation of black missing persons, coupled with the relative silence through which society greets these cases—in other words, differences at the level of event or experience—the prevailing field of knowledge does not permit such distinctions. What do such disappearances mean within the onto-epistemic conditions governing the antiblack world? How does "black missing person" indict the "figure of the unsovereign," the human figure de-domesticated from its own body?[47] Social death remains controversial precisely because its discursive deployment and the politics ensnaring it index not racial politics per se, but more to the crux of the matter, structural positionality and political solidarity with blackness, which in turn impugn performativity as the primary dimension through which black subjects experience both violence and gender-sex.

A return to Weheliye's *Habeas Viscus* on the matter of sexuality deepens my reading of the ethnic studies problematic (to borrow from Sexton). Weheliye's conception of the "flesh" both misinterprets the black studies archive that it purports to develop and corrupts its structural analysis of violence into an analysis of performance more amenable to nonblack grammars of suffering and struggle. This is the basic sexual violation of the black movement. Weheliye announces "black feminist theories of the human" as the foundation for his so-called critique of Agamben's bare life and Foucault's biopolitics. I have shown how his reading of these thinkers extends rather than interrupts the basic colonizing mission of which they are exemplary instances. Zeroing in on Weheliye's misappropriation of Spillers and Wynter further exposes the duplicity.

Weheliye draws his concept "habeas viscus" from Spillers's distinction, first introduced in her well-known essay "Mama's Baby, Papa's Maybe: An American Grammar Book," between the bodies of enslaved Africans and black flesh, "that zero degree of social conceptualization that does not escape concealment under the brush of discourse or the reflexes of iconography."[48] He claims that Spillers's designation of the flesh signals "how violent political domination activates a fleshly surplus that simultaneously sustains and disfigures said brutality, and, on the other hand," directs us "to reclaim the atrocity of flesh as a pivotal arena for the politics emanating from different traditions of the oppressed. The flesh, rather than displacing bare life or civil death, excavates the social (after)life of these categories: it represents racializing assemblages of subjection that can never annihilate the lines of flight, freedom dreams, practices of liberation, and possibilities of other worlds."[49] Weheliye, then, is asserting a creative, productive, positive dimension to the flesh: "to experience the flesh might just allow us to relate to the world differently," to inhabit the "insurgent praxes of humanity composed in the hieroglyphics of the flesh."[50] In short, Weheliye employs Spillers's concept to construct a resistant posture amid the freight of violence within which gender-sex constructs alternately form and decompose modern bodies. But is this what Spillers means by the "flesh"? Is Weheliye's use of the term aligned with her gestures to the unrepresentable, the unmade bodies thrown into "a figurative darkness that exposed their destinies to an unknown course"?[51]

Under conditions of enslavement, writes Spillers, "one is neither female, nor male, as both subjects are taken into account as *quantities*."[52] All customary aspects of sexuality are thrown into crisis in this "enforced state of breach," not only depriving black people of the pleasures and identifications of gender-sex, but more importantly, policing blackness through a sexual displacement that is originary and ongoing: "The loss of the indigenous name/land marks a metaphor of displacement for other human and cultural features and relations, including the displacement of the genitalia, the female's and the male's desire that engenders future."[53] According to this analysis, gender is a form of rule over Africans in captivity and, as Spillers observes, brands successive generations long after the body has been "liberated," "finding its various symbolic substitutions in an efficacy of meanings that repeat the initiating moments."[54] "Flesh" is Spillers's way of denoting how the profound rupture in the human world wrought by slavery also severs the African body from the human body in so many literal and metaphorical mutilations, with the "flesh" standing in for the remainder, what is left to stand outside of culture, external to meaning and value—as Spillers puts it, blackness is vestibular to culture.[55]

On the contrary, Weheliye is using "flesh" to recover into the known and empirical what cannot be known and recovered. He states: "Being vestibular to culture means that gendered blackness—though excluded from culture, and frequently violently so—is a passage to the human in western modernity because, in giving flesh to the word of Man, the flesh comes to define the phenomenology of Man, which is always already lived as unadulterated physiology."[56] For Weheliye, "flesh" not only bypasses the social death captured by Spillers's concept, but he also reverses it, discovering empowerment through a regendering along the way. I stress this correction of Weheliye's reading of Spillers because it reveals the ethnic studies paradigm creep at play. Weheliye's commitment is to "gender" as a viable category of experience through which to mobilize multicultural politics. The problem here is that gender-sex is not a productive category of black politics, which is the insight Spillers makes available. Her deconstruction of gender-sex, its refusal under the terms of black suffering, augurs an insurrection in critical thought not about gender-sex but regarding blackness itself. By subverting this insight, Weheliye tempers the insurrectionary politic it bears, and twists "flesh" into the preservation of precisely that which it is meant to mark the obliteration of—black standing in the modern world.

Habeas Viscus equally misappropriates Wynter's contribution to overturning the gender conceits of empire. When Weheliye turns to Wynter, his commitment to the preservation of gender-sex becomes more explicit. Wynter reconceptualizes the "gender" of feminism and Western social thought generally as "genre," with genre operating at a higher, or more fundamental, ontological level than feminism's "gender." For Wynter, both "race" and "gender" are featured genres of Man, different codes for a master construal of the human being in Western imperialist terms. Weheliye finds this formulation unconvincing "because it leads to the repudiation of gender analytics as such."[57] He objects, in other words, not to the merits of the argument, but rather to its conclusions, to what it requires that we give up: gender.

When Wynter does refer to "gender," explains Greg Thomas, it is not the genitalist and individualist gender of bourgeois white supremacy. It is a collective category that differentiates the West from the Rest, white from nonwhite, but more pointedly, black from nonblack, since "race" finds its most essential expression with respect to black people, the only human group "whose humanity has been totally denied," explains Wynter.[58] Wynter's use of "gender" is therefore not merely a departure from how Western feminists, gender studies, and queer studies deploy the term, whether as identity or as marker of oppression and exclusion; it also withers the ostensibly radical interventions of "women-of-color" feminism or "queer-of-color" critique that stop far short of confronting the ontic relations contained within "gender." In his "critical resource guide" to Wynter's body politics, Thomas notes that "this is how gender is defined in social practice, epochally, as ontology, for Western humanism—which does not or cannot conceive of 'human being' without its 'human gender' in tow. Like 'true heterosexuality,' or 'human sexuality,' it is cast as the race and class property of Occidentalism and its elites."[59] The gender politics of *Habeas Viscus*, in other words, is antiblack in its zealous grip on the terms of the socially alive (gendered humanity) over the social death of blackness, a genre of being human that shows up in "gender" and "sex" only as pure negation.

Weheliye's use of Spillers and Wynter, therefore, actually advances an ethnic studies agenda that is inimical to black political struggle. *Habeas Viscus* exemplifies the post–black studies disavowal of blackness that I am arguing is a central feature of the post-racial era. The interventionist critical thinker works to build upon the trail blazed by those who have come before; Weheliye, on the other hand, blocks the pathway of innovation and critical extension: his preoccupation with adapting black social death to the proprieties of multicultural formation undermines any critical eye he might apply to the work under examination. For instance, while Spillers notes the rupture of fatherhood and motherhood equally, she nevertheless privileges the open vulnerability of the female slave: "only the female stands *in the flesh*, both mother and mother-dispossessed."[60] Spillers's focus on the female slave stems from her concern with the particular uses of female blackness across the generations—an epochal discourse of slander signifying a rupture in ontic relations. "Mama's Baby" brings the infamous Moynihan Report, for instance, face-to-face with the Middle Passage to meditate on the place of the mother in black culture into the present. Her argument, therefore, stresses the ways in which "the female . . . breaks in upon the imagination with a forcefulness that marks both a denial and an 'illegitimacy'" that bequeaths a distinct heritage for black children ungendered.[61] Subsequent black studies scholars working on the path Spillers has blazed also reproduce this emphasis on the female slave as the litmus for power's extremity under the slavocracy. One advantage of this stress on female blackness is a more incisive grasp of racial formation and sexual subjection as inextricable and, in Hartman's words, as "indissociable from violence."[62] For example, this is why Hartman sees black self-determination through the lens of the black female's sexual self-defense.[63]

On the other hand, the disadvantage of holding out the female as synecdochal for black sexual subjection is the tendency to regard female enslavement as synonymous with "rape," while "emasculation" becomes the operative trope for male enslavement. Spillers does not sufficiently disrupt this gender ideology, in which female bodies are gendered while male bodies are generic and therefore only the female body can be sexually violated and the male cannot. Spillers's deconstruction of gendered violence similarly emphasizes the female body as the locus of ungendering, with the male body de-emphasized. As Thomas notes, this proposition perversely reinscribes heterosexuality as requisite for sexual exploitation and, furthermore, reduces rape to heterosexual copulation and penile penetrations of female bodies, specifically.[64] Such unchallenged gender conceits are untenable for studies of black culture and sexuality since the publication of Sexton's *Amalgamation Schemes* and Thomas's *The Sexual Demon of Colonial Power*, in the least. Sexton and Thomas reground the analysis of gender-sex on the terrain of racial violence that produces its logics and directs our reading of sexuality through the primary ontic (anti)relations of African subhumanity.

As perceptive as Spillers's discernments are, then, they nonetheless participate in a larger occlusion of the full violence of antiblackness. The black male also stands as father-dispossessed, of course, albeit within a further ghosting of his banishment under the terms of erasure wrought by the "captor father's mocking presence."[65] Although her rewriting of the female social subject in black culture enjoins a radical tradition of black women throwing the historical structure into crisis, the social milieu in the post–civil rights period into which Spillers's intervention occurs is such that the black male is not brushed with the light of her insights, but instead her treatment of gender is alloyed to a multicultural politic of "intersectionality" that actually dulls the critical pressure Spillers presents.

While black feminists note the long tradition of black women bringing their experiences with racist abuse from white society and with sexist treatment from black men to bear on black thought, black feminism in its current guise, and its deployment of "intersectional" discourse to theorize race and gender, is a product of the particular lines of force shaping COINTELPRO's afterlife, wherein black praxis is indelibly marked by the quarantine of black power. Whereas black women of the Black Power era were able to influence the black liberation movement into a nascent but burgeoning critique of gender-sex itself, the suppression of black power since that time has been insidious in its capacity to redirect black thought. Much of the black feminist political organizing during the 1970s and 1980s focused on remedying the invisibility in which black women experienced sexual violence. Members of the Combahee River Collective, widely regarded as foundational to contemporary black feminism and women of color organizing, were at the forefront of agitation against the serial murder of black women in Boston in 1979, publishing a pamphlet for the community titled, "Six Black Women: Why Did They Die?"[66] The pamphlet asserted the now definitional claim of black feminism that not just race and not just gender, but race and gender together makes black females especially and singularly vulnerable to violence. Some of the black women organizing in Boston were also involved in mobilizing support for Joan Little, on trial in 1974 for killing a white jailer who had attempted to sexually assault her while she was being held in the Beaufort County Jail in Washington, North Carolina. These developments in black feminist praxis in the 1970s continued to produce key interventions across the ensuing decades, from African American Women in Defense of Ourselves organized in support of Anita Hill's testimony against

Clarence Thomas in 1991, to #SayHerName and Black Youth Project 100, among others, in the early twenty-first century.[67] Although black feminism may be at the leading edge of political thought during this period, its focus on renovating the meaning of gender-sex, across the diversity of methods employed, indicates how the culture of politics in the afterlife of COINTELPRO remains in fee to slaveholding society's terms of order.

In "Demarginalizing the Intersection of Race and Sex," one of the earliest articulations of "intersectional" discourse, Kimberlé Crenshaw explores the various ways the courts prevent black women plaintiffs from claiming their multidirectional discriminated status under Title VII of the Civil Rights Act of 1964.[68] In *DeGraffenreid v. General Motors*, the court refused to recognize the race and gender compound status of black women and instead analyzed their claim using the historical experience of white women, obscuring the distinct discrimination of black women.[69] Conversely, the court in *Moore v. Hughes Helicopter* held that black women do not experience sex discrimination, per se, and therefore could not use employment statistics reflecting sex disparities between all women and all men, only those reflective of black women solely.[70] *Payne v. Travenol*, in yet another variation on the refusal, held that black women are so uniquely disadvantaged by race and sex discrimination that they cannot represent all black people.[71] For Crenshaw, these cases are "doctrinal manifestations" of an approach to race- and gender-based harm that marginalizes black women.[72] While this is certainly true, the courts' failure to recognize the intersectional experiences of black women merely references the fact that law is not a capacious vehicle for ameliorating the hierarchies organizing society. For instance, David Kairys observes that the courts' decisions in antidiscrimination and equal protection cases since the passage of the Civil Rights Act have made it easy for whites to invalidate good faith efforts to use race to counter racism, while making it impossible for nonwhites to prove racial discrimination, with the predictable result being that "almost all of the winning plaintiffs in equal protection race cases before the Supreme Court have been white."[73] In this reality, then, black feminism's intersectional interrogations of the race and sex violence institutionalized in state and civil society are in fact enabling of a more fundamental institution—that of slaveholding society's normative codes of being human, gender-sex.

One of the signs of this internal limit to black feminism is the ubiquity of intersectionality as multiculturalism's auxiliary, on the one hand, and on the other hand, the continued erasure of the black subject of knowledge production. Intersectionality actually swallows up the specificity of black positionality. Gender-sex categories simultaneously hide and convey the terror intrinsic to their making. Intersectionality abets this terror by erasing the racial violence subtending gender-sex and appropriating and regulating black political claims that, as Patrice Douglass explains, makes visible the long-standing power relations in which black people and other subjects enjoy qualitatively distinct theoretical mobility.[74] Weheliye uses "black feminism" in this manner, as *the* critical lens for addressing body politics while dispensing with the gendered and sexualized dynamics in which race is constituted through violence. "Mama's Baby" nods to the Nina Simone song "My Name Is Peaches": "My country needs me, and if I were not here, I would have to be invented."[75] Weheliye, in the ethnic studies vein, performs his own invention of Spillers and Wynter: where the canonization of the black female as the raped slave and the cathedralization of gender do not actually appear in their work, he invents it, transmogrifying the position of structural vulnerability and delimited self-activity that Spillers represents with the "flesh" into an experience available to all nonwhite persons: "the being of nonwhite subjects has been coded by the cultural laws in the world of Man as pure negativity."[76]

Whereas much of black feminism attempts to counter what it poses as the exclusionary practices of feminism by including black women within the privileges of gender, both Spillers's and Wynter's body of work, conversely, deduces how blackness is more than (or less than) the antithesis to whiteness; it is the absence of humanity to whiteness's human plenitude. As that singular position against which the human takes form, the void that generates presence, it is also the negation of "manhood" and "womanhood," or in feminism's terms, of "gender" and "sex" themselves. Taken together, these interventions suggest that "black feminism" is a structural impossibility, and as such, an onto-epistemic contradiction—hence my use of quotation marks around the phrase.[77] If Weheliye is doing "black feminism," then perhaps Spillers, Wynter, Hartman, and others are summoning a position that is less accountable to "black feminism" per se, and more to how black militancy has grappled with the particular modalities of gender-sex that converge on the black body as various forms of tyranny.[78]

Decomposition

Between 2005 and 2011, no fewer than ten black women went missing in Rocky Mount, North Carolina. Their bodies were discovered, many months to years after they were last seen, in various states of decomposition. In 2007, as black women were disappearing, a prominent white civic leader, Debbie Kornegay, was stabbed to death by a homeless man, leading to an immediate, massive, around-the-clock manhunt, unrelenting until the suspect was apprehended less than forty-eight hours after the incident. The police chief of Rocky Mount acknowledged that when it came to the missing and murdered black women, however, the burden for public safety and law enforcement rests with the victims' families. "They need to stay on law enforcement," said Chief John Manley. "You have to stay on us. Let us know that you're not going away until you know we've done everything we possibly could do. Because if you don't care, I don't know why we should."[79] This would be a remarkable concession from the state about the scope of black endangerment, except that the tyranny confronting blackness "clashes with the idea that all lives can be made meaningful."[80]

It took seven black women's bodies turning up in the woods before the local authorities could see that there was a pattern of violence connecting the victims. By July 2009, the black community in Rocky Mount had finally succeeded in getting a modicum of exposure on the serial murders. A producer from CNN contacted the mother of one of the victims in August to arrange for her transport to a Raleigh studio for an interview. The car never arrived, and instead CNN viewers were informed of "breaking news" out of north Georgia about a desperate search for "a young [white] mother in extreme danger."[81] This casual displacement of black suffering underscores the layers of sexual violence ordering society. Black people are barred from the symbolic order of gendered humanity such that the sexual assaults on black females, even as the death toll mounts, register merely as accumulated corpses, a collection of abandoned things, like a pile of objects one encounters in a musty corner of a cluttered basement.

Gendered violence would locate black people in the world; it would place them in an analogous relationship to human beings. The silence shrouding Rocky Mount, however, its illegibility in the face of what the world recognizes as gendered violence—that is, when a white woman is harmed—is an always present reminder that blackness is barred categorically from standing in the world, and therefore, the very categories deployed to name and differentiate human bodies, "gender" and "sexuality," are proscribed for black people. At the outset of this chapter, I referenced Assata Shakur and her communiqué "To My People" from the Middlesex County Workhouse where she was being held prior to her trial. In her opening salutation, she identifies herself through a gendered discourse of human suffering:

> Black brothers, Black sisters, i want you to know that i love you and i hope that somewhere in your hearts you have love for me. My name is Assata Shakur (slave name joane chesimard), and i am a revolutionary. A Black revolutionary. By that i mean that i have declared war on all forces that have raped our women, castrated our men, and kept our babies empty-bellied.[82]

Shakur makes critical the very concepts of human life—gender-sex—that are, in the final analysis, inapplicable to black struggle: rape and castration; or in Rocky Mount, serial sexual assault and murder. This may in fact be what is most inadmissible about the condition of social death. Black thought, across its political diversity, has felt compelled to think blackness through the human rubric of gender-sex such that Shakur and Weheliye, who may have little else in common, both enjoin this compulsory ritual of "self-making."[83]

The terror of the Rocky Mount murders, then, lies with the fact that the black women went missing long before they were abducted from their neighborhood. They had been missing from the gendered recognition that non-blackness would bestow and that would render their endangerment visible as gendered or sexual violence. In other words, to put a finer point on the matter, it would have mobilized a rescue party—"a lot of folk working around the clock, not letting up," as Chief Manley described the hunt for Kornegay's murderer.[84]

James Baldwin, when he went to Atlanta to investigate the child murders there in 1979–1981, discovered that this terror exceeds even the horrors of death: *"Never be found again*: that terror is far more vivid than the fear of death."[85]

This terror, the ongoing missing and murdered state of blackness, is not mere discrimination or injustice—crimes and affronts committed against black life. More essentially, it is a form of sustenance for human beings. In other words, it is by way of the destruction of black lives that nonblack lives gain an understanding of their place within the world: it lends the fundamental "relational positioning and articulation of identities between subjects and objects."[86] There is no relationality between the police and the black community's security needs; or between the media and the black community's stories; or between white people and their gendered dramas of value, on the one hand, and on the other hand, black people and their absence of bodily integrity as evidenced by the latter's subjection to gratuitous sexual violence. The missing and murdered—from Shakur to the women of Rocky Mount, to the symbolic destruction of blackness in Cacho and Weheliye—are caught in what David Eltis terms "violence beyond the limit," an open-ended vulnerability that exceeds all constraint, regulation, or rationality.[87] The paradigm in which Cacho, Weheliye, and others who work in the ethnic studies or multiculturalist vein situate themselves demands holding onto that which black people are barred from attaining. Accountability to blackness, conversely, demands letting go of it all: of political community with nonblacks, of legal standing and institutional recognition, of symbolic integrity in the human world, of gender-sex identity, of filiation and affiliation. The decomposition of black flesh in the backwoods, alleyways, and abandoned spaces demands decomposing the assumptive desires for black gender-sex presence. We need not conclude that such sober analysis leads to inaction, submission, or acquiescence. On the contrary, blackhood stands as an ethical position for black self-determination emergent out of precisely the destruction of the missing and murdered—out of social death.

CHAPTER THREE

From Blackland, with Love

He heaved the whole of himself at her in a torrent of words that rushed the wind from her lungs. He called himself names, ugly names he'd stored up from the devil knew where burning through the pleats of her bodice. And all she could do was breathe and hold on and declare the love of the blood. As painful as the dirty words were cleaving through her breastbone, his hiccups shuddering clear through to her spine, part of her called it shimsham. A part of her wanted to beat him down to the ground with her fists, then drag him to the road by the nape of his neck and say go on then, go on, go on. But the best part of her locked him in tight while she prayed for a long, hard driving, relentless rain.

—Toni Cade Bambara, *Those Bones Are Not My Child*, 1999

The ethnic studies paradigm's abduction of blackness indicates that the collective structural vulnerability of black people remains impermissible under the present order of knowledge and finds itself pushed aside or recruited to service nonblack political problems and ethical quandaries. The most visible black abductions appear momentarily on society's radar as police actions—as in the cases of Akai Gurley, Alton Sterling, and Jessica Williams—while others never appear at all, as with Jackie Askins, Carlesha Freeland-Gaither, and the women of Rocky Mount, North Carolina. Meanwhile, black power remains at large, as Assata Shakur reminds us. Inspected closely and ethically, social death also reveals Western conceptions of "gender" and "sexuality" as inapplicable to black existence and, consequently, as untenable itineraries for black struggle.

In this chapter, I delve further into Toni Cade Bambara's conception of "blackhood" as a more ethical and viable mode of liberation movement. Through blackhood, then, this chapter argues that displacing gender-sex in black praxis can elucidate the centrality of self-defense and political clarity for self-determination. Humanism's discourses of the body (gender-sex) stand as an intransigent impediment to an ethical embrace of the only discourse of embodiment we need for self-determination: blackness. Frantz Fanon observed in *Wretched of the Earth* that "all decolonization is successful": if it is not successful, affirms Greg Thomas, then it is not decolonization.[1] Self-determination, on the other hand, is the necessary means for getting there, the programmatic basis for an ethical confrontation with the world's ongoing violence, and as such, the genesis of the police power against blackness. The Atlanta child murders of 1979–1981, the case of black abductions that did generate sustained national attention, albeit fleetingly, will stand in this chapter for the terrain on which the seizure and fungibility of black bodies responds to Pan-African self-determination against a slaveholding society. The Atlanta "missing and murdered," as local residents referred to the case, sets the stage for my examination of how Bambara's formulation of blackhood ferrets a way through this landscape. How does blackhood stand against today's leading critical discourse on race and sex that renders black people missing and murdered?

In Atlanta, black parents and community members noted a pattern in which poor black children, men, and women were disappearing at alarming rates. Officially, the city tallied twenty-six males and two females as missing in Atlanta between summer 1979 and spring 1981, and twenty-seven murdered bodies were eventually found in various locations in and around the city. The official list excluded numerous disappearances and deaths—the black community puts the number around one hundred persons disappeared during this time—and the abductions and killings continued well after 1981. Indeed, within the overall impression of *Blackhood Against the Police Power*, the "missing and murdered" case is more consistent with, rather than a break from or an exception to, what preceded and followed it in chronological time. What matters to me here is what the Atlanta case illuminates about the structural condition of blackness, encompassing but not limited to the empirical realities that black people endure. The "Atlanta tragedy" briefly grabbed the nation's preoccupations, particularly as the murders were superficially sensationalized by the media as racially motivated. Suggestions were that the Ku Klux Klan or some other white hate group was directly responsible; many within the community also suspected police involvement in the slayings. The episode was officially closed, however, with the arrest, trial, and conviction of a young black man, Wayne Williams, for the murder of two adult males. Many people in the black community, including a number of the victims' families, remain unconvinced that Williams was the perpetrator of any, let alone all, of the murders.

The Sexual Violence against Black Studies

The ethnic studies paradigm departs from the black studies tradition that grounds this book in that it is largely mute with respect to the fact that sexualities are formulated, ritually propounded, and theorized as "race"—or rather, in the service of a global historical traffic in white supremacy and antiblackness.[2] Feminism, gender studies, and queer studies have proceeded as if the very notion and material reality of Western civilization has not been founded on a primary and sexually graphic opposition between black and nonblack persons; by contrast, black studies has always registered this fact—and not as a discrete category of analysis distinct from what it means to be racialized in an antiblack world. From the black studies perspective pursued here, therefore, histories of sexuality presuppose the history of racism in which human sexuality inhabits white bodies while sexual savagery marks black and other nonwhite ones. Contributions from black women are often depicted as occurring ahistorically outside of the black radical tradition, as if gender and sex analysis, or nonsexist, nonpatriarchal, and so-called nonheteronormative black politics are recent innovations and not themselves constitutive to the radical movements against antiblackness since the dawn of the slave trade. In short, by featuring the black studies critique of gender and sex politics I am calling upon a tradition that impugns as slanderous the widely accepted assertion that black studies has been inhospitable to women and queers specifically and to the deconstruction of gender and sexuality generally.[3] Instead, I refer to a black movement tradition that has grappled with slavery and its afterlife as sexual violence, the enslavement of Africans as a manifestation of Western sexuality, as opposed to merely documenting sexual crimes as a component of antiblackness and the police power. Additionally, this tradition beholds such violence as constitutive to what white people do to each other and to how they present themselves generally as sexual beings. Histories of sexuality, therefore, presuppose the history of racism in which human sexuality occupies white bodies while a subhuman and savage sexual bestiality typifies black and other nonwhite ones.[4]

From the earliest recorded slave narratives, the archive of black letters records the black movement's engagement with gendered and sex violence. As Christina Sharpe identifies with poetic precision, "in the beginning is sexual trauma"—meaning, prior to any narrative of black life in the so-called New World, prior to the violence through which black subjects are interpellated over and over again across time and space, and prior to the trauma that black subjects themselves reproduce, is the trauma of the beginning itself.[5] This sexual violence also precedes and begets "race," meaning that "race" only emerges in the modern world as an expression of direct relations of sexualized force, and moreover, "race" derives in the first instance—historically, ontologically, axiologically—from the sexual violence that produces racial blackness. As I noted previously, then, "race" is an expression of racism, contrary to the various propositions on offer from the multicultural milieu where racism is a function of race (as in liberal colorblindness ideology) or the two coexist and coincide only under specific conditions (as in the racial formation thesis): Alexander Weheliye, for instance, shows how this proposition remains the guiding precept for the ethnic studies paradigm when he asks, "how can racism—biopolitical or otherwise—exist without race?"[6] Accordingly—and this is the crux of the matter that the two latter positions necessarily sidestep—there is no ethical accounting of racial politics that leaves antiblack (sexual) violence by the wayside.[7] This context demands to be written into the protocols of the critical study of race and sex in terms as portentous and decisive as the crimes of rape and bestiality routinely imposed upon black people across the generations. This insight reverberates across black history, from Ida B. Wells's focus on lynching in the late nineteenth century and Callie House's leadership organizing black washerwomen and domestics in the twentieth century's first reparations movement, to blues women from Bessie Smith to Nina Simone, to black nationalisms of all kinds from Marcus Garvey, Amy Jacques Garvey, and Shirley Graham Du Bois to George Jackson and Safiya Bukhari.

Given this tradition and its deconstruction of "man," "woman," and "human sexuality" out of a specifically antiblack crucible of sexual violence, how scandalous it is to consider the onslaught of charges against black studies as one-dimensional and underdeveloped with respect to questions of gender and sex. When feminist, queer, and ethnic studies, what I refer to as the multicultural formation, announced in the 1980s that it was "freeing" critical thought and identity politics from the confines of a black/white binary, asserting that the black studies framework does not do justice to the "multiplicity" and "hybridity" of oppressed identities, academic discourse on racism was denuded of both violence and sexuality, its constituent elements.[8] In fact, this move arises out of the desire to displace the analysis of blackness on offer from black studies, proceeds apace with the general backlash against the black social movements of the long civil rights era, and lends the ideological cover for the further institutionalization of antiblack sexual violence during the ensuing decades of the wars on crime, drugs, and gangs, and their alloyed assaults on welfare, education, housing and public space, and politicized black popular culture—with putatively female, male, plus the variety of black bodies referred to as queer all coming under an intensified vulgar scrutiny in differing and overlapping ways. Or, to put it another way, the multicultural framework affirmed COINTELPRO's delegitimation of radical black politics. Black dispossession hangs in the balance: by defining the black/white binary as the problem and evacuating racism of sexuality and sexuality of racism, multiculturalism mystifies the crux of the matter—that blackness constitutes the sexual valence against which all racialized subjects implicitly take their bearing as human beings—and in so doing, has constructed a dense scaffolding of racial discourse characterized not simply by its imprecision and impotence in the face of white supremacy, but also by its declination to name black suffering for what it is.

Blackhood: Bambara's Intervention for Social Reproduction

It is at this juncture that Bambara fully intervenes in this study. Among the breadth of the black studies archive, Bambara provides one of the most incisive expositions of the production of "race" at the intersection that matters: violence and sexuality. Bambara highlights, as is often the case within the annals of black studies, the black family as a means toward exploding the sexual violence of antiblackness and fortifying social reproduction. From her treatise "On the Issue of Roles" in the landmark collection *The Black Woman*, asserting that the pathway of black revolution would need to transgress the confining threshold of sex and gender, to her encyclopedic compendium of the black freedom struggle, published posthumously, *Those Bones Are Not My Child*, not to mention her indelible early short stories and novels and later community film work, Bambara exemplifies the critical tradition of independent black radicalism in which I am locating the present project. By taking up Bambara's call for "blackhood," I am featuring a critical tradition of deconstructing gender and sex politics that exceeds the intramural violence of antiblackness that shows up within black studies and black communities as misogynist, masculinist, and homophobic violence and, in parallel time, subverts the font of this violence in forces extrinsic to the field and to the community that seek to malign its innovations on gender-sex in pathological terms. The black struggle alone has consistently supplied *the* ethical accounting of racism as the sexual violence of antiblack terror: the "missing and murdered" register this sexual terror ensnaring black bodies, at the center of the black community, and in the institutional spaces wherein black studies is increasingly ghosted. Blackhood stands against the (sexual) police power of post-racial society and its post–black studies apparatus.

In her discussion of black women and the "trickster trope of unnaming," LaMonda Stallings writes that the "process of naming Black females as 'Black women' disturbs the self-invention of the subjects and results in a confining and violent confrontation between these two separate subjects—Black woman and Black female."[9] Stallings senses both sides of the coin Bambara plays with "blackhood." On one side, the attempt to "name unnameable beings" stresses the social control mode of gender.[10] "Black" dissembles "gender" such that "black woman" bludgeons black females with a litany of pathologies, serving up a Sisyphean concourse of not-quite-human status; and likewise with "black man." For this reason, Bambara asserts the imperative to destroy gender assumption in order to realize black liberation: "The job then regarding 'roles' is to submerge all breezy definitions of manhood/womanhood (or reject them out of hand if you're not squeamish about being called 'neuter') until realistic definitions emerge through a commitment to Blackhood."[11] On the other side, Stallings is calling attention to the importance of self-naming and renaming to black struggle. Because much of black existence involves endlessly changing layers of declination, deception, or deconstruction to subvert, deny, distend, and survive oppressive regimes and "return acts of naming and meaning to the individual," Bambara's renaming of "blackhood" as *the* necessary revolutionary position attempts to throw off the dead-end distractions of gender. At the same time, by naming the most fundamental position from which to imagine and act on revolution *blackhood*, Bambara is saying that blackness is the base of the modern world and its carceral conditioning on the black community is like the veil that W. E. B. Du Bois imagined separating the black world from nonblack, and black life from *life*, psychically, physically, culturally, and structurally. Bambara did not choose "humanhood," or "true man" and "true woman," or "difference," "God," "beingness," "blood," or any other obtusely racialized label—all of which, at some point or other, have done time as the rallying sign for black freedom, to no avail.

Bambara continues to use the black family to meditate and innovate on the various obstacles and possibilities for black liberation in her two novels, *The Salt Eaters* and *Those Bones Are Not My Child*. Despite being published almost two decades apart, these two stories are so profoundly interconnected that they appear today as merely successive chapters of survival's long ordeal. *Salt* confronts the psychic and interpersonal challenges to spiritual well-being in the antiblack world, while *Bones* explores the communal consequences of these trials—what happens when the community fails to develop concerted strategies for cultivating wellness across the generations. Bambara makes the necessary move of positioning black bodies at the locus of human vulnerability—a formulation that is politically unsettling to the liberal multicultural common sense that polices antiracism. Because black bodies are more fundamentally threatened than any other bodies, the danger they face underwrites the precarity of humanity itself.[12] The full import, then, of Bambara's work is that blackhood is the only ethical pathway to full humanity.

Bones, in particular, records the violence that would quarantine blackhood and disqualify it from the court of human enquiry. Zala, the mother at the center of *Bones*, whose son is one of Atlanta's missing and murdered, struggles to get the word out about black children. She is told by a newsman that "Black boys getting killed in the South just ain't news," because attention has turned to international terrorism and the Iran hostage situation. Zala responds, "Please! There's terrorism right here in Atlanta."[13] As Rebecca Wanzo explains, "murdered black bodies lack scope because they do not translate as harms that could affect the majority of U.S. citizens."[14] Blackhood enjoins the black struggle's long-standing confrontation with this condition of social death. In a 1982 interview, Bambara expressed a sentiment echoed across the black studies archive, that "the literature in this country that confronts what is particular and peculiar about this country is black literature. . . . As Richard Wright said, if Poe and those guys were standing where *he* was standing, they would not have to invent *horror*, they would *know* it."[15] Blackhood's confrontation with the everyday terror, especially in Atlanta in 1979–1981, divulges the black family in strictly communal terms, uncontained by gender-sex regulation. In *Bones*, during one meeting of parents and community members working to find the missing and murdered children, one brother comments:

> "You know those mugs ain't gonna confirm the phone calls made to the police this morning. . . . In fact, they ain't gonna do a damn thing but cool us out. A bunch of pussies."
>
> "Is that your idea of a curse?" Leah snapped, handing the children their plates as they made bubble eyes at each other.[16]

Leah checked the brother's homophobia and misogyny, while she fed the children. Through it all, the children are party to their parents' activism on the community's behalf and to normative gender-sex constructs stripped of legitimacy—blackhood in real time.

Crime Solving in Blackland

The disappearances of black people of all ages, sexualities, and genders, into a void of violence that no language can represent, indicts the terms of social death, while the obliteration of this void in the critical study of race and sex indicates the inadmissible career of "social death." Bambara's use of "blackhood" signifies the paradigm in which this book confronts the structure of violence for which black suffering serves as both prototype and the host of generative political possibility for nonblack, post-racial politics. "Blackland" is the name of the paradigm's terrain, with "Atlanta" serving as a precinct and an illustrative mapping of this territory in which the black missing and murdered disappear not simply from streets, parks, homes, and families, but from the very order of knowledge that imbues human beings with meaning, value, and presence. Through the juxtaposition of black social death with "social death" discourse, there is a perverse relationship between the intimacies of bodily harm subjecting black people across different political economies, from the slavocracy to the present post-racial era, and how such violence is reproduced in the leading discourses on race, sex, and gender. What happens to blackness in the discursive imaginary is evidenced through the institutional assaults on black studies and is enabled by routinized violence against black communities across time and space.

Blackhood's confrontation with the Atlanta missing and murdered stands against not only the kidnappings, tortures, rapes, and murders, but also against the very order of knowledge that constitutes such violent acts against black people as no violence at all. In the present post-racial political economy, such violence is condemned and even prosecuted through various channels, legal and otherwise. My concern with the antiblackness of antiracism, however, leads me to regard such objections to violence as not the antidote to social death, but rather as a feature of its performance. In its accounting of the crime spree in Atlanta, for instance, criminology repeats the disappearances, focusing solely on the operations of criminal justice in the case. Sociology casts a slightly wider analytical net, recognizing many of the contextual factors that contributed to the vulnerability of black people in Atlanta at that time and the general impunity with which such violence occurred. Relevant factors include the changes in the political economy that were producing greater poverty, worklessness, and spatial isolation for the black community.[17] Bambara, too, makes note of the political economic forces at work in Atlanta. She observes how "the whole city was touched up, everyone falling for the ad-agency slogans created to attract out-of-town dollars."[18] She attunes the reader, moreover, to how the nascent black middle class is complicit in the seizure of black lands.

> The takeover schemes of the seventies had been foiled, for the time being at least, first by the unexpected appearance of hundreds of young Black professional couples who bought up the re-gentrified homes, second by the Black Christian Nationalist Church, which bought up a whole block on Gordon for the Shrine of the Black Madonna Center. The West End secured, community workers no longer studied the master plan of the Atlanta 2000 Project, which targeted several districts for "demographic changes," in time for the International University and the World's Fair, both slated for the turn of the century. Malik, one of the brothers who'd accompanied the caravan weeks ago, had said that if they were to study the plan, they might note a relationship between the series of fires set in the West End area, the proposed school closings there, the proposed reapportionment schemes, and the aggressive offers real-estate dealers were making to old-time residents of the neighborhood to get out.[19]

Bambara's blackhood approach, then, lends the political economic reality a specific interpretation centered on the self-activity of black people. A sociological emphasis on the political economy alone underestimates the violence of, and thus distorts, the historical structure. Antiblack animus fades into a supposedly impersonal logic of capital accumulation, with racism inverted and seen as the result of racial processes, rather than as the violent acts that enable and reproduce procedures of racial formation, with gender-sex simplistically overlaid as yet another supplementary dimension, the modality through which capital's contradictions are lived out and struggled over. Bambara's treatment, on the other hand, also pays close attention to how capital moves in on the black community: the historical continuities across eras of black subjection expose the connections between territory, institutions, and the coaccumulation of black bodies and land.

Bones charts the black community's work to recover its own, with the day-to-day struggle narrated through Zala and Spence's efforts to find their son Sundiata (Sonny) who has disappeared as part of the missing and murdered. Zala maps the killer's route, revealing the linkages between poor black neighborhoods, the financial district, borders with development zones, locations of police stations, shopping areas, parks, and schools. In one scene, Spence and Zala are driving together through the city, finding themselves drawn to the neighborhoods where many of the children disappeared. Spence, driving, finds himself stuck at an intersection.

> "It's not a light, Spence. It's just a stop sign."
>
> "I know," he said, but didn't move other than tapping his foot on the pedal and jogging them in their seats. She wanted to get going. She didn't care where.
>
> "I can't seem to shake off this . . . It's as though we're being compelled . . . or surrounded." He didn't know where they were, and that was good. But he didn't trust any direction, not left, not right, not straight ahead.
>
> "Where to?" he demanded.
>
> Lost, they were safe for the moment.[20]

There is no map to safe passage through antiblackness; it is the territory itself that threatens, not a particular route, neighborhood, policy, or political regime. Not knowing the way out, letting go of the pretense that safety is a function of staying on course, of somehow perceiving dead ends and dark corners ahead of time, may be the only security.[21] Spence's training as a soldier, his experience bringing logistics fatally to bear on an enemy, is of little use in blackland; his masculinity is irrelevant; and Zala's fiercely protective mothering—exceeded always by the menace facing her children.

It is through Bambara's blackhood and how it supersedes gender-sex itineraries that we are able to follow her alternate route into blackland. Black people have deep connections to land—the land lost and found, land wrought and land fought ("blood at the root . . . a strange and bitter crop"), and land as sanctuary in the meantime (marronage).[22] Slavery's mark of the chattel beast, instead of naturalizing black people into the environment as so much wildlife, seeks to isolate them from ecology, as if they are a species alienated from all ecosystems in the biome. Accumulated and fungible black bodies are coextensive with the accumulation of black labor, land, and geopolitical space. *Bones* should be read as an atlas of black landscape in which the pastoral overlays the urban, with the former emptied of its bucolic and the latter devoid of its systems of convenience and wealth. What remains is the necessity to survive on the move amid historical artifacts in the environment that are objectively horrific—the blood-stained root, the corner where a cousin was shot dead, the park where a child was last seen, the endlessly shifting and dialectical cartography of segregation and displacement.

Zala's mapping of the killer's route attempts to bring order and discipline to bear on the chaotic violence gripping blackland. But when she and Spence try to retrace the route, the distinctions between danger and security blur, the familiar becomes foreign. When Sonny finally returns, Zala and Spence retreat with their children to Zala's mother's home in the country. Encountering the land is to confront the ancestors. For Zala and Spence, there is succor and strength there: they can exhale from their terrible ordeal, find reprieve in the woods. They had effectively set aside their estrangement in the interest of finding Sonny and protecting the children together, but on Mama Lovey's land their intimacy is restored, albeit tenuously. For Sonny, there is accountability and continuity on the land: he can move about unmolested, but his grandmother has no truck with teenagers who run scared. New resources become available in rural blackland, self-sufficiency seems more possible, but always the route to wholeness is rifled through with the problem of property and how to unbundle sovereignty's negation. In other words, *Bones* shows that blackland is not sovereign space any more than blackhood signifies a wellspring for bodily integrity. Rather, blackhood abandons the seductive genres of antiblackness in the body in order to re-create a landscape for self-determination in the midst of the terror, never outside or beyond it.[23]

While Bambara's blackhood makes critical use of the political economic reality in blackland, the multiculturalist ethnic studies paradigm deploys it in a way that suppresses black self-determination. Jodi Melamed's *Represent and Destroy: Rationalizing Violence in the New Racial Capitalism* employs Bambara's *Bones* to recuperate a multiculturalist vision that Bambara herself does not center in her text. Melamed sees the larger problem of neoliberalism and global capitalism through Bambara's Atlanta story and views *Bones* as Bambara's literary intervention into racial capitalism's culture of difference. Melamed astutely notes that the novel aims to "decolonize the political-epistemic-cognitive domain," but her primary interest is in appropriating *Bones* as a "race radical" "activist's artifact" that "sought to teach readers how to keep the struggle going by learning what 1980s racial thinking (of the liberal-multicultural *and* neoconservative varieties) was making it easy not to know," with the intention to "thwart alienation and make possible other doings."[24] Melamed consistently repositions *Bones* in terms of a vague multicultural paradigm that is promiscuous, to say the least, with how Bambara grounds *Bones* in *black* historical struggle. Here Melamed transforms black struggle into "people-of-color social movements":

> The novel's protocol thus renews the sense of culture as potentially powerful and transformative that came out of 1970s people-of-color social movements. In the tradition of literary nationalisms and women-of-color feminism, it finds the spirit of pragmatic movement building to depend upon the creative epistemic-intellectual diagnoses of power (and self in relation to power) that culture work enables.[25]

Although Bambara is her customary rigorous social theorist in making connections throughout the novel between black history and colonialism, global terror, indigenous genocide, feminicide, war making, and so forth, she is equally diligent in establishing that the locus of these human crises is the black struggle. She never once represents the community mobilizing in Atlanta as anything other than black—the connections emanate outward from there. In this manner, Bambara is practicing black power in cultural analysis, a political lens hewn across the generations of black struggle. Blackness figures as the position of marronage in political theory: historically unthought, black power bares the truth of black positionality and its centrality for unthinking the world's foundational violence. Malcolm X, for instance, had his own way of laying down the terms of black positionality. In "The Black Revolution," in which he asked the audience to not blame him for igniting the fire of revolution when they find their doorstep aflame, Malcolm explained the relationship between the local and the global, at once an analysis of the dialectic between racial particularity and universality:

> So 1964 will see the Negro revolt evolve and merge into the worldwide black revolution that has been taking place on this earth since 1945. The so-called revolt will become a real black revolution. Now the black revolution has been taking place in Africa and Asia and Latin America; when I say *black*, I mean non-white—black, brown, red, or yellow.[26]

In Malcolm's vision, the world will be liberated under the mantle of blackness. Racial blackness, not national belonging, colonial status, or a multicultural or people-of-color coalition, is the most inclusive sign for human liberation.[27]

Melamed, on the other hand, moves in the opposite direction, extracting from the black movement "a survival guide for radical materialist antiracist cultural activism in the face of liberal multiculturalism's foreclosures."[28] Not only does she appropriate Bambara's creative act of black power for her own vision of multicultural coalition (i.e., "women-of-color feminism"), but Melamed also vacates blackness from its own struggle. She claims that the novel

> represented community activism during the murders as the last stand of 1970s social movement organizing in urban African American communities and exemplary of the kinds of discursive constraints and repressive tactics that in the 1980s drove underground the production of antiracist materialist knowledges, especially Black power, third-world Left, and women-of-color feminist orientations.[29]

The last stand of black politics? The 1970s did indeed see a potent confluence of the state's counterinsurgency program, policy changes in welfare, housing, and education, plus deindustrialization, criminalization, and the historically constant violence of antiblackness. The afterlife of COINTELPRO: black power politicos were definitely driven underground, into exile, onto the slow road to the death penalty through solitary confinement, or otherwise rendered ineffective. Nonetheless, there is a betrayal of black struggle in Melamed, despite the pretension of "oppositional antiracist movement" solidarity.[30] Her retroactive transmutation of black struggle in the 1970s and 1980s into "people-of-color social movement" or "social movement organizing in urban African American communities" is a rewriting of history loaded with and to the future. In other words, by retroactively vacating blackness from black historical struggle, Melamed is preemptively quarantining blackness in today's struggles. Black politics do not die, and yet Melamed's nostalgia for "people-of-color" solidarity reveals that it is dead on arrival in the ontic relations structuring antiracism today. Again, this is the antiblackness of the post-racial, the unconscious desire for black people to sit down and take a backseat to "people-of-color" ethical demands. As Sylvia Wynter put it, "Everyone assumed that the Black was someone who was there; they had a struggle; you join their struggle; and you push them over and move over them to the top. I call it the 'J-Lo' syndrome!"[31]

Melamed's take on *Bones* sends black politics into the void of the missing and murdered. The struggle in Atlanta richly and faithfully documented by Bambara—at considerable personal cost to her own health   is jettisoned of blackness so that blackhood today may be discredited and social movement grounded in black power overrun by the coalitions of the willing. This occurs in two ways. First, black movement is chastened to look outside itself to become relevant and legitimate to the world at large. As the newsman informed Zala, black death lacks scope. Insidiously, Melamed recruits *Bones*, an encyclopedic recording of the litany of ways black life is liminal to human ethics, to this very task of censuring blackness from humanity's ethical dilemmas. This is counterinsurgency on the order of Weheliye's *Habeas Viscus* and other post–black studies work. She asserts that the novel prompts readers "to connect domestic and foreign issues, to place race and economy in a global frame, to re-see problems posed as cultural and racial as economic and political, and to work for transnational Left solidarity."[32] In other words, what is happening in black communities only becomes legible when validated by a transnational comparison to Latin American death squads; or, organized white supremacy is posited as "resurgent" in the United States (in Melamed's words) only on evidence of American paramilitary and mercenary fighters abroad; or, the intentionality of state violence against black people needs confirmation in the form of National Security Council memos or redacted FBI documents; or, black suffering is incomprehensible as racial violence, but when viewed in economic terms alongside the dislocations wrought globally by capitalism, then all of a sudden it becomes visible as an instance of a broader human condition of exploitation.

Contra Melamed, violence wrought on the global scene is only fully called to account once it is located in the foundational violence of the transatlantic slave trade and African enslavement in the New World. For Bambara, the global connections are instructive, but the missing and murdered is foremost a function of the history of slavery. Zala's morning coffee and sorting through the day's latest evidence on the case is infiltrated by references to the father of gynecology, "a man who'd used captive African women as guinea pigs, conducting surgical experiments without anesthesia, one slave woman the subject of seventeen different operations"; and to the notorious Tuskegee Study overseen by Atlanta's very own Centers for Disease Control; and to an endless record of snipings, slashings, cross burnings, disappearances, and law enforcement's deep roots with and as white supremacist organization.[33] Bambara situates the missing and murdered, in other words, within a long-standing practice of snatching and using black bodies. "Atlanta" is not a new crisis or a "resurgent" phenomenon, but only its latest reiteration. From the vantage point of black struggle, "Atlanta" is not crisis itself, merely one of its events.

The disposition to read black struggle through the lens of other, nonblack events is the modality by which slavery and its afterlife are rendered irrelevant to contemporary social analysis. With slavery effectively quarantined from our understanding of the present, we search for answers about militarism and neoliberalism in transnational economic and political terms, as Melamed puts it, rather than in terms of the cultural and racial foundation of a slaving society. A civilization whose guiding ethical coordinates—democracy, liberty, equality, freedom—are premised on human captivity is intrinsically militaristic, terroristic, and autocratic. The fact that the society's cultural ethos is still authorized by racial slavery long after the specific institution of chattel servitude has been remodeled means that militarism and terror continue under terms of disavowal. Bambara, to the point, from a 1983 interview:

> I start with the recognition that we are at war, and that war is not simply a hot debate between the capitalist camp and the socialist camp over which economic/political/social arrangement will have hegemony in the world. It's not just the battle over turf and who has the right to utilize resources for whomsoever's benefit. The war is also being fought over the truth: what is the truth about human nature, about the human potential? My responsibility to myself, my neighbors, my family, and the human family is to try to tell the truth. That ain't easy. There are so few truth-speaking traditions in this society in which the myth of "Western civilization" has claimed the allegiance of so many.[34]

The "truth" Bambara speaks is to unravel how Western civilization has occupied, settled, and thus bastardized the concept and practice of "human nature." Black social movement implicitly confronts the Western occupation of the "human," not out of a drive to measure up to a white image or to translate black folk to whites, although these moves happen as well, but rather, simply because the doing of blackness, being fully, beautifully, and independently *black*, throws "human nature" into crisis in the most fundamental way. For this reason, black self-possession constitutes a state of emergency for nonblack society, since the latter's reigning episteme requires fungible blackness. Conversely, this is why Wilderson has argued that civil society, not merely the state's violence, represents a state of emergency for black people—because the society's very terms of order, the formation of knowledge and the ontic relations it presupposes, are organized to consume blackness.[35]

Nonblack people are not positioned in antagonistic opposition to the "human," despite the ongoing violence of white supremacy and capitalism on all peoples. For this reason, again, people-of-color coalitions do not mean the same thing to black people as they do to nonblacks. Black power has long stated its position that coalition must take a backseat to black unity. Bambara echoes this refrain: "There certainly has been a history of white/black coalitions or white/colored coalitions. Most of which have ended in betrayal."[36] In *The Salt Eaters*, Bambara presents the edge of coalition, both intramurally within the black community across its diversity and with nonblack people outside the community, as a question of culture. The answer to the disunity within the self and within the community of souls is "to stay centered in your own best traditions that will keep you in touch with the best of yourself."[37] Coalitions, notes Bambara, have resulted in a denial of self and adoption of a whole alien culture, someone else's interests and agenda.

The second way in which Melamed jettisons the blackness of *Bones* has to do with the perpetrators of the crimes against the black community. In *Represent and Destroy*, Melamed's conclusion about *Bones* goes like this: "Its goal was not to produce the real killers behind the murders but, instead, to create meaning and reference that bring to light the banal yet deadly economic, rational, and governmental forms of racialized violence that threaten the lives of African American children."[38] At first blush, perhaps, this comment seems logical, even critical, in its attention to institutionalized racism. Moreover, how could a work of fiction stand in for the investigations of the missing and murdered that authorities neglected to perform? The proper context for evaluating comments such as this one, however, is the inadmissible career of black social death sustaining post–black studies in the post-racial era. It is the ongoing status of social death for black people in a world where not only does the violence continue to this day, but no investigations are warranted because, again, ultimately black death is not a loss but rather the disavowed foundation requisite for society's coherence. For Melamed, the point of *Bones* is not to find the killers and stop the violence, because to do so would undermine the essential integrity of the terrain on which she is promoting multicultural social movement in the first place.

There is a scene in *Bones* where Zala and her two younger children, Kofi and Kenti, are discussing how the authorities are construing the missing and murdered children as juvenile delinquents. Zala complains, "So they blame the kids 'cause they can't speak up for themselves. They say the kids had no business being outdoors, getting themselves in trouble." To which Kenti responds:

"You let us go outdoors."

"Of course I do, baby. We go lots of places, 'cause a lot of people fought hard for our right to go any damn where we please. But when the children go out like they've a right to and some maniac grabs them, then it's the children's fault or the parents who should've been watching every minute, like we don't work like dogs just to put food on the table."[39]

The scene continues with Zala explaining to her children what a "hustler" is and why black children are characterized as "hustlers" whereas white kids would be described as "industrious" and "responsible." As Zala imparts another mundane lesson on racism, the children savor the moment of attention and affection, all too rare in the time since their older brother was snatched and disappeared and their parents' nerves, patience, time, and warmth has been severely taxed. There are numerous scenes such as this one throughout *Bones*, in which black parents cope with the structural prohibition against parenting black children. Black parents cannot protect their families, cannot keep them intact and stable, and black children grow up through a series of realizations that there is no secure ground on which they can depend—they are vulnerable in a structural sense to gratuitous violence, no matter how good at parenting the adults in their lives may be. Black parents in *Bones*, then, continually face the reality that the ultimate objective of the kidnappings is to return them, as a people, to captivity. In the scene above, Bambara creates a palpable feeling in Kofi and Kenti of a fleeting security. It need not be named, nor would the children know what name to give it. Unfortunately, they might mistake it for love, and when they find out how vulnerable they are to the predations of the world, they would mistake this reality for a withdrawal of mother- and father-love, as Sonny experienced when he was stolen away. Late in *Bones*, when Sonny is found and returned home to his family, he accuses his mother of abandoning him by not coming to find him, to rescue him from the world's insatiable appetite for black children. But Kofi and Kenti's experience of love as safety is no less mistaken than Sonny's experience of terror as love's withdrawal. The abandonment is not parental—it is historical, structural, and political.

While such an analysis is no solace for the child chained up in his captor's basement or for the parent searching ceaselessly, both parent and child unbroken but broken-hearted, the natal alienation of the slavocracy persistent in its effort to rupture the black family, my objection to Melamed's suggestion that the aim of *Bones* is not to find the killers of black children is that there is comfort in the belief that Bambara is not prosecuting the crimes against black humanity. It is easier to come away from *Bones* with an understanding of institutionalized racism than it is to leave with the devastation that there is no safe haven from the world for black families. It is not that it is fruitless to investigate and hunt down the killers, but instead, Bambara seems to be saying, are you prepared for what it takes? After all, the ubiquity of black subjection means not that perpetrators are difficult to name; the difficulty lies in the fact that the danger is all around us—it is society itself.

From Self-Deception to Marronage

After Sonny's return, Zala attempts to find out from him what happened and who did it. "I kept thinking you'd come, you and Dad," he says to his mom. "I kept waiting for you to come get me. But it wasn't you. It wasn't you." Zala thinks:

> A knocking at her heart, the police at the door. Always when she got close to the names, he'd accuse her and Spence. Concealment and distraction, twin ploys of deception. What had they threatened him with? And how could he be cured of deception in a place where his heroes, his leaders did it too?[40]

This theme of self-deception in *Bones* is situated within the historical structure of deception that posits black people as a problem people, not as a people with problems, as W. E. B. Du Bois famously put it.[41] *Bones*, moreover, stresses the connection between this deception and the gratuitous violence constantly endangering black communities. For this reason, Bambara emphasizes the truth-speaking traditions necessary to cut against the sham and defend black life. Truth speaking against antiblackness, therefore, is entwined with the imperative for black self-defense in two ways: speaking truth *as* self-defense, as a way of defending one's black body and the community; and also speaking the truth *about* self-defense, about the community's need for organized self-protection.

Contrary to Melamed's conclusion that the novel was not about finding the killers, when Bambara's work as a whole is taken into account, it appears ever more likely that this is precisely what she sought to do with *Bones*. Cheryl Wall reports that Bambara first presented the novel's prologue in 1982 as a freestanding first-person nonfictional account of her experiences in Atlanta.[42] Bambara and her daughter lived through the nightmare of 1979–1981 in Atlanta, and Bambara recounts how the experience affected her mental health: "There was a period too when I went utterly mad in the eighties in response to the Atlanta missing and murdered children's case."[43] The novel began as journal entries on the case and developed into pieces written for the newspaper, until she realized that she had the makings of a novel on her hands. She explains, "everybody in the world was doing research for me. People from *Newsweek* and *60 Minutes* would call me up and ask me, 'Do you have another angle on this?' I would look in my notes, I would look at something I hadn't researched yet, and I would say, 'Yeah, why don't you check out this and get back to me.'" Processing the information to solve the case led to writing the novel, but it came at a cost to her mental and physical well-being: "I stopped going out, I stopped bathing, I stopped washing my hair, I became this lunatic. My daughter would tap me every now and then and say, 'Ma, you look like hell.'"[44] In 1990, she moved from Atlanta to Philadelphia and was diagnosed with cancer in 1993. In a 1994 interview, while in a temporary period of recovery from the cancer, Bambara recalled that she knew she had cancer before she received the diagnosis from her doctor. "For several years I had been stuck—spiritually, financially, psychically, physically. Finally my intestines were blocked. I knew I had been blocked because I couldn't feel my spirit guides around me."[45] She crossed over on December 9, 1995.

Many factors can go into producing cancer in a person's body, but it is a disease that is profoundly environmental, without question. It would be foolish and arrogant to dismiss the effect of the missing and murdered case on Bambara's health. As a cultural worker whose life was devoted to the overriding lesson that spiritual and physical well-being and the health status of the community, the race, the planet, and the universe are one and the same thing, Bambara was intimately attuned to the body social.[46] Her personal vitality and power was a function of black people's collective efficacy. As a healer in the Pan-African tradition, she gave all of herself to push, knead, cajole, chastise, lead, yearn, listen, prod, teach, create, and lean into her people toward conscious wholeness. Was her physical deterioration brought about by the Atlanta case? Like a political prisoner sentenced to die by a life sentence behind bars, much of it spent in solitary confinement, did Bambara herself succumb to environmental toxicity—did her spiritual guides go missing and murdered as well as a result of the violence? "There is only one thing," writes Alexis Pauline Gumbs: the black community's living hell enduring the massacre of its children, the foreclosure of its future promise, showed up as the cancerous growths that claimed Bambara's body as part of the stamp paid for the salt in 1980s Atlanta.[47] James Baldwin, too, visited Atlanta in the early 1980s in order to report on the child murders and left irreparably debilitated. He struggled to complete his take on the period—which became *The Evidence of Things Not Seen*—and left the country, never to return to the United States alive. Having witnessed how the black community was forced to stomach the violence it was enduring, the blame-the-victim discourse culminating in Wayne Williams's conviction in 1982, Baldwin was dead from stomach cancer a few short years later, on December 1, 1987. It is without question, therefore, that Bambara wrote *Bones* in order to find the killers and arrest their wild career—her very life, black life, depended upon it.

Eleanor Traylor observes that the rite of healing conducted by the spiritual and medical healers in *The Salt Eaters* constitutes the plot of that novel.[48] I would extend this perceptive observation not only to *Bones*, but also to Bambara's life itself. As I noted earlier, and as other readers such as Traylor have previously remarked, *Bones* continues the story in *The Salt Eaters*.[49] Traylor further explicates how this continuity runs deeper than each novel's particular topics, sustained by subterranean motifs lent by ancient archetypes—such as the natural feminine and a woman's creative fire—that supersede event, place, and time. I am interested, however, in making the connection between healing and self-defense. Bambara speaks to precisely this point in her essay "Salvation Is the Issue":

> Stories are important. They keep us alive. In the ships, in the camps, in the quarters, fields, prisons, on the run, underground, under siege, in the throes, on the verge—the storyteller snatches us back from the edge to hear the next chapter. In which we are the subjects. We, the hero of the tales. Our lives

preserved. How it was; how it be. Passing it along in the relay. That is what I work to do: to produce stories that save our lives. . . . In *Salt* most particularly, in motive/content/structure/design, the question is, do we intend to have a future as sane, whole, governing people? I argue then and in "Faith" as well that immunity to the serpent's sting can be found in our tradition of struggle and our faculty for synthesis. The issue is salvation. I work to produce stories that save our lives.[50]

As with *Salt*, so too with *Bones*: it is at once a product of what Bambara termed the ongoing "split between the spiritual, psychic, and political forces in my community" as a result of the antiblack onslaught, and an attempt at salvation from this disunity.[51] While Bambara has stated that she dealt with this "wasteful and dangerous split" in the only way she knew how—writing fiction—she also goes on to explain, however, that security issues also dictated the form of her intervention. No one in Atlanta at the time of the missing and murdered, Bambara explains, could trust the kind of fact that was available. There were multiple misinformation campaigns that disseminated falsehoods and destroyed evidence, multiple law enforcement agencies working at different investigations, multiple kinds of verified killers in the mix—mercenaries, survivalists, KKK, other white renegade types, police, and so on. Publishing her investigation as a novel, then, was a strategy for personal safety: libel would be the sanitized way of saying it, but as she put it, the reality is that "security is a real question."[52] As the novel took shape, however, she realized that she did not want it for precisely this reason: "One of the reasons I didn't want it was because I knew too much, and I thought if I could reconstruct the real case, and know the difference between this and that highly selective media-police-city-hall-fiction on which someone got convicted, how safe am I?"[53]

Here Bambara herself is confronting the very question that connects all of her work—the healer's ethical dilemma. In *Salt* it was, "Do you want to be well?" In *Bones* it became, "What are we pretending not to know today, African people?"[54] Bambara admits that, beyond the research and her embeddedness within the community, she did not have access to information or insight regarding the case that was unavailable to others: "all I had was the imagination and fifty years of having lived in this country, which is a lot."[55] She had to find the courage to face what the reality was telling her: "All I'm asking, essentially, is do we understand what it means when you buy into the official version of things?" Or, as Akasha Hull pointedly rephrased it, "are we ready to know what that book is about?"[56] The question of preparedness, the preference for maroon flight over fight, and the ethical courage to know the difference, finds expression in *Bones* in numerous ways. After Sonny has returned and his parents are coping with the aftermath of his, and their, ordeal, they wonder if he acquired misplaced loyalties and was protecting his tormentors through silence. "The Stockholm syndrome, as they call it, rarely applies with freedom fighters with a passionate ideology," Bambara reminds us through her character Gerry.[57] Bambara is reiterating here the connection between healing and self-defense: a sophisticated political ideology is essential prophylactic. Seeing the world for what it is may not save you from it, but it is surely the only thing that will permit survival. And prepared, precisely, for what? From *Bones*: "War was being declared again and nothing was in place. . . . Where, then, might someone be raising an army to defend the community?"[58] The ongoing centrality of a political analysis of the world as it is, rather than as we might wish it to be, is necessary for survival because it would lead to the black community taking communal self-defense, in all of its dimensions, more seriously. In *Bones*, the scene where the daycare center at the neighborhood school is blown up by a bomb (an event that also occurred in Atlanta during the period) leads Bambara to re-collect the memories of earlier eras of black sharecroppers' modest schools torched and razed to the ground, black schoolteachers lynched, or of court-mandated school integration and white people rioting in resistance—the legacy of counterinsurgent violence directed at black education. "And still it was too much, for in the canebrakes the children taught each other counting; in the snatch rows they practiced spelling; the crops laid by, they pulled those lapboards out of root cellars and set up again."[59] Although much of the community in *Bones* does not buy the official version that the daycare bombing was an accident, Bambara is alluding to a more grave political failure of recognition: first, that such violence in the present post–civil rights period is *still* white vengeance for black self-possession; and second, that the ongoing presence of this threatening specter of destruction necessitates organized self-defense today, in the era of formal legal equality, in much the same manner that black communities organized and armed themselves in earlier periods simply for safe passage to and from work, school, shopping, worship, and pleasure.[60]

How will the community read the signs? Will it have the courage to accept the (ongoing) reality for what it is? Will the political analysis be perceptive enough to overcome the efforts to "mis-inform, mis-direct, smoke-out, screen out, black out, confound, contain, intimidate," and how are the signs controlled to this effect?[61] Early on in *Bones*, Zala struggles to develop her analysis, to clarify what the signs mean, her mind spinning with a litany of seeming coincidences and disjointed events—their connections dismissed all around as "nonsense."

> "There's no such thing as nonsense. Pay attention to these promptings," Mattie had urged, cracking a coconut open on Zala's kitchen counter and catching the milk in a saucepan, then ordering Zala to drink the milk. "It'll come clear," she said, soaking the remainder up on a washcloth and laying it across Zala's brow as she explained the clarifying properties of coconut. "It will come clear, if you just come clean," handing her four pieces to chew, as if "come clean" wasn't plenty to chew on.[62]

"Come clean": are you ready to know what you already know to be true? Wholeness must include political clarity, which is muddled by treating incidents of antiblack violence as events and not as structure. As events, the connections are easily refuted, separated by time and space, forced into the framework of causality and intentionality. As structure, they are intrinsically interdependent. At the end of the novel, the family's elder matriarch affirms the imperative of healing for self-defense. Mama Lovey confronts her grandson Sonny:

> You never were a false child. But you getting smaller every day. You need to look at that, Sundiata, 'cause could be you'll be called upon real soon to do something big that requires the kind of straight-up courage you've let strangers trash somewhere.... Whole lot of things you've yet to understand. But instead of measuring the distance between your little-boy understanding and big-boy wisdom, you standing there plotting how to get past me.[63]

At novel's end, Sonny represents what happens when the adult community does not take seriously the self-defense that political clarity would compel them to mobilize. He is snatched into the missing and murdered, traumatized and terrorized by the world. At the same time, he bears his own accountability that he is afraid to acknowledge: although well-being is a collective reality in that the conditions of possibility must be sown communally, only Sonny can chose to live to tell the tale, to tell of his living.

In addition to these leading themes in Bambara, however, *Bones* reminds us, in the end and in the main, that self-defense and whole-self living includes stealing away oneself. Kenti, Sonny's little sister, thinks how heroic "runaway" had sounded in her daddy's bedtime stories about the "folks of old fleeing captivity and setting up bases in the woods, swamps, the hills, and in the camps of the Seminoles. . . . Runaways who made a place to stand up straight in."[64] But "runaway" was being used as an epithet against black families in the present period of violence. "How soured 'runaway' had become of late in the mouths of strangers. . . . But in the face of the heart-stopping anguish of parents whose children had been murdered, how it glowed again with hope. Runaway. Not snatched, not choked, not dumped, but run away. Run away, Sonny. Rail line, hot line, steal away home."[65] Marronage, life in the midst, resistance on the move, is fight *and* flight, not the either/or false dichotomy of Western thought. Greg Thomas observes that marronage is the effaced narrative in black literature, pointing out that Toni Morrison's *Beloved*, for instance, is a novel of maroons, about a "community of runners," alive to tell the tale only because they run together in "fugitive communalism."[66] In Morrison's story, Paul D arrives from years on the road, takes off his shoes, and rubs his feet: "If a Negro got legs he ought to use them. Sit down too long, somebody will figure out a way to tie them up."[67] Assata Shakur's marronage from the women's prison in Clinton, New Jersey led to exile in Cuba. Thomas reminds us, however, that Shakur's escape to Cuba was not her first act of running—nor was she the only revolutionary whose flight began at an early age. In *Assata: An Autobiography*, Shakur tells of running away from her mother's home, chronically escaping into the streets for weeks at a time, starting as young as thirteen.[68] So too, George Jackson would recount similar passages in his youth. Ironically, his first maroon flight was being sent "down South" by his parents in an effort to "remove me from harm's way," a reversal of the stereotypical geography of marronage by slaves out of the South to the North and to Canada.[69] Afterwards, "I left home a thousand times, never to return," only to realize upon being locked up in Paso Robles by the California Youth Authority that marronage was his destiny: "It's the thing I've been running from all my life."[70]

Thomas explains that studying black revolutionary culture necessarily produces a nuanced understanding of marronage. Survival in the antiblack world compels repeated acts of marronage, continually stealing away one's self, in communion with a "community of runners," for as Morrison puts it in *Beloved*, "nobody could make it alone."[71] Flight is thus central to self-defense in the black revolutionary mold: as Jackson put it in *Soledad Brother*, "I may run, but all the time that I am, I'll be looking for a stick!"[72] Thomas writes that Jackson's flights of resistance, all the while imprisoned by the state of California, "should make it clear that maroonage is defined *not* simply by *territory* but by political *traits*, *practices* or *principles*—here a Pan-African political practice or principle of collective 'flight and resistance' for freedom, all across plantation America."[73] Furthermore, Thomas points out, Jackson's "stick is like any runner's baton in the race of struggle."[74]

With this critical tradition of marronage in mind, then, we can see that Bambara keeps the idea of the black child alive, passing on the praxis of communal runners to her reading audience. Running and running away is a persistent theme in Bambara's early works. While she seems to turn in her later work, in *Salt* and *Bones*, to a politics of standing up in place, of going within in order to heed spiritual signposts pointing the way to whole living, in fact both works are an expansive portrait of marronage, not a retreat from communal fugitivity, in that they explore the ethics of escape, refuge, and sanctuary across and within a hostile geography that knows no bounds. In *Bones*, Bambara sustains the promise of black life, allowing us to hope that Sonny will escape his captors and run away home—while stealthily allowing for the possibility that Sonny has already run away. This is how Bambara deploys blackhood to find a way through the dark night to the next porch light, in a land constituted in social death. The child perceives the toxicity of this world and strikes out intuitively for freedom, heads North, West, South even, afar, over yonder, anywhere but "Atlanta." Bambara cites an old slave song ("rail line, hot line") and a spiritual ("steal away home"), both about escaping slavery: the apparent implication is that Sonny would escape his captivity and return to his parents Zala and Spence; the inadmissible meaning is that he has escaped captivity, moved on, run away from the conditions of social death marked by mother-dispossessed and father-absence, embodying the social life of fugitivity. There is marronage somewhere in blackland, and its conditions are everywhere.

All the Things Your Movement Could Be by Now If It Were to Center Black Self-Determination

We are moving ... to create a new pool of clarifying concepts which will permit us to see and handle our own reality. In our opinion, the question of concepts is decisive. The overriding need of the moment is for us to think with our own mind and to see with our own eyes. We cannot see now because our eyes are clouded by the concepts of white supremacy. We cannot think now because we have no intellectual instruments, save those which were designed expressly to keep us from seeing.

—Lerone Bennett, *The Challenge of Blackness*, 1972

n his statements at the Brinks trial, in which he appeared as one of the defendants in a case resulting from a joint action by members of the Black Liberation Army and the Weather Underground to "reappropriate" funds from an armored car, Kuwasi Balagoon reasserted his revolutionary praxis, defending his status as a political prisoner engaged in resistance against "the American Imperialist."[1] He went on to levy the charge of black genocide against the United States, theorizing a revolutionary political program against the

cultural, economic, and political protocols of the "racist nation."[2] Balagoon's
dignified fight against oppression continued unabated until his death—but
the nightmare of the political prisoner (behind bars, in the crosshairs of state
repression, or policed in the "social incarceration" of the antiblack world)
not only does not weigh sufficiently on the collective conscience today, it
generates nary a moment of theoretical resistance in critical treatments of the
all-too-obvious problem of criminal justice. Balagoon's death in prison from
AIDS in 1986, and the similar application of capital punishment's drawn-out
schedule for many of his incarcerated comrades, is a central facet of the state's
counterinsurgency during the 1980s and into the present, the concealed un-
derpinning to the spectacles of criminal justice ("wars" on crime, drugs, gangs,
welfare, and so forth) waged on black communities and in the news headlines.
The political prisoner, the disappeared revolutionary, is an axial dilemma in
black, a clash of ethics, for not only the mainstream embrace of the criminal
law, but also for the Left critiques of "justice."

My concern in this chapter is with the hazards of "progressive" antiracist
politics that targets policing and punishment as evidence of democracy and
equality violated and seeks to realign society accordingly, albeit in terms that
are not qualitatively different from civil society's long-standing trepidation
regarding the threatening specter of black liberation. I consider the role of
politically engaged intellectual, legal, and activist work on law, policing, and
punishment in eclipsing the singular position of black people in the world.
What appear to be victories against the police power, or devastating exposés
and critiques of criminal justice practices, are revealed, in the main, as
further displacing black self-determination and the paradigmatic questions of
antiblackness that it alone raises and impugns. First, I analyze the movement
against stop-and-frisk policing, with particular focus on the 2013 court decision
in *Floyd, et al. v. City of New York, et al.* against the New York Police Department
(NYPD). The U.S. district court found the NYPD liable for a pattern of racial
profiling and unconstitutional stops of city residents. The court ordered
the city to implement "immediate reforms," and a Joint Remedial Process
is now underway toward this end. *Floyd* requires a reexamination of Fourth
Amendment jurisprudence and the origins of the constitutional protection
against unreasonable search and seizure. Hailed as a victory against racist

policing, does the *Floyd* decision augur the twilight of racial profiling? Can legal prohibition effectively curtail the practice? What does this case tell us about policing and about the police power of antiracist antiblackness both, in tandem? These questions lead to crucial insights about blackhood's antagonism with law and state power.

Second, I interrogate two prominent critical treatments of policing and punishment for the political deception of black movement that they present. Michelle Alexander's *The New Jim Crow: Mass Incarceration in the Age of Colorblindness* and Ruth Wilson Gilmore's *Golden Gulag: Prisons, Surplus, Crisis, and Opposition in Globalizing California* are two signal texts in the recent swell of intellectual engagements with the problems of policing and punishment in recent years.[3] Alexander has been in high demand on the national speaking circuit since the publication of *The New Jim Crow*, and her book is widely popular for its accessible critique of contemporary criminal justice policy. Both within and outside the academy, it is regarded as the leading treatment of the mass incarceration problem, with the phrasing "the new Jim Crow" popping up throughout mainstream discourse from popular culture to electoral politics as short-hand reference for the prison system. Gilmore has held prominent leadership roles in academia and is also well known as an antiprison activist-scholar. The high prestige that both Alexander and Gilmore enjoy, and by extension the degree of credibility accorded their books, is in part a reflection of the esteem accorded their credentials as practitioners: Alexander as a former civil rights attorney and Gilmore as a long-time activist. In addition to shaping how we think about prisons and punishment, and beyond the considerable merits of both Alexander's and Gilmore's work, both of their books are representative of the analytical pitfalls characterizing the flourishing scholarship on the topic in the post-racial period. It cannot be taken as a given that the objectives and methods of inquiry affiliated with critical studies of punishment are always aligned with those of black liberation—even in instances where the impact of incarceration and policing on the black community is the explicit topic of the study. How does it come to be that in the process of arguing for the abolition of prisons or the reform of policing, people can reinscribe the very symbolic order that positions the black community outside the human family that made possible the prison as we know it today?

The Counterrevolution of Search and Seizure

As I have noted previously, since the police are merely an appendage of power, not the seat of power itself, their operations are symptomatic of society's governing structure. My interest, therefore, is less with the apparatus of law and criminal justice and more with the structural reality in which we have the kind of policing and punishment that we do. I argue that our political energies need to be directed toward this underlying foundation on which modern society rests, because simply reforming how policing and punishment occur without a fundamental overhaul of the social structures behind it will simply reproduce the status quo under a different name. Such is the illusion of post-racialism, wherein the modern era's long-standing hostility toward black people now appears as some sort of "tolerance fatigue," a general impatience with black failure, as if historical oppression was in actuality a kind of malaise that the black community cannot shake.

Examining law and criminal justice policy, then, is only useful for my purposes insofar as it facilitates tracking power back to its source. In the land-mark Supreme Court case *Terry v. Ohio*, the court proclaimed, with customary understatement: "It is simply fantastic to urge that [a frisk] performed in public by a policeman while the citizen stands helpless, perhaps facing a wall with his hands raised, is a 'petty indignity.'"[4] The former U.S. district court senior judge for the Southern District of New York, Shira Scheindlin, employed this quotation from the *Terry* decision as an epigraph to her own decision in *Floyd, et al. v. City of New York, et al.* In *Floyd*, Judge Scheindlin found the NYPD's implementation of its stop-and-frisk policy to be in violation of the Fourth and Fourteenth Amendments to the Constitution and ordered its immediate remediation. The political establishment bristled at Judge Scheindlin's ruling: indeed, the Court of Appeals for the Second District removed Judge Scheindlin from the case and presumably was on its way to overturning her decision when the de Blasio administration came into the mayor's office and withdrew the city's appeal. On the other hand, the movement against police brutality and stop-and-frisk claimed the *Floyd* decision as a major victory.

Floyd will make little difference in ending racial profiling, as will become clear over the course of this chapter. We can, however, put it to work in analyzing the violence that the decision purports to curtail but that it in fact represents and, in so doing, construct a more ethical relationship to law than is currently on offer in the leading critical discourses about policing and punishment in activist, legal, and academic circles. One of the main obstacles to adequately assessing the power relations that express themselves through policing is an incorrect understanding about the relationship between law and the police. Customary thinking holds that law is created, and then the police enforce the law and the courts review their execution of law. In reality, things happen in reverse: policing precedes law and literally creates it as it goes along. Fourth Amendment jurisprudence verifies this point, as does the historical context for the Constitution itself.

The history of the constitutional protection against "unreasonable searches and seizures" is usually told backward. Andrew Taslitz rehearses the customary narrative found throughout the archive: "Ultimately, therefore, the use of general warrants, writs of assistance, and the like to promote collection of government levies sought to enforce an absurd system of virtual representation that came to define for the colonists the essence of tyranny."[5] There is no departure or deviation from this narrative about search and seizure: the Fourth Amendment repudiates the tyranny of generalized suspicion and invasive state power typical of colonial and undemocratic regimes. This account is historically inaccurate, however, and the lie of the paradigm is easily exposed. Historical explanations are faithful to the colonists' words and blind to their deeds. Historians continue to uncritically proclaim the colonists' perspectives and beliefs, as if recording their sensibilities suffices for historically grounded analysis. In this way, historians double down on the national mythology, and since accounts of the past are always geared toward prosecuting the present, this white nationalism continues to inform contemporary controversies. That is to say, today's movement against police brutality and racial profiling must advance the basic epistemic violence of this historical narrative: racial profiling is unconstitutional, the argument goes, because it relies upon a generalized suspicion that violates the founders' revolutionary independence from such tyranny.

The historical lie in this account, as always is the case, is the occlusion of slavery. The colonists famously presented their cause as revolutionary because it sought to throw off the shackles of enslavement—when in fact, their resistance was counterrevolutionary in that it endeavored to keep the shackles on the Africans, even at pains of war with their European motherland.[6] They condemned the writs of assistance as "instruments of slavery," in the words of John Adams, and proclaimed themselves ready to die rather than submit to British enslavement.[7] Historians generally pantomime the colonists' artificial distinction between "chattel slavery" and "political slavery." On the one hand, the colonists recognized "slavery" as "the absence of political liberty for a corporate body and loss of economic independence for the individual."[8] They experienced the imposition of the British writs, therefore, as a distinctly political effect of British domination: "The colonists became champions of the specific warrant not because it was specific but because they associated the general warrant with violent British efforts to subjugate them politically."[9] Slavery thus directly generated constitutional political thought: "'Slavery' ... as the absolute political evil ... appears in every statement of political principle, in every discussion of constitutionalism or legal rights, in every exhortation of resistance [in eighteenth-century political discourse]."[10]

Despite the recognition in early constitutionalism's preoccupation with slavery that enslavement is the result of political struggle, when it came to their own slaving practices, the colonists construed it in natural, cultural, or moral terms as a way of distancing themselves from the slavocracy they had created and on which they were wholly dependent. In this sense, they described slavery as "the inability or unwillingness to be self-governing, or more specifically, the inability to control bodily lusts and passions, above all selfishness," with "liberty" construed as the freedom from licentiousness, or subservience to the animalistic "passions," by way of command over the higher faculty of reason.[11] Thomas Jefferson said that dependence on another produces "subservience and venality, suffocates the germ of virtue, and prepares fit tools for the design of ambition." For Jefferson and the colonists, the danger for the individual lay in subjection "to the arbitrary will and pleasure of another," with arbitrariness especially offensive because it meant actions based on whim or passion, rather than rationality and reason.[12] George Washington, as well, spoke for the colonists when he said that it was vital to avoid becoming "tame and abject slaves," like the Africans they ruled "over with such arbitrary sway."[13] Of course, Jefferson and Washington intentionally disavow both their collective war-making against Africans that produced the very plantations over which they lorded and that Africans were daunting and unrelenting in their resistance—anything but subservient, venal, and tame. For the so-called founding generation, then, enslavement is unjust political repression when describing Britain's control over its colonies, but with respect to the colonists' own dominance over their African chattel, the slave is an inferior creature and it is the prerogative of the strong, rational, and civilized to possess and arbitrarily control such beings.

The hypocrisy of colonial discourse is by now unremarkable, and the continued excision of this duplicity from the history of constitutionalism is laughable, and at the same time, to be expected. Nonetheless, it remains analytically and politically instructive for unraveling the obdurate antiblackness in contemporary efforts to reform criminal law and criminal justice. The colonists' resistance to general warrants and writs of assistance was an objection to the gratuitous violence that continues to mark the policing of blackness today— the imposition of authority and punishment arbitrarily and without specific cause. As Taslitz summarizes, again representing the dominant narrative of the Fourth Amendment, "general searches were implicitly seen as insulting because they violated principles of individualized justice."[14] The so-called "principle of individualized justice" is culturally and historically specific to Western slave-holding culture. It was of such importance to the colonists precisely because as slave owners they knew better than anyone the power signified by gratuitous violence. The prohibition against arbitrariness was vital to the colonists, and likewise is a cornerstone of criminal justice reform today, because it disavows the group-based nature of power and of the social itself. In the *Floyd* decision, Judge Scheindlin notes, "reasonable suspicion requires an *individualized* suspicion of wrongdoing," and an officer "must be able to articulate something more than an inchoate and *unparticularized* suspicion or hunch" (emphasis added).[15] The colonists' objection to the use of the general warrant resonates across Fourth Amendment jurisprudence: "A police department may not target a racially identified group for stops *in general*—that is, for stops based on suspicions of general criminal wrongdoing—simply because members of that group appear frequently in the police department's suspect data."[16]

At this point, I have laid out the necessary, but not sufficient, grounds for deconstructing Fourth Amendment jurisprudence and the source of the policing of black people. To make the paradigm shift complete, we must move past a critique of white nationalist mythology to the historical struggle of the white nation against African revolutionaries that is made available to us across the eras through the black studies archive. The parallels between the colonists' objection to the general warrant and the same such objections today to racial profiling and stop-and-frisk are not to be read as a genealogy or to be taken at face value. Rather, they must be read as the police power, one and the same, against blackhood. Slavery was itself, at base, the profound and fundamental expression of search and seizure powers over black people's bodies, over black spaces, and over black lands. Colonial settlers conjured the principles of individualized justice that would become the Fourth Amendment to the Constitution only in relation to this capacity to seize blackness with impunity. Preexisting dynamics, explains Gerald Horne, especially the energies of rebellion and armed revolt, create lasting effects on which legal constructs rest. The colonists' rebellion against Britain came as London was moving toward the abolition of slave-trading, leading the United States to become the undisputed captain of the transatlantic and Pan-American slave trade. Horne's confrontation with white nationalist mythology from the vantage of black historical struggle overhauls the meaning of the Revolution, reveals the underpinnings of abolitionism, and permits an ethical assessment of the police power to which Fourth Amendment jurisprudence adheres.

Horne explains that the frequency and intensity of African rebellion in the Caribbean, let alone its periodic success and the omnipresent threat of marronage amid the plantations, had portended the collapse of Britain's slave holdings in the region. African rebelliousness had pushed European settlers from the Caribbean to the North American mainland, writes Horne, bringing with them "nerve-jangling experiences with Africans that hardened their support of slavery—just as abolitionism was arising in London."[17] Horne also notes that Europeans arriving in North America from the Caribbean brought not only their experience with African rebelliousness, but also their own slaves who were all too aware that their oppressors were vulnerable. The decades leading up to the dawn of the American Revolution in 1776 were thus marked by notable slave rebellions across North America, most significantly in Manhattan in 1712 and 1741 and South Carolina in 1739.[18] Horne compels us—consistent with the black studies archive across the eras—to understand African resistance in the New World as a unitary response to Euro-American dominance, with the United States and Britain adopting different approaches to maintaining power over seized blackness.[19] Whereas the British were eventually persuaded to adopt abolition in the face of mounting losses at the hands of African rebels in the Caribbean (and the corresponding costs to its other overseas colonies, namely India), the North American colonists dug deeper into the morass of greater investment with the slave trade and paranoia regarding black self-determination. Ben Franklin fairly represented colonist sentiment, almost two decades before the Revolution, when he asserted, "Every slave might be reckoned a domestic enemy," and a fellow Philadelphian denounced London for "not only urging savages to invade the country, but instigating Negroes to murder their masters."[20]

Greater investment in the slave trade brought exponentially larger numbers of Africans to the North American colonies. With an escalation in the slave trade came a commensurate increase in African resistance. The perpetual plots of African insurrection fomented white paranoia about the black presence, which in turn saw the colonists further militarize their society, including expanded use by the slave patrols of search and seizure against Africans on and off the plantations. Horne explains that as the slave trade increased, and revolts of the enslaved rose accordingly, abolitionism began to spread and the division between the colonists and London sharpened on the slavery question.[21] Thelma Foote affirms that the primary outcome of the American Revolution was "the reassertion of slaveowner control over the enslaved black population in the new republic."[22]

The conditions of possibility, then, for the articulation of the colonists' "principle of individualized justice" and the prohibition against the general warrant that would crystalize after 1776 as the Fourth Amendment are the following three forces. First, the American struggle for sovereignty proceeded through the struggle for slavery. For this reason, Horne describes the Revolution of 1776 as an internecine conflict, a civil war within antiblackness that would be renewed in 1836 when Texas split from Mexico following the latter's abolition of slavery, continued in 1861–1865 in the U.S. Civil War between the Union and the Confederacy, in 1888 when slavery was abolished in Brazil, and so on. More to my purpose here in this chapter, sovereignty and slavery as twin faces of the modern era should reorient our reading of sovereignty's particulars, such as the protection against unwarranted search and seizure. Second, abolitionism wherever and whenever it arose was a self-interested resolution to crisis conditions arising from African resistance, among other factors. This means that black self-determination—not white ideology, leadership, or mass action—fomented the age of emancipation, while abolitionism has always been about the preservation of power, not its redistribution or reformation or curtailment. Third, the design of the American republic compels Africans to disregard sovereignty and legal standing in the pursuit of justice. During the Revolutionary War, the colonists' principles of individualized justice were put on hold, search and seizure being viewed as a legitimate means of fighting the enemy.[23] The ongoing war against black people, accordingly, is a permanent state of breach wherein generalized suspicion and arbitrary (i.e., racialized) search and seizure reign; remedies within this structure function, like abolitionism, to extend the reach of power, not ameliorate it. Policing blackness remains a wartime problem, where the law takes a back seat to the police power. For these reasons, the Fourth Amendment is the apex of counterrevolutionary warfare. It enshrines search and seizure as a requisite tactic in the policing of black people and is the definitive case of how law retroactively codifies the actions of the police power against blackness already at work in society.

Policing Precedes Law

Policing precedes law is a paradigmatic rejection of Western ideology and antiblackness. Consider this central reformulation of law's relation to the police power in more detail. Judge Scheindlin opens her decision in *Floyd* with the assurance that the constitutionality of stops and frisks is not at issue. She affirmatively reviews the Fourth Amendment jurisprudence subsequent to *Terry v. Ohio* wherein the court created the legal fiction of "reasonable suspicion," the standard a police officer must meet in order to conduct a stop-and-frisk. *Terry*'s reasoning and the legitimacy of "reasonable suspicion" itself, in other words, do not come under examination for Judge Scheindlin. Although it is meant to apply to individual-level suspicion, the practice of suspicion itself is conceptually and empirically wedded to the social and political construction of blackness—in other words, suspicion functions at the level of populations, not the individual. "Danger," "threat," and "security" are racialized constructs that define black people as intrinsically suspicious as a group, irrespective of individual behaviors. Individual-level suspicion only attends to white behaviors, and even then police officers are loath to make the connection and criminalize whites. Judge Scheindlin cited instances where NYPD commanders explicitly directed their officers to overlook white people they actually witness breaking the law because "this is about stopping the right people, the right place, the right location."[24] The police commissioner at the time of the *Floyd* case, Ray Kelly, is quoted as saying that he "wanted [black and Latino] men to be afraid every time they left their homes."[25] When it was pointed out to the commissioner that this type of group-based suspicion was illegal, at best, he replied, "How else are we going to get rid of guns?"[26] Needless to say, it should be well known by now that the police practice of stop-and-frisk does not get rid of guns: no weapons were found in 98.5 percent of the 2.3 million frisks conducted by the NYPD after 4.4 million stops between 2004 and 2012.[27] These statistics bear out across contexts and categories of law breaking: time and again, studies verify that racial profiling simply masks criminal behavior because it shields white people, who are statistically more likely to be involved in criminal behavior, from scrutiny. It is notoriously ineffective as crime control—but then, that is precisely the point of policing: social control, not crime control.[28] The *Floyd* case occurred because an earlier case, *Daniels, et al. v. City of New York, et al.*, failed to produce changes in how the police practice stops and frisks. In the period between the city's settlement of the *Daniels* case in 2003 and the *Floyd* decision in 2013, the NYPD actually increased its stop-and-frisks dramatically, from 314,000 stops in 2004 to a high of 686,000 in 2011, joining a long line of court decisions, commission reports, and police scandal exposés that produced no lasting reforms but simply more of the same police practices.[29]

"Reasonable suspicion" is therefore either socially impossible or inherently racist. Either way, it is unconstitutional and unlawful.[30] *Floyd* may not end racial profiling, but it does represent a severe shot across the bow of the Supreme Court's decision in *Terry*. That is to say, despite Judge Scheindlin's claims that the constitutional legitimacy of stop-and-frisk was not at issue in the case, I suggest that we should read *Floyd* as laying the legal groundwork for overturning *Terry*, doing away with the legal fiction of "reasonable suspicion," and ending the legal cover for stop-and-frisk altogether. *Floyd* and *Terry* both reiterate a more fundamental principle pertinent to the case against the Fourth Amendment itself: policing does not follow law; rather, it follows the political forces at play in a historical moment that it is charged with carrying out. Take the benchmark of Fourth Amendment jurisprudence, for example. When the Supreme Court created the legal fiction of "reasonable suspicion" in its *Terry* decision, reducing the constitutional standard that police have to meet before infringing upon a person's right to privacy, scaled down from "probable cause," essentially what it did was amend the law to conform with what the police were already doing. When asked during cross-examination at the trial court on what basis did he suspect John Terry and his companions, all of whom were black, of criminal activity, the white police officer who made the arrest, Detective Martin McFadden, explained simply: "I didn't like them. . . . I was attracted to them."[31] What the court found "reasonable" in this response, then, is nothing more than classic Negrophobia, the sexual neurosis of white supremacy, a disavowed desire for and fear of "immoral shameful things"—black bodies. That this Negrophobia was accepted by the court, and henceforth has been studied by generations of law students ever since as "good law," underscores my position that policing precedes the law, not the other way around. Indeed, the courts since *Terry* have consistently declined to define "reasonable suspicion" or "probable cause," decreeing that law enforcement alone has the prerogative to determine these key elements of a lawful Fourth Amendment search and seizure. The insight of utmost consequence for movements to curtail policing and punishment is that the state and its legal apparatus as the arena for petitioning and adjudicating claims to justice, on the one hand, and the police as the agents of lethal violence with impunity, on the other hand, are in fact two sides of the same coin.[32] Things are working as intended: if the police relate to those whom they profile as "suspect" as a law unto themselves, endorsed by the judicial process, then law itself is moot, null and void—for what is the meaning of law in the face of routinized impunity before it?

The police as the law, rather than checked by and accountable to it, brings us to the problem of impunity. When NYPD officer Daniel Pantaleo applied an illegal chokehold on Eric Garner on July 17, 2014, he literally killed Garner with his bare hands. Although chokeholds have been prohibited since 1993, shortly after five officers were put on trial for asphyxiating a young man, the Civilian Complaint Review Board has received on average two hundred complaints per year by city residents of officers using chokeholds.[33] This is a clear record of impunity. Needless to say, beyond the district attorney's refusal to indict him on any charges, Officer Pantaleo not only has not been fired for conduct expressly prohibited by department regulations that caused a man's death, he has not missed a single paycheck.

After two NYPD officers were attacked and shot as they sat in their patrol car on December 20, 2014, hundreds of officers turned their backs on Mayor de Blasio as he spoke at the officers' funerals, and subsequently officers citywide engaged in what the *New York Post* described as a "virtual work stoppage." Tickets and court summons were down as much as 96 percent and arrests were down 66 percent.[34] Mayor de Blasio garnered this open rebellion by his employees for expressing his concern about discriminatory policing and his worry that his own black son is potentially endangered by his department's practices.[35] The head of the police officer's union blamed the mayor for the attacks on Officers Rafael Ramos and Wenjian Liu, as well as on the people who have protested police killings in the Garner and Brown cases, saying the mayor has "blood on the hands."[36] In Providence, Rhode Island, a similar expression of impunity by police occurred on October 2, 2015, when an employee of Dunkin' Donuts gave an officer his cup of coffee with "#blacklivesmatter" written on the cup. The Providence police department was furious, and it extracted a formal apology from Dunkin' Donuts, which in turn "counseled" its employee.[37] Similar confrontations at fast food restaurants in Texas and Florida in 2015 resulted in workers being fired for refusing service to police officers. When rank-and-file officers are able to flagrantly flaunt the directives of their bosses with no fear of consequences—and lest we not forget that the police are a paramilitary organization, what do we think would happen if a soldier in Iraq decided not to follow orders one day?—or an affirmation of life elicits condemnation and requires a formal apology, then we are dealing with a deeply entrenched structure of impunity.

Making Eye Contact

The counterrevolutionary purpose of the Fourth Amendment and the structure of impunity that law sanctions raises the question of how to understand this police behavior. Since the search and seizure of black people is not only standard police procedure, but more to the point, it is the primary historical purpose of policing, the real question becomes, what is the nature of this racism? The cultural ethos contiguous with slavery that underwrites racial profiling is the proscription against any form of black self-defense or self-possession. The slave that showed any signs of recalcitrance, disgruntlement, discontent, or resistance was guilty of nonsubmission, punishable as a criminal act, a form of theft, the act of taking over control of someone else's property.[38] Fourth Amendment principles arose out of a state of war against rebellious blackness. In terms of today's events, writes Steve Martinot, "for those profiled to claim constitutional rights in the face of police impunity are thus guilty of pretending to a superseding law which impunity has itself already superseded."[39] In other words, the law to which the survivors of policing appeal to hold the police accountable does not exist for the purpose the survivors wish to employ it; its function, rather, is to affirm police impunity and the criminality of black self-possession. The nature of this racism is terror: the construction of threatening nonhuman objects through acts of categorization and profiling, often culminating in murderous violence by the police under the auspices of self-defense and law enforcement. Jurisprudence on the police power extends the reasoning in the antebellum slave codes that society owes its security to the police power, whose importance is evidenced by its resistance to representation and limitation. The 1830 North Carolina Supreme Court case of *State v. Mann* held that the power of the master had to be absolute in order to "render the submission of the slave perfect," and that the inevitable abuses of power that come with such totalitarian authority must also be protected in order to guarantee the perpetuation of the institution of slavery.[40] In the same period, in *State of New York v. Miln*, the Supreme Court decreed the "indefinite supremacy" of the police power and that it possesses an "undeniable and unlimited jurisdiction over all persons and things."[41] The court would restate this premise, in an early interpretation of the newly ratified Fourteenth Amendment, passed to protect recently emancipated slaves in the South, in the *Slaughterhouse Cases*: "The power is, and must be from its very nature, incapable of any very exact definition or limitation."[42]

From the standpoint of the police power, blackness is imperceptible except as the danger it is presumed to pose to public welfare; acts of violence against black people are justifiable as self-defense, obligatory to ensure the stability of society, and by definition can never be excessive.[43] In the paranoia of the police power, black children are feared as fully grown adults (Tamir Rice); black men are convicted of rape solely on the basis of a white woman's dream (Clarence Moses-El); black therapists aiding their autistic patients are shot for their trouble (Charles Kinsey); black fathers are "stunned and arrested" while picking up their children from daycare (Chris Lollie); black women are body-slammed to the ground for crossing the street (Ersula Ore); incapacitated black motorists seeking assistance (Renisha McBride, Jonathan Ferrell) or lying unconscious in their cars (Tyisha Miller) are blown away by residents and police officers alike; sleeping black grandchildren become collateral damage during a police raid (Aiyana Stanley-Jones); shopping in the gun aisle of Walmart becomes an executable offense on the spot if you are black (John Crawford); a litany of everyday objects (wallets, cell phones, candy bars, and so on) are perceived as lethal weapons in the hands of black people (Amadou Diallo, Stephon Clark, Andre Burgess, and too many to name); informing an officer during a traffic stop that you have a legally permitted gun in your glove compartment is interpreted by said officer as an act of aggression, as if you were actually holding the gun (Philando Castile); and heaven help you if you are black and are having a mental collapse of some kind (Quintonio LeGrier, Philip Coleman) or happen to live next door to someone who is (Betty Jones).

While it is possible to debate the practices to which the power applies— from on-the-street racial profiling to penal policies such as three strikes, drug sentencing regimes, or even so-called administrative segregation within the prison—the power's existence has never been open to discussion. To deliberate or prevaricate over its various practices, then, let alone to worry whether it is containable or susceptible to reform, as Judge Scheindlin or the proponents of criminal justice reform such as Michelle Alexander (to whom I will turn momentarily) suggest, is to both miss the point and to find oneself in the cul-de-sac of a topic defined by its foreclosure to deliberation. The Fourth Amendment enshrines this power; it does not provide the means of confronting and undoing it.

On April 12, 2015, Freddie Gray was talking with a friend in West Baltimore when three Baltimore police officers came around a corner and "made eye contact" (in the police department's words) with him. Gray took off in the other direction. It is unclear if Gray started running immediately upon seeing the officers or if initially he was walking; but at the very least, Gray was running once the police gave chase. When the police caught him, they beat him, arrested him, and put him into the back of a police van that had been summoned to the location. At some point in the course of his arrest and transport, before arriving at the police station, the officers inflicted fatal injuries on Gray. His spinal cord was nearly severed, and his voice box was crushed. He fell into a coma and died a week later on April 19, 2015. The furor surrounding Gray's death, including the uprising by Baltimore residents and the subsequent unsuccessful prosecutions of the arresting officers, has almost entirely centered on what the police did to him while he was in their custody. Gray's death, however, was not chiefly dependent on the intentions of the officers to kill or even on their actions once he was in their custody, but instead rests on their license to pursue, the legal ability to seize his person in the first place. Pursuit and seizure eventually lead to black death in many cases, as with Gray so too with Eric Garner, Trayvon Martin, Ramarley Graham, and Sandra Bland, to cite cases discussed in this book alone; and sometimes it does not, as with Chris Lollie and Ersula Ore. The opening act of violence in police killings is always the visual act of racial profiling. This fact has been largely overlooked in the public debates about the Gray case—and not because people are unaware of racial profiling's role in black premature death, but because Fourth Amendment law makes the pursuit of Gray for "making eye contact" reasonable. Having apprehended Gray, the police claim that the search of his person produced an "illegal switchblade," providing the probable cause needed to arrest him.[44] Once he is caught, probable cause to effectuate a legitimate arrest arises easily from any number of expressions of police power that are largely impossible to disprove after the fact and outside of the moment (resisting arrest, "illegal switchblade," assaulting an officer, failure to comply, obstructing justice).

The question is how does Fourth Amendment jurisprudence cover the police seizure of Gray in the first place? That is to say, what is the counterrevolutionary rationale subtending the Gray case? On the one hand, the court seems to provide for each person's freedom to move about unfettered by unwarranted police intrusion. Donald Tibbs explains the importance of *U.S. v. Mendenhall* to the Gray case: "The Court said that every citizen has the right to forward locomotion, which means the right to go about one's business without police interference. In addition to *Mendenhall*, there are a multitude of legal decisions affirming a right to discontinue the encounter or not talk to the police officer during reasonable suspicion encounters. Further, that discontinuation (or refusal to talk) is not enough to either heighten reasonable suspicion or rise to the level of probable cause. The right to walk away resides in the citizen's right to be free from unreasonable seizures."[45] The police report provides no explanation for the pursuit, other than the after-the-fact "switchblade" and that Gray "fled unprovoked"—but *Mendenhall* seems to affirm Gray's right to avoid an encounter with the police by moving in the other direction. In other words, the reasons for his flight are irrelevant, constitutionally speaking; moreover, the mere presence of the police may be sufficient provocation for removing oneself from police presence, as *Mendenhall* permits. A friend of Gray's, Michael Robertson, states that Gray ran because "he had a history with that police beating him."[46] In this light, Gray's flight was an act of self-preservation, apparently consistent with the letter of the law.

On the other hand, additional Fourth Amendment case law circumscribes *Mendenhall*'s application to a human being such as Freddie Gray. The most important of these cases is that of *Illinois v. Wardlow*. William Wardlow was arrested in Chicago in 1995 under circumstances very similar to Gray's case. Chicago police chased and stopped Wardlow because he turned and ran in the opposite direction upon seeing an approaching caravan of police cruisers on their way to raid another part of his neighborhood. Unlike Gray in Baltimore, however, Wardlow survived his arrest and challenged the constitutionality of his seizure by the police, arguing that the police did not have reasonable suspicion to stop him in the first place. The court acknowledged its own prior rulings, holding that presence in a "high-crime area," alone, is insufficient grounds for reasonable suspicion and that refusal to cooperate with police, such as in running away, is likewise inadequate grounds for a *Terry* stop.[47] Location when combined with some other factor, however, does become sufficient basis for reasonable suspicion.[48] On the grounds that Wardlow was evading the police while in a "high-crime area," therefore, the court held that the stop-and-frisk was constitutional under the Fourth Amendment and the rules set forth in *Terry*.[49] Since crime rates are a reflection of policing, not of criminal activity, essentially the court is nullifying black self-defense on the basis of a racist geographic assignation created by the police themselves: "high-crime area" being merely a proxy for "black neighborhood." Given that this spatial construction occurs most fundamentally at the level of the body itself, we can fairly conclude that every black person, anywhere, anytime, is "stop-eligible."[50] Since this practice of seizing black bodies predates the Fourth Amendment, policing precedes law and licenses the regulation of black self-determination as an unmitigated social threat.[51] On this score, the constitutionality of Gray's arrest is taken for granted.

The counterrevolutionary context of search and seizure discloses Fourth Amendment jurisprudence, from *Terry* to *Wardlow* to *Floyd*, as a feature of the ongoing counterinsurgency of antiblack violence. More than simply gratuitousness, violence for existing as such, black people are being punished for their nonsubmission generally. Gray was hunted down and killed for "making eye contact" and for nonsubmission to the control those eyes aim to impose on all black people. In this light, *Wardlow* may not be the best legal, let alone historical, precedent for Gray's death. That distinction goes to the lynching of Emmett Till in Money, Missouri, in 1955. Although the popular narrative has it that Till, being a native of Chicago, was naïve about the South's white supremacist etiquette and committed a capital offense by whistling at a white woman, this account underestimates both Till and the norm that he violated. It is more ethical—meaning, more accurate an account of the power relations at work—to state that Till was murdered not for one thing that he did, but rather for his general presentation of nonsubmission to whiteness.[52] Whether he did this consciously or unintentionally is irrelevant: in Martinot's words, "generalizations of people never have their source in the people generalized, only in those doing the generalizing."[53]

What does this mean for *Floyd*? If the salute that some observers have given the *Floyd* decision is true, that "the worst of stop-and-frisk is over" (as one news report put it), then what does it mean to go back to prior levels of stop-and-frisk?[54] Why isn't this quantitative calculus coming under more severe scrutiny for the group-based harm it endorses? In other words, *Floyd* and "progressive" critics of the police view stop-and-frisk, or acts of collective and generalized suspicion, as permissible so long as it doesn't get out of hand. By putting *Terry* stops in the context of contemporary police killings, nineteenth- and twentieth-century lynchings, and eighteenth-century proslavery warfare, I hope to irreparably destabilize Fourth Amendment jurisprudence and political organizing.

Prosecuting Blackness in the War on the War on Drugs

Within the centuries-long counterrevolutionary drive against black liberation, the war on drugs is trivial. Within contemporary debates on criminal justice, however, it looms large because of the ongoing destruction to black communities today. Its historical significance within post-*Terry* Fourth Amendment jurisprudence, similarly, reflects its prominent role in realizing black submission in the post–civil rights period and the degree to which the courts have molded the law to fit the ever-increasing demands of the police. Policing precedes law. Since the war on drugs has been the topic for numerous book-length studies already, I will not devote any time to exploring or analyzing its particulars. My concern is with how the conceptual paradigm of this critical work dislocates the war on drugs from its proper context—the war on blackness. Michelle Alexander's *The New Jim Crow: Mass Incarceration in the Age of Colorblindness* is currently assumed to be the definitive text on the changes wrought by the war on drugs and the war on crime. Although *The New Jim Crow* is a detailed exposé of racial discrimination in modern criminal justice practice, it nonetheless ends up prosecuting blackness. Frank Wilderson has noted that in the contemporary culture of politics, the way in which black people suffer tends to get transposed and transformed into something else, something that may intersect with black experience (poverty, discrimination, landlessness), but which ultimately pushes aside the ethical demands that the abject objecthood of blackness presents the modern world.[55] With Alexander, the displacement of black suffering is adroit but no less unpleasant: she is at pains to criticize colorblind social policy and jurisprudence, and yet she reproduces the very paradigm in which colorblindness receives its sustenance, categorically discounts every single radical or revolutionary black social movement since the dawn of the slave trade, and finds every possible contradictory way of disavowing the persistence of antiblack animus and violence "in the age of colorblindness."

For instance, in her description of what she terms "the cruel hand" of criminal justice, what happens when a black person enters the criminal justice system (as if the "system" was something apart and distinct from an antiblack society), she refutes as racist the notion that "ghetto families . . . are perfectly content to live in crime-ridden communities, feeling no shame or regret about the fate of their young men." Her refutation, however, turns in on itself. She writes:

> The predictable response is: What about gangsta rap and the culture of violence that has been embraced by so many black youth? Is there not some truth to the notion that black culture has devolved in recent years, as reflected in youth standing on the street corners with pants sagging below their rears and rappers boasting about beating their "hos" and going to jail? Is there not some reason to wonder whether the black community, to some extent, has lost its moral compass?
>
> The easy answer is to say yes and wag a finger at those who are behaving badly. . . . The more difficult answer—the more courageous one—is to say yes, yes we should be concerned about the behavior of men trapped in ghetto communities, but the deep failure of morality is our own . . . are we willing to demonize a population, declare a war against them, and then stand back and heap shame and contempt upon them for failing to behave like model citizens while under attack?[56]

For Alexander, young black men are embracing the stigma of criminality, turning to crime and a culture that celebrates narcissistic self-destruction in the context of constrained life choices. Because she does not change, reject, deconstruct, or even identify the paradigm that would posit such antiblack questions in the first place, we are thrown back into the throes of the white supremacist miasma, the ethos of slavery, as Jared Sexton puts it, that "admits no legitimate black self-defense, recognizes no legitimate assertions of self-possession," autonomy, or self-determination—be it hip hop, gangsta rap, revolutionary literature, grassroots organizing, violence, or "crime."[57] There is no good answer to a paradigmatically flawed question because it inevitably leaves the construct intact—black immorality and pathology—and black humanity is left outside flailing in the wind, trying to defend itself against the ferocity of the paradigm that created it as abject in the first place.

This example emanates from *The New Jim Crow*'s incorrect structural analysis and disastrous historical analysis. In shifting our attention away from the structural to the empirical, Alexander obscures "a conceptual framework and an ethical orientation," casting black subjection as the outcome of the machinations of criminal justice policy and criminal law.[58] Here is Alexander: "One might imagine that a criminal defendant . . . would be told of the consequences of a guilty plea or conviction. . . . He will also be told little or nothing about the parallel universe he is about to enter, one that promises a form of punishment that is often more difficult to bear than prison time: a lifetime of shame, contempt, scorn, and exclusion."[59] In this sense, the "civic death," as she summarizes it, experienced by black people who have served time in prison is figured as a contingent violence, the result of the transgressive status of a guilty plea or a conviction, when in fact it is a gratuitous feature of the antiblack world to which all black people are subject, criminal record or not. To put it differently, Alexander inverts the structure: what she locates in the racially discriminatory operations of criminal justice—in other words, in being caught up in the excesses or corruptions of an otherwise ethical structure—is actually the result of black people having been accumulated through gratuitous violence and racialization. Balagoon, echoing Malcolm X before him, viewed the contemporary prison as merely one discrete institution of control that is derivative, as opposed to generative, of the historical struggle by black people to be free. Balagoon stated in 1971: "Brother Malcolm said once: 'If you black, you were born in jail.' Jail—the buildings, the cells, the bars—means only a change in the form of our restrictions and confinement. It is only a matter of degree."[60] To reiterate: imprisonment is but one among a litany of technologies across space and time valorizing antiblack gratuitous violence.

The New Jim Crow's incorrect structural analysis is grounded in a misreading of slavery as exploitation. This error is a conceptual breakdown in which the empirical registers of black oppression and resistance are dislocated from the positionality of blackness within the structure of Western ontology. As noted in an earlier chapter, Sylvia Wynter refers to it as mistaking the map for the territory: confronting the astounding costs of the Western imperial project without "coming to grips with the *real issue* (the territory rather than its maps)," much like a physician treating a patient's symptoms and not the root causes of embodied illness.[61] This failure is the result of the limitations of humanist discourse itself, which provides the basic epistemological framework for thinking about power and suffering. That is to say, humanist discourse imagines the subject's experience with violence as the outcome of transgressions and, consequently, is inarticulate about how human subjects are positioned in relation to, once again, a structure of gratuitous violence—violence attached to being, not doing. Humanism, of course, also produced colorblindness, and this inversion is precisely what colorblind ideology requires. Colorblindness needs to situate all violence on the same continuum, as differences in degree, rather than of kind. For example, Alexander asserts that "we have witnessed an evolution in the United States from a racial caste system based entirely on exploitation (slavery), to one based largely on subordination (Jim Crow), to one defined by marginalization (mass incarceration)."[62] Setting aside the fact that this historical summary bears no relation to actual history, I will simply note for my purposes here that exploitation of the slave's labor power was certainly a common experience of slavery, but it is not the primary purpose of the slave's existence. A trove of scholarship in the black studies tradition elaborates on this point, demonstrating how the fungibility of enslaved persons—for any manner of desire—takes precedence over the accumulation of surplus labor-value.[63] Accordingly, what is sorely missing in Alexander is recognition that criminalization is not the problem but rather an indication of a problem, the ongoing and indispensable deployment of blackness to suture the coherence of civil society's leading ethical dilemmas (the "crime problem," "democracy," "security," "excessive force," "racial profiling," "torture," and so forth). It is as if W. E. B. Du Bois never penned his famous paradigm-defining question: "How does it feel to *be* a problem?"[64]

Confusing the empirical for the structural, or the map for its territory, leads to the misplaced prescriptive notion on which *The New Jim Crow* rests: the recurrent suggestion that the excessive punishment of mass incarceration would not fly were it to overflow into white and middle-class communities and threaten the safety and security of the mainstream in the manner that it presently does the black community. This notion misses the point of the constitution of the mainstream itself precisely through a culture of violence against black people.[65] For this reason, critiquing the institutional composition and comprehensive social effects of the prison industrial complex is insufficient for gaining traction on the constantly shifting and deeply entrenched coordinates of antiblackness and white supremacy that sustain the carceral imagination and its evolving institutionalizations. Criminalization and the permissibility of state violence against blacks are cultural rather than simply sociological processes. The cultural components of policing are also the very same elements holding together white supremacy: paranoia (of blackness, or of the "crime problem"); violence against the black body (police impunity); and the racial solidarity that these two dimensions produce for nonblack society.[66] This culture of antiblack violence is both historically prior to the emergence of mass incarceration in the late twentieth century and the ontological condition of possibility not only for the prison-industrial complex, but also for the law itself—a basic fact that Alexander must sidestep in order to formulate her prescriptive reforms of the criminal law.

Alexander is unwilling to touch the political and ethical implications of such a structural analysis. For this reason, it is unsurprising that she entirely vacates the long history of black rebellion and revolutionary struggle in her historical account. The state's terroristic confrontation with Black Power is particularly absent. She locates the emergence of the "new Jim Crow" with the war on drugs, when in fact it is the war on African and African-descended bodies and culture, and perhaps most especially its revolutionary movements of the 1960s–1970s, that most directly gave rise to both the technologies of contemporary policing and to its legitimating discourses on colorblindness and the corresponding jurisprudence of the Fourth, Fifth, and Eighth Amendments. COINTELPRO—both the historical event and the ongoing disposition of state violence, terror, and sabotage—reminds us that colorblindness in all its variations, from the war on crime to its critics such as Michelle Alexander, has a material base in antiblack violence. Unfortunately, Alexander does not hold herself accountable to the ethical standards of black revolutionaries. As such, her vision for social change is a dead end. Alexander's analysis of "the new Jim Crow" reflects a mainstream understanding of the problem to be overcome that clips the transformative wings on which visions of reparation and abolition take flight. Her critique of criminal justice reifies the prison, solidifies black captivity, and reproduces a contorted version of history that privileges the liberal narrative of personal growth and self-awareness as the antidote to racism. As Alexander puts it, our society took a U-turn away from the path of progress it was on after the civil rights era; what we must do, she asserts, is turn the ship back around and get back to what we were doing right.

Sanitizing the Trauma

What does it tell us that these glaring problems and omissions in Alexander have been largely met with silence from progressive and antiracist activists and scholars? It suggests an unstated predilection for liberal integrationism over black power—which is synonymous with a preference for the antiblack violence of the state and civil society over the self-activity of black revolution. While various possible lines of investigation depart from this question, I consider the affinities between *The New Jim Crow* and Ruth Wilson Gilmore's *Golden Gulag: Prisons, Surplus, Crisis, and Opposition in Globalizing California*, perhaps the defining text in the emergent field of critical prison studies, not only for the invaluable instruction the text imparts, but also because of the important leadership of its author in understanding and confronting mass incarceration. While Alexander clearly did not study *Golden Gulag*, and as a result she reproduces a number of common errors in her explanation of the rise of mass incarceration, the distance between the two books is a matter of degree, not a difference in kind. Both books are situated within a political economic assessment of racism in which state policies (Alexander) and state restructuring (Gilmore) have produced a reliance on excessive punishment. While Alexander is at pains to avoid saying very much about racism at all, Gilmore's analysis of racism ends up being equally circumspect.

Gulag acknowledges the general racial violence of the prison construction project, and also the role of blackness in the story of how the post-Keynesian militarist state "makes critical" existing hierarchies to render prisoners "massively available as carceral objects."[67] The issue, however, is not whether racism but rather how racism, and on this score Gilmore fares little better than Alexander. Gilmore has coined a definition of racism that is often cited within critical race studies literature: racism is the "state-sanctioned and/or legal production and exploitation of group-differentiated vulnerabilities to premature death."[68] To paraphrase Greg Thomas's questioning of Alexander's book: Has this definition of racism been questioned at all? In addition to its materialist tenor and the striking—yet ultimately contradictory when applied to blackness—phrase "vulnerabilities to premature death," what is most noticeable about this definition is its lack of specificity. In fact, it is so generalizable that it might just as easily define patriarchy or exploitation under capital or perhaps even homophobia.[69] Gilmore's account of the prison-industrial complex, then, privileges the political economy not simply in terms of her close scrutiny of the multiscalar "prison fix," as she puts it, but it also lends a framework of alienation and exploitation through which to grasp racism's symbolic economy as well.

Gilmore's approach is perhaps best explained by Stuart Hall's famous explication of "societies structured in dominance" in which race is the "modality in which class is 'lived,' the medium through which class relations are experienced, the form in which it is appropriated and 'fought through.'"[70] In other words, racism is irreducible to other social relations, it cannot be explained in abstraction from those relations, and yet it is subsumed within class relations. It is significant, for instance, that Hall does not put it the other way around—as in, class (or gender and sex, for that matter) is the modality in which race is "lived." For her part, Gilmore quickly dispenses with racism as an explanation for prison growth because she looks for racism—in this case, the warehousing of black bodies—to fulfill an instrumental role in the capitalist political economy. She condescendingly summarizes the argument that racism is driving mass incarceration thusly: "Among many who charge racism, folk wisdom, a product of mixing the Thirteenth Amendment with thin evidence, is that prison constitutes the new slavery and that the millions in cages are there to provide cheap labor for corporations looking to lower stateside production costs."[71] She proceeds to explain that the problem with the "new slavery" argument, as she characterizes it, "is that very few prisoners work for anybody while they're locked up."[72] As with Alexander, this understanding of slavery as primarily a matter of labor exploitation suffers from a gross misreading of history and an equally grievous underestimation of the basis for slave relations into the present. Gilmore proceeds in this vein, noting that "the generally accepted goal for prisons has been incapacitation," as if that disqualifies black prisoners from the status of "slaves," and thereby demonstrating her failure to recognize that this "do-nothing theory" of incarceration, in her words, in fact performs a good deal of political, cultural, epistemological, and axiological work. Moreover, whether blackness is warehoused, exploited as surplus labor, or creates psychic value for nonblack society, such an endless variety of available uses—fungible blackness—is made possible by the a priori capture of blackness in the first place.[73]

A significant part of this work that prisons perform is the violent suppression of the black revolutionary struggle, especially its militant and armed dimensions. In ignoring this aspect of prison growth, Gilmore stands side by side with Alexander in obscuring the prison's place within the history of antiblack sexual violence. Whereas Alexander asserts that the present period is marked by "the absence of racial hostility in public discourse and the steep decline in vigilante racial violence," as if simply asserting as much will make it so, Gilmore states that "old races die, through extermination or assimilation, and new races come into being," including the "convict race."[74] These distortions of reality contrast starkly with black daily experience. The roll call of black people assaulted for being black is endless, and as Greg Thomas has written, the desire to focus on one current, illustrative example of "premature death" (in Gilmore's words) is constantly frustrated and outdated by the latest incident.[75]

One would think that the 2013 acquittal of George Zimmerman for the murder of Trayvon Martin would give one pause before minimizing the danger that black people face today from civil society. And yet, in her posttrial comments on the acquittal, Alexander sought to turn the attention onto the state and away from how the actions of Zimmerman and the members of the jury symbolize the disposition of civil society.

> You know, there has been an outpouring of anger and concern because of the actions of George Zimmerman, a private citizen who profiled a young boy and pursued him and tried to confront him, perhaps. But what George Zimmerman did is no different than what police officers do every day as a matter of standard operating procedure. We have tolerated this kind of police profiling and the stopping and frisking of young black and brown men. We have tolerated this kind of conduct for years and years, recognizing that it violates basic civil rights but allowing it to go on. . . . I believe that Trayvon Martin's life might well have been spared if many of us who care about racial justice had raised our voices much, much sooner and much, much more loudly about the routine stereotyping and profiling of young black men and boys. It is because we have tolerated these practices for so long that George Zimmerman felt emboldened, I believe, to act on a discriminatory mindset that night.[76]

In Alexander's analysis, the problem of racial profiling begins with the police. The law sets the tone for society, and she invokes some unspecific "we" of civil society that has been too accommodating of the police and, hence, too lenient with the "discriminatory mindset" in "our" midst. Alexander is expressing a leading narrative in the fields of critical legal studies and critical criminology, sometimes referred to as the "public safety pedagogy": the notion that we learn what safety means, and how to achieve it, through what the state does. This idea is merely the converse of the assertion that if there is unjust violence in our lives, we can recalibrate the state's practices in such a way as to bring that violence under control, whether it's the violence of a criminal or a terrorist or the state's own agents. Public safety pedagogy, then, oversees the dangerous contradiction of calling for police protection from crime while simultaneously calling for less harm from the police themselves.[77]

Alexander's assessment of the relationship between criminal justice and civil society is incorrect on at least three crucial levels. First, as I have already discussed at length, the police are not beholden to the law; rather, the law retroactively codifies what the police are already doing. I have also elaborated on the second counterpoint to Alexander, police impunity and the perceived danger of black self-determination. If the state is duty-bound by the structure of impunity, and the impetus for the police power is the threatening specter of blackness, then we reach the third point in response to Alexander's take on the Zimmerman verdict: the police power is merely the methodology for the organization of an antiblack society.[78] In other words, gratuitous violence against black people is one of the primary vectors of social cohesion for civil society. The postbellum era of antiblack lynchings is a primary context for understanding both the origins of the law enforcement apparatus and the social organization from which it stems. The following excerpt from an editorial published in the *Wilmington Messenger* in 1898 demonstrates the unity between the discourse on lynching and today's prevailing critical discourse on police violence:

Should a rattlesnake, or a mad dog, be tried before killing? Should a murderer, incendiary, or highwayman, caught in the act, be allowed to complete it and to appeal to all the delays and chances of law? If you, or your people, or your property, be feloniously attacked, will you await the laws, or will you act at once in self-defense? If a mad man be on the streets, marauding and slaying all he meets, must we take out a warrant for him, arrest and try him, before we disable him and stop his wild career? The negro who has just been lynched at Charlottesville was far worse than any rattlesnake or mad dog, far worse than any mad man or criminal and by his nature and course had outlawed himself utterly. To recognize in him any right to the protections and processes of law would be to mitigate his offence, aggravate the outrage upon the lady, and to add to the shame and horror already inflicted upon her. No decent white man endowed with reason and the proper respect of manhood, should or could restrain himself in the presence of so foul a crime. It would disgrace justice and defile the courts to treat him as an innocent man.[79]

As with the police power, it does not matter here whether a crime has been committed or not; the threat is self-evident in the nature of the potential perpetrator, and threats are meant to be exterminated swiftly, preemptively, and without pause for due process. The racism in this passage lies not simply with the idea that the Negro is an animal. It is foolish to put a snake on trial not because he will have nothing to say on the stand, but rather because he will bite you before you get him there. Put differently, the snake is barred from testimony not because he is an animal but because the possibility of his speaking is continually and permanently preempted by the threat he poses.[80] *This* is the racism, then: it matters not whether blackness signifies humanity or nonhuman status, but rather that the Negro will kill you if you waste time on the question in the first place.

Zimmerman attacked Martin according to this logic, and the nonblack jury concurred. There is no other explanation for how a man who attacks a teenage boy could successfully argue that he had to kill the boy in order to defend himself from a threat that he himself conjured: the jury already recognized Martin as danger personified, irrespective of his actions or his status as the hunted, and that policing relates to blackness as pure power (violence with impunity), not as practice (law enforcement), as institution (the police), or as principle ("justice"). With these elements at work prior to the trial getting underway, the jury did not need to even hear testimony from Zimmerman himself in order to identify with him, the perpetrator of the incident, rather than with Martin, the victim (a courtroom alliance that would otherwise be preposterous were the trial not in fact a public drill in the protocols of antiblackness, a spectacle by which the mundane terms of engagement are staged as a theater of necessity, as in a routine military war games exercise, where the official rhetoric is trotted out so we are reminded of the danger of blackness in our midst, and a sampling of the fortitude of the frontline—nonblack America—is vetted).

While the jury's decision in the Zimmerman case prompted outrage in many people, Michael Dunn's conviction for the murder of seventeen-year-old Jordan Davis was met with satisfaction. On November 23, 2013, in Jacksonville, Florida, Davis and his friends were sitting in their car in the parking lot of a convenience store when Dunn arrived and told the boys to turn down their music. An argument ensued, to which Dunn responded by returning to his car, retrieving a loaded handgun, and shooting ten rounds into the boys' car, fatally wounding Davis. Both reactions to these two cases, however, while understandable, each in its own right, mystify the power relations at work here. Dunn's conviction was not justice any more than Zimmerman's acquittal was a breakdown in the system. When a jury reaches a verdict, or a grand jury reaches its decision, it is civil society in conference with itself, not the manipulation of civil society by corrupt or incompetent or skilled state actors (prosecutors, district attorneys, judges, police). Where Dunn went wrong was not in his violence or his legal defense strategy; rather, it was merely his failure to perform the post-racial era's particular etiquette of antiblackness. If he had not driven off in his car after the murder, had not had pizza and beer with his girlfriend in his hotel room many miles away, and had not had a pleasant night's sleep like it was any other day, but instead had called police to tell them that his life was threatened by these "thugs," as he called Davis and his friends, his defense would have worked out much like Zimmerman's. But Dunn blew the lid on his own farce, and echoing James Baldwin here, because this is America's farce and America doesn't like to face itself, the jury could not get down with it—meaning it could not get down with its own antiblackness. Dunn's act of violence was no different than Zimmerman's: both men initiated encounters with black children to which they both brought the sensibility that black people represent walking, talking, stalking demon-dangers that must be dealt with swiftly and preemptively. As Fred Moten put it, neither Zimmerman nor Dunn consciously intended to destroy black personhood; they simply instinctively perceived Martin and Davis as representing insurgent black life, a profound threat to the social order—the danger of blackhood.[81]

Racism's Remedies as Counterinsurgency

Alexander thus misses the full import of the Zimmerman trial, its performance of antiblack solidarity, but also the structure of banal terror, the long counterterrevolution, undergirding civil society to which it refers. Certainly the most powerful moment of the Zimmerman trial was the testimony of Rachel Jeantel,

Martin's friend who was on the phone with him when Zimmerman attacked. Jeantel explained that she was fearful that Zimmerman was following Martin because Zimmerman was a rapist and that she urged Martin to run. In her posttrial interview with Piers Morgan, Jeantel elaborated that if you are a black boy and a strange man is following you, you risk ending up on the news as a missing person.[82] The disappearance of black children perhaps has particular resonance in the South, from the slave trade to Emmett Till to the Atlanta child murders of 1979–1981, but it meets up with the reality of extrajudicial killing today nationwide: as the Zimmerman trial was ending, the Malcolm X Grassroots Movement issued its annual report, *Operation Ghetto Storm*, finding that Martin was among 312 other black people who were killed during 2012 by police, security guards, and vigilantes—over one killing every twenty-eight hours.[83] What the police do, in short, is merely an expression of the antiblack violence around which society is organized in the first place, and Alexander's emphasis on reforming the law and police practice grossly underestimates the basic relationship between blackness, gratuitous violence, and the police power of civil society.

Jeantel's warning to her friend about rapists reminds us that the disappearances of black people are a function of the sexual violence of the police power. This sexual violence is as much a feature of criminal justice practice as it is a guiding force of the police power of civil society. *Ware v. City of Detroit, et al.* involved the practice by Detroit police officers of cavity searching suspects during routine *Terry* stops. The police officer reached into Mr. Ware's pants and fondled his genitals, and then reached around and attempted to stick a finger up his ass. The American Civil Liberties Union settled the case in 2009 on the day that trial was set to begin. Although unwilling to defend its officers' conduct in court due to the damning evidence against them, the city of Detroit nonetheless rewarded one of the officers with a promotion.[84] Similar reports from across the United States affirm the intrinsic sexual assault embedded within Fourth Amendment search and seizure. "Reasonable suspicion," therefore, is sexual violence, innately.

Consider, as well, the 2009 case of *Denson v. United States*, in which customs agents detained a pregnant black woman upon her return to the United States from Jamaica under suspicion of drug trafficking.[85] Not only does the court condone the use of race, gender, and nation as the sole basis for "reasonable suspicion," but in this case they endorsed body cavity searches, forced removal to a local hospital for a pelvic exam, a laxative treatment, and detention until such treatment cleared out the woman's bowels. In a classic demonstration of how white psychic fantasies become material realities (as in: today a white fantasy about recalcitrant black criminality, tomorrow a three-strikes law that removes felons permanently from society), at each step in this woman's torture-detention the suspicions of law enforcement were proven baseless, and yet at each juncture the police translated the absence of drugs as confirmation that what was not there was in fact yet to be revealed. The specter of black criminality—especially in the form of a lascivious black female sexuality—not only outweighs the endangerment of this woman's unborn child, not to mention her Fourth, Fifth, and Eighth Amendment protections, but because of its mythic quality, sexual racism proves most persuasive precisely when it fails to predict reality. In *Denson*, the legal transposition of rape as "reasonable suspicion" or "security interest" veils this violence with the implication of collusion, and positing black agency as criminality hides state terror.

This state terror is usually disconnected from reasonable suspicion, from sexual violence, and from debates about stop-and-frisk. A case of sexualized terror by police to grab headlines recently was that of Oklahoma City police officer Daniel Holtzclaw, convicted in December 2015 of multiple counts of rape, sexual battery, and other related charges. All of his victims were poor black women he assaulted during his patrols, women who do not register as having legitimate possession of their bodies in the first place. The Holtzclaw case, predictably, has been made out to be a gross exception to the norm, when in fact it is historically consistent in its sexual violence. Danielle McGuire's 2010 book *At the Dark End of the Street: Black Women, Rape, and Resistance—a New History of the Civil Rights Movement from Rosa Parks to the Rise of Black Power* documents the long history of sexual assault on black women by police officers going back to at least the 1940s. McGuire's history shows how the bus boycotts that animated the early civil rights movement were in fact based in black women's resistance to sexual assault on the buses from police officers and bus drivers.[86] The Holtzclaw case also revealed how the Oklahoma City

Police Department knew of the sexual predator on its force for over six weeks before he assaulted his final victim. This means that Holtzclaw raped half of the women he is convicted of assaulting while under investigation from his own department.[87] At work here is police impunity, normalized antiblack sexual violence, and the construal of black women as sexually open and therefore incapable of being violated. It also recalls the ordeal of Jackie Askins, where she shares that the most painful part of her experience being held captive and raped and tortured for months in her kidnapper's basement was that her absence from society was not even noticed. The Rocky Mount disappearances, as well, force the question: Had Holtzclaw been committing serial murder, instead of serial rape, would the disappearances of his victims have even registered as an absence at all? Is the disappearance of sexual terror much different from being disappeared as a human being altogether?

Since the late 1980s, the black community in Los Angeles has been mobilized to confront just such a problem, protesting police inaction and silence, in the least, and community safety, moreover, with respect to the serial murder of black women. Their efforts echo the black community's struggles in 1979–1981 in Atlanta to bring to light police complicity in the serial murders of black children in that city. Although the recent conviction in the "Grim Sleeper" case, in which Lonnie David Franklin Jr. was sentenced on June 6, 2016, to die for the murders of at least ten black women in LA, serves as official closure, much like the conviction of Wayne Williams in the Atlanta case brought an official end to serial child murders there, the black community in LA continues to mobilize for self-defense, just as many black Atlantans strived to do. During the twenty-year period of Franklin's crimes in LA, Anthony Edward Sowell was perpetrating similar serial rape and murder against poor black women in Cleveland. Many of the eleven women whose bodies were discovered buried throughout Sowell's property when he was finally arrested in 2009 were not missing despite having not been seen for many years. Atlanta, Cleveland, Los Angeles, Rocky Mount, and so on—the political and historical context for reasonable suspicion suggests that the violation of certain physical and social bodies is so reasonable as to be no violation at all. In short, state violence and police impunity are the content of Fourth Amendment search and seizure and connect my interrogation of policing in this chapter with my analysis of the police power in the rest of the book where black people are missing and murdered physically and psychically.

Alexander's dismissal of the ongoing and naked hostility of the mainstream grammar of antiblackness, despite changes to its syntax, denudes "race" of its intrinsic violence, unmitigated across time and space. But then this move is to be expected from an avowedly integrationist liberal civil rights agenda such as Alexander's. Here is where Gilmore's supposedly more progressive and radical contribution to the abolitionist agenda may be more traumatizing to black people. What does she mean when she states "old races die" and "new races come into being"?[88] In language that is more densely coded than even Alexander's, she intimates her meaning: "Sadly, even activists committed to antiracist organizing renovate commonsense divisions by objectifying certain kinds of people into a pre-given category that then automatically gets oppressed."[89] She goes on to offer that the alternative to this supposedly misguided premise for political action is to see "how the very capacities we struggle to turn to other purposes *make* races by making some people, and their biological and fictive kin, vulnerable to forces that make premature death likely and in some ways distinctive."[90] By which she means to say, the prison makes "new races" by subjecting all of us equally to its terms: "Given these practices, it should not be all that surprising that hundreds of thousands of white men are also in prison. . . . Such men, and their diverse caged brethren, might . . . be . . . the 'convict race.'"[91] To Gilmore's way of thinking, prison as a technology of social control and dehumanization may build upon past oppression, but ultimately it subjects the people under its purview to the same form of dehumanization. This conception of the prison is fundamentally ahistorical; anybody and everybody, black and white, brown, red, and yellow, can and will enter the racialization of prison and come out, as it were, part of a universal "convict race." Activists who insist on the "old" categories of oppression, such as blackness, "have become so effectively deskilled when it comes to thinking and doing what matters most."[92] This reification of the prison occurs at heights so dizzying that the ground on which we stand is no longer recognizable.

When Joy James terms the United States a "slave democracy" or a "democratic slave state," she is grounding her analysis in the history of counterrevolution for slavery that I have explored in this chapter.[93] White people went to war with themselves in North America not once, but twice, to preserve both slavery and democracy's basis in black captivity.[94] Having had emancipation forced upon it by the self-determination of black people, the slave democracy renovated itself for a new era. It is popularly understood by now that the Thirteenth Amendment to the U.S. Constitution did not actually abolish the institution of slavery, but instead relocated it into the domain of the criminal justice system. Gilmore's dismissal of this fact as related to an argument regarding mass incarceration as the new slavery sidesteps a more consequential analysis. Most discussions of the Thirteenth Amendment misconstrue the clause stating that criminal convicts can be enslaved as a "loophole." According to this narrative, the loophole has been exploited to produce the gross injustices of mass incarceration and industrialized punishment today.

This narrative is an example of bad faith. The clause in question is a design feature, not a design flaw, historically consistent with the original agenda of the Civil War to extend, not end, black unfreedom. The Thirteenth Amendment is, therefore, not the provincialization of slavery, a discrete winnowing of the scope of enslavement to criminal convicts.[95] On the contrary: since criminalization is first and foremost a political-symbolic tool, it harkens not to individual behavior but rather to the social itself, to an onto-epistemic framework structuring social relations.[96] As such, the Thirteenth Amendment oversees the reiteration of democracy's basis in social captivity—no plantations, no auction blocks, no laws, no prisons necessary. This analysis is amply on offer in the annals of black radical thought, especially from the archives of political prisoners discounted by both Alexander and Gilmore. Writing from inside prison, George Jackson defined racism in terms of "a morbid fear of both Blacks and revolutions."[97] Also writing from prison where he remains today, Sundiata Acoli observes "the Afrikan prison struggle began on the shores of Afrika behind the walls of medieval pens that held captives for ships bound west into slavery. It continues today behind the walls of modern U.S. penitentiaries where all prisoners are held as legal slaves—a blatant violation of international law."[98] Gilmore is leading the way in the study of the prison-industrial complex not only by privileging a political economic analysis of the "carceral regime" as a function principally of a crisis in capital and state capacity, but also in dismissing the knowledge of black revolutionaries as so much "folk wisdom," as she puts it.

The disappearance of race as violence and of black death as its condition of possibility is enabled by construing black agency as oppressive and standing in the way of what Gilmore terms "non-reformist reform," rather than recognizing black self-activity, in every historical moment, as that which calls the police power into being in the first place.[99] When Gilmore refers to "commonsense divisions," she is using the Gramscian notion of "commonsense" as a politically constructed category of contested meaning. To refer to blackness in this way is to imply that in the current period the black freedom movement has achieved a hegemonic stature that privileges it above and at the expense of all other oppressed groups. Even if this claim is intended only at the level of rhetoric or discourse and is not meant to refer to actual material gains, it sutures the antiprison movement to a reactionary and antiblack multicultural politics that holds black politics on the same continuum with white supremacy. In Gilmore's framework, then, a social justice movement authorized by blackness—to wit, one that is historically grounded and ethically accountable—undermines the goals of antiprison activism. As Jared Sexton has demonstrated in his study of multiracialism, this discourse of "oppressive black power," the oppression of others by blacks, attempts to have it both ways.[100] On the one hand, multiracialism derives its claims to justice from the history of black struggle, generating its affective currency from emulating the cultural politics of the black movement. On the other hand, it stridently distances itself from blackness, undermining the signal contributions of Black Power, asserting that blacks have inverted racial hierarchy—or, "reversed racism"—to the categorical disadvantage of whites, Latinos, and Asian Americans, and banking on this symbolic buffer as its path to legitimacy and purchase in civil society.[101]

Sexton's study offers further insight on Gilmore's suggestion that the prison creates "new races." Sexton observes the historical relation between the popularity of multiracial positions and the relative efficacy, perceived or actual, of black politics.

When black resistance is thought by state and civil society to be effectively contained or neutralized, both practically and symbolically, the color line becomes considerably more fluid . . . when blacks move against the structures of white supremacy, "mixed race" is revoked as a viable social identity and racial blackness is again understood as a broad spectrum.[102]

Gilmore's suggestion that today's racial politics is best served by abandoning "old" categories of oppression advances amid both a "refortified antiblackness" and the ascription that the black community bears "primary responsibility for cutting the border of race."[103] In short, it is significant that Gilmore asserts that the multiple racial identities of the American prison population constitute a new (and ostensibly *mestizo* or mixed) race—black, white, brown, yellow, and red united as the "convict race"—rather than claiming that imprisonment signifies the blackening of the racially diverse populace. Alexander and Gilmore are thus a one-two punch: black revolutionary organizing and movement is not simply hidden in their vision, it is delegitimized. The illogic of this approach, of deracinating the struggle against prisons of the historical context of black people resisting and defending themselves against antiblack terror, the very condition of possibility for the prison-industrial complex in the first place, moves under the cover of a multicultural framework that regards the "cutting edge" of antiracist praxis as that which displaces the black/white binary. But in fact, this approach is a refusal of black victimization that enjoins the antiblack paradigm in which blackness is not capable of being victimized; it is simply vanquished.[104] When Gilmore refers to racism as "group-differentiated vulnerabilities," then, she does not refer to blackness, since vulnerability infers a capacity for victimization. The "premature death" of blackness, on the other hand, is foretold, and from this perspective, the focus on the prison is overblown, a spectacle that distracts and diverts. For this reason, Gilmore's much-lauded definition of racism is contradictory when applied to blackness, while at the same time it is too imprecise to be analytically accurate when applied in any other context.

If Prison Abolition Is the Answer, Then What Is the Question?

Among all the things your movement could be by now if it were to center black self-determination is in position to deconstruct the very essence of punishment and eradicate the scourge of human commodification that has fatally compromised each and every effort to realize human equality since the dawn of the modern era. In her essay, "'All the Things You Could Be By Now, If Sigmund Freud's Wife Was Your Mother': Psychoanalysis and Race,"

Hortense Spillers notes that the Western paradigm, to which "family," "sexuality," "interiority," and all of their accompanying dynamics are tethered, can only produce a compromised protocol for black healing. Following Spillers, I suggest similarly that formulations of justice from within this paradigm are dead-on-arrival because the crisis that they imagine resolving through the abolition of prisons—or the curtailment of stop-and-frisk, or placing body cameras on police officers, and so on—is far more fundamental than Western onto-epistemic conventions can accommodate.[105] The crisis extends on both sides of the Atlantic slave trade and is therefore constitutive to the world that such movements are seeking to salvage. Spillers suggests that the missing pieces of a new "lifeworld have to do with the dimensions of the socio-ethical."[106] For this reason, I have endeavored to elucidate an ethical relationship to the problems of policing and punishment that are symptomatic of the more vital matter of black self-determination.

When Gilmore writes "old races die, through extermination or assimilation, and new races come into being," she is performing a timeworn practice of sustaining the liberal (now multicultural) polity through black death. The example of *Golden Gulag* should be particularly instructive for people committed to human liberation—contemporary organizing against the prison-industrial complex, foremost—because it demonstrates how black solidarity can be evacuated not through intentional betrayal or calculated antiblackness, but simply by subjecting black existence to a political economy framework that inevitably bends black suffering into something that it is not exclusively. In other words, black people suffer along with everyone else under the "post-Keynesian warfare state" that Gilmore identifies—and then there is yet another level of suffering that black people alone endure that this analysis is not equipped to address. This level is the precondition for what we face today, and therefore is most essential to address in carving the way out. Gilmore's rigorous study of state and economic restructuring is an invaluable contribution to explaining the prison-industrial complex; black communities are indeed severely harmed by the political economic forces she documents. Furthermore, she has publicly stated the importance of antiracism to any struggle for social change.[107] But this is not enough. The purpose of *Blackhood Against the Police Power* is to reveal how antiracism bears within its epistemic and ontic fold the imprint of antiblackness, and as such, critical thought for freedom cannot remain at the level of empirical, experiential, or material reality alone. I suggest that the question of blackness is intrinsic to the discourse on the prison promoted by the critical study of policing and punishment and does not emerge as an antagonism simply at the moment that a new ensemble of questions is raised. The antagonism is an aspect of how the problem of mass incarceration is framed; in other words, the discourse on the prison-industrial complex both communicates and is an effect of the "general system of the formation and transformation of statements" as to what is and what is not on the table for discussion.[108] *The New Jim Crow* and *Golden Gulag* are indicative of antiblack antiracism in that while they address different aspects of the racism in criminal justice, the friction between the two is simultaneously inconsequential and productive in the sense that it serves to occlude a unity of interests with respect to the political antagonism of antiblackness.

How we call attention to the genocidal coordinates of the modern world is a complicated and fraught affair. The compulsion to focus on the litany of violent events—such as the high-profile police homicide, for which there is always a current example—in order to demonstrate how bad racism can get ends up reaffirming the mainstream notion that such instances are aberrations, further obscuring the fact that racism is a mundane affair, and thereby reducing itself to the fraudulent ethics in which nonblack civil society constitutes itself.[109] The spectacles of antiblackness tend to displace recognition of the utter vulnerability of black bodies that serves as the condition of possibility for spectacular violence in the first place. Abject black bodies are mapped onto the wanton openness of black spaces; this is the essence of race displaced by the multicultural academy's antiessentialism and engulfed by the spectacles of racism such as police killing. It is precisely this banality, the operation of hunting black people as a matter of routine police business, and the contempt for black life that it expresses, that is obscured in the high-profile court case against the NYPD's stop-and-frisk practices, wherein the preoccupation with how police officers racially profile retrenches the ability of the police to do so as part of normal police procedure.[110] In the end, the one insight that both the spectacles of antiblackness and the criminal justice reform discourse mobilized against them illuminate is that the prerogative to ignore such violence is the mark of nonblack positionality. This banality of antiblackness corresponds to, and is buttressed by, the epistemological violence of the multicultural academy.

Once, many years ago, when I was a graduate student, a professor of mine asked me what I was going to do when racism was no longer a problem. It was his way of saying that I should not waste my time studying an issue that was certainly old news at best, a passing fancy, or simply a mystification of a more fundamental problem (such as the ill effects of capitalist production). I began this chapter with Balagoon and the crisis that black revolutionary political prisoners pose for the leading critical treatments of policing and punishment. My former professor would not be the only one incapable of integrating the on-going existence of political prisoners into his understanding of reality. Jasmine Abdullah might be the most recent such prisoner. An organizer with Black Lives Matter (BLM) in Pasadena, California, Abdullah was arrested in August 2015 for "felony lynching," a law passed in 1933 to criminalize the taking of someone from police custody, ostensibly by a lynch mob. The police claim that Abdullah and other BLM members rushed a police vehicle after a public protest with the intention of freeing someone from police custody, but in fact Abdullah was part of a group of BLM members objecting to the arrest of a young woman in the midst of the larger protest event—the occasion for which, not incidentally, was to protest the 2012 killing of Kendrec McDade by the Pasadena police. The media reports of Abdullah's conviction sloppily state that the application of an antilynching law against a black activist is "ironic," and yet this case perfectly illustrates my argument in this chapter about the relationship between law and policing.[111] Never used to protect black life from the lynch mob, felony lynching laws have only been applied against political activists, most recently against BLM organizers such as Abdullah. Abdullah's supporters note that the Pasadena police began harassing her after she organized a march to mark the three-year anniversary of McDade's slaying. In other words, this law provides a tidy cover for the social control operations of the police and has always been about legitimation of the police power, and never about the criminalization of antiblack violence.[112]

As with the counterrevolutionary eighteenth century when colonists escalated the slave trade and saw African rebelliousness intensify in kind, so too with the counterrevolutionary twenty-first century in which the intensification of black resistance to the police power is met with an expansive legal arsenal and a deeply entrenched antiblack culture of politics, hand in hand. In light of the world as it is, rather than the world some people like my former professor would pretend it to be, I might turn his question around, and inquire of the contemporary movements against policing and punishment, and of ourselves: What are we going to do when the prison is no longer an issue? As Spillers puts it, "the problem with this picture is that it is perfect *as far as it goes*, but it might not take us the distance."[113] The house of antiblackness can withstand renovations to its architecture as long as its foundation remains intact.

CHAPTER FIVE

On Performance and Position, Erotically

I guess that other plantation served as a warning, cause they might want your pussy, but if you do anything to get back at them, it'll be your life they be wanting, and then they make even that some kind of a sex show, all them beatings and killings wasn't nothing but sex circus.

—Gayle Jones, *Corregidora*, 1998

This chapter explores the complex, compelling, and contradictory relations between the historical context of black expressive arts, the structure of gratuitous violence, and the readings of this confrontation within the leading critical discourse on race and sex politics. To put it differently, my concern in this chapter lies with how those of us involved with problems of black revolution—that is, with the crux of what it means to liberate humanity—can further develop a critical stance that deals honestly with the ethico-political context in which black art, black performance, black social movements, and black popular culture find expression. I am, in other words, interested in configuring the critical study of performance within an accounting of the materiality of antiblack sexual violence in which the modern world is grounded, especially as hip hop in particular ushers the various transmutations of the police power's efforts at repressing black revolution's erotic program. My focus, then, is on how the context of a world in which, since the advent of racial slavery, black people are structurally positioned outside the human family and its claims to integrity, honor, and visibility can inform how we read black expressive cultures. I suggest that rigorous adherence to this context is rare in cultural critique, and that the prevailing analytic conventions of "intersectionality" and "performativity," in particular, as well as the methods of gender and sex studies in general, wilt in the face of this rigor. Moreover, I argue that a disquieting queer antiblackness has come to the fore.

The work of hip-hop superstar Lil Wayne offers an intriguing entre into examining antiblack sexual violence and presents us with an opportunity to read the cultural politics of punishment in the era of post-racialism. Although I have written elsewhere about hip hop and the emergent hip-hop studies in the academy, I am less interested here in the academic debates that hip hop has occasioned, other than to observe that the growth of hip hop as a legitimate topic of teaching and research in the university signals the importance of hip hop to cultural history, of the university to global consumer culture, and of the long-standing desire to consume black culture generally. More generously, it also represents the ongoing storm and saliency of blackness to the study of almost anything. I am more concerned, however, with clarifying a retrograde tendency at large in the study of power and performance in this post-racial moment. That is to say, this chapter is not about hip hop per se, and I admittedly skirt around the contested definitions of what is and what is not hip hop. Instead, I hope to demonstrate in this chapter how readings of black expressive culture can enhance the quarantine of blackhood's erotic radicalism even while explicitly advancing an antiracist politic. I find a discussion of black popular culture useful toward exposing the pitfalls of performance studies and a certain queer studies engagement with blackness and the prison-industrial complex in particular.

In his hit song "Mrs. Officer," from his 2008 album *Tha Carter III*, Lil Wayne (Dwayne Carter) raps about getting pulled over by a female cop who then pulls him into her patrol car and makes him have sex with her. The song celebrates his sexual prowess but does so over a jarring subtext of state power. The women who desire Lil Wayne's sexual attentions are police officers; his masculine boasting climaxes with the refrain, "Rodney King, baby, yeah, I beat it like a cop." This explicit reference to a landmark event in the history of black struggle—the 1992 beating of Rodney King, the subsequent acquittal of the Los Angeles police officers whose protracted assault on King was caught on videotape, and the uprising of inner-city LA in response—paradoxically generated no controversy whatsoever. What does it mean, then, that the most notorious instance of police brutality in the post–civil rights era becomes, in "Mrs. Officer," not prelude to rebellion, but rather a refrain of sexual conquest? Or, put differently, what do we need to know about the erotic challenge of blackhood and the antiblack culture of politics that produces this song to understand the possibilities of black performance—and its foreclosures?

The relationship between erotic practices of state violence and black popular culture's renditions of sex and gender politics is an intimate one. I consider Lil Wayne in this light: How can we read the present context of increasing black dispossession and criminalization and the historical context of black struggles for self-determination and representation within contemporary cultural production? How is a popular hip-hop song that explicitly recalls an infamous police beating, and implicitly brackets the ensuing historic urban uprising, connected to a sonic and visual landscape that consolidates black suffering and its invisibility today, that further eclipses the historical context of (ongoing) black struggles for self-determination, and that endeavors to marshal all manner of black expression into the new discourse of containment—post-racialism? How does the leading academic etiquette for analyzing race and sex politics, "intersectionality," and its elaboration in performance studies and queer studies as the privileged fields of knowledge for assessing such cultural production, lend further legitimacy to this containment?

The single most important factor in reading black expressive culture is the interpretive frame employed. I have drawn upon a critical seam in the black radical intellectual tradition that understands "race," as well as the primary categories of social analysis in Western culture ("sex," "gender," "labor," "nation"), in terms of the defining cataclysm of slavery and the Middle Passage. In this tradition, *antiblackness* signifies both the foundation of the modern world (an immutable calculus of who counts as human) and the basis for the world's proliferating elaborations of power (the ever-changing methods of policing blackness as beyond the pale). What does meticulous accountability to this paradigm look like in practice? What is the ethico-political context it unveils, and how does this terrain reshape our reading of both black revolutionary politics and black expressive cultures, which as we will see, bleed into each other, indelibly?

The Post-Racial as Counterinsurgency's Psychosexual Afterlife

Of immediate salience to these questions is the period of the 1960s–1980s, during which the black liberation struggle reached its revolutionary zenith and was countered by deadly state repression, which proceeded apace with both anticolonial movements abroad and the restructuring of the industrial economy and a revanchist welfare state domestically. Any analysis of hip hop today, then, must account for the ways in which the present state of affairs in hip-hop culture is in large measure an effect of ongoing state violence against urban black communities and their concomitant structural dispossession— even if this antiblack violence also appears as an intramural battle, reductively referred to as "black-on-black" conflict or, simplistically, as misogyny and homophobia.[1] This historical context of revolution, counterinsurgency, and political economic restructuring is also the terrain on which colorblindness emerges as official state policy and hegemonic discourse. Although colorblind ideology and its jurisprudence have been well interrogated by scholars across the legal, social sciences, and humanities faculty, and the failure of the civil rights reforms to adequately ameliorate inequality and poverty has been well documented, such critical reviews studiously avoid connecting colorblindness—the ideology and its politico-juridical structures—to its material base, to the dirty work of a white supremacist state apparatus deeply mired in criminal enterprise.[2] The repression of black revolutionary struggle, through and beyond the murderous activities of COINTELPRO, was designed to establish a legacy of intimate violence—and in this way was a clear indication of the erotic power presented in the black liberation movement. In the words of former political prisoner Dhoruba Bin Wahad, COINTELPRO was nothing less than "a program of domestic warfare" in which the black family and black children were the ultimate targets.[3] FBI documents famously declared: "The Negro youth and moderates must be made to understand that if they succumb to revolutionary teaching, they will be dead revolutionaries."[4]

When we review the testimonials of former Black Panther Party (BPP) members, portraying a more nuanced portrait of the day-to-day experiences in the organization, then we can begin to understand the FBI's stated focus on disrupting the "indoctrination" of black children in terms of a much deeper preoccupation with destroying the erotic revolution already underway within the black community. Afeni Shakur, a former section leader in the New York chapter of the party, described the interpersonal gender relations she encountered as an important factor in her joining the Panthers.

> When I first met Sekou [Odinga] and Lumumba [Shakur] it was the first time in my life that I ever met men who didn't abuse women. As simple as that. It had nothing to do with anything about political movements. It was just that never in my life had I met men who didn't abuse women, and who loved women because they were women and because they were people.[5]

Male chauvinism certainly loomed large within the BPP and played out in terms of discrimination against women, sexual manipulation and harassment, and even violence. Sexism and gender violence, on the one hand, and Shakur's experience on the other, taken together, indicate two crucial aspects about the Panthers that bear on how we understand the contextual dimension of erotic rebellion. First, divisive sexism in the party reflects the white supremacist patriarchal society in which the Panthers emerged. Former Panther and Black Liberation Army (BLA) member Safiya Bukhari put it thusly: "The division in the Black community between the Black male and Black female did not just come about on its own. It was carefully thought out and cultivated. . . . We had taken on the persona of sexist America, but with a Black hue. It was into this context that the Black Panther Party was born, declaring that we were revolutionaries and a revolutionary had no gender."[6]

Bukhari's point that "a revolutionary had no gender" amplifies the second fact about the Panthers worth noting here. The BPP was engaged in transforming the depraved meanings of sex and gender intrinsic to America's fascistic antiblackness. The organizing violence of Western civilization has entailed a graphically sexualized dichotomy between rational and sensory nature, between white and nonwhite persons, and in particular, the conceptualization of black people as an undisciplined mass of sexual savages. Frantz Fanon wrote in *Black Skin, White Masks*, "In the case of the Jew, one thinks of money and its cognates. In that of the Negro, one thinks of sex."[7] Fanon went on to name the sexual neurosis of white supremacy as "Negrophobia," instructing us to read the terror of racism as sexual revulsion, as a disavowed desire for "immoral and shameful things"—black bodies, the lusted-after objects of colonial desire, imagined by the colonizer and slave master alike as hypersexual and bestial.[8] Greg Thomas thus observes that the specific historical crucibles of racialization—slavery and colonialism—as the cultural-historical processes by which "race" is produced through violent carnality, are simultaneously the cultural-historical processes by which "sex" or "sexuality" is conferred, as if these social processes are "natural" and not in fact normative, and are not in fact one and the same.[9] For this reason, Bin Wahad astutely observes that COINTELPRO had a prominent "psycho-sexual" dimension.[10]

If we follow Fanon closely, however, we must extend and modify Bin Wahad's assessment of the psychosexual in order to calibrate it to Bukhari's genderless revolutionary. For Fanon, the psycho-political repression marked by the phallic order of white racist culture is sociogenic: it does not simply produce individual pathology, but rather generates Negrophobic genders and sexualities as a rule, constructed as they are in the phallic order of the West around "phobogenic" victims conceived not as human beings but rather as "walking, stalking, human-sized erections," to use Fanon's masculinist illustration.[11] Fanon explains that neither the white man nor the white woman, therefore, can be properly categorized as "heterosexual": "That is because the Negrophobic woman is in fact nothing but a putative sexual partner—just as the Negrophobic man is a repressed homosexual."[12] Thomas, in addressing Fanon's own Negrophobia, "internalized by a colonized elite," and typically read by the liberal academy in the West as homophobia or misogyny, notes that Negrophobia is delimited neither by gender nor by sexuality, and thus a similar analysis of phobias surrounds black females who are no less construed by white supremacy as hypersexual. Moreover, Thomas completes and distills Fanon by concluding that heterosexuality and homosexuality are racially exclusive formulations of repression in that they are reserved for white bodies alone. The erotic identities of Negrophobic white men and women are both anchored in black male and female bodies, which, as Thomas explains, since these black objects of desire "are scripted as sub-human, cannot possibly participate in the human sexuality of heterosexuality or even repressed homosexuality, proper. . . . Black people are barred from this category of human being and its specious categories of modern, human sexuality."[13] Within the context of Negrophobia, then, Thomas concludes that the "genders and sexualities of the white West can in no way conform to their own social ideals or descriptions. . . . The myth of Black *and white* heterosexuality and homosexuality should be destroyed."[14]

Is this what Bukhari means by "a revolutionary has no gender"? Was COINTELPRO an erotically violent pogrom precisely because it was responding to the profoundly destabilizing psychosexual implications of revolutionary blackness? Sex and gender politics under revolutionary struggle affirm that racial formation and sexual subjection are inextricably linked, and confirm that slave relations remain, rather than were, a vortex of sexual violence. In the era of COINTELPRO, the hydraulics of state terror continue to be formulated in terms of gender relations and sex. Bukhari notes the effect of a COINTELPRO murder of a Panther comrade in broad daylight on a busy Harlem street in March 1971.

> The person was a paid killer, receiving thousands of dollars. [Robert's] body-guard had been pistol-whipped, and he was killed, and the police did nothing. It was clear that they were working in conjunction with the killers. So our paranoia wasn't really paranoia at all—we actually had a basis in fact to be on the defensive. . . . We sandbagged the office and our living quarters, and security was beefed up. We weren't allowed to be around family members, and the children were put in safe locations. We were trying to protect our families and to continue as best we could doing our work. But finally it was decided that the Party could no longer function aboveground because of the conditions.[15]

This scene from the COINTELPRO dossier should be read alongside the history of plantation slavery, wherein black males and females were forced to produce offspring to enhance the wealth of the slave owner. The deployment of sexual crimes to reproduce the relations of slavery (motherless and fatherless breeding) points to how, in Sylvia Wynter's terms, blackness is the symbolic negation of womanhood and manhood, as much as it is of whiteness—thereby underscoring how sexual violence and the explosion of gender categorization evince the fundamental antagonism of blackness for the social formation of the United States.[16]

The absolute vulnerability of black domesticity signified by the COINTEL-PRO scene related by Bukhari above is structurally analogous to the slave quarters. We must use both "private" and "home" under erasure since there is no sanctuary for black bodies because captivity is a constituent element of black life, whether under slavery, COINTELPRO, or the present prison-industrial complex where the war on drugs and the police practice of raiding black homes and neighborhoods becomes the context for the rise of militarized policing and asset forfeiture laws that permit law enforcement to confiscate the features of the black domestic sphere without criminal conviction or even due process.[17] The notion that black home is an oxymoron, no different than prison, is an insight that echoes across the generations of black critical expression, from Malcolm X to George Jackson to hip hop; we need to nuance this analysis with the recognition that it represents sexual violence against the erotic possibilities of black liberation, wherein black family, "blood," and the integrity of human sexuality, functionally outlawed by antiblackness, is resurrected as a possibility by the radical imaginings of the Panthers. In her well-known take on this terrain, Hortense Spillers reads slavery as the institutionalization of bodily rupture. Without bodies to claim as their own, writes Spillers, the enslaved are also structurally precluded from claiming "relations" between themselves.[18] Black mothers and fathers cannot claim their children: black flesh is always already claimed by direct relations of force.[19]

COINTELPRO's intended destruction of the black family and community represents the natal alienation of enslavement: the slave is isolated from both descending and ascending generations; mothers and fathers are precluded from being able to make any claims on their children; while their descendants are deprived of the identity and belonging that genealogy provides. The generation of black children that suffered abandonment due to state violence and the restructuring of the political economy, genealogically isolated from their revolutionary parents living in exile, incarcerated, or killed by COINTELPRO, would come to be referred to as "the hip-hop generation." Hip-hop artist Tupac Shakur is unexceptional in this respect, although he may be the most well-known embodiment of this context. Tupac was aggrieved by the gruesome pattern of family interference and destruction that he witnessed growing up around the Panthers. He recounted the experience of FBI agents approaching him at school seeking the whereabouts of his stepfather, Mutulu Shakur.[20] Afeni Shakur, Tupac's mother, speaks about the disorientation and pain that Tupac endured in these situations: "When you talk about the pain that the child felt, especially when you realize that you can't change it, it is hard. It is such a deep place."[21] Similarly, Afeni Shakur discusses one of her comrades in the New York Panther 21 trial of 1970–1971 who was forced into exile in Algeria:

It's really a very cruel thing; his child now is almost two [at the time, 1970], and he's only seen her when she was very small, when she was just born. This is the beginning of the many broken hearts and broken dreams, you know, in the Party. It just was something else, something that I'll never be able to forgive this government for. I think that that's one of my biggest beefs, that Sekou is unable to walk the streets and talk to people like he's supposed to because he's so beautiful. I heard that in Algeria, the children come to the window and they're just screaming, "Sekou, Sekou, Sekou." They're always around the house because they love that man. I understand it. I could just see it. I know that it happens. I mean it's not hard for me to believe.[22]

Shakur clearly communicates the fundamental meaning of the state's war against the black community during the long civil rights era and definitively rebuts the racist discourse about black family pathology that sought to legitimate the state's rupture of black parental rights and of the rights of black children to be parented.

In Ksisay Sadiki's video documentary-in-progress called "Panther Cubs," children of the Panthers, themselves now adults with children of their own, talk about the effects of growing up under conditions of revolutionary struggle and counterinsurgency warfare. One "Panther cub" describes the experience as akin to being a survivor of domestic violence, incest, or rape, in that the state repression is so utterly disavowed by the society at large, and in addition, their parents had to impose a strict code of silence in their families for their own protection, so that the children were left with no voice with which to articulate the violence and no external reflection to affirm their experience. In *The Wretched of the Earth*, Fanon describes this as "the peaceful violence that the world is steeped in."[23]

The discourse on colorblindness, then, emerges from a context of profound anxiety and self-consciousness about the ongoing impunity and brutality of the state's relationship to black Americans. The concerted effort to define racism as merely individual acts of bias betrays a desire to hide the reality of gratuitous violence against black bodies and institutionalized oppression against black communities. Whereas colorblindness emerged from the midst of a raw and violent period of social protest and state repression, seeking to transform the meaning of these struggles from a political contest to merely a matter of criminality, post-racialism appears after four decades of law-and-order retrenchment. With respect to hip-hop culture today, the black revolution—and all meaningful assertions of black resistance—must be killed off in order that the colorblind nation, with its enormous market and cultural interest in hip hop, may live.

Lil Wayne and Erotic Rebellion

From the promises that break by themselves to the breaks with great promise, in the words of Sekou Sundiata, the hip-hop generation rose from the devastation of the state's war against black revolutionaries to carry on the tradition of irreverence and creative artistry that historians like Robin D. G. Kelley remind us have been a central component of black expressive vernacular culture since at least the baaadman tales of Jelly Roll Morton in the late nineteenth century and the age-old tradition of "signifyin."[24] Lil Wayne's "Mrs. Officer" is of this tradition and mystifies it at the same time—and in this way it is a quintessential anthem for the post-racial era. The sobering realities of economic and political pressure for artists today, however, mean that we need to read the historical milieu and the cultural text together against the grain of both Western bourgeois academic discourse on intersectionality and didactic antiracist politics.

For Thomas, evaluating black expressive culture in light of the context of gratuitous violence and the police power means recognizing that black culture embodies an "ethics of violence" that enables or encourages it to oppose, counter, and correct the antiblack violence in which the world is steeped.[25] In other words, it's not that black people are or black culture is pathologically violent; rather, the world has been pathologically violent toward blacks for over six centuries, and therefore, black expressions of violence are ethical as counterviolence. Indeed, because the formation of the modern world took place through the sexual violation of black bodies, racialization, the making of race and what that means in terms of power, occurs at the nexus of sex and violence.[26] Because of the intrinsically sexual nature of this antiblack violence, then, Thomas's study of hip hop describes what he calls "sexual poetic justice" in black expressive cultures as a doorway to rethinking black subjugation and revolution by undermining the eroticism that patriarchy invests in rape and allowing a new eroticism to emerge from the violence of resistance, from its pleasures.[27]

For example, before sending a promise note of revenge to "women abusers" everywhere, Lil' Kim raps in "Cell Block Tango (He Had It Comin')" with Queen Latifah and Macy Gray on the 2003 soundtrack to the movie *Chicago*: "I'm not guilty, just tryna protect mine / It ain't my fault he ran into my knife twenty times."[28] Thomas is clear that this unabashed affinity for sexual counterviolence in hip hop shares a tradition of outlaw sexual poetic justice with blues songstresses of an earlier era, such as Bessie Smith and Dinah Washington, who sang "Send Me to the 'Lectric Chair" "'cause I done cut my good man's throat." But sexual poetic justice in black music is also closely connected with Black Power–era women who dismissed what is legal for what is right and necessary. In the famous 1974–1975 trial of *State v. Joan Little*, the nation learned that Little had killed her sexual assailant, the jailer of the Beaufort County Jail in Washington, North Carolina, where she had been an inmate at the time. After the killing, Little became a fugitive, but she turned herself in, and just as she had on the night of her jailer's attempted rape, she defended herself again at trial: "I ran because it was self-defense. . . . If the authorities there [in Beaufort County] had gotten to me before any other body . . . I never would have been here to tell what really happened."[29] There was significant debate within the local community as to whether a young, poor, single, independent, and sexually active black woman could even be violated in the first place—reflecting, in short, that the black woman's relation to civil society is the fungible, violent, relation of an object, ontologically deprived of bodily integrity. As Genna McNeil observes, Little's decision to remain in North Carolina to defend herself at trial affirmed her status as a "self-assertive and defiant" woman of autonomy and resistance, "rather than solely self-defensive."[30]

Bukhari's experience in the BLA extends Little's description of the state's policing of black female sexuality and the necessary articulation of counterviolence and sexual justice. Imprisoned in April 1975 as a result of a COINTELPRO attack that killed two of her comrades, Bukhari writes about her ordeal trying to get medical treatment from authorities at the Virginia Correctional Center for Women. "Inside the prison, I was denied care. The general feeling was that they could not chance hospitalization for fear I would escape; as such, they preferred to take a chance on my life."[31] Noting that when "help," or the "doctor," did attend to the women in the prison, it simply wrought even greater havoc than mere neglect, Bukhari documents an inventory of abuse that we must recognize as sexual violence: "Their lives are in the hands of a 'doctor' who examines a woman whose right ovary has been removed and tells her there is tenderness in the missing ovary. This 'doctor' examines a woman who has been in prison for six months and tells her that she is six weeks pregnant and there is nothing wrong with her. She later finds her baby has died and mortified inside of her. Alternatively, he tells you that you are not pregnant and three months later, you give birth to a seven-pound baby boy." Bukhari started hemorrhaging in December 1976 and sought help at the clinic. "No help of any consequence was given, so I escaped." While on escape, a doctor counsels her that she needs surgery; two months later, Bukhari was recaptured. In a manner of resistance that recalls Little's conviction to stand trial in North Carolina to affirm her right to her body, Bukhari decides to use the lack of medical care as her defense for the escape "to accomplish two things: (1) expose the level of medical care at the prison and (2) put pressure on them to give me the care I needed." By the time she finally got medical attention in June 1978, it was too late: "I was so messed up inside that everything but one ovary had to go. . . . I was forced to have a hysterectomy."[32]

The erotic power and presence to free oneself meets up with the "repetition compulsion" that reterritorializes the black body, from rape victim to "murderer," teenager to "criminal," community activist to "terrorist," abandoned child to "gangster." As Toni Morrison notes in *Beloved*, "freeing yourself is one thing; claiming ownership of that freed self is another."[33] Black violence is a precondition for actual engagement between blacks and civil society, a fact that Fanon explained and Black Power verified. Hip hop, in its potential as a diegesis of black revolution, in its oftentimes erotic continuation in a different form of the black liberation fighters of an earlier generation, in its ongoing stance of refusal and lyrical counterviolence to the sexual terror of COINTELPRO, explores a variety of representational strategies that we should read within the context of an "ethics of violence."

Lest we think that sexual poetic justice is an extremist expression, of an earlier, more politicized period, or of the hardcore fringe in hip hop, consider the current reigning black pop diva, Rihanna. In "Man Down," Rihanna shoots dead her sexual assailant. In the video, Rihanna is confident, independent, and embraced within her community; she goes on her own to the club, dancing freely, celebrating the erotic rites of dance with other women and men—until her assailant follows her from the club and attacks her. The violence temporarily brings a darkness to Rihanna's world that is not lifted until her counterviolence. "Man Down" intentionally evokes Bob Marley's anticolonialist classic hit "I Shot the Sheriff," but from a womanist perspective. By placing the shooting at the beginning of the song, Rihanna constructs her violent act not as a denouement or undoing of her erotic power, but rather as an expression of it, a warning of the hazard facing men who violate women, or who interfere with the feminist fertility rituals of the dancehall. She champions an "undomesticated sexuality," uncontained and undisciplined by patriarchy. Although Rihanna is a now a global pop icon, filming "Man Down" in her native Caribbean facilitates her use of the lyrical gun-play popular in dancehall culture of the region and allows her to tap into the "mass-based alternative morality" in the Caribbean tradition of sexually unrepressed and aggressive women on the dance floor.[34]

The condemnation of "Man Down"—and of "Russian Roulette," "Hard," "Love the Way You Lie," and a number of other songs and videos by Rihanna— points to the centrality of an ethics of violence and sexual poetic justice to black women's representational practices, and more importantly, to the specific positionality of black female sexuality within such matrices of violence. One condemnation of "Man Down" demonstrates how Rihanna's artistic expression becomes laced with her personal life in order to construe her body as the evidence of deviance posed by black female sexuality.

> "Man Down" is an inexcusable, shock-only, shoot-and-kill theme song. In my 30
> years of viewing BET, I have never witnessed such a cold calculated execution
> of murder in primetime. Viacom's standards and practices department has
> reached another new low.[35]

This commentator, Paul Porter of the Parent Television Council, is not simply denouncing the evocative imagery as too violent. What disturbs his sensibilities—and those of both feminists and antifeminists alike—is that Rihanna is not behaving as a domestic violence survivor should act. Porter is censuring Rihanna as a survivor, and moreover, is condemning her artistic representation of gendered violence against women in general.[36] Rihanna's aesthetic and political interpretations of domestic violence transgresses survivor politics of respectability: not only does she fight back, but she represents a more complex notion of sexuality and femininity in which violence, consensual and nonconsensual, pleasurable and painful, is something that both men and women seize hold of in their intimate spaces—as defense or retaliation from a place of strength, or as offense, compensation, retaliation, connection, and instigation from the deficits, limitations, and shortcomings of the complex human condition.

The scorn heaped on Rihanna for her initial willingness to stay with Chris Brown after he assaulted her conjoins the criticism of her artistic choices. Alisa Bierria observes that Brown's assault on Rihanna was the most publicized domestic violence incident since Anita Hill and Clarence Thomas in 1991 (although Hill–Thomas was not domestic violence per se, but rather workplace sexual harassment), noting that the sentiments expressed across social media included a preponderance of concern for Brown, the abuser, rather than Rihanna, the abused; Rihanna must have provoked Brown; Rihanna's initial decision to stay with Brown disqualifies her from social concern; and her music, including her decision to appear on Eminem's song "Love the Way You Lie" shortly after her domestic violence incident, a song that depicts how violence can be a mutually attractive and painful dynamic within intimate relationships, is grounds for the assertion that she, and not Brown, was the perpetrator in their incident. As Bierria discerns, what is at work here is not the customary blame-the-victim narrative: "characterizing this dynamic as 'victim-blaming,' which salvages the notion of a 'victim' but contends that the victim enabled the violence, misses a key point. Black women who are victims of violence are not simply accused of bringing it upon themselves, they are dis-positioned as its perpetrator."[37] Rihanna's descriptions of violence, pleasure, and pain are treated as literal, conflated with her own experience with abuse, and construed as warranting her victim-displacement. By contrast, male artists such as Eminem are granted artistic license that assumes a critical distance between a creative description of an emotional state and a literal endorsement of the violent actions depicted in the music (and all of this despite the disclosure that Eminem did in fact beat his wife).[38]

The construal of Rihanna's eroticized performances of the ethics of violence as evidence that she cannot be victimized rests on the long-standing and ensnaring character of the sexual crimes perpetrated against blackness. The utter vulnerability of black sexuality during slavery dislodged the responsibility for sexual crimes onto its victim, incorporating the violations of enslavement as shame. Her sexual exploitation served as evidence of the slave woman's power to render her master weak, to become the "mistress of her own subjection."[39] Rihanna evinces Saidiya Hartman's point that the "captive female does not possess gender as much as she is possessed by gender—that is, by way of a particular investment in and use of the body."[40] The violent matrix of subjection, vulnerability, and culpability possessing black sexuality characterizes the symbolic space of popular culture precisely because it continues to underwrite the institutions that seek to control black self-determination. In the previous chapter, I argued that "reasonable suspicion" covers for a sexual violence spectacularized in the criminal law as much as it is in popular culture. Cases such as *Denson v. United States* or *Ware v. City of Detroit, et al.*, and innumerable others besides, are only possible because of the routine day-to-day sexual hostility and aggressions toward black people. The ethics of violence depicted in black popular culture confronts this violence through an articulation with the modes of self-determination black people exercise in various mundane ways.

Lil Wayne exemplifies the tradition of erotic rebellion from Smith and Washington to Little and Bukhari in some important respects, but he also betrays both a shared positioning with and an ethic divergent from that of a black woman like Rihanna. The meanings and potential meanings in "Mrs. Officer" are both well buried and hidden in plain sight, and in a playful and erotic insouciance, Lil Wayne enjoins a tradition of humor, irreverence, and illicit eroticism in which black pleasure intersects with politics, identity, and power. Lil Wayne appropriates and recasts stereotypes of black men as hypersexual beings with large penises ("my hands so big you thought I told ya to pull it over") and insatiable appetites ("my face on every wanted poster"). Where Ice-T used to refer to himself as a "white woman's dream," a tongue-in-cheek conjuring, and at the same time parodying, of the historical mythology of the black male's sexual largess and prowess, Lil Wayne's "gifts" or "skills" command the attention of all females, represented as the whole police force of "lady cops": "I'm wanted by every lady cop all over." He transforms the definitive trope of undesirability, the ubiquitous stereotype of black male criminality ("my face on every wanted poster"), into a sign of his sexual desirableness—even that he is husband material ("I know you wish your name was Mrs. Carter, huh?"). Handcuffs come to mark sexual excitement rather than state violence, and rough treatment is a welcomed expression of brimming desire and unrepressed eroticism ("put me in handcuffs / start ripping my pants off"), drawing on the well-developed play in sadomasochism between pleasure and pain. And the resulting screams of ecstasy—"Wee Ooh Wee Ooh Wee"—emitted from the "lady cop" inside the patrol car where Lil Wayne is "beating it like a cop" mimic the sound of a police siren, turning the omnipresent portent of danger in urban black communities into a gong-sound of erotic triumph.

Following Carolyn Cooper's study of Jamaican dancehall, Lil Wayne's expression of hypersexuality, typically dismissed as vulgar, obscene, or apolitical, should itself be read as an intervention in state discourses of power. In the Jamaican context, this expression would be described in terms of the dancehall reference to "slackness," which Cooper suggests should be understood as "an ideological revolt against law and order; an undermining of consensual standards of decency."[41] Moreover, Cooper sees "slackness" in terms of a specific conception of the erotic, as encompassing the aspirational desires of the economically marginalized, expressed sexually and materially. Jamaican folkways maintain that the body is a vessel transporting the soul, and as such, the body must be protected from exploitation and adorned in splendor, reflecting the "incontestable" worth of the soul it encases.[42] The history of slavery has subjected the body to grotesque forms of exploitation, of course. "For a stubborn 'hard core' of the Jamaican people," states Cooper, this historical burden means that "work must be seen as yielding reasonable rewards or it will not be done willingly."[43] Lil Wayne's "slackness," in other words, comments on racialized tropes about commodifiable bodies while marshaling the body itself toward this end.

Cooper's evocation of "slackness" connects us to Ronald Judy, who lays weight on the matter of black bodies categorically excluded from Western culture's requisite registers of human legibility, such as "labor." For Judy, hardcore black cultural forms such as hip hop convey black identity after the end of work. He evokes the hard core in this way:

> It is no longer possible to be black against the system. Black folk are dead, killed by their own faith in willfully being beyond, and in spite of, power. Will beyond power has no passion, only affect. Black folk have killed themselves by striving to conserve themselves in a willful affect—the productive labor of modern subjects, aka work. Black folk, who have always been defined in relation to work, went the way of work. . . . Real black folk are already dead, walking around consuming themselves in search of that which is no longer possible, that which defines them. . . . A nigga is that which emerges from the demise of human capital, what gets articulated when the field nigger loses value as labor. The nigga is unemployed, null and void, walking around like . . . a nigga who understands that all possibility converts from capital, and capital does not derive from work.[44]

The hypersexuality of Lil Wayne embodies aspirational desires and at the same time represents an utter disdain for civil society's rules overseeing material gain and upward mobility. In "Mrs. Officer," he erotically adorns his body with accumulated capital, as it were, as well as the symbology of social and sexual potency (e.g., luxury automobiles, jewelry, body art)—without the exploitative drag of actually exposing his labor to the alienation of surplus value, and thereby becoming someone else's private property. More to the point, however, is that Judy's notation on "work" is simultaneously a historical analysis, a cultural reading, and an ontological intervention. While labor exploitation has historically been a commonality of black existence in the West, the fact that black labor power is largely tangential (surplus) to the present era of neoliberal global capitalism does not signify a change in black positionality within the social structure. Rather, it reveals "work" to be inessential to black dispossession and incidental to antiblack violence in the modern world—after all, labor is not the primary reason for the slave's existence. In these terms, then, Lil Wayne is today's leading artisan of "slackness." While he appears to embody what critics of hip hop and youth culture tediously harp on (apathetic, amoral, and undisciplined), in fact, such slackness bespeaks an awareness *in the body* as to one's accumulation and fungibility for purposes of society's aggrandizement. Whether the rebellious slave whose humanity the law recognized only in order to ascribe criminal culpability, the Black Panther Party armed for self-defense, the hip-hop artist throwing sonic and metaphorical bombs, or the counterviolence of sexual poetic justice, lyrical or actual, the main reason why counterviolence by black people is profoundly destabilizing to civil society is what it calls into question: the gratuitous antiblack violence of the police power necessary for the coherence of our society.[45]

Lil Wayne and the Persona of Sociohistorical Violence

Although violence, and representations of violence, by black men are virtually never conceived in relation to their sexual victimization, this oversight is a scandal for critical thought given the ubiquity of antiblack sexual violence. The banality of racial profiling, stop-and-frisk, and other forms of police harassment in black communities is a feature of the sexual structural vulnerability blackness signifies. Accordingly, it is imperative that critical analysis behold hip-hop culture writ large as embodying this context of sexual violence. Within the contested field of representation and the counternarratives of black performance that I point to above, racialized policing and punishment emerges simultaneously with a traumatic sexual violence that constitutes an effaced engagement with the history of plantation slavery and its production of modes of black selfhood, its desires and practices. Deciphering how hip hop navigates this terrain can be instructive to our larger concern with antiblackness in the era of post-racialism because hip-hop masculinities are seen as always and already preoccupied with their erasure, "emasculation." The emasculation of the black male has served as a primary trope for reading both the founding scene of black male subjectivity and as an explanatory figure for a range of discussions premised on a pathological "black manhood."[46]

In "Mrs. Officer," Lil Wayne's assumption of masculine authority must pass over the structural positionality of black women, situated historically between the violent sexual aggression of both white and black men. The interdependent terms of racialized antagonism through which black and white masculinities are ideologically engendered as opposites—as subordinate and dominant subjects competing for positions of mastery—means that women are reduced to mediums for realizing male power. Although Lil Wayne begins the video as the policed subject in the scenario, this dynamic inverts itself quickly so that instead of a "lady cop," we see only black male cops policing women of color. The male cops arrest the women from their vehicles at traffic roadblocks and process them through central booking: fingerprinting, mug shots, perp lineup. The features of criminal arrest thus become the eroticized scene of captive black female sexuality, controlled by male authority.

"Mrs. Officer" aims for a degree of cross-racial male bonding in its viewing audience, and the key to understanding this bonding is Lil Wayne's urgency in suppressing the unspoken history of institutionalized sexual violence against black men; the female body, and especially the woman of color, is the medium through which this suppression is accomplished. For instance, the everyday reality of sexual violence in the form of police harassment and brutality on black and brown men, which in 1997 played out notoriously in New York City in the form of Abner Louima's brutal hours-long gang rape and torture by at least a dozen NYPD officers—essentially, as Lil Wayne raps in "Mrs. Officer," "she pulled me over / pulled me out the rover / then she pulled me closer / threw me in the back of the car / put me in handcuffs start ripping my pants off"—this racialized sexual violence by men on other men becomes impermissible knowledge.[47]

Something interesting happens during the performance of what cannot be spoken—the sexual violence of the law. Lil Wayne and the black men in the video find empowerment through the law, as police officers, not against it, affirming that while hip hop and young black men in general constitute the prototypical (sexual) threat against which civilization must defend, the gains of the post–civil rights era are such that they also must aspire to the very venues of society and state geared toward their captivity.[48] To wit, because of the uniform, not despite it, blacks remain the objects, not the subjects, of cultural narratives about policing; they are still the targets of the police power even while performing such power themselves. In this sense, then, Lil Wayne's presentation in "Mrs. Officer" of a criminalized blackness appears simultaneously as a (sexual) political problem and the apparatus marshaled to its containment. As Wilderson puts it, "few characters aestheticize White supremacy more effectively and persuasively than a Black male cop."[49] The white male viewer is thus returned to his safe place of self-identification and mastery, but at the same time has been able to indulge in that commonplace white fixation with black male sexuality as something threatening and dangerous. In short, what is happening in "Mrs. Officer," then, is that white men are alternately fantasizing about and repulsed by the conquest of women of color, the conquest of black men, and their own conquest by black men.

But none of this can be spoken. Indeed, it is nigh unrepresentable, although such relations are clearly well documented historically, albeit mostly in literature rather than in history or the social sciences. Toni Morrison's famous chain-gang scene in *Beloved* depicts the subordination of black men to the sexual gratification or dominance of white male masters in starkly oblique terms: "Chain-up completed, they knelt down. . . . Kneeling in the mist they waited for the whim of a guard, or two, or three. . . . Occasionally a kneeling man chose gunshot to his head as the price, maybe, of taking a bit of foreskin with him to Jesus. Paul D did not know that then. He was looking at his palsied hands, smelling the guard, listening to his soft grunts so like the doves."[50] According to Darieck Scott, Morrison attempts to figure both "the sexual exploitation of men and the silence surrounding" this violence.[51] Indeed, Lil Wayne himself attempts to bracket out his own personal sexual violation as a young boy, passing it off as entirely unspectacular in terms of violence.

In a scene from an unauthorized documentary, *The Carter*, released on the Internet in 2009, Lil Wayne jokes openly about his surrogate father, Baby, facilitating Lil Wayne's sexual victimization at age eleven. In the documentary, he goes on to tell Lil Twist, a fifteen-year-old member of Wayne's record label Young Money, "I loved it. . . . I'm a do you like Baby and them did me"—meaning that he is going to get Lil Twist raped too.[52] In a subsequent appearance on *Jimmy Kimmel Live!* on March 3, 2009, Kimmel asks Lil Wayne if it is true that he lost his virginity at age eleven. Clearly taken aback by the question, Wayne first attempts to laugh it off, but then tells his story. Kimmel and his other guest that evening, none other than the respected television news anchor Charlie Gibson, tease Lil Wayne about the incident, construing it as irrefutable proof of Wayne's intrinsic sexual prowess, and ignoring Wayne's concession that it was a harmful experience to him.

Although Lil Wayne's recounting of his violation on national television left out the critical role of his parent, he is acutely aware on *The Carter* that it was his putative father Baby who authorized his rape: "I'm a do you like Baby and them did me." In his reading of the 2002 film *Antwone Fisher*, another narrative that depicts black masculinity as under assault by intramural factors—namely, again, black parental figures—rather than besieged by the structural antagonism of antiblackness and the internalized violence it induces within black community, Wilderson observes the complex manner in which white supremacy exerts the technologies of accumulation and fungibility on blacks while giving the appearance that the technologies emerge from within black people themselves.[53] Ultimately, Lil Wayne's personal story stresses that "black masculinity" and "black family" are oxymorons[54]—not because Baby's overseeing of the rape violates the parent's role as protector, nor because the event indelibly impacted Lil Wayne's development of a healthy masculine identity; rather, because of Fanon's claim that blackness is a void beyond human recognition and incorporation, and therefore, the relational categories of filiation, let alone the customary aspects of sexuality such as "pleasure" and "desire" ("I loved it . . . it was good"), are inapplicable. When Fanon states that the black person has no ontological resistance in the eyes of the Other, in regards to Lil Wayne's sexual violation this means that his suffering cannot be heard or recognized for what it is. The stunning exchange on *Jimmy Kimmel Live!* illustrates as much:

> KIMMEL: Is it true that you lost your virginity at age eleven?
>
> LIL WAYNE: Wow . . . wow . . . that's very true, very very true.
>
> KIMMEL: Same with Charlie . . .
>
> GIBSON: I didn't know you *could* lose your virginity at eleven years old.
>
> (LAUGHTER ALL AROUND)
>
> KIMMEL: *We* can't (gesturing between himself and Gibson), but *he* did (indicating Lil Wayne). . . . Do you feel like that affected you negatively, in your adulthood?
>
> LIL WAYNE: Yeah, it did, yeah.
>
> KIMMEL: You have a son of your own now . . . how old is he?
>
> LIL WAYNE: He's four months.
>
> KIMMEL: Is he a virgin?
>
> (laughter)

From Paul D to Lil Wayne, black sexual subjection is pleasurable to white male dominators (and their audiences), endlessly fungible across space and time. Kimmel and Gibson may appear to be relating to Lil Wayne through the valence of masculine bonding, and yet Kimmel and Gibson note that the putative common bond with Lil Wayne—being men—is in fact a ruse: "I didn't know you *could* lose your virginity at eleven years old" . . ."*We* can't, but *he* did." The "gender conceits of empire," as Thomas puts it, bar blacks: white supremacy allocates manhood and womanhood to white bodies alone.[55] Black existence is without analog, and therefore, despite recognizing that for themselves being raped at age eleven would be bad, wrong, and indeed, grounds for someone's criminal prosecution, Kimmel and Gibson find Lil Wayne's experience humorous. In this fashion, Lil Wayne's effort to laugh off his victimization, to enjoin the (white) masculine narrative that would crowd out any manifestation of structural antagonism, is undone, unwittingly reiterating Hartman's prescient words: "every attempt to employ the slave in a narrative ultimately resulted in his or her obliteration."[56] Lil Wayne's laughter is the soundtrack of social death.

Lil Wayne's performance in "Mrs. Officer," as well as in *The Carter* if not on *Jimmy Kimmel Live!*, seems to begin with the assumption that black masculinity is the law, rather than an oxymoron indicative of a structural antagonism into which black humanity has been captured by the force of law. In order to redeem himself as such—as a man—Lil Wayne must "beat it like a cop": meaning, black women must take the rap for his "ontological excess."[57] The fourteen-year-old girl who carried out the older men's directives to "Suck Lil Wayne's little dick! Girl, you know you're such a good dick sucker!" (as Lil Wayne recalls it in *The Carter*) remains anonymous, conveniently sucked into a void of her own, alongside Lil Wayne, into the space where differing levels of consent and coercion are collapsed into the desires of more powerful men. That Lil Wayne's rape came directly at the hands of this fourteen-year-old girl makes the absence of her consent, the obliteration of her victimhood, no less significant. To consider this episode in both of their lives in any terms other than coercion is to discount the modalities of accumulation and fungibility organizing black bodies in the modern world, wherein captive flesh is "available for all manner of figuration and fantasy."[58] The assaultive power of Lil Wayne's assailant was, at best, "a displacement of the *organized* violence consistently required of captivity and, further, a dissimulation of the *institutionalized* sexual power" of slavery's afterlife.[59]

In "Mrs. Officer," then, we could decipher the "illocutionary force" of the figure of the female cop in similar terms as prepubescent Lil Wayne's fourteen-year-old "rapist."[60] Whereas the mediating role of the fourteen-year-old girl ostensibly softens the force of Lil Wayne's sexual exploitation by his surrogate father, the fact that the cop in "Mrs. Officer" is female mystifies the sexual violence of white supremacy. The woman cop (in other words, the fact that the police officer is female) is necessary to obscure the sexual desire of the white male spectator for the black male body; she is needed to soften the image (and thus mute the reality) of sexualized state violence against black bodies; she lends the black male power: Lil Wayne purports to turn surveillance by the state into a conquest of his own. The woman cop (the fact that the woman is a police officer) is requisite for obscuring the widespread realities of violence against women and making misogyny more palatable: as a cop, she deserves a beating or getting fucked; as a cop in the black community, she started it; as a cop, she is not really female and he is not really using her as a sexual object (since state power is seen as synonymous with male authority, not female). Lil Wayne is attempting to delineate his subjectivity within the crucible of antiblack violence and sexual repression, carving out a space for the embodied performance of black eroticism, always and already illicit, dangerous, and subversive. Yet what I am suggesting is significant here is how he counters state violence and the limits he quickly runs up against. He imagines a counterviolence—which, mind you, he is positioned to ethically authorize, but the form this performance takes requires successive layers of gendered and sexual repression. In other words, it is the performance of antiblackness. Hardly what we mean by "sexual poetic justice," and a marker of how male performances of blackness can be recruited to ethically diverge from that of female performances, and thereby extend the racial disunity that gender-sex instigates within the black community. Lil Wayne needs some blackhood.

Queer Post–Black Studies

I suggest that "Mrs. Officer" shows how reading black erotic struggle through hip hop is to not only consider the sexual violence of COINTELPRO, but also to confront how hip hop is today both a scene and a medium for COINTELPRO's redux. Here I am referring to more than the well-documented existence of the "hip-hop cops," the local and federal law enforcement task forces devoted to the hyperpolicing of hip-hop artists and their crews.[61] Regina Kunzel has shown that in the long history of sex in prison, it was only within the "aftermath of the civil rights movement and embattled expressions of black power, and at a time in which black men were incarcerated at increasingly disproportionate rates"—in other words, during COINTELPRO's chaperoning of the nascent prison-industrial complex—that sexual violence came to define civil society's view of the prison experience.[62] Kunzel writes:

The recognition of sexual coercion and violence behind bars, then, was far from new in the 1960s and 1970s. But writers in this period drew attention to the subject in an increasingly urgent and unrelenting way. Their accounts were newly ubiquitous, newly graphic, and newly univocal in depicting sexual violence and brutality, so much so, in fact, that rape would come to be understood as the defining practice of sex in men's prisons.[63]

According to Kunzel, the ascendance of rape as the signature violence of incarceration is construed not as a manifestation of institutionalized control over captive sexually subjected bodies. Rather, the prison is specifically imagined as a site of sexual violence as the result of an inverted racial hierarchy in which black men avenge their historic castration under white supremacist patriarchy by raping white men. This discursive context facilitates the easy fluctuation in "Mrs. Officer" between black male performers dressed as law enforcement in one scene, followed by the same performers dancing in orange prison jumpsuits in a subsequent scene. Although the latter comment critically on the violent role of the former in black life, in hegemonic discourse the signs are not at odds but rather conjoin and conform to the notion that black male sexual predators populate the nation's streets, jails, and prisons. Hip hop, then, provides more than a renewed platform on which representations of black masculinity converge with images of criminality and incarceration; it discursively secures for contemporary audiences the notion of racialized sexual violence disseminated by the slave master and lynch mob of earlier periods: the music video serves as medium for the continual circulation and "global touring" of the black male rapist.[64] It is not Lil Wayne that accomplishes this mythology, although he has been recruited to its terms. Rather, it points to a certain "apprehension about unchecked black male aggression" that remains a central feature of the contemporary period, as it has during every previous era since the dawn of Europeans' trade in African bodies.[65]

My discussion of Lil Wayne targets the significance of performativity and sexuality in contemporary interpretations of black cultural expression. Lil Wayne himself is not historically important; the point is to illustrate how to approach questions of black performance, and the politics of gender and sex therein, within the context of black social death. Different performances will present different content, but the underlying structure remains the same, and the question I have examined is how to read those dimensions of the ethico-political context in a particular performance that persist unchanged over time. The erotics of black self-determination threaten the prevailing structure in a variety of ways, but they do not exceed it. Escape is temporary, periodic, and always delimited by the paradigmatic capture of blackness. This story is difficult to tell, for marronage remains everywhere encompassed by the plantation—at least for the time being. A more sanguine tale is to chart the performance of black power episodically as if it represented a breakdown, or a shift, in the paradigm. This mystification of power is particularly true with respect to gender-sex. Hardly ever do you see gender-sex presented in anything other than its performative dimension, rather than told paradigmatically. Following on the analysis presented in previous chapters of "the flesh" and the deconstruction of gender-sex categorization altogether, and the ethical response supplied by "blackhood," blackness puts not only the normative histories of sexuality into crisis, but the critical-queer readings of gender-sex, as well.

The drive to tell a queer story of black gender-sex is perverse because it appears as antiracist and antiheteronormative when in fact it is inescapably embedded within an antiblack narrative that has become, in Wilderson's words, decreasingly available to speech and conscious discourse.[66] Cathy Cohen once made the case for black people as queer, by definition, given the regulation of black sexualities, bodies, and social formations throughout time as intrinsically nonnormative.[67] She demonstrated that the demonization of poor black women as "welfare queens," for instance, is connected not only to representations of black queers in pathological terms, but also to nonblack gays and lesbians as well. Cohen's intervention, however, is taken up only within queer studies, to the extent that it is acknowledged at all, as a reminder of the disconnects between gay and lesbian studies (as it was called in the 1990s) and the radical potentials of queer organizing "on the ground."[68] Cohen's more radical insight is rarely, if ever, employed by queer thinkers or activists to abandon their post of difference vis-à-vis blackness; and, to my knowledge, Cohen's point has never been taken up by black studies to abandon its embrace of gender-sex constructs—however critically reconstituted—as humanizing vehicles. If we take Cohen seriously, we see that the only ethical frame for queer and gender studies is as black studies. Absent such a position, however, and connecting with my analysis of the critical study of police and prisons in the preceding chapter and with the subtext of "Mrs. Officer" examined above, I point to a problem underlying the ground on which queer studies confronts the black archive. There is an evident "queer limit" to the memory of black struggle within leading queer and trans political discourse.[69] Three brief examples will illustrate my point about gender and sex politics amid antiblackness, and underscore my larger concern regarding the post-racial moment's elision of the structural constraints facing black performance.

Kunzel's *Criminal Intimacy: Prison and the Uneven History of Modern American Sexuality* is lauded within both queer studies and critical prison studies because it argues for the importance of the prison to the history of sexuality and for the centrality of sex and sexuality to modern imprisonment. From the vantage of black studies, however, there is a troubling parallel between how Kunzel discusses sex in prison and the narrative of slavery as a plantation romance in which slave masters and historians alike find "agency" in black slaves' "choices" to couple with white masters. Kunzel acknowledges that the matter of captivity calls into question any notion of consent or autonomous or self-possessed decision-making, or equally fundamental, the nature of desire itself—and yet, as with the scholars who assert that there were real affective bonds between slave and master, and that these bonds served to mitigate and moderate the terror and tyranny of slavery, Kunzel overrides this context of violence in favor of what she sees as the "complexity" of emotional and sexual "reciprocity." By critically exposing the discourse on sex in prison for its reliance on pathological blackness, and highlighting how fears and resentments about race eased concerns about the instability of sexual identity, Kunzel appears to be charting a provocative and progressive new chapter in the history of sexuality. In reality, however, she is reinscribing the canonical approach to Western sexuality that, far from producing a nonnormative construction of sex, simply normalizes the clean repression of "the erotic brutality of what is termed race."[70]

In *Criminal Intimacy*, sex is simply what two people do with their genitals, and statements of desire emanating from the archive, alone, negate the historical, institutional, and structural context of the "raw sexual terror" ceaselessly confronting black existence in the New World.[71] To put it differently, Kunzel relies entirely on a performative reading of gender-sex—what prison inmates say and do—absent the structural context in which gender and sex constructs acquire meaning. There is no accounting of the sexual violence that produced black incarceration in the first place, neither of the institution itself as sexual violence, nor of the qualitative differences between white and black inmates under captivity historically. Black prisoners are presumed to be equally in possession of their bodies and their will, while both parties to the sexual relationship are granted a "desire" unfettered by racism. In a society in which desire and sexuality are produced through a foundational antiblack sexual violence, it is doubtful whether anyone's desire, black or nonblack, exists unimpeached at some level by the carnal knowledge of black subjection. Following on Hartman's insights, on the one hand Kunzel obscures "the difference between the deployment of sexuality in the contexts of white kinship"—in other words, the putative "husband," sexual "partner," subject of "desire"—and the proprietorial relation that nonblacks enjoy to the body and its uses within the world. On the other hand, Kunzel effaces black fungibility—the embodiment of white dominance as desire, the regularity of sexual violence in the everyday, the relations of mastery and subjection embedded in gratuitous violence, and the extension of captivity, rather than its mere introduction, at the site of the prison.[72] The study of slavery, furthermore, reminds us that sexual control includes both its prohibition and its sanctioned performances. Kunzel fails to account for how all of these various mechanisms of sexual domination act in concert, and for this reason, *Criminal Intimacy* is a noteworthy example of queer post–black studies.

Kunzel's inability to situate her study within the realities of antiblack sexual violence sets forth her own desire for gender and sex to hold an analytical integrity that they do not actually bear. This desire animates much of the political pose in which queer studies flourishes—or, rather, flounders. To take one prominent example from queer theory today, Elizabeth Freeman's *Time Binds: Queer Temporalities, Queer Histories* argues that queer time is political work because it articulates a separate register from the time of modernity and capitalism; it is a temporality of slowness; and it allows bodies to meet across time, connecting "a group of people beyond monogamous, enduring couplehood."[73] Freeman's ability to queer time, however, is premised on slavery's enduring capacity to structure thought itself. In Freeman's hands, concepts such as "time binds," "time's wounds," and "history's holes" only further obscure and disavow how slavery, in Calvin Warren's words, continues to "work through temporal domination" that renders black people "temporally homeless."[74] Warren explains that "slavery is the vicious enterprise of situating a being outside the time of man and in the abyss of black time."[75] Freeman is proposing manipulations within the time of man, then, not the queering of time as it has been thought since the dawn of the trade in African bodies. *Time Binds* enjoins, rather than departs from, the violent metaphysics of Western thought that reduces black being to an object of exchange—in this instance of queer theorizing, it is objectified into the concept of time itself, queer or otherwise: to borrow from Warren, whenever we are talking about time, we are always talking through, if not about, slavery.[76] Freeman ultimately speaks slavery's name in her final chapter on sadomasochism, but her supposed derring-do in discussing a fringe eroticism is betrayed by her conservation of sadomasochism in the individualistic and "psychologistic language of identity politics," rather than as a social pathos gripping the entire slaveholding world.[77]

Eric Stanley employs queer time in a similar fashion to ontologize antiqueer violence. In his 2011 essay in *Social Text*, "Near Life, Queer Death: Overkill and Ontological Capture," Stanley examines "forms of queer (non)sociality" that he terms "the nothing, or those made to live the death of a near life."[78] Stanley's essay is a good example of the problems of how "social death" discourse is used to accentuate the oppressive conditions of nonblack people, and also of the fallacy of using Nazism or colonialism to theorize the meaning of racial violence. I have deconstructed these problems as features of post–black studies, and I need not revisit them here. Instead, I wish to highlight the lengths to which queer studies goes to invest gender and sex with an alterity sufficient to, as Stanley puts it, "understand how the queer approximates the cutting violence that marks the edges of subjectivity itself."[79] Stanley uses the term "overkill" to "indicate such excessive violence that it pushes a body beyond death." This is the "time of queer death," a temporality gauged to "not simply the end of a specific life, but the ending of all queer life."[80] Stanley argues that overkill proves that queers are nothing to begin with, like the slave. In other words, queers live the death of a near life and continue to die after death in a spectacular surplus of violence.

The world that produces the increasing incidence of antiqueer violence and the horrendous cases of destroyed lives that inform Stanley's meditations is indeed in need of urgent and radical intervention. The problem with the queer studies approach that Stanley exemplifies is that it relies upon the parasitic consumption of blackness in order to engorge its sense of "gender self-determination"—and parasitism is the mark of antiblackness, a decidedly counterrevolutionary impulse.[81] Adolph Reed Jr. once wrote in terms that are applicable to the queer post–black studies that I examine here: "Twenty years ago, the left called this sort of thing 'adventurism,' a distraction from both real politics and *real-politik*. Today, having suffered decades of intensifying political marginalization, too many of us are prepared to smile gamely and call it revolution."[82] Antiblack violence is gratuitous and banal; it does not require the "spectacular material-semiotics of overkill."[83] The latter is performative and existential, while the former is the very ground on which all performances of existence are staged. Any politics of gender or sex that does not attune itself to the violence without end that provides the condition for thinking simply forestalls revolutionary change. My use of Reed's "adventurism" comment, then, does not mean that the topics of Stanley's inquiry are frivolous; rather, it is meant to highlight Stanley's injudicious deployment of antiblackness that strikes me as counterrevolutionary, notwithstanding the revolutionary posture of queer radical discourse.

What would the analyses of "criminal intimacy" and antiqueer violence look like were they authored by the antiblack world's relations of force rather than civil society's relations of consent? In other words, what would gender-sex look like were it presented paradigmatically and not episodically? Here I am not referring to the violence of interpersonal relations within the space of the prison, which is the primary level at which Kunzel acknowledges the problem of consent, but rather to the violence of the power relations that the prison institutionalizes, the violence of the social itself for which the prison is but one site of institutionality. The black studies archive supplies copious instruction on this question. It would mean deconstructing the very notions of "sex" and "sexuality" as conceits of white supremacy, as Thomas demonstrates. It would mean grappling with the articulation of sex, violence, and use that structurally precludes black people from forming bodies, as Spillers makes critical in her conception of the "flesh." It would mean reconnecting with Scott's meditations on the silence within the black studies archive shrouding black male sexual victimization; confronting the script silently underwriting Kunzel's project invested in fantasies of interracial union as salvation from racial blackness; and encountering the transactions of sexual violence by which one is simultaneously made a subject and the author of one's own subjection, as Christina Sharpe has explored.[84] It would mean, moreover, developing Cohen's assessment of black people as inherently "queer" through Thomas's argument, building upon Fanon and Wynter, that not only are black people disqualified from Western notions of heterosexuality and homosexuality, but that the very terms of desire themselves are anchored to Negrophobia and, as such, cannot ethically name anybody's sexual identity or practice. Ultimately, an analysis of "criminal intimacy" accountable to the antiblack world's relations of force would entail integrating Wilderson's warning not to substitute performativity for positionality with Hartman's call to "liberate the performative from the closures of sentiment and contented subjection in order to engage the critical labor of redress."[85] As Hartman instructs, a vital step in this process is to reconcile the violence of the archive itself with the necessity of trying to represent what we cannot, the counternarratives that are doomed to the margins of the archive, never to be installed as history as such.[86] While Kunzel purports to be performing just such a task, she is in fact recovering marginalized white voices at the expense of reiterating the antiblack violence of the archive.

Similar redress from the black studies archive lies in wait for Stanley's "over-kill." Hartman is at pains to stress that the spectacles of antiblackness cannot be reproduced ethically precisely because black suffering is mundane and its spectacular reproduction obscures this reality. By contrast, Stanley needs to reproduce each gory detail of the cases of antiqueer violence he discusses in order to draw to them the status of ontologic suffering. That his argument relies upon the spectacular betrays an implicit distinction drawn against that which does not register as suffering at all—blackness. As Toni Morrison's *Beloved* inquires, *what is too much in a context already defined by its excessive violence?* If Stanley were to recognize that blackness dissembles gender-sex and that sexual violence is the ground of racialization, he might be able to see the true possibility of solidarity with black struggle: that black people are queer and that antiblack violence is about nonnormative gender-sex. He would need to blacken his praxis and subject his queer politics to black ethical demands. In short, at issue here in these examples of queer post–black studies is confusion between the performative and the structural coordinates of power that leads queer studies to appropriate blackness toward a politic not aligned with black suffering and struggle. Stanley's essay makes explicit what is more commonly an underground current of black fungibility running through queer and trans politics.

The crucial point that I will come to rest on in this chapter is that black performance can never simply refer to individual or even collective experiences with power, but instead must be dealt with in terms of a generalized condition of social pleasure and pain. In much the same way that "gender," "sex," "man," "woman," "queer," and so forth are not principally individual categories of experience at all, but rather index the social and historical structures of human life, as so deconstructed across the preceding pages and chapters of this book, so too with "power," "resistance," "terror," "pain," and "pleasure." Would this child still be alive if she were not black? Are white children at risk of being shot by police as they sleep on their grandmothers' couches?[87] Such rhetorical questions are as ubiquitous as the performance of antiblackness they always trail, like the tail on a dog, corroborating that where one is positioned in the social schema always trumps any individual experience with the police power. In fact, the tail wags the dog: the question expresses the parasitic relation between social life and black social death—black vulnerability to gratuitous violence affirms the sanctity of white life. Recent directions within black studies–affiliated scholarship on black performativity, afro-futurity, "afro-fabulation," "ambiguous heterotopias," and the like, necessarily sidestep this problem of parasitism.[88] Insofar as performativity denotes empowered action, it must grapple with the relations of power implied therein—to wit, with how "relations" itself is imbued with the power to render blackness abject. In other words, if black people are construed through gratuitous violence as nonentities, then there are no relations between blacks and nonblacks, just as you would not define the juxtaposition of objects with subjects as a "relationship." This does not mean that black subjects do not act and shape the world in an infinite variety of ways, but what it does mean is that these actions occur within a context in which nonblack society needs antiblack violence to attain human status. As Fanon explained in *Black Skin, White Masks*: "The white man slaves to reach a human level."[89] Analyses that generally work from a premise of black social life, rather than social death, fundamentally disavow this problem. Black performance should be read as taking the measure of this parasitism, not as an escape from it.

This point is a vital one because society's performance of black fungibility has changed considerably since the Middle Passage. The post-racial is thus not simply a return to earlier modes of racist culture, nor is it merely a continuation of an unbroken white supremacist society. It is, however, indicative of "the contemporary predicament of freedom" and the time of a "life lived in loss."[90] Considered within its proper ethico-political context, black cultural expression reveals the contemporary culture of politics, the post-racial, to be tendered in a collective antipathy toward the lived experience of black people, a political theater for the staging of discrepant structures of feeling arising from contrasting conceptions of suffering between black and nonblack, and a dexterous capacity to disavow the ethical force of black counterviolence and erotic rebellion. Lil Wayne and hip-hop performance has much to tell us about the world of the post-racial, but the lesson is clearly not that we are on the brink of a world without race, a world without blackness as the central syncretic hinge on which human recognition swings. Lil Wayne reminds us that the post-racial continues to rely upon black performances of what Nicole Fleetwood (extending Spillers) refers to as "excess flesh"—expression that, for all of its complex and queer layers of critique, sedimented resistance, and erotic longing, is useful for civil society's need to relegate blackness to humanity's abyss, and to repetitively disavow the knowledge of this bodily destruction through discourse such as post-racialism.[91] In the end, Lil Wayne's implicit cry to be free of being positioned psychically and materially outside humanity's distribution of values remains impermissible knowledge precisely because it is insatiable under the present regime of antiblackness in which our society is grounded.

CHAPTER SIX

Torture Outside of Pain
in the Black Studies Tradition

Let the world be a Black Poem.

—Amiri Baraka, "Black Art," 2014

This concluding chapter of the book will not offer a conclusion. When the history of blackness begins, in many ways, with a place known as the Door of No Return, there is no way to go back over the pain of history to make the present hurt less or to reinvest the future with a promise that the past mocks. As Dionne Brand observes, there are maps to the physical Door(s) of No Return, such as to Elmina Castle on the coast of present-day Ghana, or to Maison des Esclaves (House of Slaves) on Gorée Island, off the coast of Dakar, Senegal, or any number of points along the Slave Coast (Bight of Benin). "But to the Door of No Return which is illuminated in the consciousness of Blacks in the Diaspora there are no maps," writes Brand. "This door is not mere physicality. It is a spiritual location. It is also perhaps a psychic destination. Since leaving was never voluntary, return was, and still may be, an intention, however deeply buried. There is as it says no way in; no return."[1] The black studies and black radical traditions are fatally and productively embedded within this everyday terror of no return. If slavery itself is the story that cannot but must be told, as M. NourbeSe Philip puts it, then the black freedom struggle is the movement with "no way in" to the world as it is; it is the no-movement that nonetheless moves inexorably toward a (re)new(ed) world.[2] No return means that black liberation is not a reclamation project; nor is it based in reparation or restitution, for that matter. It is distinctively iconoclastic, both institutionally and representationally; or, in Aimé Césaire's inimitable poetics, it is "the only thing in the world that's worth the effort of starting: the end of the world, by God!"[3] From James Baldwin's observation made during the Atlanta "missing and murdered" case that being snatched away and never being found again may be a terror worse than death, to Toni Cade Bambara's refusal that "those bones are not my child," to Assata Shakur's avowal that "I'm not letting these parasites, these oppressors, these greedy racist swine make me kill my children in my mind, before they are even born," black thought has studiously confronted both black power's embers and black suffering's abscess.[4]

There is no prescription for fixing the situation, short of Césaire's apocalyptic vision of regeneration. This "deep sighting" by Césaire is itself perhaps the only form of redress available to the black community at this time.[5] I have shown how the forms of redress explored thus far in this study, outfitted as "justice" or "antiracism," are duplicitous, at worst, and incomplete, at best. The onslaught facing black people remains constant, and the inability to transform, or even ethically analyze, social relations and structures of power through the various practices reviewed in these pages marks the enormity of the breach. Saidiya Hartman writes that redress under such conditions entails three steps. First, rendering visible and bringing to voice the continued devastation of enslavement is requisite for rebuilding the social body. Hartman stresses that the violated body must be remembered in order that it may be "re-membered," put back together, so to speak, from the dis-integrated condition of chattel property. Second, Hartman explains that the efforts at redeeming the pained body's humanity relieve the desiccated and famished condition of fungible objecthood even as these acts of redress inevitably fall short. Third, redress pronounces "the history that hurts" and the needs and desires directed toward minimizing the violence of being dislocated from this history, in all of its torturous pain.[6]

Hartman's threefold course for redressing the pained black body in turn reveals three necessary techniques that I will use to turn attention away from unethical prescriptions to the problems examined in the pages of this study, and toward a politics of exhumation—or, charting an accountability to that which has already been decreed dead on arrival. First, the body is central. It is the primary terrain for torture and the ongoing scene of terror; it is, therefore, the central object of redress. Since the black body is violated socially, however, not simply personally or individually, redress of the pained body requires reconstituting the terms of subjectivity for the socially dead. One of the things that this means is that, as I have explored in other terms earlier in this study, the various discourses of the body, from "biology" to its political lexicon of "race" and "gender-sex," are points where blackness places the social structure under pressure precisely because they are expressions of socially constituted power relations, not biological or natural ones.

Second, redress is therefore itself an articulation of loss and a longing for repair and wholeness for the self and for the people. Such expressions of loss confront the "violence of historical dislocation and dissolution," in Hartman's words, the primary scenes of which are repetitively performed daily.[7] In other words, redressive actions must be grounded in accurate historical analysis; ascertaining what is missing is itself a necessary step toward redressing the loss, albeit an insufficient one. Third, acts of redress that attempt to bring the socially dead into the realm of the living document the ongoing troubled relation to the "human" even as they unequivocally establish the human station. There is no clear-cut line between the smooth surface operations of social death and the community's collective enunciation of need, solidarity, and futurity.[8] To the point: each and every one of the cases of state violence reviewed in this study occurred because the structure of antiblackness positions black people as subhuman, while at the same time, black people embody the society's willingness to accept their destruction as an admission of black humanity. This is how gratuitous violence works: black people are targeted for what blackness represents socially, not for what they may or may not be doing individually, and yet it is precisely individual actions, or black embodied performance (including dying), that emphatically asserts black humanity. On the one hand, only sentient beings constructed as nonhuman objects are subjected to gratuitous, rather than contingent, violence; on the other hand, precisely because of this gratuitousness, black humanity is irrefutable and structurally circumscribed—or it would not occasion the state of emergency in which the world remains mired. Redress must deal with the complex relation between this unavoidable reality and the equally inescapable need of the collective to fulfill desire "as an articulation of these tensions, limits, fissures, wounds, and ravages."[9]

My concern in this final chapter is with what happens to this issue of redress when blackness stands front and center—and yet still goes missing and murdered. Given both the long and the short historical context of black people discarded and disappeared—the long: slavery and its afterlife; the short: the post-racial era's prosecution of COINTELPRO's afterlife—how is black suffering and struggle rendered invisible when black representations take center stage? Consistent with the campaign against blackhood considered in the previous chapters, the answer is that blackness must first be deracinated of self-defense, self-possession, and collective self-determination—in short, stripped of black power. In its most egregious form, this process takes place through a posture of solidarity with black struggle. It is onto these erstwhile allies or ostensibly antiracist narratives that I train my lens. The many overtly racist representations of blackness emanating from quarters too numerous and diverse to even generalize are as they appear, nakedly antiblack; confronting such violence, however, is complicated and undermined by the covert and the insidious, the antiblack antiracisms.

This final chapter in *Blackhood Against the Police Power* further considers the police work of the antiracist and blackhood's stance apart from such treacherous formulations of blackness. In recognition of how the ally's cut can sometimes injure the deepest, and with a focus on the disquieting betrayal of delimited redress, I consider such transgressions in terms of *torture*. While "torture" usually marks what is out-of-bounds, in excess of permissible behaviors, the history of black struggle undermines the stability of this term. I suggest that under conditions of antiblackness, we must necessarily strip "torture" of all semblance of exceptionality. In this concluding chapter, I approach this ethical matter in terms of "black pain." After a brief reconstruction of "torture" accountable to black historical struggle, I evaluate what Emancipation's ongoing violence might mean for black pain. What counts as the pain of blackness involves the reconstructed conception of torture and rests on the interrogation of performativity levied in earlier chapters. To accentuate how the world as it is at present requires the black body to suffer outside of pain, I consider the recent documentary film by Liz Garbus, *What Happened, Miss Simone?*

Give Them Blacks to Eat: Torture Reconstructed

A black motorist is pulled over by a police officer. The stated reason is an improperly affixed front license plate. The officer asks the motorist if he has a driver's license. He replies that, yes of course he does, but he will need to reach into the glove compartment to get it out. The officer says no, don't do that, and don't make any sudden movements or reach where I can't see your hands. Instead, the officer asks for his name to run a check on his driver's record. She then asks the motorist if he has proper insurance. Again, he replies, yes of course, but he will need to reach into the glove compartment to get it out. No, no, the officer says, again, don't do that, no scary movements. After the officer returns from running the driver's record (which comes up clean), she hands him a ticket for driving without proper insurance (but not license), the proof of which he was not permitted to produce due to the officer's paralyzing fear of his black presence, which was in fact what attracted the officer and led to the traffic stop in the first place. Just another day on the job for the officer: duty fulfilled, numbers reached, revenue generated, status performed, authority flexed, subjection exacted. Or, we could call it the consumption of fungible blackness. For the black motorist, however, it is another day in the crosshairs. The trigger may not have been pulled this time, but the body was violated all the same—and therein lays the terror and the torture.[10]

Sara E. Johnson reports in her book *The Fear of French Negroes: Transcolonial Collaboration in the Revolutionary Americas* on the popularity of canine torture against black and indigenous combatants during the numerous conflicts in the Americas across the fifty-year period from the beginning of the successful black revolt on Saint-Domingue against France in the early 1790s on through the 1840s. The methods of torture employed by the French in a last-gasp effort to preserve control over Saint-Domingue are fairly summarized by an 1803 letter written by Donatien-Marie-Joseph de Vimeur, the Vicomte de Rochambeau, commander of Napoleon's forces on the island. The general writes, "I send you my commandant . . . twenty-eight 'bouledogues.' These reinforcements will allow you to entirely finish your operations. I don't need to tell you that no rations or expenditures are authorized for the nourishment of the dogs: you should give them blacks to eat."[11] The French had sent emissaries to Spain's colony in Cuba to purchase the specially bred dogs. Spain had perfected the gruesome use of canine torture in its colony long before the slave revolts that congealed into a full-blown war of independence on Saint-Domingue. The training of these dogs entailed a regimen of starvation and feeding only on the flesh of Africans such that they were constantly in a rabid frenzy for human flesh. The French employed the dogs mercilessly in Saint-Domingue; the British did the same on Jamaica in the Second Maroon War (1795–1796); and the Americans also used canine torture throughout the North American South, but especially in Florida during the Second Seminole War (1835–1842).

Johnson makes clear that the appearance of African-eating dogs is evidence of a state of war.[12] Plantation society by definition confounds the normative discourses of "war" and "torture" alike. The dogs were not simply trotted out when a slave escaped or to subdue an uprising. They were spectacles deployed at regular turns: sometimes paraded snarling through town; or used to execute an African tied up in the town square; or the remains of their work, such as the heads of gored victims, displayed as trophies—their terror was "an ambient one," as Johnson terms it, central in establishing an atmosphere of expected and extreme violence.[13] What *Fear of French Negroes* reveals (although Johnson does not expound upon) is how slavery is the very crucible through which the modern discourses on "war" and "torture" are reproduced as normative. In other words, the coherence of these terms as referring to states of exception and excess relies upon an off-handed disavowal of the very black pain that is its modus operandi. The fact that "war" and "torture" are routine descriptions of a state of affairs in which grotesque violence can befall a black person at any time means that they must be qualified as exceptional for nonblack society.

The role of canine torture in the long history of antiblack violence does not end with the 1840s, or even with the coming of Emancipation, of course. The many images from the long civil rights era depicting police dogs attacking black children or the police deployment of drug-sniffing dogs today to circumvent the probable cause requirement that police must meet before they can search and seize black persons and property are but two examples that come to mind—but I am not interested in writing the history of canine violence. Instead, my purpose here is to rewrite the discourse on torture, and the dogs are only useful insofar as placing the history of Europeans nourishing these beasts on black flesh under the slavocracy alongside an account of an unspectacular traffic stop today can destabilize the received meaning of the latter event in terms of "torture." Toward this end, *Fear of French Negroes* raises two issues that connect canine torture during the plantation era in the Americas with contemporary expressions of the police power. The dogs tended to offend the civilized sensibilities of the colonial elites at the time. Marcus Rainsford was a British captain in the Third West India Regiment stationed in Saint-Domingue during the Haitian Revolution and in 1805 wrote one of the few sympathetic portraits of the Haitian people to appear in the nineteenth century. In *An Historical Account of the Black Empire of Hayti*, Rainsford singled out canine warfare for condemnation, charging the French for "not merely returning to the barbarism of the earliest periods, but descending to the characters of assassins and executioners; and removing the boundaries which civilization had prescribed even to war, rendering it a wild conflict of brutes and a midnight massacre."[14]

Johnson not only observes the hypocrisy of critics of canine torture such as Rainsford, but she also logs the deeper deception in which they pitched their objections. Rainsford criticizes the French canine torture practices even while his own country of Britain had made extensive use of canine warfare during the Second Maroon War in Jamaica less than a decade prior. Of greater significance, however, as Johnson perceptively notes, is that critics like Rainsford engaged in a more fundamental disavowal by displacing the brutality of slavery itself onto one discrete feature of its structure, canine torture. Their focus on the means of subduing rebellious Africans rather than on the system that would necessitate their perfect subjection in the first place was duplicitous and betrays the fatally compromised ethical universe in which they perceived moral questions.

Rainsford's compassionate pretensions elide an obdurate reality: in his view, his fellow Europeans are barbaric not because of their compulsion to hunt, acquire, use, ravish, exploit, deplete, and destroy African people and culture, but merely because they use dogs to do so. The contorted ethics of condemning but one feature of a patently unethical system applies to contemporary discourse on "police brutality." The focus on the spectacles of policing in which officers kill unarmed black people, rather than on the routine hunt that precedes it or the larger structure that necessitates it, performs the same deception that Johnson identifies with Rainsford and other nineteenth-century critics of canine torture. The hunt for black suspects (euphemistically called "racial profiling" or "criminal profiling") is the opening act of violence and the disavowed condition of possibility for each and every subsequent act of violence by the police. The drug-sniffing or African-eating dogs may not be deployed in each and every instance, but the "ambient" terror effect, as Johnson put it, is for all intents and purposes the same. To focus on law enforcement rather than on the system that deputizes police officers with impunity and sends them out to subdue black life, already marked elsewhere as disposable and fungible, is a deception most fundamental to the operation of modern ethics.

The second issue that Johnson's discussion of canine warfare divulges is identified in a quotation she employs from C. L. R. James. To underscore her point that slave societies were by definition in a state of war, Johnson refers her readers to *The Black Jacobins* where James writes that

> though one could trap them like animals, transport them in pens, work them alongside an ass or a horse and beat both with the same stick, stable them and starve them, they remained, despite their black skins and curly hair, quite invincibly human beings; with the intelligence and resentment of human beings. To cow them in the necessary docility and acceptance necessitated a regime of calculated brutality and terrorism, and it is this that explains the usual spectacle of property-owners apparently careless of preserving their property: *they had first to ensure their own safety.*[15]

James's point that torture in the black–white paradigm bespeaks a base struggle over life and death recalls points I have made throughout this study regarding antiblack violence as prerequisite for the establishment of society in the first place. Since black people are construed as violence personified, antiblack assaults are always justified self-defense and can never be preemptive since by definition the society is intrinsically at risk from blackness. Police officers always claim self-defense when they shoot black people; that they act in the larger defense of society against the de-civilizing danger of blackness is implicit.

If we read James more broadly, however, the meaning of torture clarifies. The safety of the planters, slavers, and varied merchant-mercenary-militia of the slavocracy was tied not simply to the effective preemption of black revolt. More fundamentally, their existence as men and women, as civilized and propertied human beings, rested on captive and fungible blackness. The supreme authority of these human beings required the total submission of enslaved Africans, who existed merely as "surrogate selves," in Toni Morrison's words, for the master race.[16] Antiblack violence, in short, is the methodology for reproducing society. To return to James, then, they had first to ensure their own *survival* as human beings. The very existence of the plantation society constituted black torture; it follows that slavery's afterlife, in which each successive political economy is organized to contain black liberation, depends upon the reproduction of black torture. Torture and survival, black and white, by turns: it is generative, not simply defensive.

From slavery to lynching to the contemporary prison-industrial complex and the variety of antiblack institutional violence it features, torture retains its mundane role in social reproduction. The examples proliferate without end: the long history of medical experimentation on blacks, the preponderance of solitary confinement in the prison system, the contemporary assault on black families through the child welfare systems and the criminalization of black mothering, the usurpation of blackland, the gentrification of black schools, and so on.[17] Again, the body is central and the violence is sexual. The reconstruction of torture that I have unfolded here stands at odds with the hegemonic narrative of torture's developmental arc within criminal justice practice. This narrative typically conforms to Michel Foucault's history of modern punishment in which corporal punishment was replaced over time by a disciplinary regime designed not to injure the body but to produce its conformity. As noted earlier in this book, Joy James has definitively corrected this genealogy as erroneous for its occlusion of the gratuitous and corporeal punishment against black people that has remained constant despite the rise of the modern penitentiary.

Despite James's intervention, accounts of torture in criminal justice practice continue to claim that violence against the body is largely something of a bygone era. For instance, Jerome Skolnick claims that police use of the "third degree," physical coercion to elicit information and confessions from criminal suspects, has mainly given way to deception and trickery by the police in the post–*Miranda v. Arizona* era.[18] While police deception and psychological torture tactics may be the new standard in criminal interrogations, physical violence remains typical when the police engage with black people. The case of Jon Burge, the Chicago police commander who tortured more than two hundred suspects between 1972 and 1991 in order to coerce confessions, stands out as one prominent example of post-*Miranda* torture. As the Chicago police's torture tactics came to light, then governor George Ryan was compelled to order a moratorium on capital punishment in 2000, and eventually to clear Illinois's death row entirely in 2003, as many of the capital defendants were convicted on the basis of coerced confessions.[19]

From Foucault to Skolnick, the actual empirical record of torture exceeds the grasp of hegemonic discourse—but this is not even the half of it. The debate on torture that took shape after the Iraq War began with the U.S. invasion in 2003 bespoke how torture discourse can quarantine blackness by evoking black historical struggle and suffering. Evidence about torture practices at Abu Ghraib and other U.S. military prisons in Iraq and throughout the Persian Gulf region were revelatory and shocking to an American public deeply committed to disavowal about the role of violence in the formation and functioning of U.S. society. Even critical contributions from the political Left to the torture debate that sought to place the crimes of Abu Ghraib in the historical context of U.S. foreign policy and war making abroad betrayed the same ethical ruin these commentators share with the torturers themselves: torture, we are told by Left commentators, is what U.S. military personnel do abroad in zones of imperial occupation.[20] The analogic comparison hides more than it reveals and is symptomatic of the general dispensation toward the foreclosure of black struggle. The most earnest condemnations of torture at Abu Ghraib claimed that it was reminiscent of slavery and lynching, while some commentators went so far as to claim that military prisons abroad reflect the domestic prison regime. As Jared Sexton and Elizabeth Lee explained in their perceptive essay "Figuring the Prison: Prerequisites of Torture at Abu Ghraib," however, these facile references to history and the uncritical parallels only act as supplements to the comparison between black experience and nonblack oppression. With the source relegated to the past, black suffering serves as little more than an incubator for insight or outrage, while the realities of how Abu Ghraib stands as a diagnostic for the internal organization of a society that has been at war with itself since at least the dawn of the slave trade remain well hidden. As with the spectacles of the slave-eating dogs, this war has a crucial theatrical dimension, a performance designed to terrorize and discipline (black and white, alternately), while the violent operations of which are sometimes disavowed and rendered invisible and at other times presented in plain sight with the presumption that it is in excess of the normal, not the norm itself. Either way, Sexton and Lee remind us, blacks are distinctly debased, and the use of black historical pain to make the suffering of oppressed others more real only renders black struggle more illegible, and thereby naturalizes most forcefully "the prerequisites of torture," the constitution of structures whereby torture victims are misrecognized as such.[21]

The disappearance of black torture victims from historical memory reflects a constituent element of torture's basic structure and takes us toward the font of violence itself. In mundane events like a traffic stop, such as with the black motorist in the story above, the incident is typically described as though its primary element—black embodied suffering—were not there at all. To borrow from Elaine Scarry, black pain is transmuted into the fiction of absolute power: "law enforcement," "crime prevention," "community safety"—even "racial profiling" or "driving while black," which imply a procedural glitch—each perform a clinical conversion in which the black suffering body becomes the torture implement wielded against the motorist. As Scarry explains, the interrogation is internal to torture, not an extrinsic component of it. The police officer's standard request for "license and registration" turns out to be incidental to her assertion of dominance over the black motorist: the form of interrogation, not the content, is what matters.[22]

In similar fashion, the answers demanded by the interrogating officer are less important than the form of the answering; the fact of being compelled to answer on terms that pave the way toward physical demise supersede what is actually spoken between the two parties. In the above scenario, the officer's arbitrary issuance of a ticket for the registration but not for the license, and despite the presence of both as stipulated by law, dismisses the driver's affirmative answers to the interrogation, his compliance with the law, as a means toward breaking his standing in the world, calling upon a metaphysical violence efficacious enough to simultaneously render bodily suffering invisible and convert it into the officer's power. Compliance with the law is irrelevant; subjection to the existential dominance of the officer is what matters.

When Sandra Bland was pulled over by a Texas state trooper in Waller County on July 10, 2015, the officer performed this contorted moral universe of antiblack torture. According to witnesses and to the trooper's own dashboard camera, he made a U-turn immediately upon spotting Bland drive by.[23] Having hunted her down, the trooper instigated a confrontation with Bland, recorded by the dashboard camera, and paved the way for her eventual death. After he returns to Bland's car from writing her up for an improper lane change, he begins by asking her, "Are you OK?"

> BLAND: I'm waiting on you, this your job.
>
> TROOPER: You seem irritated.
>
> BLAND: I am, I really am. Because I don't see what I'm getting a ticket for. I was getting out of your way, you was speeding up, tailing me, so I moved over, and you stopped me. So yeah I'm irritated. But that doesn't stop you from giving me a ticket.
>
> TROOPER: Are you done?
>
> BLAND: You asked me why I was irritated and I told you. So now I'm done, yeah.
>
> TROOPER: You mind putting out your cigarette please.
>
> BLAND: I'm in *my* car, I don't have to put out my cigarette.
>
> TROOPER: You can step on out now. Step out of the car.[24]

The trooper's baiting of Bland demonstrates the premium of interrogation's form over its content. Scarry explains how the formal qualities of interrogation mystify the power relations at work, flipping causality and agency on their respective heads: the victim's answer lends the torturer justification for his cruelty, making her rather than the torturer the cause of her pain, turning responsibility and moral reality upside down.[25] After the trooper has Bland cuffed and standing on the sidewalk he makes this inversion of responsibility explicit when he yells at her, "*you* started creating the problem!" Of course, this statement is a gratuitous moment on top of gratuitous violence: the law has already displaced the responsibility for the trooper's violence onto Bland, the object of policing, a priori, before Bland even responds to the interrogation. It is this vexation of agency that requires me to reconstruct torture beyond Scarry's own study of it in her book *The Body in Pain*.

Scarry's book has become a leading theoretical resource in the Western academy for examining torture, but *The Body in Pain* is itself an index of the mountain to be scaled before "torture" can be made accountable to black suffering and struggle. Whereas Scarry asserts that torture's objective is to enact a metaphysical violence that strips the prisoner of all coordinates of existence, this is a fraudulent scenario where black people are concerned, for the world is already constituted in metaphysical violence against blackness. In Patrice Douglass and Frank Wilderson's words, the status of blackness is "homologous with the 'unmade' world of the torture victim."[26] The black subject exists in a state of constant metaphysical violence such that when the black person enters the torture chamber (a la the police encounter) she is too deracinated, too stripped of ontological presence, to register as a victim of torture or even "to be credited a prior torture."[27] You cannot have your humanity reduced to bare physical trauma and wielded against you like a plastic bag over your head or cattle prongs to the genitals or 24/7 sensory deprivation—in short, to be tortured—if you are not honored as human in the first place.

The maroons hunted down by slave-catching dogs, the lynch victim, Sandra Bland, and the black motorist of the story that opened this section, however, are illegible in Scarry's examination of "the making and unmaking of the world." As are, moreover, the relatives left behind in each instance. Say the black motorist has his five-year-old daughter in her car seat in the back of the car; her experience witnessing her father's structural vulnerability at the hands of the police, the inkling of a suspicion that he may not be able to protect her from this violence, does not register as torture to Scarry. Of course, reality always exceeds the hypothetical: when police killed Philando Castile with four point-blank shots during a traffic stop in Falcon Heights, Minnesota, on July 6, 2016, his fiancée Diamond Reynolds and her four-year-old daughter were in the car as well.[28] Where the Texas state trooper correctly read from Bland's persona that she saw straight through his performance of power and was uncowed by it, and proceeded to implement "a grotesque piece of compensatory drama," obsessively wringing from her body a compliance that he could not enjoy from her in attitude, so too Scarry displays her agency through her obsessive attempts to bring the torture victim's suffering near as if it were the extremity of human pain and her narrative was powerful enough to hold it. In so doing, her study of torture implicitly effaces black pain and, by extension, lets the agents who implement it off the hook, as well as augments the master-narrative of Western civilization that authorizes her to name her Other as another human being while black people are positioned off the scale of human value altogether.[29]

Redress in the Breach

In her outrage at the trooper's reminder that she had no standing in the world as a human being protected from gratuitous violence, Bland repeatedly called out the fiction of his power. "Y'all are interesting . . . you feelin' good about yourself . . . I cannot *wait* to go to court . . . you going to throw me to the floor now, that make you feel better about yourself . . . you pussy-ass . . . you feel real good . . . you a real man now, huh . . . y'all real strong." His masculinity debunked, the discrepancy between his actions and the law highlighted, the sexual violence of policing laid bare, and the parasitic relationship of his pleasure to her pain exposed by Bland, the trooper moved to amplify his authority and fortify his identity through the infliction of physical injury that translated Bland's pain into the visible suffering his depravity demanded. She refused to the very end to submit to his unethical power, so he had to satisfy himself with her physical abjection.

Torture reconstructed entails breaking down the walls of the torture chamber so that the world itself is seen as the torture chamber. Redress remains central to this reconstruction. Bland's practice of insurgent blackness, for instance, requires careful recollection in order to delineate redress. At one point, as she is being handcuffed, Bland pronounces of the trooper, and of police officers generally, "y'all scared . . . South Carolina got y'all scared." Presumably, she is referring to North Charleston, South Carolina, police officer Michael Slager's fatal shooting of Walter Scott in the back as Scott ran away from a traffic stop on April 4, 2015. The incontrovertible video evidence from the incident in the immediate context of a sustained outcry against police impunity across the United States led to Slager's indictment on first-degree murder charges. Back to Waller County, Texas: after the backups from local police have arrived to assist the state trooper with Bland, the officers are seen and heard conferring in front of the camera about what happened. The trooper tells one officer that he took Bland to the ground because she kicked him; he and another officer are heard enumerating his scratches and injuries supposedly inflicted by Bland; and at one point, an officer looks in the direction of the dashboard camera and states, "one thing is sure, it's on video." Bland died in the midst of a remedial period of redressive action against the police power in this country. Video evidence against the cops, and the popular consumption of its images of black trauma, do not redress the situation: at best, they are a much belated admission of a long-standing state of affairs; at worst, they reiterate the ongoing fungibility of the black body in pain. Bland's reference to the murder of Walter Scott and the arrest of Officer Slager for murder swiftly following the appearance of the video evidence, as well as the on-camera behavior of the officers in Waller County, underscores how crimes against black people are invisible until and unless there is nonblack corroborating testimony. Black voices are perpetually held in doubt, and the pained body must be made to speak in tongues that white people summon: during slavery, it was through portraits of the scarred back of the slave; in the present period, it is through the video documentation of assaults on black personhood.

I turn now to Hartman's discussion of the slave woman Sukie in order to wed insurgent blackness to the issues of redress and reconstructed torture. Sukie was sold to slave traders for fighting off her master's attempt to rape her, "one day [while] in the kitchen making soap."[30] On the auction block she pulled up her dress and challenged the white men to see if they could find any teeth "down there," simultaneously restaging her threat to potential buyers-cum-rapists and exposing the sexual violence of property.[31] While exploring the multiple layers of sexual revolt and subversion practiced by Sukie, Hartman nonetheless concludes that her "deconstructive performance . . . was nothing less than slavery itself."[32] In other words, while transgressive acts large and small are not to be underestimated for their indictment of the system's terror precisely because they are unrealizable under these conditions, their significance lies not in "eluding the violence" (as Alexander Weheliye terms it in *Habeas Viscus*), but in lodging a collective record of embodied suffering.[33] Insurgent blackness and its redressive actions can only and always be accounted for under erasure.

By reading redressive actions within the constraints of the structure, following Hartman, Bland's death in a Waller County, Texas, jail cell stands as one grossly typical recent moment in which a black person's humanity is affirmed in its cold finality, enunciating her objectified position relative to the category "human."[34] Sukie's resistance to the "debasing exhibition of the black body" on the auction block, or to the "promiscuous uses of property" in the plantation kitchen, does not exceed or even distend the structure of slavery, but rather is encompassed by it; her subsequent disappearance from the archive signals her engulfment by the banal terror of property's order.[35] Likewise, Bland's resistance is not an act of "volition or self-possession but a rudimentary form of action harnessed by constraint," to apply Hartman's words.[36] Bland's death in jail, having been criminalized for her enactment of a kind of freedom, which is to say, for her gesture of black power, cloaks this condition of violent subjection with the assignation of complicity. The state's assertion that Bland died by her own hand conflates the difference between freedom and slavery in which the emancipated black person's "choice to labor dutifully, bend one's back joyfully, or act willingly as one's own inquisitor" negates the recapitulation of sexual violence that marked Bland's captivity.[37] The official decree of suicide merely underscores how repression is without limit, that terror limns the bounds of social acceptability, and the structure of gratuitous violence regards black self-defense as an aggressive act of assault: as Hartman puts it, "how is resistance registered in a context in which being found with a pen or pencil is almost as bad as having murdered your master?"[38] Or, as Bland herself put it from jail before her death, "How did switching lanes without a signal turn into all of this?" Neither Sukie nor Bland possess their redressive performances of blackness and neither did they long survive them.

In the end, Bland's family will forever be denied official admission of the truth of exactly how their beloved died at the hands of the Waller County Sheriff's Department. This suffering may be extended, and only somewhat offset, by the knowledge that they join thousands of other black families whose relatives died unceremoniously in police custody and have had to endure the official denials despite what they know to be true. They will cope with doubt, fear, shame, hopelessness, sorrow, and rage. They will likely hold at bay, on the periphery of consciousness, the continuities of their daughter's death swing in a jail cell with the thousands of black people strung up and swinging from trees, bridges, railway trestles, and makeshift gallows across the generations. Torture and survival, by turns, course through the insuperable no-movement of black struggle.

From Sukie to Bland, redressive actions spring as much from how we recollect them as they do from the severely limited capacity they bear for meeting the needs of the pained body in a given moment. Survival, therefore, lies in the terms of recollection. It is clear that the present popularity of police violence in the various medias is a reflection not of a sudden clarity about antiblack violence or an abrupt solidarity with black struggle, but rather of the crisis in witnessing that has always attached itself to black truth telling. Does the attention on police violence since Ferguson, people want to know, mean progress? No, it does not mean progress: it is a cynical use of black suffering for objectives incompatible with black liberation. For most of the nonblack world, the spectacles of black pain, the titillation of torture, simply signal a desire for a vicarious proximity to, and principled stance against, cruelty and injustice, and hence, to feel more human, more alive, more ethical. Bearing this in mind, and with the imperative to recollect in terms that situate black insurgency within the enormity of the breach, I turn now to how blackness goes missing and murdered when it occupies the center of documentary melodrama apparently created for antiracist purposes.

What Happened, Liz Garbus?

Liz Garbus has produced an extensive oeuvre during a relatively short time period: thirty-four producer credits and twenty-two director credits between 1986 and 2015. While the political grammar of Garbus's work, and what Wilderson terms the "metacommentaries on ontology" to which it is in fee, is to be found in any of her films, I focus my analysis on Garbus's most recent film, *What Happened, Miss Simone?*, about the extraordinary musician-singer Nina Simone. *What Happened, Miss Simone?* was nominated for an Academy Award for Best Documentary Feature in 2016. Garbus's films are torturous performances of white aggrandizement at the expense of black power. Her recipe for redressing black suffering is to individualize the terror and chaos of the antiblack world onto her black subjects and then oversee an internal disorder management on them. Her films typify when redress is not redressive: she occupies black power in order to turn it into nonblack psychic fuel. I suggest that despite the accouterments of antiracism and empathy with the black lives she depicts, Garbus's films are, in fact, about white people: the bad white people who do her black subjects wrong, the good white people who work to save them, and ultimately, her own station as an auteur of white redemption. In this way, her films are complicit in the reproduction of what is displaced from view in them: the structures of antiblackness that conjure the violence that she treats reductively.

Garbus has explained that the premise behind her title *What Happened, Miss Simone?* is that Simone abandoned the civil rights movement. "Nina had been this leader in the '60s, omnipresent, this voice that was so needed by people on the streets, and then she disappeared."[39] The implication is that there is a moral responsibility that Simone has shirked, a set of right actions to which she was not up to task. That she owed the movement, or the nation, or her fans—inclusive, presumably, of the liberal whites who paid to hear her music. Or more fundamentally, that she failed as a mother. From what position can one rightly judge the conduct of a black person in the throes of the antiblack world?[40] To borrow from Sexton, it is the immorality of the slave system and its afterlife that warrants consideration, not the morality of black people (there is a forum for such debate among black revolutionaries, not among nonblacks).

"To do otherwise," explains Sexton, "is to substitute moralizing for political analysis."[41] Garbus's implicit moralizing of Simone confuses the scales of coercion and consent in which black people exist, and her approach illustrates Sexton's key observation that a disavowal of actual power relations leads to wild conflations between the interpersonal and the structural. This method rests on narrowing the power encounter to a small enough stage, "that is, so long as we suspend consideration of the 'barren and brutal' conditions" of black oppression, Sexton expounds, "we can say nearly anything about it we wish."[42] If only the movement had been less militant, less sexist, or more accommodating of multicultural coalition—and all such criticisms that have been levied about the black struggle of the long civil rights period derive from a thinly veiled "moral economy of submission and servitude" positioning blacks as debtors, obliged and duty bound to nonblacks in return for inclusion, standing, and freedom.[43]

Despite the power of this discourse against blackhood, corralled and deployed by Garbus in her film, the problems Simone and the black struggle encountered are irreducible to protest strategies, interracial relations, or any other contradictions internal to the movement. Freedom was not forestalled due to individual personalities, frailties, or pathologies; Simone was not brought to heel (to use Hillary Clinton's phrase) by mental illness or misogyny or the pressures of fame.[44] The movement that produced Simone was squashed by a full frontal assault of the combined powers of state and civil society. Under such conditions, "between the crosshairs and without sanctuary," individual black revolutionaries could not remain standing and moving forward as they were.[45] Simone and others did not simply disappear or drop out; they were stomped out, terrorized by a dreadful apparatus of violence that infiltrated the most intimate spaces of the black community and continues its tilt against black power to this day.

At the height of her powers—which is to say, at the height of the movement—Simone addressed her audience at one of the massive outdoor civil rights rallies. Before singing, she asked the people gathered, "Are you ready to kill if necessary? Is your mind ready? Is your body ready?"[46] Getting our minds ready, cultivating a consciousness accountable to blackhood, requires close and careful reconsideration of both the structural violence arrayed against blackness and the performative acts of survival and redress destabilizing this edifice of power. For *What Happened, Miss Simone?*, this reevaluation means repositioning ex-husband Andrew Stroud's abuse and Simone's mental illness as part and parcel of not only the structure's counterinsurgency moves against the black movement, but also as central to the film's contribution to this quarantine of black power. Although at the time of my writing, there has been no extended critical engagement with *What Happened, Miss Simone?*, reviews on the blogosphere have lodged succinct objections to Stroud's prominent presence in the film. Tanya Steele, for instance, puts it thusly:

> Imagine this: A documentary about Rihanna where Chris Brown gets to talk about Rihanna's temperament. Where Brown admits to hitting Rihanna as if it was par for the course because she was a difficult personality. Nina Simone's husband was described in this way: "He would step out of his car and people ran." Nina, in her own words said: "He put a gun to my head, then he tied me up and raped me." Would we let Chris Brown complicate the narrative of the abuse? Why do we allow Nina Simone's abuser to be part of the telling of her story?[47]

Of course, Brown was permitted to shape the narrative of the abuse he perpetrated on Rihanna. Or, rather, more accurately, the narrative was already available and ready to go, thanks to our antiblack and misogynist culture. Nonetheless, Steele's analogy is apt and her point is well taken. The presence and credibility given to Stroud indicts Garbus's liberalism and mocks the sensitivity to women's stories on which her credentials are based. In fact, more is at stake here, and close evaluation of how Garbus deploys Stroud will unravel how the film renders blackness missing and murdered.

Garbus frames the introduction of Simone to Stroud with a recording of Simone singing "I Loves You, Porgy" in the background. Garbus's use of "Porgy" here is uncritical, un-self-conscious, and a grotesque play for dominant cinema's romantic melodrama where it does not belong. "Porgy" is a love song that helped make *Porgy and Bess* a hit in white society. For the black community, on the other hand, George Gershwin's opera was controversial at best, and reviled by many. Simone was deeply reticent about recording it when she was first asked to do so. The very first woman to sing the role of Bess in 1935,

Anne Brown (at the time, a twenty-one-year-old Julliard student), said, "When my father saw the premier of *Porgy and Bess*, he was very disappointed and sad that Negroes had been pictured in usual clichés, ignorant dope peddlers and users, criminals. We have had enough of that. It's time to stop."[48] Garbus seems to think that as a famous love song, and Simone's first popular hit, it provides appropriate backdrop to the nascent relationship between Simone and Stroud. But Garbus unwittingly betrays herself: "Porgy" signals how Garbus is the overseer of Simone's narrative, while Stroud was enlisted to serve as the overseer of Simone during her time on the plantation she referred to as the "United Snakes of America." Simone's version of "Porgy" reinterprets Gershwin's spectacle of what he termed "high-spirited" black folk culture; such was her musical brilliance. But this reinterpretation is only possible in the fleeting moments of performance when Simone controls the image. Garbus's use of the image, however, undermines Simone's control. It is telling that Garbus did not frame the Stroud segment with "Sinnerman," "Strange Fruit," or even "Black Is the Color."

Stroud was a police officer known for a level of violence and authoritarianism exceptional even in that line of work. He did not simply rape and batter Simone, he actively sought to punish her blackhood. His violent presence in her life coincided with Simone's strengthening black consciousness. Stroud's perspective: "She wanted to align herself with the extreme terrorist militants who were influencing her. . . . She's putting down the white people like a barking dog." In addition to this dehumanization of his wife and black social movement, Stroud reveals his clear intentions to manage not simply her career but her political consciousness: her politics "cut the legs out of all the work that I had done." As is the way with abusers, rapists, colonizers, and white supremacists, Stroud displaces the physical, psychic, and political violence he enacted onto Simone: "I told her that's not the way and it began to manifest in her feelings toward me." Simone's diaries, however, reveal the true consequences of the abuse: "Andrew and I talked of my possible suicide, and he let me know that not only would he NOT suffer, but he would be relieved. I hate him. I hate him. I have every intention of leaving him, if I live." Simone's sentiments resonate with every survivor of domestic violence. In this light, the very fact that she escaped his death wish should be attributed in no small measure to her prominent standing in a Pan-African movement that was ready and willing to lend her sanctuary just about anywhere in the diaspora. This dimension of her survival underscores the fact that Stroud's violence is much more significant than mere gender-sex exploitation: it is violence against blackhood. It is irrelevant whether or not Stroud would have attacked Simone had she not become politicized; the fact is that his violence was aimed at subordinating her awareness of black power to some subservient conception of blackness. Stroud was the personification of COINTELPRO in Simone's life. That this counterinsurgency warfare played out in the intimate spaces of black-on-black relations, and appeared to both their close circle of friends and to the outside world as the bumps and fissures of marriage, or as the excesses of masculinity, or the pressures of celebrity life, or as Stroud and Garbus would have it, as much a testament to Simone's difficult persona as to Stroud's depravities, merely obscures the antiblackness from which the violence actually draws its fuel.

Garbus's film never places Stroud's antiblack violence in a critical light. Garbus turns instead to an interview with Ilyshah Shabazz, daughter of Malcolm X and Betty Shabazz, who relates, "activism during the sixties rendered chaos in any individuals' lives. People sacrificed sanity, well-being, life. Nina Simone was a free spirit in an era that didn't really appreciate a woman's genius. So what does that do to a household and a family, not because of income but because of your soul not being able to do what you're meant to do?" True enough, and who would know better than Malcolm and Betty's children? Placing rape, sexual assault, character slander, and the death threats that Simone endured from her husband, however, along the same continuum of trauma that Betty and her children survived as a result of Malcolm's leadership in the movement requires clarification. The intimate violence wrought by COINTELPRO was in fact the main objective of the state's counterinsurgency program and, moreover, was precisely the manner in which it tied into earlier eras of lynching. There may be a forum for debating how to allocate blame within the black community for some of this intimate violence, but once again, that forum is among black revolutionaries or within black families. Since she belongs to neither of these constituencies, the only ethical thing for Garbus to do is to construct a narrative that portrays the world as it is, not as she would like it to be. Shabazz's comments lent political cover for Stroud's blame-the-victim posture, and both Shabazz and Stroud converge on the discourse of mental illness that Garbus would mobilize as the defining lens for evaluating Simone's life.

When Simone finally shed herself of Stroud and arrived in Liberia, she said, "now I am free," harkening, of course, to one of her famous songs of the period, "I Wish I Knew How It Would Feel to Be Free," which concludes with the line, "I sing 'cause I know how it feels to be free." Prior to that time, she had divulged ample sentiments that lent meaning to her relief at arriving in Africa. The diagnosis: "To me American society is nothing but a cancer, and it must be exposed before it can be cured. I am not the doctor to cure it; all I can do is expose the sickness." The urgency: "Really gets down to reality, not performance . . . we can't afford any more losses . . . they're shooting us down one by one." The necessary means: "Black people are never going to get their rights unless we have a separate state, and if we have an armed revolution there would be a lot of blood but I think we'd have a separate state." And the toll: "They don't know I'm dead and my ghost is holding on." Garbus never permits this political analysis to define the conditions in which Simone declares herself finally free. If it had, certainly the only conclusion would have been mental clarity, not madness. Clearly, freedom is not as simplistic as back-to-Africa; rather, it is a more fugitive, delimited, and yet clairvoyant and Pan-Africanist sensibility that ties in with maroons and the persistent flight home of the ancestors. Equally egregious on this score is the utter lack of discussion of Simone's artistry itself as evidence of an elevated consciousness to which madness could not apply. The film does not discuss in anything other than superficial ways why her particular talents were so uniquely powerful during a revolutionary era. For instance, Simone noted, "we don't know anything about ourselves. . . . we can't talk about where we came from, we don't know, it's like a lost race," echoing a theme reverberating throughout the black struggle from Carter G. Woodson and Marcus Garvey to Malcolm X. Simone, however, was able to take it a step further, singing in "Ain't Got No—I Got Life," a medley she created by combining two separate songs from the Broadway musical production *Hair*, "Ain't got nothing, I got life . . . got my nose, my blood . . . got life," elevating historical analysis into the realm of embodied resistance. A survival ode to the social life of social death.

What do you do when revolution is suddenly aborted? How do you go on living your life after you have given your life to the revolution? In other words, how do you live a life aborted? How does one settle back into social death after having been part of the mobilization for its death? Or, as Deborah Bowen writes, "How does a black woman live amidst the paradox of what makes us weary—the truth of our lives, our existence, our survival in a world that tries to ruin us, tries to use us up, all the while praising us with paternalistic fervor?"[49] Garbus employs this paternalism in her portrayal of Simone's mental illness once she departs the United States. First we hear Simone's daughter Lisa Kelley describe her mother as "struggling with demons." Simone is temporarily estranged from her daughter when she first leaves the United States, but eventually Kelley goes to Liberia to live with her mother. Kelley recalls this period of her life as awful: Simone becomes abusive toward her daughter, both physically and emotionally. Kelley is relieved to return to her father. Then, we hear from Al Shackman, Simone's long-time guitarist, who shares that something was eating at Simone—but what was it, he could not say. Again, Bowen pointedly counters:

> Is it too far a stretch to see how the disempowerment one feels at the constant reminder that your skin predetermines your success might make a human being, a black woman, feel pain and rage and anger? Madness and demons— language that brings to mind issues of mental instability and fragility, of a person living with a distorted sense of the world and her place in it, so much so that their perceptions are not to be trusted. Once a black person is overcome by the constant presence of racism, and reacts with anger, then their ability to think of their experiences is filtered through the lens of socially acceptable behavior, as defined by whiteness' rationality. This lens distorts the hurtness, rage-ness, mad-ness that black people readily recognize as a legitimate response to racism, construing it outside of a racial context and into a mental health one, a context where one can claim that Nina had demons, that Nina is mad.[50]

Why is Stroud not the crazy one? Not only for his violence, but for driving Simone to her wits-end exhaustion with his management of her performing career? Why not Simone's daughter Kelley? She ran back to her father's arms, the rapist and policeman of black consciousness: Why is the mother's abuser (a vessel for white patriarchal society) not perceived as a threat to the black daughter? Is it because the daughter is already formed through a larger abuse of blackness, whereas Simone resisted such repression? Kelley also deemed it appropriate to allow Garbus to divulge and narrate details about her mother's life that Simone herself chose not to share in her own 1991 autobiography *I Put a Spell on You*. Or, a la Fanon, why is it not the world that has gone mad?

According to the Garbus film, Simone's listing ship is finally righted when she is rescued by two white men in Europe who agree to set up her living and guide her performing—provided she does what they say, namely that she take psychotropic medication to keep her even and predictable. This is seen in the film as a sad but necessary response to her diagnosed mental instability. From the perspective of blackhood, however, this amounts to medicating her artistry in order to control her blackness, especially the volatile postrevolutionary self for whom destruction and dashed dreams are around every corner. What does framing Simone in terms of mental illness accomplish for Garbus? First, it bypasses her radicalism, treating it as a trite feature of an idiosyncratic and unstable mind. Second, it hides the ongoing war against black radicalism, the real costs to people's lives, the family as the ultimate target in this warfare, and how Simone's own family experience with violence was not atypical. Third, it renders invisible how counterinsurgency continues to debilitate long after the movement has effectively been curtailed. Being a revolutionary in a postrevolution era can be a lonely affair. For Simone, as for many movement people living in counterrevolutionary times, this played out in unexpected, confusing, and painful ways. She writes in her autobiography:

> I turned to stone inside. Lucille, who'd stepped into Momma's shoes and taught me to be a woman, was gone. I tried to cry. I wanted to but tears wouldn't come. What sort of a person was I when sometimes I could cry for hours without knowing why and yet couldn't find a tear for Daddy and my beloved Lucille? What sort of person could break down and cry on stage in Europe over the deaths of political leaders and then refuse to visit her father's grave? What sort of person could do this? What happened to make me this way?[51]

Fourth, Garbus's use of mental illness to frame Simone's story is a rejection of black radical thought in favor of the Western consciousness that it has laboriously deconstructed over the generations. The blueprint for deconstructing and displacing mental illness discourse is available from many quarters in black letters, including Audre Lorde's analysis of the Master's tools, Sylvia Wynter's realization that it is a war against consciousness, W. E. B. Du Bois's double-consciousness and two warring ideals, Aimé Césaire's argument that Europe is indefensible, and Frantz Fanon's explanation of self-alienation.

The Third Rail

The final thing that framing Simone in terms of mental illness accomplishes for Garbus is that it recenters white people, recovers white ethicality, and gently refortifies a national narrative based on depoliticizing black cultural icons and destroying black power. The film permits the pall of madness to fall over Simone after she left her hard-working and honorable family, after she stopped singing white pop tunes, after she immerses herself in the civil rights movement, after she leaves her husband and child, and after she leaves her country. Garbus thus permits the two Europeans to save Simone from herself. In the end, however, the real savior of Nina Simone, the film asserts, is Liz Garbus. It is she who has labored to repair the damage done to the nation-state by the black rebellion, of which Simone was its "patron saint," according to Stanley Crouch. Any vestiges of black power have been exposed by Garbus as outrageous and mad. The litmus for this is always the matter of black self-defense. Simone was of a clear mind about what was necessary for liberation. "I was never non-violent," she states in the Garbus film, "I thought we should get our rights by any means necessary." In her autobiography, she recounts the period in the immediate aftermath of the 1963 bombing of the 16th Street Baptist Church in Birmingham that killed the four schoolgirls. Her husband discovered her attempting to fabricate a zip gun in their basement. "I had it in my mind," she writes, " to go out and kill someone, I didn't know who, but someone I could identify as being in the way of my people getting some justice for the first time in three hundred years."[52] And in the Garbus film, Simone states:

If I'd had my way I'd a been a killer, I woulda had guns and gone to the south and give em violence for violence, shotguns for shotguns. But my husband told me I didn't know anything about guns and he refused to teach me, and the only thing I had was music so I obeyed him. But if I had my way I wouldn't be sitting here today; I'd be probably dead.

What would it have meant for Garbus to treat this commitment to black self-defense respectfully rather than dismissively?

Garbus believes that her film is significant in part because it is timely: "We were in our edit room when the events of Ferguson were unfolding. It reminds you that the struggle is ongoing and that her music and her words are as necessary and as relevant as they were then. It doesn't shape the film, but it is certainly a ripe moment for the film to be coming out. Nina's is a voice that is very needed today."[53] What does this mean, exactly? To say "the struggle is ongoing" is to say nothing more remarkable than "the sky is still blue." Would Garbus join the chorus that has been asserting that Sandra Bland suffered from mental illness and that as a result she acted wildly and ended her own life?[54] Or would she permit Simone's clear belief in the necessity of black self-defense to portend a more complex discussion about Bland's right to defense as the Texas state trooper follows up his threat—"I will light you up!"—by forcibly reaching around her to unbuckle her seatbelt and pull her from her vehicle? Joy James has rightfully called self-defense the "third rail" of contemporary black politics; elsewhere I have written that the priority on black self-defense is what precludes black people from the protective ambit of human rights doctrine.[55] Self-defense is the no-fly zone in protests against police violence; and yet it is for precisely this reason that it is the litmus for blackhood's stance against the police power, a position that Simone clearly articulated and that Garbus cowers in the face of.

If Bland had been armed and exercised her right to self-defense against this state trooper, the chances are great that she would have been shot dead. In the best-case scenario, she survives the gun standoff or gunfight, survives police custody, and at her trial is able to articulate her self-defense—before being sentenced to a lengthy prison term for standing her ground. But what happens when a black person is not armed and cannot defend herself? She still ends up in one of these two situations. This is why James calls it the "third rail" of black politics: to advocate self-defense is to automatically invite the law's lethal force upon you while simultaneously rejecting its legitimacy—and who is prepared to willingly stand outside the law as a means of engaging it? To not advocate for self-defense, on the other hand, is to swallow the reality of this structural vulnerability and hope for the best, an exercise in bad faith and self-abdication if ever there was one, although the realities of self-preservation make this a profoundly difficult dilemma.

The ethical coherence of the white nation, meanwhile, depends on dis-avowing the third rail's existence altogether. The black revolutionary, on the other hand, is devoted to the third rail's exposure: as Simone put it, "I am not the doctor to cure it; all I can do is expose the sickness." Garbus, therefore, must work carefully to recruit the life of the black revolutionary to her agenda of burying the ethical antagonism that revolution represents. Garbus says of Simone, "At every moment there were these kind of oppositional forces that were ruling her, so she literally has quite a bipolar existence."[56] The reality of the third rail means that civil society is founded on the fundamental exclusion of black people; what Garbus is doing in brushing Simone with "a bipolar existence" is demonstrating the inclusiveness of civil society by showing that black people too have the same problems and mental health issues that human beings endure. America's racist structures that bounce her between the polarities of adoring fame on one end, to lethal violence on the other, are instantly adjusted into a matter of how Simone copes with her mind. To put it differently, in order for Simone as a black person with no standing as a human being in an antiblack society to have a story, a nonblack person must provide that narration as if she were a human being and not a natally alienated being. Garbus's narrative strategies affirm Simone's natal alienation by dislocating her from the historical context of blackhood. Simone must go missing and murdered in order to become visible through dominant cinema's matrix of darkness, blackness, and femaleness signified as dread, sin, and evil, and requiring containment by white nationalist discourses of either punishment, paternalism, or medicalization. Simone was treated with all three in spades.

The trappings of cinematic narrative and human relationality in *What Happened, Miss Simone?* are unsuccessful in hiding the reality of tortured black bodies—Simone's, Garbus's representation of her, and the black social body generally. *What Happened, Miss Simone?* illustrates how the displacement of blackness in critical thought and the Stroud-esque counterinsurgency against black self-determination in general constitute the conditions of possibility for the slanderous misrepresentations of black art and leadership such as that exemplified in the life of Nina Simone. There is no redress here. In other words, Garbus can successfully snuff out black power in the cultural realm only because the life of black power in the political arena today has gone missing and murdered. Her torturous cinematic rendering of the black movement to which we are subjected in *What Happened, Miss Simone?* is thus as a reflection of the torture imposed on everyday black people. Bambara, reliably, assists in deciphering how Garbus's film mystifies the antiblack reality, as well as the general mystification enshrouding torture itself. Toward the end of *Those Bones Are Not My Child*, after Sonny has returned and the family has retreated to Zala's mother's home in the country for refuge, Aunt Gerry talks about the banal presence of torture in the black freedom struggle and yet how this violence escapes language.

> "It's the same with us and the sixties. Neither Maxwell nor I dwelt on the beatings. I'm sure we spoke of the fear. We didn't want to shield you from that."
>
> "Mostly I remember the singing," Zala said.
>
> "Yes, the singing. Perhaps there is no way to talk about torture and hatred, because they aren't images, they're un-images. I don't mean I can't picture the clubs and the guns and the electric prods. But it's all an un-image. Half the people I work with have been political prisoners in one liberation struggle or another—and even with ANC members in numbers transforming prison conditions . . . torture is an un-image. That's as far as I can get. It's similar to your situation, isn't it? You've not spoken of the yearlong torment nearly as much as . . ." Gerry could not find the words.[57]

Torture exceeds our capacity to name it as long as we do not step out of the paradigm that reproduces it as a mundane and unmarked feature of the landscape, like the way civil society calls upon black bodies as so many props for its collective nurturance.

Coda

What happened to our sweet song—making love
making love wanting to make revolution?

— Ifi Amadiume, "Grassroots Revolution," 1995

This study has revealed that black power remains the "ghost in the machine," the "shadow book," the host on which all of civil society's ethical questions are premised—and moreover, it is the basis for blackhood's ethical confrontation with a world debauched beyond redemption.[1] The parasitism of civil society always comes back to the forbidden question of black power. Each of the discrete topics covered in this study underscores how black power remains profoundly present no matter how assiduously it is disavowed, expunged, and (seemingly) destroyed. The police power of state and civil society, including its various antiracist discourses and formations, must seek blackhood's suppression in order for nonblack intracommunal narratives of transformation to vouchsafe the unethical terms of nonblack life. In other words, as I have endeavored to emphasize throughout this study, the passage of time only makes this generalized condition of social superexcrescence less apparent, decreasingly available to speech, and further from the grasp of collective consciousness. For this reason, the black studies and black radical traditions are pressed into urgent service today like never before in the history of the modern world. Our counterrevolutionary era is thus as profoundly anti-intellectual as it is antiblack. Rediscovering blackhood and confronting social death entails becoming socially alive anew—thinking as if for the first time. Toni Cade Bambara describes this process for us in *Those Bones Are Not My Child* through Zala's awakening to the afterlife of Sonny's torture, which was her own.

> She eased around, lifting her leg and placing her knee carefully on the bed. She was learning how to do things in slow motion. She would have to learn other things too. How to open her lungs again, retrain them after a year of shallow breathing. How to unclench her thighs, teach her back to relax. And she would have to learn to call him Sonny again.
>
> "I couldn't . . ."
>
> It was a croak. And the sound seemed to scare him as much as it did her. He fell back against the pillows and clamped his mouth shut, though she hadn't shushed him this time. This time she looked at him squarely, to show that she could, to show that whatever he'd been through he was seeable.
>
> . . . Meanwhile, she would learn how to hem up the dragging flesh of her life with careful, tiny stitches.[2]

That is to say, the daily wrestle with death's omnipresence requires considerable consciousness, intention, courage, and breath.

Insofar as *Blackhood Against the Police Power* aims to "hem up" our dragging collective consciousness, where does its vigilant stitches leave us? Chapter 6 began with a warning against conclusions, and so too, the coda signs off this study with a few measures of expanded cadence shorn of the customary prescriptions. The present state of affairs is produced through (1) a direct confrontation against independent black thought, the suppression of which contributes to (2) communal disarray and collective vulnerability, which in turn, is requisite for (3) the attenuation of black power and (4) the ensuing political delusion that (5) leaves isolated acts of marronage misrecognized and undersupported.

On the first score, although *Blackhood Against the Police Power* is linked with academic fields of study, it stands accountable to the independent black studies tradition that carries on despite the institutionalized withering of black studies in the academy. As such, it bears remembering that the Atlanta "missing and murdered" case took place in the interval between, on the one hand, the isolation of the only independent black studies venture to emerge out of the Black Power movement, Atlanta's Institute of the Black World (IBW), and on the other hand, the unrestrained abductions of black children, women, and men in Atlanta during the so-called wars on crime, drugs, and gangs. The IBW sought to shepherd the black movement through the 1970s and into the 1980s, articulating a vision for independent black thought and social movement unencumbered by the co-optations of white institutions and the disciplinary power of colorblindness. Following Malcolm X's lead, and referencing Ralph Ellison's *Invisible Man*, the former director of the IBW, Vincent Harding, projected the course for independent black studies out of the devastating reality: "You have looked upon chaos and are not destroyed!"[3]

> As we read the black past, and meditate upon our present, we sense that our manhood will not ever be fulfilled through full participation in *this* America, through entry into *this* mainstream. We see America as counter-life, counter-joy, in league with ultimate nothingness and death. So we have seen the emptiness. Black History is our journey into the void where our fathers believed America to be. Black History plunges us into the chasm, into the darkness, where we can depend upon no saga called America.[4]

Harding explains that at the point where it no longer draws back from the brink of utter destruction, but instead reaches out into it to "grasp our blackness," "Black history moves into Black Studies and becomes part of the search for the new land, the new society, the new being."[5] In this way, black studies for Harding teaches us that we are on *blackland*, territory in which the past and present seamlessly articulate and future horizons remain the fruit of only the most sober and ethical of analyses.

The IBW ultimately succumbed to counterinsurgency's various modalities—and shortly after it closed its doors, black Atlantans began to take note of an alarming increase in the violence on blackland. The "missing and murdered" case was underway. The terror of this period was its own form of counterinsurgency that left the black community as a whole further divided, devastated, de-politicized, and vulnerable. By the 1990s, in the afterlife of the "missing and murdered" case, if you will, the forces of antiblack violence in Atlanta had transmuted yet again under the nascent prison-industrial complex; or, we might say they became institutionalized for a post-racial period. It took three shuddering and deathly decades, then, to effectively quarantine the crisis-at-large of blackness-on-a-move as it manifest out of the civil rights and Black Power periods. In addition to the frontal assault on black organizations, leadership, and rank-and-file movement, counterinsurgency needed to squelch independent black critical thought, which it did by forcing the IBW to shutter its doors, dispersing black intellectual workers back into isolation in largely white (or white-indebted) institutions. The abductions and terror against black children and parents were all the more feasible having rendered the IBW itself missing and murdered. Hence, again, my interest in "Atlanta" here is not as an event or as a discrete place bounded in space and time, but rather for how it represents a paradigm in effect across antiblack society. Suppressing blackhood entails a war on consciousness, with communal disarray and collective vulnerability its costly byproducts.

Bambara, a leading voice of the Black Arts and Black Studies Movements, and an associate at the IBW, was a resident of Atlanta during the time of the missing and murdered, as previously noted in chapter 3. Elaine Brown, former chairwoman of the Black Panther Party, was also a resident of Atlanta in the 1990s, where she returned to grassroots organizing around children's educational opportunities and juveniles prosecuted as adults in the state of Georgia. Brown's book, *The Condemnation of Little B*, is an account of the 1990s as definitive as *Bones* was of the late 1970s–early 1980s. These works of independent black studies carry on the IBW's tradition of intellectual marronage. Bambara and Brown make plain that the forces at work in blackland during 1970–2000 were nothing less than an attack on *blackhood*. Blackland viewed through the rise and fall of the institute, Bambara's account of the "missing and murdered" case, and Brown's analysis of the conviction of a thirteen-year-old black boy, Michael "Little B" Lewis, to life in prison recount the manner in which Black Power was ambushed and the post-racial was erected over the violated body of the black community. Moreover, these accounts present a studious dissent from the hegemonic discourse on race and sex emergent from this period and an epistemic counterviolence against the constitution of the post-racial that the sequestration of institutionalized black studies permits. *Blackhood Against the Police Power* strives to supplement this collective dissension and contribute to sustaining an independent intellectual and political practice.

Third, the suppression of self-determining black thought is necessary for disarming black power. As Michel-Rolph Trouillot's study of "power and the production of history" shows, black revolutionary action is simply unthinkable to the world even as the events that constitute it are unfolding. Instead of recognizing black self-determination for what it is, explains Trouillot, it is made to enter into narratives that make sense to the antiblack mind. Then, even as revolutionary praxis becomes an indisputable fact of human history, it is erased as such. Finally, when the events are too singular to ignore, they are emptied "of their revolutionary content so that the entire string of facts, gnawed from all sides, becomes trivialized."[6] The problem we now face in the post-racial period is precisely this diminution of black power.

The consequence of black power's mitigation, fourthly, is political delusion—and it is on display every day, inviting the danger inside. In a 1982 interview about her first novel, *The Salt Eaters*, Bambara explained political delusion in terms of the salt:

> It finally all goes back to the African flying myth. . . . But as the old folks tell it, we got grounded because we ate too much salt. But as *some* of the old folks say, we got grounded because we opened ourselves up to horror, to certain kinds of horror, we invited it onto the Continent and then that created tears, occasion for tears, and it was *that* salt that finally drowned our wings and made us earth-bound.[7]

Missing and murdered bodies and revolutionary ideas, alike, teach us that the price of emancipation has been the burdened condition of complicity, compromise, and bad faith—delusionary practices for a besieged people. Why was Dylann Roof welcomed into the Emanuel AME Church in Charleston, South Carolina, on June 17, 2015, a historic sanctuary of black refuge, a congregation that counts among its founders Denmark Vesey, no less, one of black history's famous revolutionaries? For how long has the congregation been "grounded" and opened up "to certain kinds of horror," such that it no longer recognized the hate even as it sat among them in Bible study for an entire hour before announcing itself from the barrel of a gun that had gone undetected? A belated reminder of too much salt? Roof's persona and behavior not only fit a self-evident profile of the white supremacist hate criminal but also follow a long pattern of assaults against blackness: Why was the church not armed and vigilant to check such expected threats at its door? What happened to the traditions of healing and self-defense organized to recognize and fortify against precisely the kind of predatory attack that Roof carried out in Charleston? Spiritually, they are still coming for Vesey, counterinsurgency against any space of black self-possession, be it the body, family home, house of worship, or neighborhood school. The community's grief turned to disgrace in the memorializing period as the first black head of the "democratic slave state," Barack Obama, sang "Amazing Grace," while Hillary Clinton, the aspiring first female head of the "slave democracy," finally acceded, "Yes, black lives matter."[8] These performances of post-racialism and postpatriarchy nimbly displace the fact that such scenes of black death are integral to the coherence of the nation-state's "penal democracy."[9]

In *Bones*, the black community school is terrorized by a white supremacist's bomb. Due to the political delusion stemming from the suppression of independent black thought and the evisceration of black power, against which Bambara and Brown have railed, reality is far more odious than fiction can imagine. When a sheriff's deputy assaulted a black girl at a South Carolina high school on October 26, 2015, he was answering the summons of the classroom teacher, which means that the officer was merely carrying out the violence authorized by this black man in charge of the classroom. As in Charleston, the violence has already been invited inside community institutions; it controls and corrodes from within. In the video footage of the South Carolina assault, most of the other students are cowering at their desks, shell-shocked and terrified; but one black female student bravely stands up to the officer to protest her classmate's treatment. Both girls were arrested on a charge of "disturbing schools." The video footage compelled the Richland County Sheriff to fire the deputy, but at the press conference where he announced the deputy's termination, the sheriff reiterated that it was in fact the assaulted student who is culpable: "We must not lose sight that this whole incident started by this student. She is responsible for initiating this action."[10]

This policing rhetoric is historically constant in its goal of transfiguring black people into the perpetrators of the harms they endure. This is nothing new. In the present period, however, the police power has been able to render the long-standing practice of black self-defense illegitimate—as when Korryn Gaines used a shotgun to defend herself, her family, and her home against police intrusion on August 1, 2016. The arrest warrant that the police were attempting to serve stemmed from a traffic stop five months earlier. Gaines replaced her license plates with placards reading "freedom traveler" and "any government official who compromises this pursuit to happiness and right to travel, will be held criminally responsible and fined, as this is a natural right and freedom," and during the traffic stop she refused to comply with any directives from officers, explaining that the officers did not have any authority over her.[11] In August, officers obtained illegal entry into her home where Gaines met them with an armed shotgun and threatened to shoot if they did not leave. Eventually the police opened fire, killing Gaines and injuring her son.

The fifth point in this Coda, then, lies with the abandonment of Gaines. The discussion of this case has largely focused on how the police leveraged control over social media to block Gaines from broadcasting in real-time the stand-off with police at her home. That corporate media outlets such as Facebook and Instagram function as arms of the police power is unremarkable, however, and one of the ways in which this policing works is to focus public attention on the thwarting of efforts to document the violence of policing—and away from Gaines's expressions of irrepressible blackness, her ethical counterviolence.[12] Again, this is why Joy James has termed armed self-defense the third rail of black self-determination: the surveillance of blackness and its dissemination of the blood-stained record swallows, and thus stands at odds with, the acts of marronage by everyday black folk like Gaines. While her expressions of autonomy were more spectacular than the numerous daily such acts by people like Chris Lollie (picking up his kids from daycare and resisting police interference) or Sandra Bland (driving down the highway and questioning police baiting) or Ramarley Graham (retreating to the safety of his home to avoid police interdiction), the outcomes are essentially the same.

The language on the placards she affixed to her license plates has led to speculation that Gaines was a member of, or at least influenced by, the "sovereign citizen" movement.[13] Indeed, many of Gaines's statements recorded on video or posted to her Instagram account utilize some of the same arguments against state authority popularized by sovereign citizens. I hope that it is obvious, however, that when black people express some of the ideas associated with the sovereign citizens movement, it turns everything on its head. White expressions of sovereignty in the face of government authority, especially since the passage of the Fourteenth Amendment, should be read to mean the right to possess black people, or at least to possess dominance over them, as a feature of the right to self-possession. On the other hand, when black people utilize the sovereign citizen ideology, they are directly contesting the antiblackness intrinsic to not only the U.S. nation-state, but to the very notion of "sovereignty" itself. Since black people represent the position of the "unsovereign" in the modern world, as Jared Sexton has explained, Gaines was attempting to strike the fungible blackness at the heart of the modern world.[14] Of course, not only was this gesture symbolic on her part since she had no means to make it real, but her belief, in line with sovereign citizen ideology, that "Constitutional law is the only true law" (as she stated on her Instagram account) is a dead end for black people, as I have endeavored to show in this book and elsewhere.[15]

Political clarity, spiritual well-being, and self-preservation are one thing. George Jackson affirms precisely why the protocols of black social death constitute inadmissible evidence for the leading critical discourses on race and sex politics today.

> As soon as all this became clear to me and I developed the nerve to admit it to myself, that we were defeated in war and are now captives, slaves or actually that we inherited a neoslave existence, I immediately became relaxed, always expecting the worst, and started working on the remedy.[16]

Paula Giddings makes an observation about Bambara that echoes Jackson's sentiments: "The thing about Toni Cade, I realized years later, was that she could face the fact that her condition placed her at the edges of the world."[17] Life at the edge is a condition of marronage and ethical honesty about structural vulnerability.

Study. Know your paradigms. Understand present political problems in terms of black historical struggle.

Divest from law, from policing, from capitalist culture, from the false freedoms of gender-sex, and from any program that does not hold itself accountable to blackness.

Hands off Assata!

Hands off Claudette! Hands off Jamil!

Hands off Sandra! Hands off Rekia!

Hands off Chris, Eric, Michael, Ramarley, Freddie, Tamir, et al.!

Hands off Trayvon! Hands off Marissa!

Hands off Assana, Naomi, and Deborah!

Hands off Ersula! Hands off Joy!

Hands off all the children!

Hands off Blackhood!

Hands off Blackland!

Blackhood against the police power.

Notes

PREFACE

1. Wahneema Lubiano, "Black Ladies, Welfare Queens, and State Minstrels: Ideological War by Narrative Means," in *Race-ing Justice, En-gendering Power: Essays on Anita Hill, Clarence Thomas, and the Social Construction of Reality*, ed. Toni Morrison (New York: Pantheon, 1992), 232–252.

2. See Ishmael Reed, "'Hamilton: The Musical': Black Actors Dress Up Like Slave Traders . . . and It's Not Halloween," *CounterPunch*, August 21, 2015, http://www.counterpunch.org.

3. See Utrice Leid, *Leid Stories* (podcast), https://leidstories.podbean.com.

4. Thank you to Joy James for instructing me on this point.

5. Frank B. Wilderson III, Samira Spatzek, and Paula von Gleich, "'The Inside-Outside of Civil Society': An Interview with Frank B. Wilderson, III," *Black Studies Papers* 2 no. 1 (2016): 20.

6. Jared Sexton, "The Social Life of Social Death: On Afro-Pessimism and Black Optimism," *InTensions* 5 (Fall 2011): 1–47.

INTRODUCTION

1. Kevin Johnson, "FBI: Justifiable Homicides at Highest in More than a Decade," *USA Today*, October 15, 2008.

2. "Fruitvale Station (2013)," The Numbers, http://www.the-numbers.com.

3. Peter Hartlaub, "There's a 'Fruitvale Station' Movie Poster at Fruitvale Station," *SFGATE*, July 10, 2013, https://www.sfgate.com.

4. Sylvia Wynter, "No Human Involved: An Open Letter to My Colleagues," *Forum N.H.I.* 1, no. 1 (fall 1994): 44.

5. Ibid., 58, 69.

6. Quoted in Aisha Harris, "How Accurate Is *Fruitvale Station*?," *Slate*, July 12, 2013, http://www.slate.com.

7. Quoted in Esther Zuckerman, "Ryan Coogler on Humanizing a Movement for *Fruitvale Station*," *The Atlantic*, July 12, 2013, http://www.theatlantic.com.

8. Quoted in Zuckerman, "Ryan Coogler."

9. James Baldwin, *Tell Me How Long the Train's Been Gone* (New York: Vintage, 1968), 331.

10. Wynter, "No Human Involved," 65.

11. Ibid.

12. Greg Thomas, *The Sexual Demon of Colonial Power: Pan-African Embodiment and Erotic Schemes of Empire* (Bloomington: Indiana University Press, 2007), 1.

13. Percy Howard, "Frank B. Wilderson, 'Wallowing in the Contradictions,' Part 1," *A Necessary Angel* (blog), https://percy3.wordpress.com.

14. The journalist Utrice Leid makes this point in her coverage of the ongoing spectacles of policing violence and the civil court settlements with victims' families. See *Leid Stories* (podcast), https://leidstories.podbean.com/.

15. Kristian Williams, *Our Enemies in Blue: Police and Power in America* (Boston: South End, 2007), 20. Williams cites Bureau of Labor Statistics, "National Census of Fatal Occupational Injuries in 2000."

16. The political economy behind Obama's election is not relevant to the present study, but would begin with reports of Obama's mother's family's involvement with the CIA and Obama's subsequent grooming for leadership of the global corporate-security state apparatus—factors, needless to say, quite divergent from the narratives of "hope," "change," and racial reconciliation on which the president's candidacy was sold to and consumed by the public.

17. Joy James, "Campaigns against 'Blackness': Criminality, Incivility, and Election to Executive Office," *Critical Sociology* 36, no. 1 (2010): 26.

18. These two tendencies may appear contradictory and countervailing, but I suggest that they are in fact wholly consistent with each other. Although I do not address capital punishment policy and procedure directly, the argument I present in this study suggests that the ethical life of civil society necessarily calls into question the fairness of the death penalty, while at the same time, it remains untroubled by the overwhelmingly black lives that sit condemned on death row. This is how the concern for the status of law equals a disregard for the standing of blackness before it.

19. Lewis Gordon, *Her Majesty's Other Children: Sketches of Racism from a Neocolonial Age* (Lanham, MD: Rowman & Littlefield, 1997), 76.

20. Ibid., 65.

21. See, for example, the Leadership Conference on Civil and Human Rights report, *Wrong Then, Wrong Now: Racial Profiling Before and After September 11, 2001* (Washington, DC: Leadership Conference on Civil and Human Rights, 2002).

22. Fred Moten, "The Case of Blackness," *Criticism* 50, no. 2 (2008): 177.

23. James, "Campaigns against 'Blackness,'" 26.

24. June Cross and Henry Louis Gates Jr., "The Two Nations of Black America," *Frontline* (PBS, 1998), https://www.pbs.org/wgbh/frontline.

25. Cornel West, "Black Strivings in a Twilight Civilization," in Henry Louis Gates Jr. and West, *The Future of the Race* (New York: Knopf, 1996), 72.

26. Frank B. Wilderson III, "Gramsci's Black Marx: Whither the Slave in Civil Society?" *Social Identities* 9, no. 2 (2003): 232.

27. Jared Sexton, *Amalgamation Schemes: Antiblackness and the Critique of Multiracialism* (Minneapolis: University of Minnesota Press, 2008), 53.

28. Ibid., 50–54, citing Steve Martinot, *The Rule of Racialization: Class, Identity, Governance* (Philadelphia: Temple University Press, 2002) and David Theo Goldberg, *The Racial State* (New York: Blackwell, 2002), 5. I take my use of "quarantine" from Sexton's *Amalgamation Schemes*.

29. Sexton, *Amalgamation Schemes*, 12.

30. Gordon, *Her Majesty's Other Children*, 67.

31. See P. Khalil Saucier and Tryon P. Woods, "Introduction: Where Is the Danger in Black Studies and Can We Look at It Again (and Again)?," in *On Marronage: Ethical*

Confrontations with Antiblackness, ed. Saucier and Woods (Trenton, NJ: Africa World Press, 2015), 1–32.

32. Elizabeth Alexander, "'Can You Be BLACK and Look at This?' Reading the Rodney King Videos," in *Black Male: Representations of Masculinity in Contemporary American Art*, ed. Thelma Golden (New York: Whitney Museum, 1995), 95.

33. On "the Negro as an exorbitance for thought," see Nahum D. Chandler, "Of Exorbitance: The Problem of the Negro as a Problem for Thought," *Criticism* 50, no. 3 (2008): 355.

34. Nahum D. Chandler, *X: The Problem of the Negro as a Problem for Thought* (New York: Fordham University Press, 2014).

35. Sylvia Wynter, "On How We Mistook the Map for the Territory, and Re-Imprisoned Ourselves in Our Unbearable Wrongness of Being, of *Desetre*: Black Studies Toward the Human Project," in *Not Only the Master's Tools: African-American Studies in Theory and Practice*, ed. Lewis R. Gordon and Jane Anna Gordon (Boulder: Paradigm, 2006), 108.

36. Wynter cites the National Association for African-American Research, the Black Academy of Arts and Letters, the Institute of the Black World, the New School of Afro-American Thought, the Institute of Black Studies in Los Angeles, and Forum 66 in Detroit. To this list we can also add the informal study groups run by the Black Panther Party.

37. Wynter, "On How We Mistook the Map for the Territory," 109.

38. Noliwe Rooks, *White Money/Black Power: The Surprising History of African American Studies and the Crisis of Race in Higher Education* (Boston: Beacon Press, 2007).

39. Wynter, "On How We Mistook the Map for the Territory," 111.

40. Ibid., 110.

41. On capital's global crisis, see Midnight Notes Collective, ed., *Midnight Oil: Work, Energy, War 1973–1992* (Brooklyn: Autonomedia, 1992).

42. Wynter, "On How We Mistook the Map for the Territory," 113–114.

43. Thomas, *The Sexual Demon of Colonial Power*, 2.

44. Wynter, "On How We Mistook the Map for the Territory," 115.

45. Toni Cade Bambara, "On the Issue of Roles," in *The Black Woman: An Anthology*, ed. Bambara (New York: Penguin, 1970), 103.

46. See Saidiya Hartman, "The Time of Slavery," *South Atlantic Quarterly* 101, no. 4 (2002): 757–777; Frank B. Wilderson III, "Grammar & Ghosts: The Performative

Limits of African Freedom," *Theatre Survey* 50, no. 1 (2009): 119–125; Johannes Fabian, *Time and the Other: How Anthropology Makes Its Object* (New York: Columbia University Press, 2002).

47. Walter Rodney, *Walter Rodney Speaks: The Making of an African Intellectual*, ed. Robert A. Hill (Trenton, NJ: Africa World Press, 1990), 84.

48. See Stephen Steinberg, *Turning Back: The Retreat from Racial Justice in American Thought and Policy* (Boston: Beacon Press, 1995). Steinberg's analysis of Moynihan, William Julius Wilson, and Cornel West draws important connections that bear on my discussion of black feminism here.

49. On the development of a national law enforcement apparatus, see Center for Research on Criminal Justice, *The Iron Fist and the Velvet Glove: An Analysis of the U.S. Police* (Berkeley: Center for Research on Criminal Justice, 1977).

50. Thomas, *The Sexual Demon of Colonial Power*, 1, 2.

51. Hortense Spillers, "Peter's Pans: Eating in the Diaspora," in *Black, White, and in Color: Essays on American Literature and Culture* (Chicago: University of Chicago Press, 2003), 8.

52. Hortense Spillers, with Saidiya Hartman, Farah Jasmine Griffin, Shelley Eversley, and Jennifer L. Morgan, "'Whatcha Gonna Do?': Revisiting 'Mama's Baby, Papa's Maybe: An American Grammar Book,'" *Women's Studies Quarterly* 35, nos. 1/2 (2007): 306.

53. A la Anna Julia Cooper, "Only the black woman can say, when and where I enter, in the quiet, undisputed dignity of my womanhood, without violence and without suing or special patronage, then and there the whole . . . race enters with me." See Cooper, *A Voice from the South* (Xenia, OH: Aldine, 1892); and Paula Giddings, *When and Where I Enter: The Impact of Black Women on Race and Sex in America* (New York: Morrow, 2007).

54. Spillers, "Peter's Pans," 7.

55. Lisa Gail Collins and Margo Natalie Crawford, "Introduction: Power to the People!," in *New Thoughts on the Black Arts Movement*, ed. Collins and Crawford (New Brunswick: Rutgers University Press, 2008), 11; Spillers, "Peter's Pans," 5.

56. See the website of the Fire!! Press, http://firepress.com/index.html; Amiri Baraka and Larry Neal, eds., *Black Fire: An Anthology of Afro-American Writing* (1968; repr. Baltimore: Black Classic, 2008); Beverly Guy-Sheftall, ed., *Words of Fire: An Anthology of African-American Feminist Thought* (New York: New Press, 1995); Charlotte Watson-Sherman, ed., *Sisterfire: Black Womanist Fiction and Poetry* (New

York: HarperCollins, 1994).

57. Kalamu ya Salaam, "Black Arts Movement," in *The Oxford Companion to African American Literature*, ed. William L. Andrews, Frances Smith Foster, and Trudier Harris (New York: Oxford University Press, 1997), 73.

58. Spillers, "Peter's Pans," 5.

59. See, for instance, Angela Y. Davis, *Violence Against Women and the Ongoing Challenge to Racism* (New York: Kitchen Table/Women of Color Press, 1988); and Beth E. Richie, *Arrested Justice: Black Women, Violence, and America's Prison Nation* (New York: New York University Press, 2012).

60. Margo Natalie Crawford, "Black Light on the *Wall of Respect*," in Collins and Crawford, *New Thoughts on the Black Arts Movement*, 28.

61. Angela Y. Davis, *Women, Race, and Class* (New York: Vintage, 1983). See Thomas's chapter, "The Madness of Gender in Plantation America: Sex, Womanhood, and U.S. Chattel Slavery, Revisited," in *The Sexual Demon of Colonial Power*, for an insightful comparison between Davis's "Reflections" and its later rewriting as "The Legacy of Slavery: Standards for a New Womanhood," in *Women, Race, and Class*.

62. Davis, "Reflections on the Black Woman's Role in the Community of Slaves," in *The Angela Y. Davis Reader*, ed. Joy James (Malden, MA: Blackwell, 1998), 116, 123.

63. Davis, "The Legacy of Slavery," in *Women, Race, and Class*, 29; Thomas, *The Sexual Demon of Colonial Power*, throughout.

64. Spillers, with Hartman et al., "'Whatcha Gonna Do?'" 301.

65. Sylvia Wynter, "PROUD FLESH Inter/Views: Sylvia Wynter," *PROUD FLESH: A New Afrikan Journal of Culture, Politics, and Consciousness* 4 (2006): 4.

66. Gloria T. Hull and Barbara Smith, "Introduction: The Politics of Black Women's Studies," in *All the Women Are White, All the Blacks Are Men, But Some of Us Are Brave: Black Women's Studies*, ed. Hull, Patricia Bell Scott, and Smith (New York: Feminist Press, 1982), xxi.

67. Anita Patterson, Review of *Scenes of Subjection: Terror, Slavery, and Self-Making in Nineteenth-Century America*, by Saidiya V. Hartman, *African American Review* 33, no. 4 (1999): 683.

68. Saucier and Woods, *On Marronage*; P. Khalil Saucier and Tryon P. Woods, eds., *Conceptual Aphasia in Black: Displacing Racial Formation* (Lanham, MD: Lexington, 2016). Although scholars working in an afro-pessimist vein have appeared in a variety of journals here and there in recent years, there has only been one journal

that has devoted an entire special issue to the framework (again, by the time of my writing): Dalton Anthony Jones, ed., "Black Holes: Afro-Pessimism, Blackness, and the Discourses of Modernity," special issue, *Rhizomes: Cultural Studies in Emerging Knowledge* 29 (2016)." Other journals have begun to publish critical engagements with afro-pessimism: see "Afro-Pessimism and Black Feminism," special issue, *Theory & Event* 21, no. 1 (2018); and Lewis R. Gordon et al., "Critical Exchange: Afro pessimism," *Contemporary Political Theory* 16 (2017).

69. See Sexton, "The Social Life of Social Death"; and Jared Sexton, "Afro-Pessimism: The Unclear Word," in Jones, "Black Holes," special issue, *Rhizomes: Cultural Studies in Emerging Knowledge* 29 (2016): 1–23.

70. Deborah Bowen, personal communication, November 24, 2017.

71. Frank B. Wilderson III, "'The Position of the Unthought': An Interview with Saidiya V. Hartman," *Qui Parle* 13, no. 2 (2003): 185.

72. Malcolm X, "Message to the Grassroots," in *Malcolm X Speaks: Selected Speeches and Statements*, ed. George Breitman (New York: Grove, 1965), 14–17.

73. See Mari Matsuda, Charles R. Lawrence III, Richard Delgado, and Kimberlé Williams Crenshaw, *Words That Wound: Critical Race Theory, Assaultive Speech, and the First Amendment* (Boulder: Westview Press, 1993).

74. Derrick Bell, *Faces at the Bottom of the Well: The Permanence of Racism* (New York: Basic, 1993).

75. Derrick Bell, "Racial Realism," *Connecticut Law Review* 24, no. 2 (1992): 377.

76. Wilderson, "'The Position of the Unthought,'" 183.

77. W. E. B. DuBois, "Editorial," *The Crisis: Record of the Darker Races* 1, no. 1 (November 1910): 10.

78. E. Franklin Frazier, "The Pathology of Race Prejudice," *The Forum*, June 1927, 856–861.

79. Nathan Hare, "The Challenge of the Black Scholar," in *The Death of White Sociology*, ed. Joyce A. Ladner (New York: Vintage, 1973), 70. Hare's role in the institutionalization of black studies in the academy is tied to this ongoing crisis. Hare was fired in 1967 from his faculty position at one of the preeminent historically black universities, Howard University, because the administration objected to his embrace of Black Power politics. Subsequently hired in 1968 by San Francisco State University to lead the first Department of Black Studies in the nation, Hare ended up coining the term "ethnic studies" to replace the "minority studies" label then

being considered by the university administration. In true Oedipal fashion, Hare's support for an autonomous Department of Black Studies led to his firing by SFSU in 1969, while Black Studies would come to be subsumed within the College of Ethnic Studies. See Rooks, *White Money/Black Power.*

80. Lerone Bennett Jr., *The Challenge of Blackness* (Chicago: Johnson, 1972), 57; Frantz Fanon, *The Wretched of the Earth* (New York: Grove Press, 1968), 49.

81. Adolph Reed Jr., "'What Are the Drums Saying, Booker?': The Curious Role of the Black Public Intellectual," in *Class Notes: Posing as Politics and Other Thoughts on the American Scene* (New York: New Press, 2000), 79.

82. Ibid., 80, 81.

83. Greg Thomas, "Afro-Blue Notes: The Death of Afro-Pessimism (*2.0*)?," in "Afro-Pessimism and Black Feminism," special issue, *Theory & Event* 21, no. 1 (2018): 287.

84. V. Y. Mudimbe, *The Invention of Africa: Gnosis, Philosophy, and the Order of Knowledge* (Indianapolis: Indiana University Press, 1988).

85. See Cheik Anta Diop, *Civilization or Barbarism: An Authentic Anthropology* (Chicago: Chicago Review, 1991). On the postcolonial afro-pessimism, see "The Afropessimism Phenomenon," special issue, *Critical Arts* 25, no. 3 (2011); Gloria Emeagwali, "Six Types of Afro-Pessimists," Udadisi, December 24, 2012, https://udadisi.blogspot.com.

86. Toussaint Nothias, "Definition and Scope of Afro-Pessimism: Mapping the Concept and Its Usefulness for Analysing News Media Coverage of Africa," *Leeds African Studies Bulletin* 74 (December 2012): 54–62.

87. The sum total of Wilderson's take on the connection between old and new afro-pessimisms: "My use of the word bears no resemblance to this definition." Frank B. Wilderson III, *Red, White & Black: Cinema and the Structure of U.S. Antagonisms* (Durham, NC: Duke University Press, 2010), 346 n. 9.

88. Thomas, "Afro-Blue Notes," 284.

89. As Thomas has pointed out on at least two occasions, afro-pessimism draws upon Fanon's *Black Skin, White Masks* at the expense of his full corpus: see Greg Thomas, "The Body Politics of '*Man*' and '*Woman*' in an 'Anti-Black' World: Sylvia Wynter on Humanism's Empire (A Critical Resource Guide)," in Saucier and Woods, *On Marronage*, 67–108, and Thomas, "Afro-Blue Notes"; see Frank B. Wilderson III, "Biko and the Problematic of Presence," in *Biko Lives! Contesting the Legacies of Steve Biko*, ed. Andile Mngxitama, Amanda Alexander, and Nigel Gibson (New York: Palgrave, 2008), 95–114; see Jared Sexton, "People-of-Color-Blindness: Notes on the Afterlife of

Slavery," *Social Text* 28, no. 2 (2010): 31–56.

90. As cited in Thomas, "Afro-Blue Notes," 285, 312–313 n. 15; Cheikh Anta Diop, *The Cultural Unity of Black Africa* (London: Karnak House, 1989), 177, 134–135; Diop, *Civilization or Barbarism*, 361.

91. Thomas, "Afro-Blue Notes," 286.

92. Ibid., 288.

93. Fred Moten, "Black Op," *PMLA* 123, no. 5 (2008): 1743–1747.

94. See Moten, "The Case of Blackness"; Moten, "Black Op"; and Sexton, "The Social Life of Social Death."

95. See Calvin L. Warren, "Black Mysticism: Fred Moten's Phenomenology of (Black) Spirit," *Zeitschrift für Anglistik und Amerikanistik: A Quarterly of Language, Literature and Culture* 65, no. 2 (2017). doi: https://doi.org/10.1515/zaa-2017-0022.

96. Thank you to Khalil Saucier for instructing me on the Hurston–Wright exchange.

97. Marlon Riggs, director, *Tongues Untied* (California Newsreel, 1989).

98. More work would need to be done to trace the specific contribution of the old afro-pessimism to the process by which the black studies movement was denuded of its black power ethos, thereby contributing to the conditions of possibility for the new afro-pessimism. I suggest, however, that key points awaiting connection include the repression of black internationalists, from Paul Robeson to Du Bois to William Patterson to the League of Revolutionary Black Workers and others in the Black Power era; the U.S. role in suppressing decolonization on the African continent (e.g., the CIA assassination of Patrice Lumumba in the Congo, American mercenaries fighting on the side of white Rhodesia, multinational corporate interests across the continent); and the active role of U.S.-based philanthropic foundations in formulating apartheid in southern Africa, segregation in North America, the institutionalization of black studies, and the constriction of academic freedom in African universities. See, variously, the numerous works of Gerald Horne, including *Paul Robeson: The Artist as Revolutionary* (London: Pluto, 2016), *Black Revolutionary: William Patterson and the Globalization of the African American Freedom Struggle* (Champaign: University of Illinois Press, 2013), *Race Woman: The Lives of Shirley Graham Du Bois* (New York: New York University Press, 2000), and *From the Barrel of a Gun: The United States and the War Against Zimbabwe, 1965–1980* (Chapel Hill: University of North Carolina Press, 2001); Dayo Gore, *Radicalism at the Crossroads: African American Women Activists in the Cold War* (New York: New York University

Press, 2012); Dan Georgakas and Marvin Surkin, *Detroit: I Do Mind Dying; A Study in Urban Revolution* (Boston: South End, 1999); Tiffany Willoughby-Herard, *Waste of a White Skin: The Carnegie Corporation and the Racial Logic of White Vulnerability* (Berkeley: University of California Press, 2015); and Silvia Federici, George Caffentzis, and Ousseina Alidou, eds., *A Thousand Flowers: Social Struggles Against Structural Adjustment in African Universities* (Trenton, NJ: Africa World Press, 2000).

99. As Hull and Smith write, for instance, "Because we are so oppressed as Black women, every aspect of our fight for freedom, including teaching and writing about ourselves, must in some way further our liberation." In "Introduction," xxi.

100. See "Afro-Pessimism and Black Feminism."

101. Patrick Wolfe, introduction to *The Settler Complex: Recuperating Binarism in Colonial Studies*, ed. Wolfe (Los Angeles: UCLA American Indian Studies Center, 2016), 2.

102. The increasing appearance of books and articles that address both settler colonialism and antiblackness testifies to the salience of thinking them together in the post-racial period. Although I have not done an exhaustive literature review, I have noticed two tendencies. On the one hand, there is a small number of scholars who have put in the time to study recent scholarship on antiblackness and slavery's afterlife, but for whom this foray into black studies is useful in fortifying their investment in the ethnic studies paradigm. Iyko Day's *Alien Capital: Asian Racialization and the Logic of Settler Colonial Capitalism* (Durham, NC: Duke University Press, 2016) and Day's "Being or Nothingness: Indigeneity, Antiblackness, and Settler Colonial Critique," *Critical Ethnic Studies* 1, no. 2 (2015): 102–121, are good examples of this approach, as is other work on the topic published in *Critical Ethnic Studies*. On the other hand, there is an even smaller number of scholars attempting to straddle paradigms. Tiffany Lethabo King's work exemplifies this approach: see "Labor's Aphasia: Toward Antiblackness as Constitutive to Settler Colonialism," Decolonization: Indigeneity, Education & Society, June 10, 2014, https://decolonization.wordpress.com; and "The Labor of (Re)reading Plantation Landscapes Fungible(ly)," *Antipode: A Radical Journal of Geography* 48, no. 4 (2016): 1022–1039. Both approaches are generative in the sense that they bear the potential for productive engagement, but the problem is that paradigms do not bend well. Paradigms are hard to reconcile with each other because they reflect deeply drawn political desires. Political antagonism being what it is at this historical juncture, either one paradigm wins out over the other in a particular instance, or the earnest

effort to balance both ends up simply treading water. In other words, the antagonism forces a confrontation: as I note in chapter 2, you cannot have it both ways—slavery took that possibility off the table long ago.

103. For instance, Patrick Wolfe, one of the internationally recognized leading voices in settler colonial studies, makes these assertions in *Traces of History: Elementary Structures of Race* (London: Verso, 2016), 63–67. Alternatively, on North American marronage, see for example, Sylviane A. Diouf, *Slavery's Exiles: The Story of the American Maroons* (New York: New York University Press, 2016); and Daniel O. Sayers, *A Desolate Place for a Defiant People: The Archaeology of Maroons, Indigenous Americans, and Enslaved Laborers in the Great Dismal Swamp* (Gainesville: University Press of Florida, 2016). The work of Pan-African filmmaker Haile Gerima is also important in the recovery of maroon traditions. The practice of constructing sub-Saharan Africa as the place where you go to turn human beings into commodified flesh begins at least as far back as the eighth century under Arab slave traders. See, for example, Ronald Segal, *Islam's Black Slaves: The Other Black Diaspora* (New York: Farrar, Strauss & Giroux, 2001). The African slave trade in the Mediterranean region prior to the opening of the transatlantic trade routes was instrumental both in producing the wealth that would later make possible the European "voyages of discovery" to the so-called New World beginning in the fifteenth century and in solidifying racial slavery as the basis for the emergent modern world's culture of politics. See, for example, Cedric Robinson, *Black Marxism: The Making of the Black Radical Tradition* (Chapel Hill: University of North Carolina Press, 2000).

104. See, for example, Jodi A. Byrd, *The Transit of Empire: Indigenous Critiques of Colonialism* (Minneapolis: University of Minnesota Press, 2011), xix, xxv, xxiv. Byrd takes the term "arrivants" from Caribbean poet Kamau Brathwaite, but her use of the term aligns with the basic premise of indigenous studies and settler colonial studies that Africans in the New World are complicit with native dispossession and empire's ongoing terms, and as such are obstacles to indigenous self-determination. Although the "coeval conditions of slavery and indentureship" comes from Lisa Lowe, Byrd endorses the "coeval" status of racial slavery with other conscripted labor regimes, only objecting to the "coeval" status of American Indians and African slaves. See Lisa Lowe, *The Intimacies of Four Continents* (Durham, NC: Duke University Press, 2015).

105. Wolfe, introduction to *The Settler Complex*, 3. On today's iteration of the black "migrant" crisis in the Mediterranean region, see P. Khalil Saucier and Tryon P.

Woods, "Ex Aqua: The Mediterranean Basin, Africans on the Move, and the Politics of Policing," *Theoria: A Journal of Social and Political Theory* 61, no. 141 (2014): 55–75.

106. See Tryon P. Woods, "Pedagogy in Revolution, for the Anti-Revolutionary Stretch: Pan-African Correspondence across Space and Time," in *A Luta Continua: (Re)Introducing Amilcar Cabral to a New Generation of Thinkers*, ed. P. Khalil Saucier (Trenton, NJ: Africa World Press, 2016), 173–204.

107. Jared Sexton, "The *Vel* of Slavery: Tracking the Figure of the Unsovereign," *Critical Sociology* 42, nos. 4–5 (2016): 592.

108. Gwendolyn Brooks, "The Blackstone Rangers—I. As Seen By Disciplines," in *In the Mecca* (New York: Harper & Row, 1968), 44.

CHAPTER ONE. The Time of Blackened Ethics

1. Fred Moten, "The Case of Blackness," *Criticism* 50, no. 2 (2008): 177; Jared Sexton, "Ante-Anti-Blackness: Afterthoughts," *Lateral* 1 (2012): 3.

2. Audre Lorde, *Sister Outsider* (New York: Ten Speed Press, 1984), 39.

3. Ibid., 38.

4. Lewis Gordon, *Disciplinary Decadence: Living Thought in Trying Times* (Boulder: Paradigm, 2006), 1–2.

5. Frantz Fanon, *Black Skin, White Masks* (New York: Grove Press, 1967), 12.

6. Gordon, *Disciplinary Decadence*, 8.

7. Sander L. Gilman, *Difference and Pathology: Stereotypes of Sexuality, Race, and Madness* (Ithaca: Cornell University Press, 1985); Gustav Jahoda, *Images of Savages: Ancient Roots of Modern Prejudice in Western Culture* (London: Routledge, 1999); Bernard Lewis, *Race and Slavery in the Middle East: An Historical Enquiry* (Oxford: Oxford University Press, 1992); R. I. Moore, *The Formation of a Persecuting Society: Power and Deviance in Western Europe, 950–1250* (Oxford: Basil Blackwell, 1987); Ronald Segal, *Islam's Black Slaves: The Other Black Diaspora* (New York: Farrar, Strauss & Giroux, 2001).

8. Jared Sexton, "'The Curtain of the Sky': An Introduction," *Critical Sociology* 36, no. 1 (2010): 18.

9. Saidiya V. Hartman, *Scenes of Subjection: Terror, Slavery, and Self-Making in Nineteenth-Century America* (New York: Oxford University Press, 1997), 79–112; Hortense Spillers, "Mama's Baby, Papa's Maybe: An American Grammar Book," in *Black, White, and in Color: Essays on American Literature and Culture* (Chicago:

University of Chicago Press, 2003), 203–229.

10. Frank B. Wilderson III, *Red, White & Black: Cinema and the Structure of U.S. Antagonisms* (Durham, NC: Duke University Press, 2010), 127.

11. Orlando Patterson, *Slavery and Social Death: A Comparative Study* (Cambridge, MA: Harvard University Press, 1982), 5.

12. Dorothy E. Roberts, *Killing the Black Body: Race, Reproduction, and the Meaning of Liberty* (New York: Pantheon, 1997); Roberts, *Shattered Bonds: The Color of Child Welfare* (New York: Basic Books, 2002).

13. Patterson, *Slavery and Social Death*, 13.

14. Russ Buetner, "At Sentencing, Judge Puts Twins' Crimes in Perspective," *New York Times*, August 23, 2012, A23.

15. Ronald A. T. Judy, *(Dis)Forming the American Canon: African-Arabic Slave Narratives and the Vernacular* (Minneapolis: University of Minnesota Press, 1993), 20–21; Wilderson, *Red, White & Black*, 40.

16. W. E. B. Du Bois, *Black Reconstruction in America: An Essay Towards a History of the Part Which Black Folk Played in Reconstructing Democracy in American, 1860–1880* (New York: Atheneum, 1979), 121.

17. Fanon, *Black Skin, White Masks*; Jared Sexton, "The Social Life of Social Death: On Afro-Pessimism and Black Optimism," *InTensions* 5.0 (fall 2011): 29.

18. Jared Sexton and Huey Copeland, "Raw Life: An Introduction," *Qui Parle* 13, no. 2 (2003): 53.

19. Bryan Wagner, *Disturbing the Peace: Black Culture and the Police Power after Slavery* (Cambridge, MA: Harvard University Press, 2009), 1.

20. Nahum Chandler, *X: The Problem of the Negro as a Problem for Thought* (New York: Fordham University Press, 2014), 139.

21. Michel Foucault, *Language, Counter-Memory, Practice: Selected Essays and Interviews* (Ithaca: Cornell University Press, 1980), 139.

22. Michel Foucault, *The Essential Foucault: Selections from Essential Works of Foucault, 1954–1984* (New York: New Press, 2003), 306.

23. See Evelyn M. Hammonds, "Toward a Genealogy of Black Female Sexuality: The Problematic of Silence," in *Feminist Genealogies, Colonial Legacies, Democratic Futures*, ed. M. Jacqui Alexander and Chandra Talpade Mohanty (New York: Routledge, 1997), 93–104; Roderick A. Ferguson, *The Reorder of Things: The University and Its Pedagogies of Minority Difference* (Minneapolis: University of Minnesota

Press, 2012), 76 and throughout; Roderick A. Ferguson, "Of Our Normative Strivings: African American Studies and the Histories of Sexuality," *Social Text* 23, nos. 3–4 (2005): 85–100. Ferguson's work is the most concentrated exposition of how Foucault haunts contemporary ethnic studies.

24. Sylvia Wynter, "The Re-Enchantment of Humanism: An Interview with Sylvia Wynter," by David Scott, *Small Axe: A Journal of Caribbean Criticism* 8 (September 2000): 199.

25. Moten, "The Case of Blackness," 181.

26. Ibid., 182; Fred Moten, "Black Op," *PMLA* 123, no. 5 (October 2008): 1743–1747.

27. Cornel West, "The New Cultural Politics of Difference," in *Out There: Marginalization and Contemporary Cultures*, ed. Russell Ferguson, Martha Gever, Trinh T. Minh-ha, and Cornel West (New York: The New Museum of Contemporary Art; Cambridge, MA: MIT Press, 1990), 19–38.

28. Greg Thomas, *The Sexual Demon of Colonial Power: Pan-African Embodiment and Erotic Schemes of Empire* (Bloomington: Indiana University Press, 2007), 156; Cheikh Anta Diop, *The African Origin of Civilization: Myth or Reality* (Chicago: Lawrence Hill, 1974); Walter Rodney, *How Europe Underdeveloped Africa* (Washington, DC: Howard University Press, 1982); Saidiya V. Hartman, *Lose Your Mother: A Journey along the Atlantic Slave Route* (New York: Farrar, Strauss & Giroux, 2007); Hartman, "Venus in Two Acts," in *On Marronage: Ethical Confrontations with Antiblackness*, ed. P. Khalil Saucier and Tryon P. Woods (Trenton, NJ: Africa World Press, 2015), 47–66.

29. M. NourbeSe Philip, *A Genealogy of Resistance and Other Essays* (Toronto: Mercury, 1997), 28.

30. Wilderson, *Red, White & Black*, 40–41.

31. Wynter, "The Re-Enchantment of Humanism," 169.

32. Ibid.

33. Ibid., 197–198.

34. David Marriott, "Inventions of Existence: Sylvia Wynter, Frantz Fanon, Sociogeny, and 'the Damned,'" *CR: The New Centennial Review* 11, no. 3 (2011): 48.

35. Chandler, *X*, 130.

36. Marriott, "Inventions of Existence," 47.

37. Malcolm X, "Message to the Grassroots," in *Malcolm X Speaks: Selected Speeches and Statements*, ed. George Breitman (New York: Grove Press, 1965), 8.

38. Marriott, "Inventions of Existence," 52.

39. Sexton, "The Social Life of Social Death," 10.

40. Chandler, *X*, 140–141; Sexton, "The Social Life of Social Death," 11.

41. Fanon, *Black Skin, White Masks*, 77–78.

42. Moten, "The Case of Blackness," 180.

43. Three videos exist for the Lollie case. The first video is from a skyway security camera that shows Lollie arriving in the skyway and sitting in a lobby area that he mistakenly assumes is public space; a security guard tells him to move, which he does; the guard proceeds to call the police anyway. Lollie records the second video with his cell phone, beginning a few minutes after the first police officer arrives. The third video is from a different skyway security camera located near where the police assault occurred. All three videos can be found online: Conor Friedersdorf, "Man Arrested While Picking Up His Kids: 'The Problem Is I'm Black,'" *The Atlantic*, August 29, 2014, http://www.theatlantic.com; Laura Yuen, "Panel Questioned after Cops Cleared in St. Paul Stun Gun Arrest," *MPR News*, November 23, 2014, http://www.mprnews.org.

44. Mike Murashige, "Haile Gerima and the Political Economy of Cinematic Resistance," in *Representing Blackness: Issues in Film and Video*, ed. Valerie Smith (New Brunswick: Rutgers University Press, 1997), 192.

45. For more on the case of the New Jersey 4, see the dedicated *Free the NJ4* blog https://freenj4.wordpress.com/, the documentary film *Out in the Night* (dir. blair doroshwalther, 2014) produced about the case, http://www.outinthenight.com/, as well as Aishah Shahidah Simmons, "Who Will Revere US? (Black LGTBQ People, Straight Women, and Girls) (Part 1)," Feminist Wire, April 23, 2012, http://thefeministwire.com.

46. Laura S. Logan, "The Case of the 'Killer Lesbians,'" The Public Intellectual, July 18, 2011, http://thepublicintellectual.org.

47. Wynter, "The Re-Enchantment of Humanism," 180.

48. Wilderson, *Red, White & Black*, 38.

49. Ibid., 138.

50. Judy, *(Dis)Forming the American Canon*, 89, 107.

51. *State of Missouri v. Darren Wilson*, Grand Jury Volume V, September 16, 2014, 224–225, http://apps.npr.org/documents/document.html?id=1370569-grand-jury-volume-5.

52. *State of Missouri v. Darren Wilson*, Grand Jury Volume V, 216.

53. *State of Missouri v. Darren Wilson*, Grand Jury Volume V, 212.

54. https://www.youtube.com/watch?v=xXonpyOdS3A.

55. *State of Missouri v. Darren Wilson*, Grand Jury Volume V, 228–229.

56. Wynter, "The Re-Enchantment of Humanism," 186.

57. Steve Martinot and Jared Sexton, "The Avant-Garde of White Supremacy," *Social Identities* 9, no. 2 (2003): 175.

58. Hartman, *Scenes of Subjection*, 52.

59. Jamiles Lartey, "Alabama Police Shot a Teen Dead, But His Friend Got 30 Years for the Murder," *The Guardian*, April 15, 2018, https://www.theguardian.com/us.

60. See the numerous reports around the media regarding "Witness 40," Sandra McElroy, first reported by *The Smoking Gun*, "'Witness 40': Exposing a Fraud in Ferguson," December 15, 2014, http://www.thesmokinggun.com.

CHAPTER TWO. The Inadmissible Career of Social Death

1. Evelyn A. Williams, *Inadmissible Evidence: The Story of the African-American Trial Lawyer Who Defended the Black Liberation Army* (Lincoln, NE: Self-published, iUniverse.com, 2000), 84.

2. Ibid.

3. Elaine Brown, *The Condemnation of Little B: New Age Racism in America* (Boston: Beacon, 2002).

4. Assata Shakur, as quoted in Williams, *Inadmissible Evidence*, 88.

5. National Crime Information Center, "NCIC Missing Person and Unidentified Person Statistics for 2013," Federal Bureau of Investigation, http://www.fbi.gov/services/cjis/ncic.

6. Louise Boyle, "The Faces of the Forgotten: Heartbreaking Plight of the 64,000 Black Women Missing Across America . . . As the Country Turns a Blind Eye," DailyMail.com, January 12, 2012, http://www.dailymail.co.uk. Also see the Black and Missing Foundation, http://www.blackandmissinginc.com/cdad/index.cfm, and Black and Missing But Not Forgotten, http://blackandmissing.org.

7. Polly Klaas was abducted from her bedroom on October 1, 1993, in Petaluma, California, and later found strangled to death. For more than two months, over four thousand people searched for Klaas, including one of the largest law enforcement searches ever deployed in California; her case was featured on *20/20* and *America's Most Wanted* and led to the passage of California's Three Strikes Law. See *The Legacy:*

Murder and Media, Politics and Prisons (Michael J. Moore, dir., 1999). Elizabeth Smart was abducted from her bedroom in Salt Lake City, Utah, on June 5, 2002. She was rescued nine months later on March 12, 2003, partly due to *America's Most Wanted* featuring her case. Thousands of people participated in the search for Smart. After her rescue there were national media interviews, books published about the case, and a made-for-television movie. Smart went to Congress to successfully promote passage of sexual predator legislation and the AMBER alert system.

8. Hortense Spillers, "Black, White, and in Color, or Learning How to Paint: Toward an Intramural Protocol of Reading," in *Black, White and In Color: Essays on American Literature and Culture* (Chicago: University of Chicago Press, 2003), 280.

9. Kali Gross, "Missing Black Women Are Usually Ignored Until They're Proved Worthy," The Root, November 10, 2014, http://www.theroot.com.

10. See, "Jackie Returns to the House Where She Was Held Captive," *Our America with Lisa Ling*, season 4, episode 407, aired July 31, 2014, http://www.oprah.com.

11. Frank B. Wilderson III, *Red, White & Black: Cinema and the Structure of U.S. Antagonisms* (Durham, NC: Duke University Press, 2010), 38.

12. Lewis Gordon, *Her Majesty's Other Children: Sketches of Racism from a Neocolonial Age* (Lanham, MD: Rowman & Littlefield, 1997), 63.

13. Lewis Gordon, *Existentia Africana: Understanding Africana Existential Thought* (New York: Routledge, 2000), 87.

14. Orlando Patterson, *Slavery and Social Death: A Comparative Study* (Cambridge, MA: Harvard University Press, 1985), 4; Jared Sexton, "The Social Life of Social Death: On Afro-Pessimism and Black Optimism," *InTensions* 5.0 (fall 2011): 31.

15. C. L. R. James, "African Independence and the Myth of African Inferiority," in *Education and Black Struggle: Notes from the Colonized World*, ed. Institute of the Black World (Cambridge, MA: Harvard Educational Review, 1974), 34.

16. See chapter 1, "The Ruse of Analogy," in Wilderson, *Red, White & Black*. Eugene Genovese, writing in the *Boston Review* (October/November 1993): "The black experience in this country has been a phenomenon without analog."

17. Lisa Marie Cacho, *Social Death: Racialized Rightlessness and the Criminalization of the Unprotected* (New York: New York University Press, 2012), 166.

18. Ibid., 13; citing Lindon Barrett, *Blackness and Value: Seeing Double* (Cambridge, MA: Harvard University Press, 1998), 19, 21 (citing, in turn, Jacques Derrida).

19. Barrett, *Blackness and Value*, 28.

20. Ibid., 148.

21. On aphasia, see Frank B. Wilderson III, "The Vengeance of Vertigo: Aphasia and Abjection in the Political Trials of Black Insurgents," in *On Marronage: Ethical Confrontations with Antiblackness*, ed. P. Khalil Saucier and Tryon P. Woods (Trenton, NJ: Africa World Press, 2015), 213–240; and Saucier and Woods, eds., *Conceptual Aphasia in Black: Displacing Racial Formation* (Lanham, MD: Lexington Books, 2016).

22. Wilderson, *Red, White & Black*, 50.

23. Barrett, *Blackness and Value*, 147.

24. W. E. B. Du Bois, *The Souls of Black Folk* (New York: Dover Publications, 1994), 3.

25. Sylvia Wynter, "PROUD FLESH Inter/Views: Sylvia Wynter," *PROUD FLESH: A New Afrikan Journal of Culture, Politics, and Consciousness* 4 (2006): 4 (emphasis in the original).

26. Wilderson, *Red, White & Black*, 18.

27. Saidiya V. Hartman, *Scenes of Subjection: Terror, Slavery, and Self-Making in Nineteenth-Century America* (New York: Oxford University Press, 1997), 22.

28. Social death as the condition of human negation—life in the crosshairs of gratuitous violence, the nonrelations of structural antagonism—is profoundly generative of both tensions internal to the black community and the (anti)relations between black and nonblack. Disagreement within black studies about what to do about social death, analytically speaking, tends to rally around a rejection of "social death" as an appropriate, accurate, or strategic frame with which to analyze and forward black social movement. The discomfort with "social death" in fact betrays an uneasiness with the "ethics of violence" subtending any approach to black studies, and the politics of social death, therefore, is a proxy for how to relate to black political agendas. This issue demands closer consideration than space permits me here. *Blackhood Against the Police Power* stands as my opening venture into confronting this political problem: by doing the analysis that social death compels, I aim to offer an intervention that can be accountable to the debates internal to black struggle.

29. Cacho, *Social Death*, 81.

30. Ibid., 82.

31. See, for example, Patricia Ticineto Clough and Craig Willse, eds., *Beyond Biopolitics: Essays on the Governance of Life and Death* (Durham, NC: Duke University Press, 2011).

32. Michel Foucault, *Society Must Be Defended: Lectures at the Collège de France, 1975–1976*, trans. David Macey (New York: Picador, 2003). See, as well, David Theo Goldberg, *Racist Culture: Philosophy and the Politics of Meaning* (Malden: Blackwell, 1993) and Falguni A. Sheth, *Toward a Political Philosophy of Race* (Albany: SUNY Press, 2009).

33. See Achille Mbembe, "Necropolitics," *Public Culture* 15, no. 1 (2003): 11–40; and Mbembe, *On the Postcolony* (Berkeley: University of California Press, 2001).

34. See, for example, Giorgio Agamben, *Homo Sacer: Sovereign Power and Bare Life* (Palo Alto: Stanford University Press, 1998); Agamben, *State of Exception* (Chicago: University of Chicago Press, 2005); Hannah Arendt, *The Origins of Totalitarianism* (New York: Harcourt, Brace, Jovanovich, 1973); Arendt, *Eichmann in Jerusalem: A Report on the Banality of Evil* (New York: Penguin Classics, 2005); and Jean-Paul Sartre, *Anti-Semite and Jew: An Exploration of the Etiology of Hate* (New York: Shocken Books, 1948).

35. Alexander G. Weheliye, *Habeas Viscus: Racializing Assemblages, Biopolitics, and Black Feminist Theories of the Human* (Durham, NC: Duke University Press, 2014), 1.

36. See Joy James, *Resisting State Violence: Radicalism, Gender, and Race in U.S. Culture* (Minneapolis: University of Minnesota Press, 1996) and Jared Sexton, "People-of-Color-Blindness: Notes on the Afterlife of Slavery," *Social Text* 28, no. 2 (2010): 31–56.

37. P. Khalil Saucier and Tryon P. Woods, "Ex Aqua: The Mediterranean Basin, Africans on the Move, and the Politics of Policing," *Theoria: A Journal of Social and Political Theory* 61, no. 141 (2014): 61–62. Aimé Césaire, *Discourse on Colonialism* (New York: Monthly Review Press, 2001); Oliver Cromwell Cox, *Race: A Study in Social Dynamics* (New York: Monthly Review Press, 2000); Du Bois, *The Souls of Black Folk*; Frantz Fanon, *The Wretched of the Earth* (New York: Grove Press, 1968); C. L. R. James, *Beyond a Boundary* (Durham, NC: Duke University Press, 2013); George Padmore, *Pan-Africanism or Communism* (New York: Doubleday, 1972); Richard Wright, *White Man, Listen!* (New York: Perennial, 1995).

38. Sexton, "People-of-Color-Blindness," 48.

39. David Marriott has described *Habeas Viscus* as "brutally written." See Marriott, "Black Critical and Cultural Theory," *Year's Work in Critical and Cultural Theory* 23, no. 1 (2015): 111.

40. Weheliye, *Habeas Viscus*, 37.

41. Ibid., 72.

42. Ibid., 131.

43. Ibid., 44–45.

44. Ibid., 131.

45. Cited in Fred Jerome, "Einstein, Race, and the Myth of the Cultural Icon," *Isis: Journal of the History of Science Society* 95, no. 4 (2004): 628–629.

46. Weheliye, *Habeas Viscus*, 135.

47. Jared Sexton, "The *Vel* of Slavery: Tracking the Figure of the Unsovereign," *Critical Sociology* 42, nos. 4–5 (2016): 583–597.

48. Hortense Spillers, "Mama's Baby, Papa's Maybe: An American Grammar Book," in *Black, White, and in Color*, 206.

49. Weheliye, *Habeas Viscus*, 2.

50. Ibid., 112, 113.

51. Spillers, "Mama's Baby, Papa's Maybe," 215.

52. Ibid.

53. Ibid., 217.

54. Ibid., 207.

55. Ibid.

56. Weheliye, *Habeas Viscus*, 43–44.

57. Ibid., 40.

58. Sylvia Wynter, "On How We Mistook the Map for the Territory, and Re-Imprisoned Ourselves in Our Unbearable Wrongness of Being, of *Desetre*: Black Studies Toward the Human Project," in *Not Only the Master's Tools: African-American Studies in Theory and Practice*, ed. Lewis R. Gordon and Jane Anna Gordon (Boulder: Paradigm, 2006), 153.

59. Greg Thomas, "The Body Politics of '*Man*' and '*Woman*' in an 'Anti-Black' World: Sylvia Wynter on Humanism's Empire (A Critical Resource Guide)," in Saucier and Woods, *On Marronage*, 67–108.

60. Spillers, "Mama's Baby, Papa's Maybe," 228.

61. Ibid., 228.

62. Hartman, *Scenes of Subjection*, 86.

63. Ibid.; Sexton, "People-of-Color-Blindness," 33.

64. Greg Thomas, *The Sexual Demon of Colonial Power: Pan-African Embodiment and Erotic Schemes of Empire* (Bloomington: Indiana University Press, 2007), 46.

65. Spillers, "Mama's Baby, Papa's Maybe," 228.

66. See Combahee River Collective, "The Combahee River Collective Statement," in *Homegirls: A Black Feminist Anthology*, ed. Barbara Smith (New Brunswick: Rutgers University Press, 2000), 264–274; Terrion L. Williamson, "Who Is Killing Us," Feminist Wire, January 18, 2012, http://www.thefeministwire.com; and Williamson, "Why Did They Die? On Combahee and the Serialization of Black Death," *Souls: A Critical Journal of Black Culture, Politics, and Society* 19, no. 3 (2017): 328–341.

67. See Kimberlé Williams Crenshaw, "Black Women Still in Defense of Ourselves," *The Nation*, October 5, 2011, https://www.thenation.com; "#SayHerName: Resisting Police Brutality against Black Women," African American Policy Forum, July 16, 2015, http://www.aapf.org; "About BYP100," Black Youth Project 100, https://byp100.org.

68. Title VII of the Civil Rights Act of 1964 prohibits employment discrimination based on race, color, religion, sex, and national origin. See "Title VII of the Civil Rights Act of 1964," Equal Employment Opportunity Commission, https://www.eeoc.gov. See Kimberlé Williams Crenshaw, "Demarginalizing the Intersection of Race and Sex: A Black Feminist Critique of Antidiscrimination Law, Feminist Theory, and Antiracist Politics," *University of Chicago Legal Forum* 1989, no. 1, article 8 (139–167); and Crenshaw, "Mapping the Margins: Intersectionality, Identity Politics, and Violence against Women of Color," *Stanford Law Review* 43 (1991): 1241–1299.

69. *DeGraffenreid v. General Motors*, 413 F Supp 142 (E D Mo 1976).

70. *Moore v. Hughes Helicopter*, 708 F2d 475 (9th Cir 1983).

71. *Payne v. Travenol*, 673 F2d 798 (5th Cir 1982).

72. Crenshaw, "Demarginalizing the Intersection of Race and Sex," 150.

73. David Kairys, "Unconscious Racism," *Temple Law Review* 83 (2011): 857–866. Also see Kairys, "A Brief History of Race and the Supreme Court," *Temple Law Review* 79 (2006): 751–771.

74. Patrice D. Douglass, "At the Intersections of Assemblages: Black Gendered Violence in Theory and in Thought," in Saucier and Woods, *Conceptual Aphasia in Black*, 103–126.

75. Spillers, "Mama's Baby, Papa's Maybe," 203.

76. Weheliye, *Habeas Viscus*, 28.

77. See P. Khalil Saucier and Tryon P. Woods, "Upgrade and Upstage: Injunctions against Stephanie Rawlings-Blake, 'Black Feminism,' and Hip Hop Studies at the Ledge (A Response to Forster)," *Journal of Popular Music Studies* 27, no. 3 (2015): 353–363.

78. Of course, Spillers, Wynter, and Hartman would each readily acknowledge their

debts to black feminists of all kinds, as I have in the introduction. The emphasis of my argument, however, reflects the need to underscore a submerged intellectual tradition.

79. Quoted in Robert Draper, "The Lost Girls of Rocky Mount," *GQ*, June 9, 2010, http://www.gq.com. This case was brought to my attention by Kristen Maye, for which I am grateful.

80. Frank B. Wilderson III, "The Black Liberation Army and the Paradox of Political Engagement," in *Postcoloniality-Decoloniality-Black Critique*, ed. Sabine Broeck and Carsten Junker (Frankfurt: Campus Verlag, 2014), 175–210.

81. Draper, "The Lost Girls of Rocky Mount."

82. Assata Shakur, *Assata: An Autobiography* (Chicago: Lawrence Hill, 2001), 49.

83. Wilderson, "The Black Liberation Army," 180.

84. Draper, "The Lost Girls of Rocky Mount."

85. James Baldwin, *The Evidence of Things Not Seen* (New York: Henry Holt, 1995), xiv.

86. Allen Feldman, *Formations of Violence: The Narrative of the Body and Political Terror in Northern Ireland* (Chicago: University of Chicago Press, 1991), 289, as cited in Wilderson, "The Black Liberation Army," 200.

87. David Eltis, "Europeans and the Rise and Fall of African Slavery in the Americas: An Interpretation," *American Historical Review* 98, no. 5 (1993): 1423; as cited in Wilderson, "The Black Liberation Army," 210.

CHAPTER THREE. From Blackland, with Love

1. Frantz Fanon, *The Wretched of the Earth* (New York: Grove Press, 1968), 37; Greg Thomas, *The Sexual Demon of Colonial Power: Pan-African Embodiment and Erotic Schemes of Empire* (Bloomington: Indiana University Press, 2007), 95.

2. Thomas, *The Sexual Demon of Colonial Power*.

3. Following P. Khalil Saucier and Tryon P. Woods, "Introduction: Where Is the Danger in Black Studies and Can We Look at It Again (and Again)?" in *On Marronage: Ethical Confrontations with Antiblackness*, ed. Saucier and Woods (Trenton, NJ: Africa World Press, 2015), 1–32, I acknowledge that of course there is sexism and homophobia within the black studies quarter, but I resist the mischaracterization of the field as a whole in these terms. This mischaracterization is an example of precisely the sexual violence of antiblackness that I am interested in countering. And, of course, I do not refer to the interpersonal dynamics within specific black studies–related

departments across the U.S. academy. The elitism, sexism, and homophobia—or, as Frantz Fanon and Greg Thomas might call it, internalized Negrophobia—in these institutional spaces can be notorious and disgusting. For treatments of this sexism and homophobia within black studies or black communities or with respect to black people, see variously Kathleen Neal Cleaver "Women, Power, and Revolution." *New Political Science* 21, no. 2 (1999): 231–236; Cathy J. Cohen, "Punks, Bulldaggers, and Welfare Queens: The Radical Potential of Queer Politics," *GLQ: A Journal of Lesbian and Gay Studies* 3 (1997): 437–465; Carol Boyce Davies, "The Persistence of Institutional Sexism in Africana Studies," Black Perspectives, September 17, 2018, https://www.aaihs.org/the-persistence-of-institutional-sexism-in-africana-studies/; Angela Y. Davis, "Reflections on the Black Woman's Role in the Community of Slaves," in *The Angela Y. Davis Reader*, ed. Joy James (Malden, MA: Blackwell, 1998); Gloria T. Hull, Patricia Bell Scott, and Barbara Smith, eds., *All the Women Are White, All the Blacks Are Men, But Some of Us Are Brave: Black Women's Studies* (New York: Feminist Press, 1982); Joy James, *Resisting State Violence: Radicalism, Gender, and Race in U.S. Culture* (Minneapolis: University of Minnesota Press, 1996); Barbara Ransby and Tracye Matthews, "Black Popular Culture and the Transcendence of Patriarchal Illusions," *Race & Class* 35, no. 1 (1993): 57–68; Beth Richie, *Compelled to Crime: The Gender Entrapment of Battered Black Women* (New York: Routledge, 1996); Dorothy E. Roberts, *Killing the Black Body: Race, Reproduction, and the Meaning of Liberty* (New York: Pantheon, 1997); Ida B. Wells-Barnett, *On Lynchings* (New York: Courier Dover Publications, 2014); Ida B. Wells-Barnett, *Southern Horrors: Lynch Law in All Its Phases* (New York: Floating Press, 2014); Sylvia Wynter, "Genital Mutilation or Symbolic Birth—Female Circumcision, Lost Origins, and the Aculturalism of Feminist/Western Thought," *Case Western Reserve Law Review* 47 (1996): 501–552. Do not miss Thomas's exemplary dissection of "Sexual Imitation and the 'Greedy Little Caste': Race and Class as Erotic Conflict in Frantz Fanon" in *The Sexual Demon of Colonial Power.*

4. Thomas, *The Sexual Demon of Colonial Power*, 7, 23.

5. Christina Sharpe, *Monstrous Intimacies: Making Post-Slavery Subjects* (Durham, NC: Duke University Press, 2010), 56.

6. Alexander G. Weheliye, *Habeas Viscus: Racializing Assemblages, Biopolitics, and Black Feminist Theories of the Human* (Durham, NC: Duke University Press, 2014), 55.

7. Jared Sexton, *Amalgamation Schemes: Antiblackness and the Critique of*

Multiracialism (Minneapolis: University of Minnesota Press, 2008), 9.

8. See, for example, Lisa Lowe, *Immigrant Acts: On Asian American Cultural Politics* (Durham, NC: Duke University Press, 1996); Cherrie Moraga and Gloria Anzaldua, eds., *This Bridge Called My Back: Writings by Radical Women of Color* (New York: Kitchen Table/Women of Color, 1983).

9. LaMonda Horton Stallings, *Mutha' Is Half a Word: Intersections of Folklore, Vernacular, Myth, and Queerness in Black Female Culture* (Columbus: Ohio State University, 2007), 37.

10. Ibid.

11. Toni Cade Bambara, "On the Issue of Roles," in *The Black Woman: An Anthology*, ed. Bambara (New York: Penguin, 1970), 109.

12. On "precarity," see Franco Barchiesi, "Precarity as Capture: A Conceptual Deconstruction of the Worker-Slave Analogy," in Saucier and Woods, *On Marronage*, 183–212.

13. Toni Cade Bambara, *Those Bones Are Not My Child* (New York: Pantheon, 1999), 274.

14. Rebecca Wanzo, "Terror at Home: Naturalized Victimization in *Those Bones Are Not My Child*," in *Savoring the Salt: The Legacy of Toni Cade Bambara*, ed. Linda Janet Holmes and Cheryl A. Wall (Philadelphia: Temple University Press, 2007), 247.

15. Kay Bonetti, "An Interview with Toni Cade Bambara," in *Conversations with Toni Cade Bambara*, ed. Thabiti Lewis (Jackson: University Press of Mississippi, 2012), 47.

16. Bambara, *Bones*, 298.

17. One of the few extended sociological treatments of the case: Bernard Headley, *The Atlanta Youth Murders and the Politics of Race* (Carbondale: Southern Illinois University Press, 1999).

18. Bambara, *Bones*, 227–228.

19. Ibid., 226.

20. Ibid., 206.

21. Aside, this insight from Bambara should be extrapolated to undermine the discourse on "safe space" that predominates in white institutions of higher learning (in particular).

22. See Billie Holiday's version of "Strange Fruit," https://www.youtube.com/watch?v=Web007rzSOI.

23. Although the black studies archive features notable treatments of space and geography, theoretical work on the black land–body connection remains

underdeveloped. My discussion of *Bones* is not meant to fill this void, although I gesture in a direction that I believe may yet prove fruitful. An indispensable resource for thinking about blackness and land is the Black/Land Project, Mistinguette Smith, founder and director, http://www.blacklandproject.org.

24. Jodi Melamed, *Represent and Destroy: Rationalizing Violence in the New Racial Capitalism* (Minneapolis: University of Minnesota Press, 2011), 123, 126.

25. Ibid., 125.

26. Malcolm X, "The Black Revolution," in *Malcolm X Speaks: Selected Speeches and Statements*, ed. George Breitman (New York: Grove Press, 1965), 49–50.

27. For more on Malcolm X and racial blackness, see Tryon P. Woods, "A Re-appraisal of Black Radicalism and Human Rights Doctrine," in Saucier and Woods, *On Marronage*, 268–269.

28. Melamed, *Represent and Destroy*, 117.

29. Ibid.

30. Ibid., 134.

31. Sylvia Wynter, "PROUD FLESH Inter/Views: Sylvia Wynter," *PROUD FLESH: A New Afrikan Journal of Culture, Politics, and Consciousness* 4 (2006): 18.

32. Melamed, *Represent and Destroy*, 134.

33. Bambara, *Bones*, 182, 183.

34. Claudia Tate, "Toni Cade Bambara," in Lewis, *Conversations with Toni Cade Bambara*, 53.

35. See Frank B. Wilderson III, "Gramsci's Black Marx: Whither the Slave in Civil Society?," *Social Identities* 9, no. 2 (2003): 225–240.

36. Bonetti, "Interview with Toni Cade Bambara," 47.

37. Kalamu ya Salaam, "Searching for the Mother Tongue," in Lewis, *Conversations with Toni Cade Bambara*, 26.

38. Melamed, *Represent and Destroy*, 135.

39. Bambara, *Bones*, 200.

40. Ibid., 582.

41. W. E. B. Du Bois, *The Souls of Black Folk* (New York: Dover Publications, 1994).

42. Cheryl A. Wall, "Toni's Obligato: Bambara and the African American Literary Tradition," in Holmes and Wall, *Savoring the Salt*, 37.

43. Louis Massiah, "How She Came By Her Name," in Lewis, *Conversations with Toni Cade Bambara*, 133.

44. Ibid.

45. Ibid., 134.

46. Alexis Pauline Gumbs, "One Thing: Toni Cade Bambara in the Speaking Everyday," Feminist Wire, March 25, 2014, http://www.thefeministwire.com.

47. Ibid.

48. Eleanor Traylor, "The Language of Soul in Toni Cade Bambara's Re/Conceived Academy," in Holmes and Wall, *Savoring the Salt*, 79.

49. Ibid., 77.

50. Toni Cade Bambara, "Salvation Is the Issue," in *Black Women Writers 1950–1980: A Critical Evaluation*, ed. Mari Evans (Garden City, NY: Anchor-Doubleday, 1984), 41–47 (as cited in Traylor, "The Language of Soul," 77).

51. Toni Cade Bambara, "What It Is I Think I'm Doing Anyhow," in *The Writer on Her Work: Contemporary Women Reflect on Their Art and Their Situation*, ed. Janet Sturnberg (New York: W.W. Norton, 1980), 165.

52. Akasha (Gloria) Hull, "A Conversation with Toni Cade Bambara," in Lewis, *Conversations with Toni Cade Bambara*, 105.

53. Massiah, "How She Came By Her Name," 133.

54. Bambara, *Bones*, 167, 168.

55. Hull, "A Conversation with Toni Cade Bambara," 105.

56. Ibid., 101.

57. Stockholm syndrome is where prisoners come to identify with their captors. Bambara, *Bones*, 560.

58. Ibid., 222, 226.

59. Ibid., 328–329.

60. See, variously, Lance Hill, *The Deacons for Defense: Armed Resistance and the Civil Rights Movement* (Chapel Hill: University of North Carolina Press, 2006); Nicholas Johnson, *Negroes and the Gun: The Black Tradition of Arms* (New York: Prometheus, 2014); Akinyele Omowale Umoja, *We Will Shoot Back: Armed Resistance in the Mississippi Freedom Movement* (New York: New York University Press, 2014); Robert F. Williams, *Negroes with Guns* (Detroit: Wayne State University Press, 1998).

61. Toni Cade Bambara, "Black English," in *Curriculum Approaches from a Black Perspective* (Atlanta: Black Child Development Institute, 1972), 78.

62. Bambara, *Bones*, 183.

63. Ibid., 565, 568.

64. Ibid., 104.

65. Ibid.

66. Greg Thomas, "'Neo-Slave Narratives' and Literacies of Maroonage," in *Toni Morrison: au-dela du visible ordinaire / Beyond the Ordinary Visible*, ed. Andree-Anne Kekeh-Dika, Maryemma Graham, and Janis A. Mayes (Paris: Presses Universitaires de Vincennes, 2015), 214.

67. Toni Morrison, *Beloved* (New York: Vintage, 2004), 11.

68. Assata Shakur, *Assata: An Autobiography* (Chicago: Lawrence Hill, 2001), 99–117.

69. George L. Jackson, *Soledad Brother: The Prison Letters of George Jackson* (Chicago: Chicago Review Press, 1994), 8.

70. Ibid., 10, 13.

71. Morrison, *Beloved*, 159.

72. Jackson, *Soledad Brother*, as cited in Thomas, "'Neo-Slave Narratives,'" 203.

73. Thomas, "'Neo-Slave Narratives,'" 217.

74. Ibid., 205.

CHAPTER FOUR. All the Things Your Movement Could Be by Now If It Were to Center Black Self-Determination

1. Kuwasi Balagoon, "Brink's Trial Closing Statement," in *A Soldier's Story: Writings by a Revolutionary New Afrikan Anarchist* (Montreal: Kersplebedeb, 2003), 27, 32.

2. Ibid., 33.

3. Elsewhere I examine these works as part of the nascent academic field of "critical prison studies." See "'Something of the Fever and the Fret': Antiblackness in the Critical Prison Studies Fold," in *Conceptual Aphasia in Black: Displacing Racial Formation*, ed. P. Khalil Saucier and Tryon P. Woods (Lanham, MD: Lexington, 2016), 127–154. Despite the diversity of the burgeoning scholarship affiliated with CPS, it all shares with Alexander and Gilmore two basic problems: a reification of the prison or the police as the problem to be overcome; and a subsumption of the specificity of blackness within other rubrics of power that inevitably and necessarily eclipse black ethical claims. The recent scholarship to which these problems apply includes work by Jordan T. Camp, Robert T. Chase, Dennis Childs, Keith Feldman, Luis Fernandez, Sarah Haley, Kelly Lytle Hernandez, Elizabeth Hinton, Julilly Kohler-Hausmann, Jenna Loyd, Anoop Mirpuri, Khalil Muhammad, Micol Seigel, Stuart Schrader, Jonathan Simon, Dean Spade, Eric Stanley, David Stein, and Heather Thompson,

among others.

4. *Terry v. Ohio*, 392 U.S. 1, 16–17 (1968).

5. Andrew E. Taslitz, *Reconstructing the Fourth Amendment: A History of Search and Seizure, 1789–1868* (New York: New York University Press, 2006), 32.

6. Gerald Horne, *The Counter-Revolution of 1776: Slave Resistance and the Origins of the United States of America* (New York: New York University Press, 2014).

7. From the legal papers of John Adams, as cited in Taslitz, *Reconstructing the Fourth Amendment*, 39n78.

8. Ibid., 39 and 39n81.

9. William Cuddihy, "The Fourth Amendment: Origins and Original Meaning" (Ph.D. Diss., University of Claremont, California, 1990), 1171; as cited in Taslitz, *Reconstructing the Fourth Amendment*, 39.

10. Bernard Bailyn, *The Ideological Origins of the American Revolution* (New York: Belknap, 1967), 232; as cited in Taslitz, *Reconstructing the Fourth Amendment*, 39n81.

11. As cited in Taslitz, *Reconstructing the Fourth Amendment*, 39.

12. Thomas Jefferson, *Notes on the State of Virginia* (New York: Harper & Row, 1964), 157; as cited in Taslitz, *Reconstructing the Fourth Amendment*, 40. Jefferson not only was the owner, trader, and pillager of hundreds of Africans on his plantation at Monticello (Sally Hemings being but a young girl when Jefferson first began raping her), he also lived such an utterly gluttonous life that he was the equivalent of four million dollars in debt at the time of his death. See Kimberly Juanita Brown, "Saving Mr. Jefferson: Slavery and Denial at Monticello," in *On Marronage: Ethical Confrontations with Antiblackness*, ed. P. Khalil Saucier and Tryon P. Woods (Trenton, NJ: Africa World Press, 2015), 109–130.

13. George Washington, "Letter to Bryan Fairfax," in *George Washington: A Collection*, ed. W. B. Allen (Indianapolis: Liberty Fund, 1988), 38; as cited in Taslitz, *Reconstructing the Fourth Amendment*, 40. Gerald Horne surmises that Washington was at least as concerned with policing the rebellious slaves on his plantation at Mount Vernon as he was with leading the nascent nation, noting that "by 1764, he owed one of his London creditors a still hefty eighteen hundred pounds sterling and certainly had an incentive to both preserve his slave property and escape from the Crown which seemed to be calling it into question." The same point would also apply to Jefferson, whose debts were far more substantial. Horne, *The Counter-Revolution of 1776*, 19.

14. Taslitz, *Reconstructing the Fourth Amendment*, 41.

15. *Floyd, et al., v. City of New York, et al.*, 959 F. Supp. 2d 540, 23 (2013); *Alabama v. White*, 496 U.S. 325, 329 (1990).

16. *Floyd*, 14–15.

17. Horne, *The Counter-Revolution of 1776*, 9.

18. Ibid., viii. Also see Thomas J. Davis, *Rumor of Revolt: The "Great Negro Plot" in Colonial New York* (New York: Free Press, 1985); Thelma Wills Foote, *Black and White Manhattan: The History of Racial Formation in Colonial New York City* (New York: Oxford University Press, 2004); John Hope Franklin and Loren Schweninger, *Runaway Slaves: Rebels on the Plantation* (New York: Oxford University Press, 1999); Peter Charles Hoffer, *Cry Liberty! The Great Stono River Slave Rebellion of 1739* (New York: Oxford University Press, 2011); and David Robertson, *Denmark Vesey: The Buried Story of America's Largest Slave Rebellion and the Man Who Led It* (New York: Vintage, 2000).

19. On African resistance connected across space and time, see in particular, W. E. B. Du Bois and Cedric Robinson.

20. Cited in Horne, *The Counter-Revolution of 1776*, 19.

21. Ibid., 27, 149, 152, 156, 159.

22. Foote, *Black and White Manhattan*, 18; as cited in Horne, *The Counter-Revolution of 1776*, 245.

23. Taslitz, *Reconstructing the Fourth Amendment*, 42.

24. *Floyd*, 82. See Jennifer Gonnerman, "Officer Serrano's Hidden Camera," *New York*, May 19, 2013, http://nymag.com.

25. Kristen Gwynne, "Sen. Eric Adams: NYPD Commissioner Told Me Cops Use Stop-and-Frisk to Instill Fear in Youths of Color," *AlterNet*, April 1, 2013, http://www.alternet.org.

26. Shanikka, "When a Judge 'Gets It' on Racism: The Decision in *Floyd v. City of New York*," Daily KOS, August 18, 2013, http://www.dailykos.com.

27. *Floyd*, 6–7.

28. See David A. Harris, *Profiles in Injustice: Why Racial Profiling Cannot Work* (New York: New Press, 2001).

29. See, for example, the Kerner, Mollen, and Christopher Commissions, and the Rampart Corruption Task Force.

30. See Donald F. Tibbs and Tryon P. Woods, "Requiem for Laquan: Policing as Punishment and Prosecuting 'Reasonable Suspicion,'" *Temple Law Review*,

Rethinking Punishment Symposium Edition, 89, no. 4 (spring 2017): 101–117.

31. Transcript of oral argument, *Terry v. Ohio* 392 U.S. 1 (1968), available online at http://www.soc.umn.edu/~samaha/cases/terry_v_ohio_oral_arguments.htm.

32. Steve Martinot and Jared Sexton, "The Avant-Garde of White Supremacy," *Social Identities* 9, no. 2 (2003): 170.

33. Roberto A. Ferdman, "Why Quibbling about the Cause of Eric Garner's Death Misses the Point," *Washington Post*, December 3, 2014, https://www.washingtonpost.com. A history of chokehold deaths is not unique to the NYPD. In Los Angeles, chokeholds were applied no less than 975 times by LAPD officers between 1975 and 1980, killing sixteen people, twelve of whom were black. Los Angeles is only 9 percent black, but black people have been the victims of 75 percent of LAPD chokehold deaths. See Tracy Maclin, "'Black and Blue Encounters,' Some Preliminary Thoughts about Fourth Amendment Seizures: Should Race Matter?," *Valparaiso University Law Review*, 26, no. 1 (1991): 243–279; and Coramae Richey Mann, *Unequal Justice: A Question of Color* (Indianapolis: Indiana University Press, 1993).

34. Larry Celona, Shawn Cohen, and Bruce Golding, "Arrests Plummet 66% with NYPD in Virtual Work Stoppage," *New York Post*, December 29, 2014, http://nypost.com. Needless to say, the crime rate was unaffected by the temporary reprieve from policing. In other words, if the work stoppage was intended to drive home how indispensable police officers are to everyday safety in the city, it backfired grandly.

35. As with President Obama's White House Beer Summit, Mayor de Blasio was also regulated by the police power of antiblackness. His role as Head Racial Profiler, the chief executive of the city's policing apparatus, trumped his status as the father of black children. He was compelled to make conciliatory statements about the tragedy of Officers Ramos and Liu, but said nothing about the NYPD's killing of one of its own, an off-duty black police officer.

36. Douglas Ernst, "De Blasio Has 'Blood on the Hands' after NYPD Shooting, Says Union President," *Washington Times*, December 21, 2014, http://www.washingtontimes.com/news/2014/dec/21/de-blasio-has-blood-hands-after-nypd-shooting-says/.

37. Mary Bowerman, "Dunkin' Donuts Apologizes Over #Blacklivesmatter on Officer's Cup," *USAToday*, October 6, 2015, http://www.usatoday.com.

38. Saidiya V. Hartman, *Scenes of Subjection: Terror, Slavery, and Self-Making in Nineteenth-Century America* (New York: Oxford University Press, 1997), 94; Steve Martinot, "The Militarization of the Police," *Social Identities* 9, no. 2 (2003): 217.

39. Martinot, "The Militarization of the Police," 217.

40. *State v. Mann* 13 N.C. 263 (1830); Hartman, *Scenes of Subjection*, 91.

41. *State of New York v. Miln*, 36 U.S. 102 (1837); Bryan Wagner, *Disturbing the Peace: Black Culture and the Police Power After Slavery* (Cambridge, MA: Harvard University Press, 2009), 10.

42. *Slaughterhouse-House Cases*, 83 U.S. 36, 49 (1873).

43. Wagner, *Disturbing the Peace*, 6–7.

44. The claim of a concealed "illegal switchblade" opens the door to a whole room full of historical and political issues relevant to the present study, but which demand more space than present constraints permit. Is the police claim creditable? If not, why is the fictional contraband a switchblade? What is the history of fictional blades and pathological blackness? If the switchblade was real, what does this have to do with questions of black self-defense? How did such a weapon come to be contraband in the first place, and what does the proscription against armed self-defense have to do with the police power against blackhood? Marlon Riggs's 1986 film *Ethnic Notions* provides a good analysis of the stereotype about black switchblades.

45. *United States v. Mendenhall*, 446 U.S. 544 (1980). Donald F. Tibbs, personal communication, June 4, 2016.

46. Kevin Rector, "The 45-Minute Mystery of Freddie Gray's Death," *Baltimore Sun*, April 25, 2015, http://www.baltimoresun.com.

47. *Brown v. Texas*, 443 U.S. 47 (1979); *Florida v. Bostick*, 501 U.S. 429 (1991).

48. *Adams v. Williams*, 407 U.S. 143 (1972) (presence in a "high-crime area" is an appropriate consideration in *Terry* analysis); *United States v. Sokolow*, 490 U.S. 1 (1989) (evasive behavior similarly pertinent); *Florida v. Rodriguez*, 469 U.S. 1 (1984) (same); *United States v. Brignoni-Ponce*, 422 U.S. 873 (1975) (same); as cited in Adam B. Wolf, "The Adversity of Race and Place: Fourth Amendment Jurisprudence in *Illinois v. Wardlow*," *Michigan Journal of Race & Law* 5 (2000), 715.

49. *Illinois v. Wardlow*, 528 U.S. 119 (2000).

50. "Stop-eligible" comes from Margaret Raymond, "Down on the Corner, Out in the Street: Considering the Character of the Neighborhood in Evaluating Reasonable Suspicion," *Ohio State Law Journal* 60, no. 1 (1999): 99. I amend Raymond's race-neutral use of "the character of the neighborhood."

51. In his otherwise instructive case note on *Illinois v. Wardlow*, Adam Wolf runs afoul of the paradigm that I am endeavoring to illuminate in *Blackhood Against the Police*

Power. After running down the basic flaws in the court's reasoning in *Wardlow*, Wolf concludes: "While the plight of the urban poor is great, and the need for law enforcement officials to protect themselves is vital, we cannot strip poor people of color of their Fourth Amendment rights to solve these problems, lest we forget that the Fourth Amendment is an individual right" (725). Its counterrevolutionary history, as I have been arguing in this chapter, shows that the Fourth Amendment is not a right that attaches to individuals, but rather an index of group-based power. Wolf's own argument makes this very case, but he retreats from the logical conclusion of the evidence he presents. Analyses such as Wolf's that seek to advance an antiracist politics from within an antiblack paradigm must be addressed as part of the problem. See Wolf, "The Adversity of Race and Place." Thank you, again, to Donald Tibbs for bringing this article to my attention.

52. The woman to whom Till supposedly whistled or made his flirtatious advances, Carolyn Bryant, later admitted that she had fabricated the entire story of Till's behavior. See Timothy B. Tyson, *The Blood of Emmett Till* (New York: Simon & Schuster, 2017); and Sheila Weller, "How Author Timothy Tyson Found the Woman at the Center of the Emmett Till Case," *Vanity Fair*, January 26, 2017, https://www.vanityfair.com. The world did not need Bryant's admission in order to reject the given explanation for Till's murder, however, as long as we remember that violence against black people is gratuitous, not contingent. The narrative that Till had to do something to occasion the antiblack violence that ended his life has been as harmful as the lynching itself.

53. Martinot, "The Militarization of the Police," 206.

54. Justin Peters, "The Worst of Stop-and-Frisk Is Over. But Why Didn't the NYPD End the Racist Policy Itself?" *Slate*, August 12, 2013, http://www.slate.com.

55. Frank B. Wilderson III, *Red, White & Black: Cinema and the Structure of U.S. Antagonisms* (Durham, NC: Duke University Press, 2010).

56. Michelle Alexander, *The New Jim Crow: Mass Incarceration in the Age of Colorblindness* (New York: New Press, 2010), 165.

57. Jared Sexton, *Amalgamation Schemes: Antiblackness and the Critique of Multiracialism* (Minneapolis: University of Minnesota Press, 2008), 148–149.

58. Ibid., 103.

59. Alexander, *The New Jim Crow*, 139.

60. Kuwasi Balagoon in Balagoon et al., *Look For Me in the Whirlwind: The Collective*

Autobiography of the New York 21, ed. Haywood Burns (New York: Random House, 1971), 326.

61. Sylvia Wynter, "On How We Mistook the Map for the Territory, and Re-Imprisoned Ourselves in Our Unbearable Wrongness of Being, of *Desetre*: Black Studies Toward the Human Project," in *Not Only the Master's Tools: African American Studies in Theory and Practice*, ed. Lewis R. Gordon and Jane Anna Gordon (Boulder: Paradigm, 2006), 161.

62. Alexander, *The New Jim Crow*, 207.

63. See, for example, Lerone Bennett Jr., *Before the Mayflower: A History of the Negro in America, 1619–1962* (Chicago: Johnson, 1962); Robin Blackburn, *The Making of New World Slavery: From the Baroque to the Modern, 1492–1800* (London: Verso, 2010); David Eltis, *The Rise of African Slavery in the Americas* (New York: Cambridge University Press, 2000); Simon Gikandi, *Slavery and the Culture of Taste* (Princeton, NJ: Princeton University Press, 2014); Vincent Harding, *There Is a River: The Black Struggle for Freedom in America* (New York: Harcourt Brace, 1981).

64. W. E. B. Du Bois, *The Souls of Black Folk* (New York: Dover Publications, 1994), 7.

65. Steve Martinot, *The Rule of Racialization: Class, Identity, Governance* (Philadelphia: Temple University Press, 2002), 232n32.

66. Martinot, "The Militarization of the Police," 218.

67. Ruth Wilson Gilmore, *Golden Gulag: Prisons, Surplus, Crisis, and Opposition in Globalizing California* (Berkeley: University of California Press, 2007), 130.

68. Ibid., 28.

69. This point owes to an observation made by Jared Sexton, personal correspondence with the author, November 2011.

70. Stuart Hall, "Race, Articulation, and Societies Structured in Dominance," in *Sociological Theories: Race and Colonialism*, by UNESCO (Paris: UNESCO, 1980), 342.

71. Gilmore, *Golden Gulag*, 20–21.

72. Ibid., 21.

73. Ibid. .

74. Alexander, *The New Jim Crow*, 197; Gilmore, *Golden Gulag*, 243–245, quoting Staughton Lynd, *Lucasville: The Untold Story of a Prison Uprising* (Philadelphia: Temple University Press, 2004).

75. Greg Thomas, *The Sexual Demon of Colonial Power: Pan-African Embodiment and Erotic Schemes of Empire* (Bloomington: Indiana University Press, 2007), 1.

76. "Michelle Alexander: 'Zimmerman Mindset' Endangers Young Black Lives with Poverty, Prison & Murder," Democracy Now!, July 17, 2013, http://www. democracynow.org.

77. In Ava DuVernay's documentary *13ᵗʰ* (Netflix, 2016), Alexander performs a similar contortion by claiming that "police brutality" is authorized by the system of mass incarceration. In other words, if we address the prison-industrial complex, according to Alexander, we will see the problems with policing go away. This claim is merely asserted in the film, with no argument or evidence to support it, and contradicts the history that informs *Blackhood Against the Police Power*. Policing is historically prior to the prison in any form; it remains the first moment of punishment today; and it will continue in its many diffuse forms throughout civil society regardless of how criminal justice reforms alter the modality of institutionalized punishment. Policing, in short, is the ontological condition of possibility for incarceration at any scale, not its byproduct.

78. Martinot and Sexton, "The Avant-Garde of White Supremacy," 171.

79. As quoted in Wagner, *Disturbing the Peace*, 19.

80. Ibid., 20.

81. "Do Black Lives Matter? Robin DG Kelley and Fred Moten in Conversation," Critical Resistance, December 13, 2014, http://criticalresistance.org/do-black-lives-matter-robin-dg-kelley-and-fred-moten-in-conversation/.

82. See interview transcripts, "Piers Morgan Live," *CNN*, July 19, 2013, http://transcripts. cnn.com/TRANSCRIPTS/1307/19/pmt.01.html.

83. Arlene Eisen, *Operation Ghetto Storm: 2012 Annual Report on the Extrajudicial Killings of 313 Black People by Police, Security Guards and Vigilantes* (Atlanta: Malcolm X Grassroots Movement, 2013), http://www.operationghettostorm.org/.

84. Since the case was settled just prior to trial, there is no official legal citation. See the American Civil Liberties Union, Michigan chapter website and docket history for 2009–2010: http://www.aclumich.org/past-legal-dockets; and http://www.aclumich. org/sites/default/files/file/SWDETROITPOLICEBRUTALITY.pdf. Thank you, once again, to Donald Tibbs for sharing this case with me.

85. *Denson v. United States*, 574 F.3d 1318. Thank you, yet again, to Donald Tibbs for sharing this case.

86. Danielle L. McGuire, *At the Dark End of the Street: Black Women, Rape, and Resistance—a New History of the Civil Rights Movement from Rosa Parks to the Rise of*

Black Power (New York: Vintage, 2011).

87. Molly Redden, "Police Officials Were Investigating Daniel Holtzclaw before Final Attack, Suit Claims," *The Guardian*, December 11, 2015, https://www.theguardian.com/us. The Associated Press reports that in a six year period, over one thousand officers lost their badges for sexual crimes, although only a very small fraction of this number ever faced criminal prosecution. The AP notes that the total is likely a gross underreporting of the sex crimes by police. Matt Sedensky and Nomaan Merchant, "AP: Hundreds of Officers Lose Licenses Over Sex Misconduct," *AP News*, November 1, 2015, http://bigstory.ap.org/article/fd1d4d05e561462a85abe50e7eaed4ec/ap-hundreds-officers-lose-licenses-over-sex-misconduct.

88. Gilmore, *Golden Gulag*, 243.

89. Ibid., 244.

90. Ibid.

91. Ibid., 244–245.

92. Ibid., 242.

93. Joy James, "Introduction: Democracy and Captivity," in *The New Abolitionists: (Neo) Slave Narratives and Contemporary Prison Writings*, ed. James (Albany: SUNY Press, 2005), xxi–xlii.

94. Du Bois explains that the U.S. Civil War was originally a war to preserve slavery's place in the union, not to end it. The ends of war only came to include emancipation as a result of the enslaved Africans' acts of self-possession: abandoning the plantations and withholding their labor from the Confederacy's war effort; shadowing the Northern army across the South; and proving themselves the lynchpin for a Northern victory. W. E. B. Du Bois, *Black Reconstruction in America: An Essay Towards a History of the Part Which Black Folk Played in Reconstructing Democracy in American, 1860–1880* (New York: Atheneum, 1979). Also, as discussed above, Horne explains how the Revolutionary War was, at base, about preserving white slaveholding power in North America.

95. The 2016 documentary by Ava DuVernay, *13ᵗʰ*, is but one prominent recent example of this mythology. Among the harmful effects of this narrative is the conclusion that we can correct the problem of racialized punishment, and finally end slavery, by creating "good" law. See Tryon P. Woods, "Campaign Cover Stories and Fungible Blackness, Part 2," *Abolition Journal*, November 8, 2016, https://abolitionjournal.org.

96. P. Khalil Saucier and Tryon P. Woods, "Ex Aqua: The Mediterranean Basin, Africans

on the Move, the Politics of Policing," *Theoria: A Journal of Social and Political Theory* 61, no. 141 (2014): 55–75; Woods, "Surrogate Selves: Notes on Anti-Trafficking and Anti-Blackness," *Social Identities* 19, no. 1 (2013): 120–134.

97. George L. Jackson, *Blood in My Eye* (Baltimore: Black Classic Press, 1990), 111.

98. Sundiata Acoli. "A Brief History of the New Afrikan Prison Struggle (Parts 1 and 2)," Sundiata Acoli Freedom Campaign, 1992, http://www.sundiataacoli.org/a-brief-history-of-the-new-afrikan-prison-struggle-parts-1-and-2-19.

99. Gilmore, *Golden Gulag*, 242; also see Fred Moten, *In the Break: The Aesthetics of the Black Radical Tradition* (Minneapolis: University of Minnesota Press, 2003). What is "non-reformist reform" anyway? Is it not still reform? Gilmore defines it as "changes that, at the end of the day, unravel rather than widen the net of social control through criminalization" (242). But it reminds me of Malcolm X's response to a reporter who asked, "Do you feel we're making progress?" Malcolm replied: "If you stick a knife in my back nine inches and pull it out six inches there's no progress; you pull it all the way out that's not progress. The progress is healing the wound that the blow made, and they haven't even begun to pull the knife out much less try to heal the wound. They won't even admit that the knife's there." See Finifinito, "Malcolm X—If You Stick a Knife in My Back," YouTube, https://www.youtube.com/watch?v=XiSiHRNQlQo.

100. Sexton, *Amalgamation Schemes*, 53.

101. Ibid., 52.

102. Ibid., 12.

103. Ibid., 13.

104. João H. Costa Vargas and Joy James, "Refusing Blackness-as-Victimization: Trayvon Martin and the Black Cyborgs," in *Pursuing Trayvon Martin: Historical Contexts and Contemporary Manifestations of Racial Dynamics*, ed. George Yancey and Janine Jones (Lanham, MD: Lexington, 2012), 193–204.

105. I am aware that serious prison abolitionists are clear that such a goal is coterminous with comprehensive and radical social change. See Prison Research Education Action Project, *Instead of Prisons: A Handbook for Abolitionists* (Oakland: Critical Resistance, 2005). Despite its vital importance, this programmatic approach is not specific enough regarding the problem that produced a social reliance on mass incarceration, as this chapter and book endeavor to show and prove.

106. Hortense J. Spillers, "'All the Things You Could Be by Now, If Sigmund Freud's Wife

Was Your Mother': Psychoanalysis and Race," in *Black, White, and in Color: Essays on American Literature and Culture* (Chicago: University of Chicago Press, 2003), 384.

107. At the 2011 annual meeting of the American Studies Association in Baltimore, MD, Gilmore responded to my presentation of some of the ideas in this chapter about Alexander's *The New Jim Crow* by claiming that racism is nothing new and that organizers have been addressing it for many years now. While this is true, her response sought to blunt my analysis and patrol the discursive and institutional spaces wherein these political discourses of race and punishment are debated and reproduced. In person and in print, then, Gilmore underscores my argument that there is a clash in explanatory frameworks that demands closer scrutiny than is currently being afforded in practically all but the most marginal of venues.

108. Gayatri Spivak, *A Critique of Postcolonial Reason: Toward a History of the Vanishing Present* (Cambridge, MA: Harvard University Press, 1999), 3n5; Jared Sexton, "Proprieties of Coalition: Blacks, Asians, and the Politics of Policing," in *On Marronage: Ethical Confrontations with Antiblackness*, ed. P. Khalil Saucier and Tryon P. Woods (Trenton, NJ: Africa World Press, 2015), 301n4.

109. Martinot and Sexton, "The Avant-Garde of White Supremacy," 173.

110. Ibid., 175.

111. Jason Henry, "'Lynching' Laws Were Meant to Protect Black People. Removing the Word Changed Everything," *Pasadena Star-News*, June 11, 2016, http://www. pasadenastarnews.com; "Black Lives Matter Activist Sentenced on Felony 'Lynching' Charges," Free Speech Radio News, June 7, 2016, https://fsrn.org.

112. For an excellent analysis of felony lynching and the Abdullah case, see Erin Gray, "Anti-Lynching Laws Were Never Meant to Defend Black Lives: The Case of Jasmine Abdullah," Truthout, June 15, 2016, http://www.truthout.org.

113. Spillers, "All the Things,'" 390.

CHAPTER FIVE. On Performance and Position, Erotically

1. On the one hand, I would refer readers to the extensive corpus of political economic analyses of the post–civil rights era that I have held up in the previous chapters as inadequate, generally speaking, for the task at hand. Among the many important and pertinent studies, see work by Patricia Hill Collins, George Lipsitz, Joe Feagin, David Harvey, Manning Marable, Douglas Massey and Nancy Denton, Melvin Oliver and Thomas R. Shapiro, Michael Omi and Howard Winant, Neil Smith, Stephen

Steinberg, Rhonda Y. Williams, and Clyde Woods. On the other hand, consistent with the intervention *Blackhood Against the Police Power* aims to make on this terrain, I am also gesturing to the gaps *within* this body of work. In other words, while I argue that, overall, political economic frameworks for analyzing black struggle are the necessary but insufficient grounds for advancing ethical confrontations with the worlds of antiblackness, such accounts are also frequently deficient on their own terms because they usually fail to interpret the ideologies of "race" and racism emergent from this period as themselves key features of the regime of exploitation and alienation (incompletely) identified as the source of black immiseration.

2. On the collective intervention of the critical race theorists regarding the limitations of civil rights era antidiscrimination law, see Kimberlé Crenshaw, Neil Gotanda, Gay Peller, and Kendall Thomas, eds., *Critical Race Theory: The Key Writings That Formed the Movement* (New York: New Press, 1996).

3. Dhoruba Bin Wahad, Assata Shakur, and Mumia Abu-Jamal, *Still Black, Still Strong: Survivors of the War Against Black Revolutionaries*, ed. Jim Fletcher, Tanaquil Jones, and Sylvère Lotringer (New York: Semiotext(e), 1993), 18.

4. Cited in Bin Wahad, Shakur, and Abu-Jamal, *Still Black, Still Strong*, back cover.

5. Afeni Shakur, in Kuwasi Balagoon et al., *Look For Me in the Whirlwind: The Collective Autobiography of the New York 21*, ed. Haywood Burns (New York: Random House, 1971), 292.

6. Safiya Bukhari, *The War Before: The True Life Story of Becoming a Black Panther, Keeping the Faith in Prison, and Fighting for Those Left Behind* (New York: Feminist Press, 2010), 54–55. Sex and gender formation are complex issues for black communities the world over, and a more in-depth treatment of this issue with regards to black revolutionary struggle than I can provide here would need to analyze the radical imaginings of the Panthers within a Pan-African context that does not take Western gender constructs and sexual violence for granted, and that attends to the organizational and strategic moves of the party themselves as expressions of gender and sex politics—all the while, of course, recognizing that the conditions of unrelenting state terror under which black power was elaborated brooked no sanctuary or respite.

7. Frantz Fanon, *Black Skin, White Masks* (New York: Grove Press, 1967), 160.

8. Ibid., 154–156.

9. Greg Thomas, "Erotics of Aryanism/Histories of Empire: How 'White Supremacy'

and 'Hellenomania' Construct 'Discourses of Sexuality,'" *CR: The New Centennial Review* 3, no. 3 (2003): 239.

10. Dhoruba Bin Wahad, "War Within," in Bin Wahad, Shakur, and Abu-Jamal, *Still Black, Still Strong*, 24–25.

11. Greg Thomas, *The Sexual Demon of Colonial Power: Pan-African Embodiment and Erotic Schemes of Empire* (Bloomington: Indiana University Press, 2007), 88.

12. Fanon, *Black Skin, White Masks*, 156.

13. Thomas, *The Sexual Demon of Colonial Power*, 88, 89.

14. Ibid., 88.

15. Bukhari, *The War Before*, 29.

16. Cited in Greg Thomas, "The 'S' Word: Sex, Empire, and Black Radical Tradition (After Sylvia)," in *Caribbean Reasonings: After Man, Towards the Human; Critical Essays on Sylvia Wynter*, ed. Anthony Bogues (Kingston: Ian Randle, 2005), 79–80.

17. Frank B. Wilderson III, *Red, White & Black: Cinema and the Structure of U.S. Antagonisms* (Durham, NC: Duke University Press, 2010), 127.

18. Hortense J. Spillers, "Mama's Baby, Papa's Maybe: An American Grammar Book," in *Black, White, and in Color: Essays on American Literature and Culture* (Chicago: University of Chicago Press, 2003), 203–229.

19. Wilderson, *Red, White & Black*, 138.

20. *Tupac Shakur: Thug Angel: The Life of an Outlaw* (Peter Spirer, dir., Image Entertainment, 2002).

21. Quoted in Michael Eric Dyson, *Holler If You Hear Me: Searching for Tupac Shakur* (New York: Basic Civitas, 2006), 57.

22. Afeni Shakur, in Balagoon et al., *Look For Me in the Whirlwind*, 294–295.

23. Frantz Fanon, *The Wretched of the Earth* (New York: Grove, 1968), 81; Wilderson, *Red, White & Black*, 120–122.

24. Sekou Sundiata, "Shout Out," *Blue Oneness of Dreams* (Polygram 1997); Robin D. G. Kelley, *Race Rebels: Culture, Politics, and the Black Working Class* (New York: Free Press, 1994), 187.

25. Greg Thomas, "Fire and *Damnation*: Hip-Hop ('Youth Culture') and 1956 in Focus," *Presence Africaine: Revue Culturelle du Monde Noir* 175–176–177, no. 2 (2007): 310.

26. Jared Sexton, *Amalgamation Schemes: Antiblackness and the Critique of Multiracialism* (Minneapolis: University of Minnesota Press, 2008).

27. Greg Thomas, *Hip-Hop Revolution in the Flesh: Power, Knowledge, and Pleasure in Lil'*

Kim's Lyricism (New York: Palgrave, 2009), 44.

28. Ibid.

29. Genna Rae McNeil, "The Body, Sexuality, and Self-Defense in *State vs. Joan Little,* 1974–75," *Journal of African American History* 93, no. 2 (2008): 237, 235.

30. Ibid., 245.

31. Bukhari, *The War Before*, 9.

32. Ibid.

33. Toni Morrison, *Beloved* (New York: Vintage, 2004), 95.

34. Carolyn Cooper, *Sound Clash: Jamaican Dancehall Culture at Large* (New York: Palgrave, 2004).

35. Quoted in Kismet Nuñez, "In the Future, We Kill Our Attackers: Rihanna's 'Man Down' as Afrofuturist Text," The AntiJemima Life, June 9, 2011, http://nunezdaughter. wordpress.com.

36. Alisa Bierria, "'Where Them Bloggers At?': Reflections on Rihanna, Accountability, and Survivor Subjectivity," *Social Justice* 37, no. 4 (2010): 101–124.

37. Ibid., 106.

38. Ibid., 118.

39. Saidiya V. Hartman, *Scenes of Subjection: Terror, Slavery, and Self-Making in Nineteenth-Century America* (New York: Oxford University Press, 1997), 87.

40. Ibid., 100.

41. Carolyn Cooper, "Erotic Maroonage: Embodying Emancipation in Jamaican Dancehall Culture," paper presented at the Ninth Annual Gilder Lehrman Center International Conference, "The Legacies of Slavery and Emancipation: Jamaica in the Atlantic World," Yale University, New Haven, CT, November 1–3, 2007, https://glc. yale.edu, 1.

42. Ibid., 2.

43. Ibid., 3.

44. Ronald A. T. Judy, "The Question of Nigga Authenticity," *boundary 2* 21, no. 3 (1994): 212.

45. Wilderson, *Red, White & Black*, 123.

46. Darieck Scott, *Extravagant Abjection: Blackness, Power, and Sexuality in the African American Literary Imagination* (New York: New York University Press, 2010), 131.

47. Related to this point is the basic fact that whites comprise approximately 75 percent of the hip-hop consumer base. Dipannita Basu, "Hip Hop: Cultural Clout,

Corporate Control, and the 'Carceral Cast,'" in *The Vinyl Ain't Final: Hip Hop and the Globalization of Black Popular Culture*, ed. Dipannita Basu and Sidney Lemelle (London: Pluto, 2006), 27–55.

48. Jared Sexton, "The Ruse of Engagement: Black Masculinity and the Cinema of Policing," *American Quarterly* 61, no. 1 (2009): 49.

49. Wilderson, *Red, White & Black*, 103.

50. Morrison, *Beloved*, 107, 108.

51. Scott, *Extravagant Abjection*, 132–133.

52. Amanda Hess, "Lil Wayne Jokes about His Own Rape," *Washington City Paper*, January 12, 2010, http://www.washingtoncitypaper.com.

53. Wilderson, *Red, White & Black*, 104.

54. Ibid., 100.

55. Thomas, *The Sexual Demon of Colonial Power*, 46.

56. Frank B. Wilderson III, "'The Position of the Unthought': An Interview with Saidiya V. Hartman," *Qui Parle* 13, no. 2 (2003): 185.

57. Wilderson, *Red, White & Black*, 100.

58. Sexton, *Amalgamation Schemes*, 114.

59. Ibid., 113–114.

60. Sylvia Wynter, "Rethinking 'Aesthetics': Notes Towards a Deciphering Practice," in *Ex-Iles: Essays on Caribbean Cinema*, ed. Mbye Cham (Trenton, NJ: Africa World Press, 1992), 267.

61. Salim Muwakkil, "Hip-Hop Cops," *In These Times*, June 28, 2004, http://www.inthesetimes.com/article/806; Dasun Allah, "The Hiphop Cop," *Village Voice*, March 30, 2004, http://www.villagevoice.com; Don Sikorski, director, *Rap Sheet: Hip Hop and the Cops* (Screen Media, 2006).

62. Regina Kunzel, *Criminal Intimacy: Prison and the Uneven History of Modern American Sexuality* (Chicago: University of Chicago Press, 2008), 151.

63. Ibid., 153.

64. Nicole R. Fleetwood, *Troubling Vision: Performance, Visuality, and Blackness* (Chicago: University of Chicago Press, 2011), 133.

65. Sexton, *Amalgamation Schemes*, 144.

66. Frank B. Wilderson III, "Social Death and Narrative Aporia in *12 Years a Slave*," *Black Camera* 7, no. 1 (2015): 134–149.

67. Cathy J. Cohen, "Punks, Bulldaggers, and Welfare Queens: The Radical Potential of

Queer Politics," *GLQ: A Journal of Lesbian and Gay Studies* 3 (1997): 437–465.

68. For an example of queer studies that cites Cohen without ever acknowledging her fundamental point about blackness as queer, see Liat Ben-Moshe, Che Gossett, Nick Mitchell, and Eric A. Stanley, "Critical Theory, Queer Resistance, and the Ends of Capture," in *Death and Other Penalties: Philosophy in a Time of Mass Incarceration*, ed. Geoffrey Adelsberg, Lisa Guenther, and Scott Zeman (New York: Fordham University Press, 2015), 271.

69. Matt Richardson, *The Queer Limit of Black Memory: Black Lesbian Literature and Irresolution* (Columbus: Ohio State University Press, 2013). There is a vital archival project underway to rewrite black history in nonnormative terms, in language that acknowledges queer realities that have always impacted the freedom struggle. Omise'eke Natasha Tinsley describes it as a "queer, unconventional and imaginative archive" of resistance, while Richardson claims that these "queer archiving practices" seek to remember lives past in order to "celebrate ourselves while we can still witness the celebration." Tinsley, "Black Atlantic, Queer Atlantic: Queer Imaginings of the Middle Passage," *GLQ: A Journal of Lesbian and Gay Studies* 14, nos. 2–3 (2008): 193, as cited in Richardson, *Queer Limit of Black Memory*, 11; Richardson, 167. Although I come at the problem differently, I am less concerned with critiquing this project and more interested in showing how its performative terms rely upon a humanist framework that necessarily disavows black positionality.

70. Thomas, *The Sexual Demon of Colonial Power*, 2.

71. Ibid.

72. Hartman, *Scenes of Subjection*, 84.

73. Elizabeth Freeman, *Time Binds: Queer Temporalities, Queer Histories* (Durham, NC: Duke University Press, 2010), 3.

74. Ibid., 1, 7, 9; Calvin L. Warren, "Black Time: Slavery, Metaphysics, and the Logic of Wellness," in *The Psychic Hold of Slavery: Legacies in American Expressive Culture*, ed. Soyica Diggs Colbert, Robert J. Patterson, and Aida Levy-Hussen (New Brunswick: Rutgers University Press, 2016), 60, 61.

75. Warren, "Black Time," 62.

76. Ibid., 58.

77. Adolph Reed Jr., *Class Notes: Posing as Politics and Other Thoughts on the American Scene* (New York: New Press, 2000), 176.

78. Eric Stanley, "Near Life, Queer Death: Overkill and Ontological Capture," *Social Text*

29, no. 2 (2011): 15.

79. Ibid., 3.

80. Ibid., 9.

81. Eric Stanley, "Fugitive Flesh: Gender Self-Determination, Queer Abolition, and Trans Resistance," in *Captive Genders: Trans Embodiment and the Prison Industrial Complex*, ed. Eric Stanley and Nat Smith (Oakland: AK Press, 2011), 5.

82. Reed, *Class Notes*, 169.

83. Stanley, "Near Life, Queer Death," 10.

84. Scott, *Extravagant Abjection*; Sexton, *Amalgamation Schemes*; Christina Sharpe, *Monstrous Intimacies: Making Post-Slavery Subjects* (Durham, NC: Duke University Press, 2010).

85. Wilderson, *Red, White & Black* and "Social Death and Narrative Aporia"; Hartman, *Scenes of Subjection*, 50.

86. Saidiya V. Hartman, "Venus in Two Acts," in *On Marronage: Ethical Confrontations with Antiblackness*, ed. P. Khalil Saucier and Tryon P. Woods (Trenton, NJ: Africa World Press, 2015), 47–66.

87. Aiyana Mo'Nay Stanley-Jones, age seven, was sleeping on her grandmother's couch when she was killed by Detroit police in a SWAT team raid on the home on May 16, 2010.

88. An ever-growing roster of work falls under these terms, and afro-futurism— especially in music and the literary arts—has a rich history that complicates ascriptions of utopianism and that cannot be reduced to accusations of escapism. The recent directions in "black performance theory," however, are only nominally connected to this history and present a new set of problems specific to the post-racial and post–black studies period. *Blackhood Against the Police Power* begins, but in no way exhausts, an ethical critique of this work. The short of it is, as I noted in the present volume's introduction, the only ethical utopian vision entails situating oneself and one's analysis within the dystopia of black struggle.

89. Fanon, *Black Skin, White Masks*, 9.

90. Stephen Best and Saidiya V. Hartman, "Fugitive Justice," *Representations* 92 (fall 2005): 5, 2.

91. Fleetwood, *Troubling Vision*, 127.

CHAPTER SIX. Torture Outside of Pain in the Black Studies Tradition

1. Dionne Brand, *A Map to the Door of No Return: Notes to Belonging* (Toronto: Vintage, 2002), 1.

2. See M. NourbeSe Philip, *Zong!* (Middletown, CT: Wesleyan University Press, 2008).

3. Aimé Césaire, *Discourse on Colonialism* (New York: Monthly Review, 2001), as cited in Frantz Fanon, *Black Skin, White Masks* (New York: Grove Press, 1967), 96; and in Frank B. Wilderson III, "Biko and the Problematic of Presence," in *Biko Lives! Contesting the Legacies of Steve Biko*, ed. Andile Mngxitama, Amanda Alexander, and Nigel Gibson (New York: Palgrave, 2008), 96.

4. James Baldwin, *The Evidence of Things Not Seen* (New York: Henry Holt, 1995); Toni Cade Bambara, *Those Bones Are Not My Child* (New York: Pantheon, 1999); Assata Shakur, *Assata: An Autobiography* (Chicago: Lawrence Hill, 2001), 93.

5. Toni Cade Bambara, *Deep Sighting and Rescue Missions: Fiction, Essays, and Conversations*, ed. Toni Morrison (New York: Pantheon, 1996).

6. Saidiya V. Hartman, *Scenes of Subjection: Terror, Slavery, and Self-Making in Nineteenth-Century America* (New York: Oxford University Press, 1997), 76–77.

7. Ibid., 77.

8. Ibid., 78.

9. Ibid.

10. This incident happened to James Wells of Racine, Wisconsin, in June 2015. The video Wells created during the traffic stop can be seen on YouTube: https://www.youtube.com/watch?v=-b902vuwvLM. The officer attempts to get Wells to submit his fingerprint in lieu of the driver's license that she would not allow him to give her and tells him to remove a tinted cover on his license plate. He refuses on both accounts and successfully stands his ground. In this case, when the officer was unable to produce the existential subjection from Wells that she was seeking (and that her position demands), she relented and withdrew rather than exact the physical submission from Wells that is usually necessary to compensate for resistant blackness. Afterward, Wells posted a photo showing that the local police chief's own personal vehicle does not bear a front license plate, which was the officer's stated reason for pulling him over in the first place. Matt Agorist, "VIDEO: Cop Pulls Man Over, Refuses to Let Him Show Insurance, Gives Him Ticket for No Insurance," Freethought Project, June 26, 2015, http://thefreethoughtproject.com.

11. Cited in Sara E. Johnson, *Fear of French Negroes: Transcolonial Collaboration in the*

Revolutionary Americas (Berkeley: University of California Press, 2012), 26.

12. Ibid., 43.

13. Ibid., 28.

14. Cited in Johnson, *Fear of French Negroes*, 25.

15. C. L. R. James, *The Black Jacobins* (New York: Vintage, 1989), 12, as cited in Johnson, *Fear of French Negroes*, 29. Emphasis added.

16. Toni Morrison, *Playing in the Dark: Whiteness and the Literary Imagination* (New York: Vintage, 1993), 37.

17. See Harriet A. Washington, *Medical Apartheid: The Dark History of Medical Experimentation on Black Americans from Colonial Times to the Present* (New York: Doubleday, 2007); Terry Kupers, *Prison Madness: The Mental Health Crisis Behind Bars and What We Must Do about It* (San Francisco: Jossey-Bass, 1999); Lorna Rhodes, *Total Confinement: Madness and Reason in the Maximum Security Prison* (Berkeley: University of California Press, 2004); Dorothy E. Roberts, *Killing the Black Body: Race, Reproduction, and the Meaning of Liberty* (New York: Pantheon, 1997) and *Shattered Bonds: The Color of Child Welfare* (New York: Basic Books, 2002); and Tryon P. Woods, "Pedagogy in Revolution, for the Anti-Revolutionary Stretch: Pan-African Correspondence across Space and Time," in *A Luta Continua: (Re)Introducing Amilcar Cabral to a New Generation of Thinkers*, ed. P. Khalil Saucier (Trenton, NJ: Africa World Press, 2016), 173–204.

18. Jerome Skolnick, "American Interrogation: From Torture to Trickery," in *Torture: A Collection*, ed. Sanford Levinson (New York: Oxford University Press, 2004), 105–128. *Miranda v. Arizona*, 384 U.S. 436 (1966), is the Supreme Court's definitive statement on Fifth Amendment protections against police coercion. *Miranda* stipulates that *before* the police can interrogate criminal suspects, they must inform them of their constitutional rights to not speak to the police and to be advised by legal counsel. As Skolnick notes, *Miranda* has simply given rise to a host of police deceptions geared to evade the "waiver paradox," the reality that no criminal suspect who actually knows his or her rights, and actually understands them, would ever speak to the police. Since the courts have simultaneously validated that the police can legally lie to suspects, including misrepresenting themselves, the evidence, and the law itself, *Miranda* may stand as the most perversely prestigious constitutional standard: the court has unequivocally reaffirmed its centrality to Fifth Amendment jurisprudence in subsequent cases—e.g., *Dickerson v. United States*, 530 U.S. 428

(2000)—and yet its prestige is perverse as police routinely circumvent and flaunt its intentions, enabled by court imprimatur of expansive police powers. This critique notwithstanding, there is a larger question as to why the legal and criminal justice academies even regard *Miranda* as a turning point in police behavior in the first place.

19. For a dossier of articles on the Burge case from 2011 to 2015, see *The Huffington Post*, http://www.huffingtonpost.com/news/jon-burge-police-torture/. Chicago has paid millions of dollars to settle lawsuits resulting from torture and incarceration in the Burge case: e.g., Carol Marin and Don Moseley, "City Settles 2 Burge Cases for $7.1M," NBC Chicago, July 23, 2012, http://www.nbcchicago.com; Zach Stafford, Spencer Ackerman, and Joanna Walters, "Chicago Agrees to Pay $5.5m to Victims of Police Torture in 1970s and 80s," *The Guardian*, May 6, 2015, http://www.theguardian.com/us.

20. See, for example, Margaret Power, ed., *Torture, American Style*, HAW Pamphlet #3, May 2006, http://www.historiansagainstwar.org. For a more comprehensive account of torture and empire, see Marnia Lazreg, *Torture and the Twilight of Empire: From Algiers to Baghdad* (Princeton: Princeton University Press, 2008).

21. Jared Sexton and Elizabeth Lee, "Figuring the Prison: Prerequisites of Torture at Abu Ghraib," *Antipode: A Radical Journal of Geography* 38, no. 5 (2006): 1005–1022.

22. Elaine Scarry, *The Body in Pain: The Making and Unmaking of the World* (New York: Oxford University Press, 1985), 28.

23. Debbie Nathan reports that the preponderantly black students in the vicinity of the historically black Prairie View A&M University, from which Bland was an alum and to which she was headed at the time of her traffic stop to start a new job, are targeted by officers for routine traffic stops in order to generate revenue for Waller County. Nathan, "The Real Reason Sandra Bland Got Locked Up," *The Nation*, December 18, 2015.

24. The entire encounter can be seen and/or heard via this complete recording of the dashboard camera posted by the Texas Department of Public Safety on YouTube: https://www.youtube.com/watch?v=CaW09Ymr2BA (all subsequent quotations from this incident come from this video). You can see the officer finish a different traffic stop; Bland then drives by, the trooper immediately makes a U-turn and speeds up right behind her, she switches to the right lane, and he then pulls her over.

25. Scarry, *The Body in Pain*, 35.

26. Patrice Douglass and Frank B. Wilderson III, "The Violence of Presence: Metaphysics in a Blackened World," *The Black Scholar* 43, no. 4 (2013): 121.

27. Ibid.

28. Reynolds recorded the traffic stop and narrated her fiancé's death at the hands of the police. Eliott C. McLaughlin, "Woman Streams Aftermath of Fatal Officer-Involved Shooting," CNN, July 8, 2016, http://www.cnn.com.

29. Scarry, *The Body in Pain*, 28.

30. Hartman, *Scenes of Subjection*, 40.

31. Ibid.

32. Ibid., 41.

33. Alexander G. Weheliye, *Habeas Viscus: Racializing Assemblages, Biopolitics, and Black Feminist Theories of the Human* (Durham, NC: Duke University Press, 2014), 113.

34. Hartman, *Scenes of Subjection*, 78.

35. Ibid., 41.

36. Ibid., 112.

37. Ibid., 141.

38. Ibid., 63.

39. Jay Fernandez, "Knowing Nina Simone: A Q/A w/ Liz Garbus about Her Netflix Doc," *Signature*, June 24, 2015, http://www.signature-reads.com.

40. Jared Sexton, *Amalgamation Schemes: Antiblackness and the Critique of Multiracialism* (Minneapolis: University of Minnesota Press, 2008), 118.

41. Ibid.

42. Ibid., 120.

43. Hartman, *Scenes of Subjection*, 131.

44. In a January 1996 speech, then first lady Hillary Clinton spoke about her husband's crime policies, referring to neighborhood gangs as "superpredators," and asserting that "we have to bring them to heel." See Hillary Clinton, "Mrs. Clinton Campaign Speech," January 25, 1996, Keene State University, C-SPAN, https://www.c-span.org/video/?69606-1/mrs-clinton-campaign-speech&start=1531.

45. Wilderson, "Biko and the Problematic of Presence," 112.

46. Unless otherwise noted, quotations are from Liz Garbus, dir., *What Happened, Miss Simone?* (Netflix, 2015).

47. Tanya Steele, "The Irresponsibility of 'What Happened, Miss Simone?'" IndieWire, June 29, 2015, http://www.indiewire.com/2015/06/

the-irresponsibility-of-what-happened-miss-simone-153559. A second commentator, at the now defunct Clever Bastard blog, inquired: "The question isn't rhetorical: who thought Andrew Stroud was a good idea? Allowing a rapist to tell the story of his victim seems far more than irresponsible, insensitive, and inhumane.".

48. Quoted in Seymour Stark, *Men in Blackface: True Stories of the Minstrel Show* (Bloomington: Xlibris, 2000), n.p.

49. Deborah Bowen, personal communication with the author, August 2015.

50. Bowen, personal communication with the author, August 2015. Bowen goes on to point out that the same analysis of how Simone is constructed applies to how Lauryn Hill is misconstrued: "What is the obsession with peering into the lives of brilliant black women, using a euro-centric psychological metric to assess stability and success, based on a model which excludes the context into which a Nina Simone or a Lauryn Hill was born. . . . We live like everyone else does—with the paradox. Smashing it, rejecting it, dismissing it, holding it, and ultimately reclaiming it as ours, partly because it isn't so uncommon to live with paradox, so that truth must be told in the reclaiming, so that we ourselves, as black women, will no longer wonder and gawk in amazement at the tragedy of Nina Simone or Lauryn Hill. No longer does their rise to stardom and decline to a reclusive life perplex us, we get real with the true lens and understand the nasty business of racism in entertainment, how it works, and get on with the business of doing our damn thing. But first an adjustment to the paradigmatic lens is required."

51. Nina Simone, *I Put a Spell On You: The Autobiography of Nina Simone* (New York: Da Capo, 1993), 128.

52. Ibid., 89.

53. Jamie Ludwig, "Director of Nina Simone Documentary: 'We Were in Our Edit Room When the Events of Ferguson Were Unfolding. It Reminds You That the Struggle Is Ongoing.'" *Salon*, June 28, 2105, http://www.salon.com/2015/06/28/director_of_nina_simone_documentary_we_were_in_our_edit_room_when_the_events_of_ferguson_were_unfolding_it_reminds_you_that_the_struggle_is_ongoing/.

54. See for example: Meghan Keneally, "Sandra Bland Had 'Lows and Highs,' Her Sister Says," *ABCNews*, July 23, 2015, http://abcnews.go.com.

55. Joy James makes her insightful comments in "Imprisoned People and Ideas with Dr. Joy James," on Jared Ball's internet radio program *I Mix What I Like*, July 31, 2015, https://imixwhatilike.org. My argument about black self-defense and human rights

can be found in Tryon P. Woods, "A Re-appraisal of Black Radicalism and Human Rights Doctrine," in *On Marronage: Ethical Confrontations with Antiblackness*, ed. P. Khalil Saucier and Tryon P. Woods (Trenton, NJ: Africa World Press, 2015), 241–278.

56. Ludwig, "Director of Nina Simone Documentary."
57. Bambara, *Bones*, 560–561.

CODA

1. Arthur Koestler, *The Ghost in the Machine* (New York: Macmillan, 1967)—"the ghost in the machine" was originally coined by Gilbert Ryle to describe Cartesian mind–body dualism; Kevin Young, *The Grey Album: On the Blackness of Blackness* (Seattle: Graywolf, 2012).
2. Toni Cade Bambara, *Those Bones Are Not My Child* (New York: Pantheon, 1999), 518, 519.
3. Ralph Ellison, *Invisible Man* (New York: Random House, 1995), 51.
4. Vincent Harding, *Beyond Chaos: Black History and the Search for the New Land*, Black Paper No. 2 (Atlanta: Institute of the Black World, 1970), 25.
5. Ibid., 26.
6. Michel-Rolph Trouillot, *Silencing the Past: Power and the Production of History* (Boston: Beacon Press, 1995), 96.
7. Kay Bonetti, "An Interview with Toni Cade Bambara," in *Conversations with Toni Cade Bambara*, ed. Thabiti Lewis (Jackson: University Press of Mississippi, 2012), 39.
8. Joy James, "Introduction: Democracy and Captivity," in *The New Abolitionists: (Neo) Slave Narratives and Contemporary Prison Writings*, ed. James (Albany: SUNY Press, 2005), xxi–xlii. Thank you to James for highlighting the post-racial moment of Obama's performance for me.
9. Joy James, ed., *Warfare in the American Homeland: Policing and Prison in a Penal Democracy* (Durham, NC: Duke University Press, 2007).
10. Holly Yan and Mariano Castillo, "Attorney Defends Actions of Fired School Officer as 'Justified and Lawful,'" *CNN*, October 29, 2015, http://www.cnn.com. Policing blackness in the school system is a major problem in and of itself. See Connie Wun, "Anti-Blackness as Mundane: Black Girls and Punishment Beyond School Discipline," in *Conceptual Aphasia in Black: Displacing Racial Formation*, ed. P. Khalil Saucier and Tryon P. Woods (Lanham, MD: Lexington, 2016), 69–86.
11. Saliqa Khan, "Police: Korryn Gaines Involved in Police Incident in March," WBALTV,

August 3, 2016, http://www.wbaltv.com/news/police-korryn-gaines-involved-in-police-incident-in-march/41016216.

12. For an analysis of the Gaines case in terms of the state of black self-defense before the law, see Tryon P. Woods, "The Implicit Bias of Implicit Bias Theory," *Drexel Law Review*, Symposium Edition 10, no. 3 (2018): 631–672.

13. See Stephen A. Crockett, "Korryn Gaines May Have Been a Sovereign Citizen. Here's What You Need to Know," The Root, August 5, 2016, http://www.theroot. com. Crockett writes that "the majority of sovereign citizens are African American," incorrectly citing the Southern Poverty Law Center (SPLC). Crockett links to the "Sovereign Citizens Movement" page at the SPLC website (https://www.splcenter. org) that, instead, states the following: "The movement is rooted in racism and anti-Semitism, though most sovereigns, many of whom are African American, are unaware of their beliefs' origins."

14. Jared Sexton, "The *Vel* of Slavery: Tracking the Figure of the Unsovereign," *Critical Sociology* 42, nos. 4–5 (2016): 583–597.

15. See Woods, "The Implicit Bias of Implicit Bias Theory"; Donald F. Tibbs and Tryon P. Woods, "Requiem for Laquan: Policing as Punishment and Prosecuting 'Reasonable Suspicion,'" *Temple Law Review*, Rethinking Punishment Symposium Edition, 89, no. 4 (2017): 101–117.

16. George Jackson, *Soledad Brother: The Prison Letters of George Jackson* (Chicago: Chicago Review Press, 1994), 111.

17. Paula Giddings, "At the Edges of the World," in *Savoring the Salt: The Legacy of Toni Cade Bambara*, ed. Linda Janet Holmes and Cheryl A. Wall (Philadelphia: Temple University Press, 2007), 127.

Bibliography

Court Cases, Briefs, and Legal Papers

Adams v. Williams, 407 U.S. 143 (1972).

Alabama v. White, 496 U.S. 325 (1990).

Brown v. Texas, 443 U.S. 47 (1979).

DeGraffenreid v. General Motors, 413 F Supp 142 (E D Mo 1976).

Denson v. United States, 574 F.3d 1318 (2009).

Dickerson v. United States, 530 U.S. 428 (2000).

Florida v. Bostick, 501 U.S. 429 (1991).

Florida v. Rodriguez, 469 U.S. 1 (1984).

Floyd, et al., v. City of New York, et al., 959 F. Supp. 2d 540 (2013).

Illinois v. Wardlow, 528 U.S. 119 (2000).

Miranda v. Arizona, 384 U.S. 436 (1966).

Moore v. Hughes Helicopter, 708 F2d 475 (9th Cir 1983).

Payne v. Travenol, 673 F2d 798 (5th Cir 1982).

Slaughterhouse-House Cases, 83 U.S. 36 (1873).

State v. Mann, 13 N.C. 263 (1830).

State of Missouri v. Darren Wilson, Grand Jury Volume V, September 16, 2014.

State of New York v. Miln, 36 U.S. 102 (1837).

Terry v. Ohio, 392 U.S. 1 (1968).

Transcript of oral argument, *Terry v. Ohio*, 392 U.S. 1 (1968).

United States v. Brignoni-Ponce, 422 U.S. 873 (1975).

United States v. Mendenhall, 446 U.S. 544 (1980).

United States v. Sokolow, 490 U.S. 1 (1989).

Podcast

Leid, Utrice. *Leid Stories*. https://leidstories.podbean.com.

Films

Bagwell, Orlando, dir. *Malcolm X: Make It Plain*. PBS, 1994.

DuVernay, Ava, dir. *13th*. Netflix, 2016.

Garbus, Liz, dir. *What Happened, Miss Simone?* Netflix, 2015.

Moore, Michael J., dir. *The Legacy: Murder and Media, Politics and Prisons*. PorchLight Entertainment, 1999.

Riggs, Marlon, dir. *Ethnic Notions*. California Newsreel, 1986.

Riggs, Marlon, dir. *Tongues Untied*. California Newsreel, 1989.

Sikorski, Don, dir. *Rap Sheet: Hip Hop and the Cops*. Screen Media, 2006.

Spirer, Peter, dir. *Tupac Shakur: Thug Angel. The Life of an Outlaw*. Image Entertainment, 2002.

Publications

Acoli, Sundiata. "A Brief History of the New Afrikan Prison Struggle (Parts 1 and 2)." Sundiata Acoli Freedom Campaign. 1992. http://www.sundiataacoli.org/a-brief-history-of-the-new-afrikan-prison-struggle-parts-1-and-2-19.

Agorist, Matt. "VIDEO: Cop Pulls Man Over, Refuses to Let Him Show Insurance, Gives Him Ticket for No Insurance." Freethought Project, June 26, 2015. http://thefreethoughtproject.com.

Alexander, Elizabeth. "'Can You Be BLACK and Look at This?' Reading the Rodney King Videos." In *Black Male: Representations of Masculinity in Contemporary American Art*, edited by Thelma Golden, 91–110. New York: Whitney Museum, 1995.

Alexander, Michelle. *The New Jim Crow: Mass Incarceration in the Age of Colorblindness*. New York: New Press, 2010.

Amadiume, Ifi. "Grassroots Revolution." In *Ecstasy*. Lagos: Longman Nigerian, 1995.

Bailyn, Bernard. *The Ideological Origins of the American Revolution*. New York: Belknap Press, 1967.

Balagoon, Kuwasi. "Brink's Trial Closing Statement." In *A Soldier's Story: Writings by a Revolutionary New Afrikan Anarchist*, 57–68. Montreal: Kersplebedeb, 2003.

Acoli, Sundiata, Kuwasi Balagoon, Dhoruba bin Wahad, Joan Bird, Jamal Joseph, Sekou Odinga, Afeni Shakur, Lumumba Shakur, et al. *Look For Me in the Whirlwind: The Collective Autobiography of the New York 21*. Edited by Haywood Burns. New York: Random House, 1971.

Baldwin, James. *The Evidence of Things Not Seen*. New York: Henry Holt, 1995.

———. *Tell Me How Long the Train's Been Gone*. New York: Vintage, 1968.

Bambara, Toni Cade. "Black English." In *Curriculum Approaches from a Black Perspective*. Atlanta: Black Child Development Institute, 1972.

———. *Deep Sighting and Rescue Missions: Fiction, Essays, and Conversations*. Edited by Toni Morrison. New York: Pantheon, 1996.

———. "On the Issue of Roles," In *The Black Woman: An Anthology*, edited by Bambara, 101–110. New York: Penguin, 1970.

———. "Salvation Is the Issue." In *Black Women Writers 1950–1980: A Critical Evaluation*, edited by Mari Evans, 41–47. Garden City, NY: Anchor-Doubleday, 1984.

———. *Those Bones Are Not My Child*. New York: Pantheon, 1999.

———. "What It Is I Think I'm Doing Anyhow." In *The Writer on Her Work: Contemporary Women Reflect on Their Art and Their Situation*, edited by Janet Sturnberg, 153–168. New York: W.W. Norton, 1980.

Baraka, Amiri. "Black Art." In *SOS: Poems 1961–2013*, 149–150. New York: Grove Press, 2014.

Baraka, Amiri, and Larry Neal, eds. *Black Fire: An Anthology of Afro-American Writing*. 1968; repr. Baltimore: Black Classic, 2008.

Barchiesi, Franco. "Precarity as Capture: A Conceptual Deconstruction of the Worker-Slave Analogy." In *On Marronage: Ethical Confrontations with Antiblackness*, edited by P. Khalil Saucier and Tryon P. Woods, 183–212. Trenton, NJ: Africa World Press, 2015.

Barrett, Lindon. *Blackness and Value: Seeing Double*. Cambridge, MA: Harvard University Press, 1998.

Basu, Dipannita. "Hip Hop: Cultural Clout, Corporate Control, and the 'Carceral Cast.'" In *The Vinyl Ain't Final: Hip Hop and the Globalization of Black Popular Culture*, edited by Dipannita Basu and Sidney Lemelle, 27–55. London: Pluto, 2006.

Bell, Derrick. *Faces at the Bottom of the Well: The Permanence of Racism*. New York: Basic Books, 1993.

———. "Racial Realism." *Connecticut Law Review* 24, no. 2 (1992): 363–379.

Bellware, Kim. "This Cop Oversaw the Torture of More Than 100 Black Men. Now He's Out After Less Than Four Years in Jail." *Huffington Post*, October 2, 2014.

Ben-Moshe, Liat, Che Gossett, Nick Mitchell, and Eric A. Stanley. "Critical Theory, Queer Resistance, and the Ends of Capture." In *Death and Other Penalties: Philosophy in a Time of Mass Incarceration*, edited by Geoffrey Adelsberg, Lisa Guenther, and Scott Zeman, 266–295. New York: Fordham University Press, 2015.

Bennett, Lerone, Jr. *Before the Mayflower: A History of the Negro in America, 1619–1962*. Chicago: Johnson, 1962.

———. *The Challenge of Blackness*. Chicago: Johnson, 1972.

Best, Stephen, and Saidiya V. Hartman. "Fugitive Justice." *Representations* 92 (fall 2005): 1–15.

Bierria, Alisa. "'Where Them Bloggers At?': Reflections on Rihanna, Accountability, and Survivor Subjectivity." *Social Justice* 37, no. 4 (2010): 101–124.

Bin Wahad, Dhoruba, Assata Shakur, and Mumia Abu-Jamal. *Still Black, Still Strong: Survivors of the War Against Black Revolutionaries*. Edited by Jim Fletcher, Tanaquil Jones, and Sylvère Lotringer. New York: Semiotext(e), 1993.

"Black Lives Matter Activist Sentenced on Felony 'Lynching' Charges." Free Speech Radio News. June 7, 2016. https://fsrn.org.

Blackburn, Robin. *The Making of New World Slavery: From the Baroque to the Modern, 1492–1800*. London: Verso, 2010.

Bonetti, Kay. "An Interview with Toni Cade Bambara." In *Conversations with Toni Cade Bambara*, edited by Thabiti Lewis, 30–48. Jackson: University Press of Mississippi, 2012.

Bowerman, Mary. "Dunkin' Donuts Apologizes Over #Blacklivesmatter on Officer's Cup." *USA Today*, October 6, 2015. http://www.usatoday.com.

Boyle, Louise. "The Faces of the Forgotten: Heartbreaking Plight of the 64,000 Black Women Missing Across America . . . As the Country Turns a Blind Eye." DailyMail.com. January 18, 2012.

Brand, Dionne. *A Map to the Door of No Return: Notes to Belonging*. Toronto: Vintage, 2002.

Brooks, Gwendolyn. *In the Mecca*. New York: Harper & Row, 1968.

Brown, Elaine. *The Condemnation of Little B: New Age Racism in America.* Boston: Beacon, 2002.

Brown, Kimberly Juanita. "Saving Mr. Jefferson: Slavery and Denial at Monticello." In *On Marronage: Ethical Confrontations with Antiblackness*, edited by P. Khalil Saucier and Tryon P. Woods, 109–130. Trenton, NJ: Africa World Press, 2015.

Buetner, Russ. "At Sentencing, Judge Puts Twins' Crimes in Perspective." *New York Times*, August 23, 2012, A23.

Bukhari, Safiya. *The War Before: The True Life Story of Becoming a Black Panther, Keeping the Faith in Prison, and Fighting for Those Left Behind.* New York: Feminist Press, 2010.

Byrd, Jodi A. *The Transit of Empire: Indigenous Critiques of Colonialism.* Minneapolis: University of Minnesota Press, 2011.

Cacho, Lisa Marie. *Social Death: Racialized Rightlessness and the Criminalization of the Unprotected.* New York: New York University Press, 2012.

Celona, Larry, Shawn Cohen, and Bruce Golding. "Arrests Plummet 66% with NYPD in Virtual Work Stoppage." *New York Post*, December 29, 2014. http://nypost.com.

Center for Research on Criminal Justice. *The Iron Fist and the Velvet Glove: An Analysis of the U.S. Police.* Berkeley: Center for Research on Criminal Justice, 1977.

Cesaire, Aime. *Discourse on Colonialism.* New York: Monthly Review Press, 2001.

Chandler, Nahum D. "Of Exorbitance: The Problem of the Negro as a Problem for Thought." *Criticism* 50, no. 3 (2008): 345–410.

———. *X: The Problem of the Negro as a Problem for Thought.* New York: Fordham University Press, 2014.

Cleaver, Kathleen Neal. "Women, Power, and Revolution." *New Political Science* 21, no. 2 (1999): 231–236.

Clough, Patricia Ticineto, and Craig Willse, eds. *Beyond Biopolitics: Essays on the Governance of Life and Death.* Durham, NC: Duke University Press, 2011.

Cohen, Cathy J. "Punks, Bulldaggers, and Welfare Queens: The Radical Potential of Queer Politics." *GLQ: A Journal of Lesbian and Gay Studies* 3 (1997): 437–465.

Collins, Lisa Gail, and Margo Natalie Crawford. "Introduction: Power to the People!" In *New Thoughts on the Black Arts Movement*, edited by Lisa Gail Collins and Margo Natalie Crawford, 1–22. New Brunswick: Rutgers University Press, 2008.

Combahee River Collective. "The Combahee River Collective Statement." In *Homegirls: A Black Feminist Anthology*, ed. Barbara Smith, 264–274. New Brunswick: Rutgers University Press, 2000.

Cooper, Anna Julia. *A Voice from the South*. Xenia, OH: Aldine, 1892.

Cooper, Carolyn. "Erotic Maroonage: Embodying Emancipation in Jamaican Dancehall Culture." Paper presented at the Ninth Annual Gilder Lehrman Center International Conference, "The Legacies of Slavery and Emancipation: Jamaica in the Atlantic World," Yale University, New Haven, CT, November 1–3, 2007. https://glc.yale.edu.

———. *Sound Clash: Jamaican Dancehall Culture at Large*. New York: Palgrave, 2004.

Cox, Oliver Cromwell. *Race: A Study in Social Dynamics*. New York: Monthly Review Press, 2000.

Crawford, Margo Natalie. "Black Light on the *Wall of Respect*." In *New Thoughts on the Black Arts Movement*, edited by Lisa Gail Collins and Margo Natalie Crawford, 25–42. New Brunswick: Rutgers University Press, 2008.

Crenshaw, Kimberlé Williams. "Black Women Still in Defense of Ourselves." *The Nation*, October 5, 2011. https://www.thenation.com.

———. "Demarginalizing the Intersection of Race and Sex: A Black Feminist Critique of Antidiscrimination Law, Feminist Theory, and Antiracist Politics." *University of Chicago Legal Forum* 1989, no. 1, article 8 (139–167).

———. "Mapping the Margins: Intersectionality, Identity Politics, and Violence Against Women of Color." *Stanford Law Review* 43 (1991): 1241–1299.

Crenshaw, Kimberlé, Neil Gotanda, Gay Peller, and Kendall Thomas, eds. *Critical Race Theory: The Key Writings That Formed the Movement*. New York: New Press, 1996.

Cuddihy, William. "The Fourth Amendment: Origins and Original Meaning." Ph.D. Diss., Claremont Graduate School, 1990.

Davis, Angela Y. "Reflections on the Black Woman's Role in the Community of Slaves." In *The Angela Y. Davis Reader*, edited by Joy James, 111–128. Malden, MA: Blackwell, 1998.

———. *Women, Race, and Class*. New York: Vintage, 1983.

Davis, Thomas J. *Rumor of Revolt: The "Great Negro Plot" in Colonial New York*. New York: Free Press, 1985.

Day, Iyko. *Alien Capital: Asian Racialization and the Logic of Settler Colonial Capitalism*. Durham, NC: Duke University Press, 2016.

———. "Being or Nothingness: Indigeneity, Antiblackness, and Settler Colonial Critique." *Critical Ethnic Studies* 1, no. 2 (2015): 102–121.

Diop, Cheikh Anta. *The African Origin of Civilization: Myth or Reality*. Chicago: Lawrence Hill, 1974.

———. *Civilization or Barbarism: An Authentic Anthropology*. Chicago: Chicago Review,

1991.

———. *The Cultural Unity of Black Africa*. London: Karnak House, 1989.

Diouf, Sylviane A. *Slavery's Exiles: The Story of the American Maroons*. New York: New York University Press, 2016.

"Do Black Lives Matter? Robin DG Kelley and Fred Moten in Conversation." Critical Resistance. December 13, 2014. http://criticalresistance.org/do-black-lives-matter-robin-dg-kelley-and-fred-moten-in-conversation/.

Douglass, Patrice D. "At the Intersections of Assemblages: Black Gendered Violence in Theory and in Thought." In *Conceptual Aphasia in Black: Displacing Racial Formation*, edited by P. Khalil Saucier and Tryon P. Woods, 103–126. Lanham, MD: Lexington, 2016.

Douglass, Patrice, and Frank B. Wilderson III. "The Violence of Presence: Metaphysics in a Blackened World." *The Black Scholar* 43, no. 4 (2013): 117–123.

Draper, Robert. "The Lost Girls of Rocky Mount." *GQ*, June 9, 2010. http://www.gq.com.

Du Bois, W. E. B. *Black Reconstruction in America: An Essay Towards a History of the Part Which Black Folk Played in Reconstructing Democracy in American, 1860–1880*. New York: Atheneum, 1979.

———. "Editorial." *The Crisis: Record of the Darker Races* 1, no. 1 (November 1910): 10–11.

———. *The Souls of Black Folk*. New York: Dover Publications, 1994.

Dyson, Michael Eric. *Holler If You Hear Me: Searching for Tupac Shakur*. New York: Basic Civitas, 2006.

Ebanda de B'béri, Boulou, and P. Eric Louw, eds. "The Afropessimism Phenomenon." Special issue, *Critical Arts* 25, no. 3 (2011).

Eisen, Arlene. *Operation Ghetto Storm: 2012 Annual Report on the Extrajudicial Killings of 313 Black People by Police, Security Guards and Vigilantes*. Atlanta: Malcolm X Grassroots Movement, 2013. http://www.operationghettostorm.org/.

Ellison, Ralph. *Invisible Man*. New York: Random House, 1995.

Eltis, David. "Europeans and the Rise and Fall of African Slavery in the Americas: An Interpretation." *American Historical Review* 98, no. 5 (1993): 1399–1423.

———. *The Rise of African Slavery in the Americas*. New York: Cambridge University Press, 2000.

Emeagwali, Gloria. "Six Types of Afro-Pessimists." Udadisi. December 24, 2012. https://udadisi.blogspot.com.

Ernst, Douglas. "De Blasio Has 'Blood on the Hands' after NYPD Shooting, Says Union

President." *Washington Times*, December 21, 2014. http://www.washingtontimes.com/
news/2014/dec/21/de-blasio-has-blood-hands-after-nypd-shooting-says/.

Fabian, Johannes. *Time and the Other: How Anthropology Makes Its Object*. New York:
Columbia University Press, 2002.

Fanon, Frantz. *Black Skin, White Masks*. New York: Grove Press, 1967.

———. *The Wretched of the Earth*. New York: Grove Press, 1968.

Federici, Silvia, George Caffentzis, and Ousseina Alidou, eds. *A Thousand Flowers: Social
Struggles Against Structural Adjustment in African Universities*. Trenton, NJ: Africa
World Press, 2000.

Feldman, Allen. *Formations of Violence: The Narrative of the Body and Political Terror in
Northern Ireland*. Chicago: University of Chicago Press, 1991.

Ferdman, Roberto A. "Why Quibbling about the Cause of Eric Garner's Death Misses the
Point." *Washington Post*, December 3, 2014. https://www.washingtonpost.com.

Ferguson, Roderick A. *The Reorder of Things: The University and Its Pedagogies of Minority
Difference*. Minneapolis: University of Minnesota Press, 2012.

Fernandez, Jay A. "Knowing Nina Simone: A Q&A w/ Liz Garbus about Her Netflix Doc."
Signature. June 24, 2015. http://www.signature-reads.com.

Fleetwood, Nicole R. *Troubling Vision: Performance, Visuality, and Blackness*. Chicago:
University of Chicago Press, 2011.

Foote, Thelma Wills. *Black and White Manhattan: The History of Racial Formation in
Colonial New York City*. New York: Oxford University Press, 2004.

Foucault, Michel. *The Essential Foucault: Selections from Essential Works of Foucault,
1954–1984*. New York: New Press, 2003.

———. *Language, Counter-Memory, Practice: Selected Essays and Interviews*. Ithaca:
Cornell University Press, 1980.

———. *Society Must Be Defended: Lectures at the College de France, 1975–1976*. Translated
by David Macey. New York: Picador, 2003.

Franklin, John Hope, and Loren Schweninger. *Runaway Slaves: Rebels on the Plantation*.
New York: Oxford University Press, 1999.

Frazier, E. Franklin. "The Pathology of Race Prejudice." *The Forum*, June 1927, 856–861.

Freeman, Elizabeth. *Time Binds: Queer Temporalities, Queer Histories*. Durham, NC: Duke
University Press, 2010.

Friedersdorf, Conor. "Man Arrested While Picking Up His Kids: 'The Problem Is I'm
Black.'" *The Atlantic*. August 29, 2014. http://www.theatlantic.com.

Georgakas, Dan, and Marvin Surkin. *Detroit: I Do Mind Dying; A Study in Urban Revolution.* Boston: South End Press, 1999.

Giddings, Paula. "At the Edges of the World." In *Savoring the Salt: The Legacy of Toni Cade Bambara,* edited by Linda Janet Holmes and Cheryl A. Wall, 127–128. Philadelphia: Temple University Press, 2007.

———. *When and Where I Enter: The Impact of Black Women on Race and Sex in America.* New York: Morrow, 2007.

Gikandi, Simon. *Slavery and the Culture of Taste.* Princeton, NJ: Princeton University Press, 2014.

Gilman, Sander L. *Difference and Pathology: Stereotypes of Sexuality, Race, and Madness.* Ithaca: Cornell University Press, 1985.

Gilmore, Ruth Wilson. *Golden Gulag: Prisons, Surplus, Crisis, and Opposition in Globalizing California.* Berkeley: University of California Press, 2007.

Goldberg, David Theo. *The Racial State.* New York: Blackwell, 2002.

———. *Racist Culture: Philosophy and the Politics of Meaning.* Malden: Blackwell, 1993.

Gonnerman, Jennifer. "Officer Serrano's Hidden Camera." *New York Magazine,* May 19, 2013, http://nymag.com.

Gordon, Lewis. *Disciplinary Decadence: Living Thought in Trying Times.* Boulder: Paradigm, 2006.

———. *Existentia Africana: Understanding Africana Existential Thought.* New York: Routledge, 2000.

———. *Her Majesty's Other Children: Sketches of Racism from a Neocolonial Age.* Lanham, MD: Rowman & Littlefield, 1997.

Gordon, Lewis R., Annie Menzel, George Shulman, and Jasmine Syedullah "Critical Exchange: Afro pessimism." *Contemporary Political Theory* 17, no. 1 (2018): 105–137.

Gore, Dayo. *Radicalism at the Crossroads: African American Women Activists in the Cold War.* New York: New York University Press, 2012.

Gray, Erin. "Anti-Lynching Laws Were Never Meant to Defend Black Lives: The Case of Jasmine Abdullah." Truthout. June 15, 2016. http://www.truthout.org.

Gross, Kali Nicole. "Missing Black Women Are Usually Ignored Until They're Proved Worthy." The Root. November 10, 2014. https://www.theroot.com.

Gumbs, Alexis Pauline. "One Thing: Toni Cade Bambara in the Speaking Everyday." Feminist Wire. March 25, 2014. http://www.thefeministwire.com/2014/03/one-thing-toni-cade/.

Guy-Sheftall, Beverly, ed., *Words of Fire: An Anthology of African-American Feminist Thought*. New York: New Press, 1995.

Gwynne, Kristen. "Sen. Eric Adams: NYPD Commissioner Told Me Cops Use Stop-and-Frisk to Instill Fear in Youths of Color." *AlterNet*, April 1, 2013. http://www.alternet.org.

Hall, Stuart. "Race, Articulation, and Societies Structured in Dominance." In *Sociological Theories: Race and Colonialism*, by UNESCO, 305–345. Paris: UNESCO, 1980.

Harding, Vincent. *Beyond Chaos: Black History and the Search for the New Land*. Black Paper No. 2. Atlanta: Institute of the Black World, 1970.

———. *There Is a River: The Black Struggle for Freedom in America*. New York: Harcourt Brace, 1981.

Hare, Nathan. "The Challenge of the Black Scholar." In *The Death of White Sociology*, edited by Joyce A. Ladner, 67–80. New York: Vintage, 1973.

Harris, Aisha. "How Accurate Is *Fruitvale Station*?" *Slate*, July 12, 2013. http://www.slate.com.

Harris, Cheryl, and Devon Carbado. "Loot or Find: Fact or Frame?" In *After the Storm: Black Intellectuals Explore the Meaning of Hurricane Katrina*, edited by David Dante Troutt, 87–110. New York: New Press, 2006.

Harris, David A. *Profiles in Injustice: Why Racial Profiling Cannot Work*. New York: New Press, 2001.

Hartlaub, Peter. "There's a 'Fruitvale Station' Movie Poster at Fruitvale Station." *SFGATE*, July 10, 2013. https://www.sfgate.com.

Hartman, Saidiya V. *Lose Your Mother: A Journey along the Atlantic Slave Route*. New York: Farrar, Strauss & Giroux, 2007.

———. *Scenes of Subjection: Terror, Slavery, and Self-Making in Nineteenth-Century America*. New York: Oxford University Press, 1997.

———. "The Time of Slavery." *South Atlantic Quarterly* 101, no. 4 (2002): 757–777.

———. "Venus in Two Acts." In *On Marronage: Ethical Confrontations with Antiblackness*, edited by P. Khalil Saucier and Tryon P. Woods, 47–66. Trenton, NJ: Africa World Press, 2015.

Headley, Bernard. *The Atlanta Youth Murders and the Politics of Race*. Carbondale: Southern Illinois University Press, 1999.

Henry, Jason. "'Lynching' Laws Were Meant to Protect Black People. Removing the Word Changed Everything." *Pasadena Star-News*, June 11, 2016. http://www.pasadenastarnews.com.

Hess, Amanda. "Lil Wayne Jokes about His Own Rape." *Washington City Paper*, January 12, 2010. http://www.washingtoncitypaper.com.

Hill, Lance. *The Deacons for Defense: Armed Resistance and the Civil Rights Movement.* Chapel Hill: University of North Carolina Press, 2006.

Hoffer, Peter Charles. *Cry Liberty! The Great Stono River Slave Rebellion of 1739.* New York: Oxford University Press, 2011.

Horne, Gerald. *Black Revolutionary: William Patterson and the Globalization of the African American Freedom Struggle.* Champaign: University of Illinois Press, 2013.

———. *The Counter-Revolution of 1776: Slave Resistance and the Origins of the United States of America.* New York: New York University Press, 2014.

———. *From the Barrel of a Gun: The United States and the War Against Zimbabwe, 1965–1980.* Chapel Hill: University of North Carolina Press, 2001.

———. *Paul Robeson: The Artist as Revolutionary.* London: Pluto, 2016.

———. *Race Woman: The Lives of Shirley Graham DuBois.* New York: New York University Press, 2000.

Howard, Percy. "Frank B. Wilderson, 'Wallowing in the Contradictions,' Part 1." *A Necessary Angel* (blog). https://percy3.wordpress.com.

Hull, Akasha (Gloria). "A Conversation with Toni Cade Bambara." In *Conversations with Toni Cade Bambara*, edited by Thabiti Lewis, 97–111. Jackson: University Press of Mississippi, 2012.

Hull, Gloria T., Patricia Bell Scott, and Barbara Smith, eds. *All the Women Are White, All the Blacks Are Men, But Some of Us Are Brave: Black Women's Studies.* New York: Feminist Press, 1982.

Hull, Gloria T., and Barbara Smith. "Introduction: The Politics of Black Women's Studies." In *All the Women Are White, All the Blacks Are Men, But Some of Us Are Brave: Black Women's Studies*, ed. Gloria T. Hull, Patricia Bell Scott, and Barbara Smith, xvii–xxxii. New York: Feminist Press, 1982.

Interview with Rachel Jeantel (transcript). "Piers Morgan Live." *CNN.* July 19, 2013. http://transcripts.cnn.com/TRANSCRIPTS/1307/19/pmt.01.html.

Jackson, George L. *Blood in My Eye.* Baltimore: Black Classic Press, 1990.

———. *Soledad Brother: The Prison Letters of George Jackson.* Chicago: Chicago Review Press, 1994.

Jahoda, Gustav. *Images of Savages: Ancient Roots of Modern Prejudice in Western Culture.* London: Routledge, 1999.

James, C. L. R. "African Independence and the Myth of African Inferiority." In *Education and Black Struggle: Notes from the Colonized World*, edited by Institute of the Black World, 33–41. Cambridge, MA: Harvard Educational Review, 1974.

———. *Beyond a Boundary*. Durham, NC: Duke University Press, 2013.

———. *The Black Jacobins*. New York: Vintage, 1989.

James, Joy. "Campaigns Against 'Blackness': Criminality, Incivility, and Election to Executive Office." *Critical Sociology* 36, no. 1 (2010): 25–44.

———. "Introduction: Democracy and Captivity." In *The New Abolitionists: (Neo)Slave Narratives and Contemporary Prison Writings*, edited by Joy James, xxi–xlii. Albany: SUNY Press, 2005.

———. *Resisting State Violence: Radicalism, Gender, and Race in U.S. Culture*. Minneapolis: University of Minnesota Press, 1996.

———, ed. *Warfare in the American Homeland: Policing and Prison in a Penal Democracy*. Durham, NC: Duke University Press, 2007.

Jefferson, Thomas. *Notes on the State of Virginia*. New York: Harper & Row, 1964.

Jerome, Fred. "Einstein, Race, and the Myth of the Cultural Icon." *Isis: Journal of the History of Science Society* 95, no. 4 (2004): 627–639.

Johnson, Kevin. "FBI: Justifiable Homicides at Highest in More than a Decade." *USA Today*, October 15, 2008.

Johnson, Nicholas. *Negroes and the Gun: The Black Tradition of Arms*. New York: Prometheus, 2014.

Johnson, Sara E. *Fear of French Negroes: Transcolonial Collaboration in the Revolutionary Americas*. Berkeley: University of California Press, 2012.

Jones, Dalton Anthony, ed. "Black Holes: Afro-Pessimism, Blackness, and the Discourses of Modernity." Special issue, *Rhizomes: Cultural Studies in Emerging Knowledge* 29 (2016).

Jones, Gayle. *Corregidora*. New York: Griot Editions, 1998.

Judy, Ronald A. T. *(Dis)Forming the American Canon: African-Arabic Slave Narratives and the Vernacular*. Minneapolis: University of Minnesota Press, 1993.

———. "The Question of Nigga Authenticity." *boundary 2* 21, no. 3 (1994): 211–230.

Kairys, David. "A Brief History of Race and the Supreme Court." *Temple Law Review* 79 (2006): 751–771.

———. "Unconscious Racism." *Temple Law Review* 83 (2011): 857–866.

Kelley, Robin D. G. *Race Rebels: Culture, Politics, and the Black Working Class*. New York:

Free Press, 1994.

Kenan, Randall. *A Visitation of Spirits*. New York: Vintage, 2000.

Keneally, Meghan. "Sandra Bland Had 'Lows and Highs,' Her Sister Says." *ABC News*. July 23, 2015. http://abcnews.go.com.

Khan, Saliqa. "Police: Korryn Gaines Involved in Police Incident in March." WBALTV. August 3, 2016. http://www.wbaltv.com/news/police-korryn-gaines-involved-in-police-incident-in-march/41016216.

King, Tiffany Lethabo. "The Labor of (Re)reading Plantation Landscapes Fungible(ly)." *Antipode: A Radical Journal of Geography* 48, no. 4 (2016): 1022–1039.

———. "Labor's Aphasia: Toward Antiblackness as Constitutive to Settler Colonialism." Decolonization: Indigeneity, Education & Society. June 10, 2014. https://decolonization.wordpress.com.

Koestler, Arthur. *The Ghost in the Machine*. New York: Macmillan, 1967.

Kunzel, Regina. *Criminal Intimacy: Prison and the Uneven History of Modern American Sexuality*. Chicago: University of Chicago Press, 2008.

Kupers, Terry. *Prison Madness: The Mental Health Crisis Behind Bars and What We Must Do about It*. San Francisco: Jossey-Bass, 1999.

Lartey, Jamiles. "Alabama Police Shot a Teen Dead, But His Friend Got 30 Years for the Murder." *The Guardian*. April 15, 2018. https://www.theguardian.com.

Lazreg, Marnia. *Torture and the Twilight of Empire: From Algiers to Baghdad*. Princeton: Princeton University Press, 2008.

Leadership Conference on Civil and Human Rights. *Wrong Then, Wrong Now: Racial Profiling Before and After September 11, 2001*. Washington, DC: Leadership Conference on Civil and Human Rights, 2002.

Lewis, Bernard. *Race and Slavery in the Middle East: An Historical Enquiry*. Oxford: Oxford University Press, 1992.

Logan, Laura S. "The Case of the 'Killer Lesbians.'" The Public Intellectual. July 18, 2011. http://thepublicintellectual.org.

Lorde, Audre. *Sister Outsider*. New York: Ten Speed Press, 1984.

Lowe, Lisa. *Immigrant Acts: On Asian American Cultural Politics*. Durham, NC: Duke University Press, 1996.

———. *The Intimacies of Four Continents*. Durham, NC: Duke University Press, 2015.

Lubiano, Wahneema. "Black Ladies, Welfare Queens, and State Minstrels: Ideological War by Narrative Means." In *Race-ing Justice, En-gendering Power: Essays on Anita*

Hill, Clarence Thomas, and the Social Construction of Reality, edited by Toni Morrison, 232–252. New York: Pantheon, 1992.

Ludwig, Jamie. "Director of Nina Simone Documentary: 'We Were in Our Edit Room When the Events of Ferguson Were Unfolding. It Reminds You That the Struggle Is Ongoing.'" *Salon*, June 28, 2015, http://www.salon.com/2015/06/28/director_of_nina_ simone_documentary_we_were_in_our_edit_room_when_the_events_of_ferguson_ were_unfolding_it_reminds_you_that_the_struggle_is_ongoing/.

Lynd, Staughton. *Lucasville: The Untold Story of a Prison Uprising*. Philadelphia: Temple University Press, 2004.

Maclin, Tracy. "'Black and Blue Encounters,' Some Preliminary Thoughts about Fourth Amendment Seizures: Should Race Matter?" *Valparaiso University Law Review* 26, no. 1 243–279.

Malaklou, M. Shadee, and Tiffany Willoughby-Herard, eds. "Afro-Pessimism and Black Feminism." Special issue, *Theory & Event* 21, no. 1 (2018).

Malcolm X. *Malcolm X Speaks: Selected Speeches and Statements*. Edited by George Breitman. New York: Grove Press, 1965.

Malcolm X with Alex Haley. *The Autobiography of Malcolm X*. New York: Grove Press, 1965.

Mann, Coramae Richey. *Unequal Justice: A Question of Color*. Indianapolis: Indiana University Press, 1993.

Marin, Carol, and Don Moseley. "City Settles 2 Burge Cases for $7.1M." NBC Chicago, July 23, 2012. http://www.nbcchicago.com.

Marriott, David. "Black Critical and Cultural Theory." *Year's Work in Critical and Cultural Theory* 23, no. 1 (2015): 109–206.

———. "Inventions of Existence: Sylvia Wynter, Frantz Fanon, Sociogeny, and 'the Damned.'" *CR: The New Centennial Review* 11, no. 3 (2011): 45–89.

Martinot, Steve. "The Militarization of the Police." *Social Identities* 9, no. 2 (2003): 205–224.

———. *The Rule of Racialization: Class, Identity, Governance*. Philadelphia: Temple University Press, 2002.

Martinot, Steve, and Jared Sexton. "The Avant-Garde of White Supremacy." *Social Identities* 9, no. 2 (2003): 169–181.

Massiah, Louis. "How She Came By Her Name." In *Conversations with Toni Cade Bambara*, edited by Thabiti Lewis, 112–138. Jackson: University Press of Mississippi, 2012.

Matsuda, Mari, Charles R. Lawrence III, Richard Delgado, and Kimberle Williams Crenshaw. *Words That Wound: Critical Race Theory, Assaultive Speech, and the First Amendment*. Boulder: Westview Press, 1993.

Mbembe, Achille. "Necropolitics." *Public Culture* 15, no. 1 (2003): 11–40.

———. *On the Postcolony*. Berkeley: University of California Press, 2001.

McGuire, Danielle L. *At the Dark End of the Street: Black Women, Rape, and Resistance—a New History of the Civil Rights Movement from Rosa Parks to the Rise of Black Power*. New York: Vintage, 2011.

McLaughlin, Eliott C. "Woman Streams Aftermath of Fatal Officer-Involved Shooting." CNN, July 8, 2016. http://www.cnn.com.

McNeil, Genna Rae. "The Body, Sexuality, and Self-Defense in *State vs. Joan Little*, 1974–75." *Journal of African American History* 93, no. 2 (2008): 235–261.

Melamed, Jodi. *Represent and Destroy: Rationalizing Violence in the New Racial Capitalism*. Minneapolis: University of Minnesota Press, 2011.

"Michelle Alexander: 'Zimmerman Mindset' Endangers Young Black Lives with Poverty, Prison & Murder." Democracy Now!, July 17, 2013, http://www.democracynow.org.

Midnight Notes Collective, ed. *Midnight Oil: Work, Energy, War 1973–1992*. Brooklyn: Autonomedia, 1992.

Moore, R. I. *The Formation of a Persecuting Society: Power and Deviance in Western Europe, 950–1250*. Oxford: Basil Blackwell, 1987.

Moraga, Cherrie, and Gloria Anzaldua, eds. *This Bridge Called My Back: Writings by Radical Women of Color*. New York: Kitchen Table/Women of Color, 1983.

Morrison, Toni. *Beloved*. New York: Vintage, 2004.

———. *Playing in the Dark: Whiteness and the Literary Imagination*. New York: Vintage, 1993.

Moten, Fred. "Black Op." *PMLA* 123, no. 5 (2008): 1743–1747.

———. "The Case of Blackness." *Criticism* 50, no. 2 (2008): 177–218.

———. *In the Break: The Aesthetics of the Black Radical Tradition*. Minneapolis: University of Minnesota Press, 2003.

Mudimbe, V. Y. *The Invention of Africa: Gnosis, Philosophy, and the Order of Knowledge*. Indianapolis: Indiana University Press, 1988.

Murashige, Mike. "Haile Gerima and the Political Economy of Cinematic Resistance." In *Representing Blackness: Issues in Film and Video*, edited by Valerie Smith, 183–204. New Brunswick: Rutgers University Press, 1997.

Muwakkil, Salim. "Hip-Hop Cops." *In These Times*, June 28, 2004, http://www.inthesetimes.com/article/806.

National Crime Information Center. "NCIC Missing Person and Unidentified Person Statistics for 2013." Federal Bureau of Investigation. http://www.fbi.gov/services/cjis/ncic.

Nathan, Debbie. "The Real Reason Sandra Bland Got Locked Up." *The Nation*, December 18, 2015.

Nothias, Toussaint. "Definition and Scope of Afro-Pessimism: Mapping the Concept and Its Usefulness for Analysing News Media Coverage of Africa." *Leeds African Studies Bulletin* 74 (December 2012): 54–62.

Nuñez, Kismet. "In the Future, We Kill Our Attackers: Rihanna's 'Man Down' as Afrofuturist Text." The AntiJemima Life. June 9, 2011. http://nunezdaughter.wordpress.com.

Padmore, George. *Pan-Africanism or Communism*. New York: Doubleday, 1972.

Patterson, Anita. Review of *Scenes of Subjection: Terror, Slavery, and Self-Making in Nineteenth-Century America*, by Saidiya V. Hartman. *African American Review* 33, no. 4 (1999): 683–686.

Patterson, Orlando. *Slavery and Social Death: A Comparative Study*. Cambridge, MA: Harvard University Press, 1982.

Peters, Justin. "The Worst of Stop-and-Frisk Is Over. But Why Didn't the NYPD End the Racist Policy Itself?" *Slate*, August 12, 2013. http://www.slate.com.

Philip, M. NourbeSe. *A Genealogy of Resistance and Other Essays*. Toronto: Mercury, 1997.
———. *Zong!* Middletown, CT: Wesleyan University Press, 2008.

Power, Margaret, ed. *Torture, American Style*. HAW Pamphlet #3. May 2006. http://www.historiansagainstwar.org.

Prison Research Education Action Project. *Instead of Prisons: A Handbook for Abolitionists*. Oakland: Critical Resistance, 2005.

Ransby, Barbara, and Tracye Matthews. "Black Popular Culture and the Transcendence of Patriarchal Illusions." *Race & Class* 35, no. 1 (1993): 57–68.

Raymond, Margaret. "Down on the Corner, Out in the Street: Considering the Character of the Neighborhood in Evaluating Reasonable Suspicion." *Ohio State Law Journal* 60, no. 1 (1999): 99–143.

Rector, Kevin. "The 45-Minute Mystery of Freddie Gray's Death." *Baltimore Sun*, April 25, 2015. http://www.baltimoresun.com.

Redden, Molly. "Police Officials Were Investigating Daniel Holtzclaw before Final Attack, Suit Claims." *The Guardian*, December 11, 2015. https://www.theguardian.com.

Reed, Adolph, Jr. *Class Notes: Posing as Politics and Other Thoughts on the American Scene.* New York: New Press, 2000.

Reed, Ishmael. "'Hamilton: The Musical': Black Actors Dress Up Like Slave Traders . . . and It's Not Halloween," *CounterPunch*, August 21, 2015. http://www.counterpunch.org.

Rhodes, Lorna. *Total Confinement: Madness and Reason in the Maximum Security Prison.* Berkeley: University of California Press, 2004.

Richardson, Matt. *The Queer Limit of Black Memory: Black Lesbian Literature and Irresolution.* Columbus: Ohio State University Press, 2013.

Richie, Beth. *Compelled to Crime: The Gender Entrapment of Battered Black Women.* New York: Routledge, 1996.

Roberts, Dorothy E. *Killing the Black Body: Race, Reproduction, and the Meaning of Liberty.* New York: Pantheon, 1997.

———. *Shattered Bonds: The Color of Child Welfare.* New York: Basic Books, 2002.

Robertson, David. *Denmark Vesey: The Buried Story of America's Largest Slave Rebellion and the Man Who Led It.* New York: Vintage, 2000.

Robinson, Cedric. *Black Marxism: The Making of the Black Radical Tradition.* Chapel Hill: University of North Carolina Press, 2000.

Rodney, Walter. *How Europe Underdeveloped Africa.* Washington, DC: Howard University Press, 1982.

———. *Walter Rodney Speaks: The Making of an African Intellectual.* Edited by Robert A. Hill. Trenton, NJ: Africa World Press, 1990.

Rooks, Noliwe. *White Money/Black Power: The Surprising History of African American Studies and the Crisis of Race in Higher Education.* Boston: Beacon Press, 2007.

Ryman, Anne. "ASU Officer Resigns Over Incident with Professor." *The Republic,* February 16, 2015. http://www.azcentral.com.

Salaam, Kalamu ya. "Black Arts Movement." In *The Oxford Companion to African American Literature*, edited by William L. Andrews, Frances Smith Foster, and Trudier Harris, 70–74. New York: Oxford University Press, 1997.

———. "Searching for the Mother Tongue." In *Conversations with Toni Cade Bambara*, edited by Thabiti Lewis, 20–29. Jackson: University Press of Mississippi, 2012.

Sanchez, Sonia. *"I'm Black When I'm Singing, I'm Blue When I Ain't" and Other Plays.* Durham, NC: Duke University Press, 2010.

Saucier, P. Khalil, and Tryon P. Woods, eds. *Conceptual Aphasia in Black: Displacing Racial Formation*. Lanham, MD: Lexington Books, 2016.

———. "Ex Aqua: The Mediterranean Basin, Africans on the Move, and the Politics of Policing." *Theoria: A Journal of Social and Political Theory* 61, no. 141 (2014): 55–75.

———. "Introduction: Where Is the Danger in Black Studies and Can We Look at It Again (and Again)?" In *On Marronage: Ethical Confrontations with Antiblackness*, edited by P. Khalil Saucier and Tryon P. Woods, 1–32. Trenton, NJ: Africa World Press, 2015.

———. *On Marronage: Ethical Confrontations with Antiblackness*. Trenton, NJ: Africa World Press, 2015.

———. "Upgrade and Upstage: Injunctions Against Stephanie Rawlings-Blake, 'Black Feminism,' and Hip Hop Studies at the Ledge (A Response to Forster)." *Journal of Popular Music Studies* 27, no. 3 (2015): 353–363.

Sayers, Daniel O. *A Desolate Place for a Defiant People: The Archaeology of Maroons, Indigenous Americans, and Enslaved Laborers in the Great Dismal Swamp*. Gainesville: University Press of Florida, 2016.

Scarry, Elaine. *The Body in Pain: The Making and Unmaking of the World*. New York: Oxford University Press, 1985.

Scott, Darieck. *Extravagant Abjection: Blackness, Power, and Sexuality in the African American Literary Imagination*. New York: New York University Press, 2010.

Sedensky, Matt, and Nomaan Merchant. "AP: Hundreds of Officers Lose Licenses Over Sex Misconduct." *AP News*. November 1, 2015. http://bigstory.ap.org/article/fd1d4d05e561462a85abe50e7eaed4ec/ap-hundreds-officers-lose-licenses-over-sex-misconduct.

Segal, Ronald. *Islam's Black Slaves: The Other Black Diaspora*. New York: Farrar, Strauss & Giroux, 2001.

Sexton, Jared. "Afro-Pessimism: The Unclear Word." In "Black Holes: Afro-Pessimism, Blackness, and the Discourses of Modernity," edited by Dalton Anthony Jones. Special issue, *Rhizomes: Cultural Studies in Emerging Knowledge* 29 (2016): 1–23.

———. *Amalgamation Schemes: Antiblackness and the Critique of Multiracialism*. Minneapolis: University of Minnesota Press, 2008.

———. "Ante-Anti-Blackness: Afterthoughts." *Lateral* 1 (2012): http://csalateral.org.

———. "'The Curtain of the Sky': An Introduction." *Critical Sociology* 36, no. 1 (2010): 11–24.

————. "People-of-Color-Blindness: Notes on the Afterlife of Slavery." *Social Text* 28, no. 2 (2010): 31–56.

————. "Proprieties of Coalition: Blacks, Asians, and the Politics of Policing." In *On Marronage: Ethical Confrontations with Antiblackness*, edited by P. Khalil Saucier and Tryon P. Woods, 279–312. Trenton, NJ: Africa World Press, 2015.

————. "The Ruse of Engagement: Black Masculinity and the Cinema of Policing." *American Quarterly* 61, no. 1 (2009): 39–63.

————. "The Social Life of Social Death: On Afro-Pessimism and Black Optimism." *InTensions* 5 (Fall 2011): 1–47.

————. "The *Vel* of Slavery: Tracking the Figure of the Unsovereign." *Critical Sociology* 42, nos. 4–5 (2016): 583–597.

Sexton, Jared, and Huey Copeland. "Raw Life: An Introduction." *Qui Parle* 13, no. 2 (2003): 53–62.

Sexton, Jared, and Elizabeth Lee. "Figuring the Prison: Prerequisites of Torture at Abu Ghraib." *Antipode: A Radical Journal of Geography* 38, no. 5 (2006): 1005–1022.

Shakur, Assata. *Assata: An Autobiography*. Chicago: Lawrence Hill, 2001.

Shanikka. "When a Judge 'Gets It' on Racism: The Decision in *Floyd v. City of New York*." Daily KOS. August 18, 2013. http://www.dailykos.com.

Sharpe, Christina. *Monstrous Intimacies: Making Post-Slavery Subjects*. Durham, NC: Duke University Press, 2010.

Sheth, Falguni A. *Toward a Political Philosophy of Race*. Albany: SUNY Press, 2009.

Simmons, Aishah Shahidah. "Who Will Revere US? (Black LGTBQ People, Straight Women, and Girls) (Part 1)." Feminist Wire. April 23, 2012. http://thefeministwire.com.

Simone, Nina. *I Put a Spell On You: The Autobiography of Nina Simone*. New York: Da Capo, 1993.

Skolnick, Jerome. "American Interrogation: From Torture to Trickery." In *Torture: A Collection*, edited by Sanford Levinson, 105–128. New York: Oxford University Press, 2004.

Spillers, Hortense J. *Black, White, and in Color: Essays on American Literature and Culture*. Chicago: University of Chicago Press, 2003.

————. Review of *Black Popular Culture*, edited by Michele Wallace and Gina Dent; *Black Macho and the Myth of the Superwoman*, by Michele Wallace; *Invisibility Blues–from Pop to Theory*, by Michele Wallace. *African American Review* 29, no. 1 (1995): 123–126.

Spillers, Hortense, with Saidiya Hartman, Farah Jasmine Griffin, Shelley Eversley, and Jennifer L. Morgan. "'Whatcha Gonna Do?': Revisiting 'Mama's Baby, Papa's Maybe: An American Grammar Book.'" *Women's Studies Quarterly* 35, no. 1/2 (2007): 299–309.

Spivak, Gayatri. *A Critique of Postocolonial Reason: Toward a History of the Vanishing Present*. Cambridge, MA: Harvard University Press, 1999.

Stafford, Zach, Spencer Ackerman, and Joanna Walters. "Chicago Agrees to Pay $5.5m to Victims of Police Torture in 1970s and 80s." *The Guardian*, May 6, 2015. http://www.theguardian.com/us.

Stallings, LaMonda Horton. *Mutha' Is Half a Word: Intersections of Folklore, Vernacular, Myth, and Queerness in Black Female Culture*. Columbus: Ohio State University, 2007.

Stanley, Eric. "Fugitive Flesh: Gender Self-Determination, Queer Abolition, and Trans Resistance." In *Captive Genders: Trans Embodiment and the Prison Industrial Complex*, edited by Eric Stanley and Nat Smith, 1–14. Oakland: AK Press, 2011.

———. "Near Life, Queer Death: Overkill and Ontological Capture." *Social Text* 29, no. 2 (2011): 1–19.

Stark, Seymour. *Men in Blackface: True Stories of the Minstrel Show*. Bloomington: Xlibris, 2000.

Steele, Tanya. "The Irresponsibility of 'What Happened, Miss Simone?'" IndieWire. June 29, 2015. http://www.indiewire.com/2015/06/the-irresponsibility-of-what-happened-miss-simone-153559.

Steinberg, Stephen. *Turning Back: The Retreat from Racial Justice in American Thought and Policy*. Boston: Beacon Press, 1995.

Sundiata, Sekou. "Shout Out." In *Blue Oneness of Dreams*. Polygram, 1997.

Taslitz, Andrew E. *Reconstructing the Fourth Amendment: A History of Search and Seizure, 1789–1868*. New York: New York University Press, 2006.

Tate, Claudia. "Toni Cade Bambara." In *Conversations with Toni Cade Bambara*, edited by Thabiti Lewis, 49–72. Jackson: University Press of Mississippi, 2012.

Thomas, Greg. "Afro-Blue Notes: The Death of Afro-Pessimism (*2.0*)?" In "Afro-Pessimism and Black Feminism." Special issue, *Theory & Event* 21, no. 1 (2018): 282–314.

———. "The Body Politics of '*Man*' and '*Woman*' in an 'Anti-Black' World: Sylvia Wynter on Humanism's Empire (A Critical Resource Guide)." In *On Marronage: Ethical Confrontations with Antiblackness*, edited by P. Khalil Saucier and Tryon P. Woods, 67–108. Trenton, NJ: Africa World Press, 2015.

———. "Erotics of Aryanism/Histories of Empire: How 'White Supremacy' and

'Hellenomania' Construct 'Discourses of Sexuality.'" *CR: The New Centennial Review* 3, no. 3 (2003): 235–255.

————. "Fire and *Damnation*: Hip-Hop ('Youth Culture') and 1956 in Focus." *Presence Africaine: Revue Culturelle du Monde Noir* 175–176–177, no. 2 (2007): 300–312.

————. *Hip-Hop Revolution in the Flesh: Power, Knowledge, and Pleasure in Lil' Kim's Lyricism*. New York: Palgrave, 2009.

————. "'Neo-Slave Narratives' and Literacies of Maroonage." In *Toni Morrison: au-dela du visible ordinaire / Beyond the Ordinary Visible*, edited by Andree-Anne Kekeh-Dika, Maryemma Graham, and Janis A. Mayes. Paris: Presses Universitaires de Vincennes, 2015.

————. *The Sexual Demon of Colonial Power: Pan-African Embodiment and Erotic Schemes of Empire*. Bloomington: Indiana University Press, 2007.

————. "The 'S' Word: Sex, Empire, and Black Radical Tradition (After Sylvia)." In *Caribbean Reasonings: After Man, Towards the Human; Critical Essays on Sylvia Wynter*, edited by Anthony Bogues. Kingston: Ian Randle, 2005.

Tibbs, Donald F., and Tryon P. Woods. "The Jena Six and Black Punishment: Law and Raw Life in the Domain of Nonexistence." *Seattle Journal for Social Justice* 7, no. 1 (2008): 235–283.

————. "Requiem for Laquan: Policing as Punishment and Prosecuting 'Reasonable Suspicion.'" *Temple Law Review*, Rethinking Punishment Symposium Edition 89, no. 4 (2017): 101–117.

Tinsley, Omise'eke Natasha. "Black Atlantic, Queer Atlantic: Queer Imaginings of the Middle Passage." *GLQ: A Journal of Lesbian and Gay Studies* 14, nos. 2–3 (2008): 191–214.

Traylor, Eleanor. "The Language of Soul in Toni Cade Bambara's Re/Conceived Academy." In *Savoring the Salt: The Legacy of Toni Cade Bambara*, edited by Linda Janet Holmes and Cheryl A. Wall, 70–80. Philadelphia: Temple University Press, 2007.

Trouillot, Michel-Rolph. *Silencing the Past: Power and the Production of History*. Boston: Beacon Press, 1995.

Tyson, Timothy B. *The Blood of Emmett Till*. New York: Simon & Schuster, 2017.

Umoja, Akinyele Omowale. *We Will Shoot Back: Armed Resistance in the Mississippi Freedom Movement*. New York: New York University Press, 2014.

Vargas, João H. Costa, and Joy James. "Refusing Blackness-as-Victimization: Trayvon Martin and the Black Cyborgs." In *Pursuing Trayvon Martin: Historical Contexts and*

Contemporary Manifestations of Racial Dynamics, edited by George Yancey and Janine Jones, 193–204. Lanham, MD: Lexington, 2012.

Wagner, Bryan. *Disturbing the Peace: Black Culture and the Police Power after Slavery.* Cambridge, MA: Harvard University Press, 2009.

Wall, Cheryl A. "Toni's Obligato: Bambara and the African American Literary Tradition." In *Savoring the Salt: The Legacy of Toni Cade Bambara*, edited by Linda Janet Holmes and Cheryl A. Wall, 27–44. Philadelphia: Temple University Press, 2007.

Wanzo, Rebecca. "Terror at Home: Naturalized Victimization in *Those Bones Are Not My Child*." In *Savoring the Salt: The Legacy of Toni Cade Bambara*, edited by Linda Janet Holmes and Cheryl A. Wall, 244–255. Philadelphia: Temple University Press, 2007.

Warren, Calvin L. "Black Mysticism: Fred Moten's Phenomenology of (Black) Spirit." *Zeitschrift für Anglistik und Amerikanistik: A Quarterly of Language, Literature and Culture* 65, no. 2 (2017). doi: https://doi.org/10.1515/zaa-2017-0022.

———. "Black Time: Slavery, Metaphysics, and the Logic of Wellness." In *The Psychic Hold of Slavery: Legacies in American Expressive Culture*, edited by Soyica Diggs Colbert, Robert J. Patterson, and Aida Levy-Hussen, 55–68. New Brunswick: Rutgers University Press, 2016.

Washington, George. "Letter to Bryan Fairfax." In *George Washington: A Collection*, edited by W. B. Allen, 33–39. Indianapolis: Liberty Fund, 1988.

Washington, Harriet A. *Medical Apartheid: The Dark History of Medical Experimentation on Black Americans from Colonial Times to the Present.* New York: Doubleday, 2007.

Watson-Sherman, Charlotte, ed., *Sisterfire: Black Womanist Fiction and Poetry*. New York: HarperCollins, 1994.

Weheliye, Alexander G. *Habeas Viscus: Racializing Assemblages, Biopolitics, and Black Feminist Theories of the Human.* Durham, NC: Duke University Press, 2014.

Wells-Barnett, Ida B. *On Lynchings.* New York: Courier Dover Publications, 2014.

———. *Southern Horrors: Lynch Law in All Its Phases.* New York: Floating Press, 2014.

West, Cornel. "Black Strivings in a Twilight Civilization." In Henry Louis Gates Jr. and Cornel West, *The Future of the Race*, 53–114. New York: Knopf, 1996.

———. "The New Cultural Politics of Difference." In *Out There: Marginalization and Contemporary Cultures*, edited by Russell Ferguson, Martha Gever, Trinh T. Minh-ha, and Cornel West, 19–38. New York: The New Museum of Contemporary Art; Cambridge, MA: MIT Press, 1990.

Wilderson, Frank B., III. "Biko and the Problematic of Presence." In *Biko Lives! Contesting the Legacies of Steve Biko*, edited by Andile Mngxitama, Amanda Alexander, and Nigel Gibson, 95–114. New York: Palgrave, 2008.

———. "The Black Liberation Army and the Paradox of Political Engagement." In *Postcoloniality-Decoloniality-Black Critique*, edited by Sabine Broeck and Carsten Junker, 175–210. Frankfurt: Campus Verlag, 2014.

———. "Grammar & Ghosts: The Performative Limits of African Freedom." *Theatre Survey* 50, no. 1 (2009): 119–125.

———. "Gramsci's Black Marx: Whither the Slave in Civil Society?" *Social Identities* 9, no. 2 (2003): 225–240.

———. "'The Position of the Unthought': An Interview with Saidiya V. Hartman." *Qui Parle* 13, no. 2 (2003): 183–201.

———. "The Prison Slave as Hegemony's (Silent) Scandal." In *Warfare in the American Homeland: Policing and Prison in a Penal Democracy*, edited by Joy James, 23–34. Durham, NC: Duke University Press, 2007.

———. *Red, White & Black: Cinema and the Structure of U.S. Antagonisms*. Durham, NC: Duke University Press, 2010.

———. "Social Death and Narrative Aporia in *12 Years a Slave*." *Black Camera* 7, no. 1 (2015): 134–149.

———. "The Vengeance of Vertigo: Aphasia and Abjection in the Political Trials of Black Insurgents." In *On Marronage: Ethical Confrontations with Antiblackness*, edited by P. Khalil Saucier and Tryon P. Woods, 213–240. Trenton, NJ: Africa World Press, 2015.

Wilderson, Frank B., III, Samira Spatzek, and Paula von Gleich. "'The Inside-Outside of Civil Society': An Interview with Frank B. Wilderson, III." *Black Studies Papers* 2, no. 1 (2016): 4–22.

Williams, Evelyn A. *Inadmissible Evidence: The Story of the African-American Trial Lawyer Who Defended the Black Liberation Army*. Lincoln, NE: Self-published, iUniverse.com, 2000.

Williams, Kristian. *Our Enemies in Blue: Police and Power in America*. Boston: South End, 2007.

Williams, Robert F. *Negroes with Guns*. Detroit: Wayne State University Press, 1998.

Williamson, Terrion L. "Who Is Killing Us." Feminist Wire. January 18, 2012. http://www.thefeministwire.com.

———. "Why Did They Die? On Combahee and the Serialization of Black Death." *Souls: A Critical Journal of Black Culture, Politics, and Society* 19, no. 3 (2017): 328–341.

Willoughby-Herard, Tiffany. *Waste of a White Skin: The Carnegie Corporation and the Racial Logic of White Vulnerability*. Berkeley: University of California Press, 2015.

Wolf, Adam B. "The Adversity of Race and Place: Fourth Amendment Jurisprudence in *Illinois v. Wardlow*, 528 S. Ct. 673 (2000)." *Michigan Journal of Race & Law* 5 (2000): 711–726.

Wolfe, Patrick, ed., *The Settler Complex: Recuperating Binarism in Colonial Studies*. Los Angeles: UCLA American Indian Studies Center, 2016.

———. *Traces of History: Elementary Structures of Race*. London: Verso, 2016.

Woods, Tryon P. "Pedagogy in Revolution, for the Anti-Revolutionary Stretch: Pan-African Correspondence across Space and Time." In *A Luta Continua: (Re)Introducing Amilcar Cabral to a New Generation of Thinkers*, edited by P. Khalil Saucier, 173–204. Trenton, NJ: Africa World Press, 2016.

———. "A Re-appraisal of Black Radicalism and Human Rights Doctrine." In *On Marronage: Ethical Confrontations with Antiblackness*, edited by P. Khalil Saucier and Tryon P. Woods, 241–278. Trenton, NJ: Africa World Press, 2015.

———. "'Something of the Fever and the Fret': Antiblackness in the Critical Prison Studies Fold." In *Conceptual Aphasia in Black: Displacing Racial Formation*, edited by P. Khalil Saucier and Tryon P. Woods, 127–154. Lanham, MD: Lexington, 2016.

———. "Surrogate Selves: Notes on Anti-Trafficking and Anti-Blackness," *Social Identities* 19, no. 1 (2013): 120–134.

Woodson, Carter G. *The Mis-Education of the Negro*. Trenton, NJ: Africa World Press, 1998.

Wright, Richard. *White Man, Listen!* New York: Perennial, 1995.

Wun, Connie. "Anti-Blackness as Mundane: Black Girls and Punishment Beyond School Discipline." In *Conceptual Aphasia in Black: Displacing Racial Formation*, edited by P. Khalil Saucier and Tryon P. Woods, 69–86. Lanham, MD: Lexington, 2016.

Wynter, Sylvia. "Genital Mutilation or Symbolic Birth—Female Circumcision, Lost Origins, and the Aculturalism of Feminist/Western Thought." *Case Western Reserve Law Review* 47 (1996): 501–552.

———. "No Human Involved: An Open Letter to My Colleagues." *Forum N.H.I.* 1, no. 1 (fall 1994): 42–73.

———. "On How We Mistook the Map for the Territory, and Re-Imprisoned Ourselves in Our Unbearable Wrongness of Being, of *Desetre*: Black Studies Toward the Human Project." In *Not Only the Master's Tools: African-American Studies in Theory and Practice*, edited by Lewis R. Gordon and Jane Anna Gordon, 107–172. Boulder:

Paradigm, 2006.

———. "PROUD FLESH Inter/Views: Sylvia Wynter." *PROUD FLESH: A New Afrikan Journal of Culture, Politics, and Consciousness* 4 (2006): 1–36.

———. "The Re-Enchantment of Humanism: An Interview with Sylvia Wynter." By David Scott. *Small Axe: A Journal of Caribbean Criticism* 8 (September 2000): 119–207.

———. "Rethinking 'Aesthetics': Notes Towards a Deciphering Practice." In *Ex-Iles: Essays on Caribbean Cinema*, edited by Mbye Cham, 236–279. Trenton, NJ: Africa World Press, 1992.

Yan, Holly, and Mariano Castillo. "Attorney Defends Actions of Fired School Officer as 'Justified and Lawful.'" *CNN*, October 29, 2015. http://www.cnn.com.

Young, Kevin. *The Grey Album: On the Blackness of Blackness.* Seattle: Graywolf, 2012.

Yuen, Laura. "Panel Questioned after Cops Cleared in St. Paul Stun Gun Arrest." *MPR News.* November 23, 2014. http://www.mprnews.org.

Zuckerman, Esther. "Ryan Coogler on Humanizing a Movement for *Fruitvale Station*." *The Atlantic*, July 12, 2013. http://www.theatlantic.com.

Index